Economic Freedom

IEA Masters of Modern Economics

Series editor: Cento Veljanovski

James M. Buchanan   *Constitutional Economics*
Milton Friedman   *Monetarist Economics*
Friedrich A. Hayek   *Economic Freedom*

Economic Freedom

Friedrich A. Hayek

Basil Blackwell

Copyright © Institute of Economic Affairs 1991

First published 1991

Basil Blackwell Ltd
108 Cowley Road, Oxford, OX4 1JF,UK

Basil Blackwell, Inc.
3 Cambridge Center
Cambridge, Massachusetts O2142, USA

British Library Cataloguing in Publication Data

A CIP catalogue record for this book is available from the British Library.

Library of Congress Cataloging-in-Publication Data

Hayek, Friedrich A. von (Friedrich August), 1899–
   Economic freedom / Friedrich A. Hayek.
     p. cm.——(IEA masters of modern economics)
   Includes bibliographical references.
     Contents: Introduction / Norman Barry——A tiger by the tail——Denationalisation of money——Market standards for money——Choice in currency——Inflation: causes, consequences, cures——Full employment at any price?——The repercussions of rent restrictions——1980s unemployment and the unions——The confusion of language in political thought——Economic freedom and representative government ——Will the democratic ideal prevail?
    ISBN 0–631–17109–6
   1. Free enterprise. 2. Economic policy. I. Title. II. Series.
HB95.H389 1990
338.9——dc20   89–78252 CIP

Typeset in 10½ on 12 pt Sabon
by Butler & Tanner Ltd, Frome and London
Printed in Great Britain by Butler & Tanner Ltd, Frome and London

Contents

Introduction

Norman Barry

Friedrich Hayek is more than just an economist, and more than just an advocate of market economics and limited government, as so many of his critics erroneously, and mischievously, assert. All that he says about the virtues of the private enterprise system, and its necessary framework of property rights and the rule of law, is embedded in a complex philosophy of man and society that he has developed over the past 40 years. As he has remarked, the economist who makes recommendations for social reform in ignorance of those ordering mechanisms that govern free societies is more likely to be a 'nuisance' than a help in the generation of that improvement he so ardently desires. Thus in this collection of Hayek's essays, the familiar problems of inflation, of government-inspired impediments to the co-ordinating functions of the market and those unintended and malign consequences that follow from short-sighted attempts to manipulate economic variables so as to promote (artificially) intrinsically desirable economic goals, such as full employment, are analysed alongside less familiar (for the professional economist) issues concerning law, morality, government and the nature of democracy.

The organising principle of Hayek's philosophy of economic freedom is based upon a profound insight into the nature and limits of human knowledge. The perfect organisation of economic systems, in which factors of production (land, labour, and capital) are allocated exactly to satisfy individual wants, and in which those factors are paid that income just sufficient to ensure the maximum productivity with no 'excess' profit, is a Nirvana yearned for by many economists, ranging from socialists and

This essay was written when the author was Visiting Scholar at the Social Philosophy and Policy Center, Bowling Green State University, Ohio.

other economic 'rationalists', through to Keynesian macro-economists. However, all mistake the purpose of a market system: it is a 'discovery procedure', a co-ordinating process by which individuals, through the signalling function of prices, make the best use of necessarily *decentralised* knowledge. Since a human society is subject to constant change, and the knowledge contained within it is of a fleeting and ephemeral kind, it cannot be 'objectified' in the manner required for quasi-scientific planning.

Hayek could not have made clearer his objection to that hubris about knowledge (and indeed, power) that characterises so much of modern economic thinking, than in his Nobel Prize Lecture, 'The Pretence of Knowledge' (reprinted here as part II of *Full Employment at Any Price?*). In arguing forcefully that unemployment is largely a consequence of some distortion in the structure of *relative* prices, Hayek suggests that we do have some theoretical knowledge of the process that tends, in an unhampered market, to restore stability, but says that

> ... when we are asked for quantitative evidence for the particular structure of prices and wages that would be required to assure a smooth continuous sale of the products and services offered, we must admit that we have no such information. We know ... the *general* conditions in which what we call, somewhat misleadingly, an 'equilibrium' will establish itself; but we never know the *particular* prices or wages that would exist if the market were to bring about such an equilibrium. (below, p. 283)

Hayek's comments here are addressed to any form of intervention, such as precise micro-economic planning, or 'fine-tuning', and demand management policies at the macro level, which depends upon knowledge: yet such knowledge must remain forever locked in the interstices of market society and hence be incommunicable to the directors of a *dirigiste* order. Economic freedom is valued, amongst other reasons, because under it the actions of decentralised traders are much more responsive to changes in the data of economic life than are political authorities. Entrepreneurs are indeed the bearers of this 'tacit' knowledge in their eagerness to exploit price differentials, without which co-ordination is scarcely possible at all.

One of the errors of modernistic and scientistic economic and social thought is its misdescription of certain key phenomena. In the above economic example, theorists treat a national economy as if it were an entity to which we can attribute a specific purpose, such as higher production, economic growth or full employment, when in fact a *catal-*

laxy or exchange system has no particular purpose, it is simply a network of *economies*, e.g. firms, individual enterprises, even 'co-operatives', each of which, of course, does have a specific end. Economics is, then, the science, not of production, but of exchange. The malign consequences of regarding a *catallaxy* as if it were 'one big company' are both economic and moral. The economic one is the failure to exploit local and dispersed knowledge, but the moral effect is even worse; for in the absence of genuine social ends that over-ride individual preferences as revealed in exchange, the organisers of an economy and planned society will impose their own. This phenomenon was first sketched by Hayek in his justly famous, and rightly alarmist, *The Road to Serfdom*, first published in 1944.

Some of the misuses of language, to which social theorists are prone, are explored and exposed in *The Confusion of Language in Political Thought*. As in economic theory, so in legal and political thought, Hayek observes the same phenomenon of confusing spontaneous and purposeless processes with directed and over-arching organisations. Although Hayek's own language in this area may be a bit complex and forbidding, the argument is clear enough. Every economic system requires a framework of stable and predictable rules: in an economic world which is necessarily uncertain, transactors require some security in the form of more or less permanent guidelines in the shape of rules of property, contract, and tort. They constitute what Hayek called the *law*, and are to be contrasted with that which he identifies as 'made law' or legislation.

Here Hayek's jurisprudence nicely parallels his economic theory; for law proper has no purpose, it is simply a set of rules required for the fulfilment of individual plans. However, legislation does have a purpose: it is to direct and control that *limited* range of activities (the supply of public goods) that is essential in the modern state. In Hayek's view law proper is better provided in common or case law (a legal analogue to the spontaneity of the market) than by statute, which is, of course, the only way that legislation can be provided. Although there is inevitably some unpredictability in emerging common law systems, it is likely to be less than that which emanates from capricious legislatures, governed as they are by parties and coalitions of pressure groups.

The error in modern jurisprudence is to interpret all law as if it were of one type – legislation flowing from more or less sovereign parliaments and subject to little in the way of judicial review. Thus it is that statute law now covers a vast area of social and economic life: welfare legislation has partially-monopolised spheres which were once governed by private insurance, paternalist statutes have undermined the common-law principle of *caveat emptor*, and public plans, often in the form of edicts and ukases, have repeatedly been imposed on private individuals.

Furthermore, the rise of statute law has also been accompanied by the specific exemption of politically favoured groups from the rules of just conduct. One of the features of law proper is that it is *perfectly general* and impartial between essentially anonymous agents. Although it is logically possible for legislation to be so structured, it is less likely. A spectacular example of the particularistic bent of legislation is the 1906 Trade Disputes Act, which renders trade unions immune from tort actions in industrial disputes. Hayek has maintained in a number of IEA publications (see especially *Unemployment and the Unions* in this collection) that this has produced malign political and economic effects. Its political effect is to introduce a significant breach in the rule of law; it exempts a particular group (largely because of its political power) from those general rules of just conduct on which all our freedoms ultimately depend. Its economic effect is quite obviously to impede the co-ordinating processes of the market by permitting unions to keep the price of labour above the market-clearing price through the use of the strike threat. In addition to this *de jure* privilege, there are some important *de facto* advantages which have accumulated over the years to unions. None of these phenomena helps the working class; they simply cause unemployment in certain sections of it.

In recent years circumstances have improved considerably: the extra immunities granted to unions in the 1970s have been removed, picketing laws have been tightened, and union membership has fallen. Most important, employers have been more eager to exercise their common-law right to dismiss workers for breach of contract (an additional reason why Britain should be wary of European 'social' codes with their legally protected 'right to strike'). Nevertheless, Hayek is to be commended for a life-long, and most often unpopular, struggle against legal privilege.

Again, the mistakes in public policy have a deep institutional explanation. In the case of perverse 'laws', these are largely a consequence of the gradual distortion of the democratic ideal, and its mutation in practice into a system of rule by coalitions of minorities, a process that has proceeded relentlessly throughout the 20th century. It would be false to say that Hayek is opposed to the principle of democracy: for those areas of social and economic life which have to be subjected to political control, the subjective choice of the voters is the only procedure compatible with liberal individualism. However, as he points out, in *Economic Freedom and Representative Government*, democracy has come to mean unlimited majority rule, and hence temporary coalitions can form which secure for named groups exemptions from the market process and the rule of law; even though they are to the long-run disadvantage of individuals as anonymous members of the general public. Thus his preferred form of government is *demarchy*, a democratic system qualified by a complex system of constitutional constraints; without this, Hayek argues, the perverse and anti-social outcomes of unlimited majoritarian procedures will lead to a disenchantment with the democratic ideal itself and the essential political freedoms that it embodies.

It is only then in the context of an understanding of Hayek's philosophy of freedom that we can appreciate the full significance of his controversial views on money and inflation. This collection contains a wide selection of his theories of the causes of inflation, the distortions it produces in the economy, and its arbitrary redistribution of income between various groups in society. Above all, Hayek has highlighted these institutional arrangements that have, in the 20th century, granted governments discretion in the supply of money. This acquired power of government to 'play on the monetary instrument', largely in the pursuit of short-run political advantage, has been the major concern of Hayek's career as an economist.

Although Hayek has always stressed the 'elementary truth' of the quantity theory of money, it would be a serious error to call him a monetarist in the broad Chicago tradition, from Irving Fisher (who was actually at Yale) to Milton Friedman. He has been as much concerned with the disequilibrating effect throughout the whole of the economy brought about by monetary injection as he has by changes in the general price level. It is true that orthodox monetarists did notice that money was not 'neutral' in the short run but produced relative price effects; however, they did not develop a causal theory of the trade cycle out of this, as Hayek and the 'Austrian' economists did. The *particular* patterns of disruption that occurred in the 1930s, with heavy unemployment in capital goods industries, have not been a feature of the post-war era, which has been characterised by misallocations of resources in all sectors of the economy, but they are illustrations of the same general phenomenon. The politically depressing message of Hayek's monetary theory is that such disruptions cannot be corrected without a painful, in terms of temporary recessions, process of readjustment. There is no short-cut solution to the problems of widespread unemployment by the manipulation of macro-economic aggregates, as is proposed by the Keynesian economists.

Among the many malign effects of inflation is that once the process is started it is very difficult to get it under control; as he graphically put it, it is like having a 'tiger by the tail'. There is no better illustration of this than the repeated failures of 'prices and incomes policies' to stem inflation. Again, in another colourful simile, a government's use of inflation to secure economic benefits is rather like drug addiction – it takes larger and larger doses to secure decreasingly smaller amounts of bliss. Hayek was never persuaded by 'money illusion', the idea that workers would not notice a cut in real wages that inflation brings about, thus producing more employment. He always said that the unions would quickly learn to include anticipated inflation in their wage demands so that the temporary benefits of inflation are soon frittered away in higher prices. He was not at all surprised by 'stagflation', the phenomenon of rising unemployment *and* rising prices.

The reader can chart for himself the progress of Hayek's radical proposal for the abolition of government's monopoly of money from his first suggestion in *Choice in Currency* (1976) through to his theory of a commodity-backed monetary Standard ('Market Standards for Money', 1986). What is distinctive of the approach is its explicit recommendation of the abolition of *monetary policy*; since governments cannot be relied upon to follow rules, monetary stability must then be produced by the market itself. Even if they could, the insuperable difficulty of measuring 'money' would make the classic Chicago solvent for inflation, a rule that ties increases in money to increases in productivity, impracticable. In fact, the development of modern international monetary institutions and the ready convertibility of currencies makes Hayek's proposal sound less radical. People are choosing currencies anyway, in the absence of Hayek's Standard. It would not be a dramatic step to allow people to trade in dollars, pounds, or marks, etc., in the High Street as well as in the international money markets.

Hayek's philosophy of economic freedom is an intricate, complex architectonic intellectual structure in which (superficially) minor as well as major recommendations for public policy are elegant inferences from a coherent set of realistic premises about man and society. Over and above the economic concerns there is a profound and morally uplifting case for liberty, the rule of law, and the respect we owe to one another not just as 'vulgar' traders but as citizens of the 'Great Society'.

1

A Tiger by the Tail

Introduced and selected by Sudha Shenoy

I The Debate, 1931–1971

The roots of current economic ideas and of those guiding wages policy lie in the 1930s, in discussion inspired by the publication of the *General Theory*. Though Keynes's ideas diverged significantly from the theoretical structure of Pigou and Marshall, with which he was most familiar, 'Keynesian' ways of thinking had been fairly widespread in Britain and the USA before the *General Theory* appeared in 1936.[1] Keynes provided a theoretical foundation for these new ways of thinking.

Since the publication of the *General Theory* there has been an extensive elaboration of the theoretical system outlined in or generally associated with it, together with a further development of an alternative system of concepts called the Classical system. This was close to a mirror-image of the Keynesian system,[2] in the main relationships (e.g. between the quantity of money and total expenditure, between interest, saving and investment, between the wage level and the level of employment, and so on). But whereas the Keynesian system was couched wholly in terms of aggregates, the so-called 'Classical' system contained what may be termed a price dimension: the changes in the price 'level' associated with changes in the total money stock were held by the Classical system to imply equi-proportional changes in *all* prices, and variations in the price level in turn were associated with changes in the level of economic activity. In a sense the Keynesian approach may be regarded as a logical extension and elaboration of this rather crudely aggregative element in the 'Classical' system.

Published originally as *Hobart Paperback* No. 4, 2nd Edition, IEA (1978).

1 Challenge to Keynes

The doctrines generally accepted among English economists contemporaneous with Keynes were challenged, in fundamental respects, by an alternative analysis, developed on the Continent, and propounded in Britain by Professor Hayek. But by the 1940s, the Keynesian approach was almost universally adopted by economists. Initially, many appeared to believe that the 'macro' problems of unemployment and depression were solved and that few other major economic problems would emerge. The only problem remaining, it seemed, was the methods required to ensure 'full' employment:

> 'Now that the principle of adequate effective demand is so firmly established,' declared Professor Arthur Smithies, 'economists should devote particular attention to defining the responsibilities of the state.'[3]

The British White Paper on Employment Policy in 1944 and the full employment commitment in the UN Charter reflected this belief, as did the 1946 Employment Act in the USA.[4]

A few dissenting voices warned of trouble ahead. Professor Jacob Viner observed of a report to the Economic and Social Council of the United Nations, *National and International Measures for Full Employment*, prepared by a group of distinguished economists (J. M. Clark, A. Smithies, N. Kaldor, P. Uri, and E. R. Walker):

> The sixty-four dollar question with respect to the relations between unemployment and full employment policy is what to do if a policy to guarantee full employment leads to chronic upward pressure on money wages through the operation of collective bargaining. The authors take a good look at the question – and run away.

Effective demand to provide employment was the 'key concept' in recommendations which Professor Viner rated as 'much more Keynesian than was the final Keynes himself . . .'[5]

Shortly after *The General Theory* appeared, Professor W. H. Hutt argued that it was a specific for inflation.[6]

Even Keynes had doubts, a few years after *The General Theory*. In his essay *How to Pay for the War* (Macmillan, 1940) he warned the trade unions of the 'futility' of demanding an increase in money rates of wages to compensate for every increase in the cost of living. To prevent inflation, he insisted,

Some means must be found for withdrawing purchasing power from the market; or prices must rise until the available goods are selling at figures which absorb the increased quantity of expenditure – in other words, the method of inflation.

And in a discussion of financing war expenditure:

> ... a demand on the part of the trade unions for an increase in money rates of wages to compensate for every increase in his cost of living is futile, and greatly to the disadvantage of the working class. Like the dog in the fable, they lose the substance in grasping at the shadow. It is true that the better organised might benefit at the expense of other consumers. But except as an effort at group selfishness, as a means of hustling someone else out of the queue, it is a mug's game....

2 The Approach to an Incomes Policy

Over the following 25-odd years, the early Keynesian theory was further elaborated and refined and a highly sophisticated series of macro-economic models developed. The 1950s more especially saw the discovery of 'cost inflation', in which a rise in wages pushed up the cost level. As prices were determined by costs, and, in crucial sectors of the economy, were 'administered' on the cost-plus-mark-up practice, prices rose to protect profit margins. But since wages were also incomes the cost and price increases had no deflationary effect, as effective demand rose simultaneously.[7] In these circumstances a contractionary monetary/fiscal policy would be deflationary: it would lead to socially intolerable levels of unemployment and excess capacity; an alternative measure, directed specifically at rising costs, would have to be devised. If price stability and full employment could both be achieved by keeping wage increases within the limits set by rises in productivity, this implied an 'incomes policy'. Further investigation into the implications for the price and wage level of linking sectoral wage increases with productivity strengthened the case for a nationally determined 'wages policy' covering both relative wage rates *and* the general wage level. If wages rose in the sectors where productivity was rising, the result would be a rise in demand for the outputs of other sectors, resulting in a rise in their prices.[8]

Economic policy in the UK and the USA, from 1950 on, reflected the adoption of these views; there was a gradual shift from exhortations, guidelines, and pay pauses to more direct attempts to influence and control wages.[9]

That such direct control of wages and prices would be needed to forestall the 'vicious wage–price spiral'[10] resulting from full employment had been forecast by Lord Beveridge as early as 1944.

By the late 1960s and early 1970s more economists came to favour an incomes policy, some reluctantly (Robbins, Meade, Paish, Brittan, Morgan),[11] others enthusiastically (Balogh, Streeten, Opie).[12]

Lord Robbins's case is particularly interesting. In the early 1950s he analysed clearly the inflationary implications of the full employment policy contemplated by Beveridge: it gave union leaders a virtual guarantee that

> *whatever [wage] rates they succeeded in getting, unemployment would not be permitted to emerge.*[13]

It would give them a continuous incentive to push wages beyond increases in productivity, setting off a 'vicious spiral' of 'more inflation'. This, in turn, might force governments to act directly on wage rates.

> The present determination of wages by bargain between employer and employed would be suspended. Wage-fixing by the state would take its place.

He believed, however, that this alternative would be rejected 'on the ground that in the end its efficient operation would prove to be incompatible with the continuation of political democracy ...'[14] Seventeen years later he argued[15] for an incomes policy as temporary '*shocktactics*', to afford a 'breathing space' in which fundamental monetary–fiscal reforms might be 'advanced and understood'.

Despairing of the good sense of union leaders, he sought to bring pressure on them indirectly, suggesting that businessmen be restrained from granting inflationary wage increases by restrictions on aggregate demand, even to the point of precipitating bankruptcies, thus preventing the payment of higher wages that would simply be recouped by higher prices. A suggested alternative or parallel measure would be to tax inflationary wage increases granted by firms. He hoped that union leaders' expectations of automatic increases in wages would thereby be frustrated. (A similar view is taken by Professors E. Victor Morgan, F. W. Paish, and Sidney Weintraub.)[16]

An alternative type of incomes policy was proposed by Mr Samuel

Brittan.[17] The government would control the level to which wage rates would be permitted to rise while allowing employers short of labour to offer higher rates, but *without* pretending to determine relative wage rates on the basis of social justice. Such a policy, he said, must be treated as a *supplement* to monetary and fiscal policies that provide sufficient demand to prevent unemployment, but prevent the emergence of excess demand. He suggested as a stop-gap a temporary price and wage freeze until these policies are implemented.

Two possible implications of this suggestion may be considered. First, if such a brake on wage increases is to be more than advice, unions must be willing to accept the guidance of the incomes authority – implying a permanent watchdog rôle for the authority (or at least an existence parallel to that of the unions-as-wage-fixers). If the unions refuse to co-operate presumably the authority will have to take over their wage-fixing function. . . .

Secondly, in common with other recommendations for incomes policies, this proposal would perpetuate a given structure of *relative* wage rates since *all* the rates to which it applied would be allowed to rise only by a given percentage (save in 'labour scarcity'). This relative wage structure today reflects not so much the allocative forces of the market[18] but the relative power or 'pushfulness' of the different unions. Can we assume that they would be content to retain indefinitely whatever relative positions they had achieved at the moment the incomes policy came into existence?

3 'Micro' Dimensions Acknowledged

The common thread running through these discussions is the alleviation of specific *wage-rate* maladjustments. They have moved some distance from the aggregative analysis. The 'macro' problem of adequate demand management has, it now appears, a 'micro' dimension: that of establishing (or obtaining) an 'appropriate' scale of prices. In other words, from the viewpoint of practical policy, the 'macro' problem of a persistent upward push (or pull) on the price 'level' is now seen to have 'micro' roots, in the specific 'pricing' methods used by specific groups of workers. 'Macro' measures acting on aggregate expenditure may have allowed us hitherto to ignore this basic micro *dis*-co-ordination,[19] but events seemingly have brought the issue forward unavoidably. 'Macro' measures, it would appear, may *offset* micro problems but are no substitute for appropriate micro solutions.

The significance of co-ordination at the micro-level appears here, in the light of a third type of analysis, which Professor Hayek developed, on foundations laid by the 'Austrians': Menger, Wieser, and Böhm-Bawerk, culminating in the works of von Mises. Hayek concentrated on an analysis of the structure of relative prices and their inter-relations. He did not adopt the framework of a general equilibrium system, nor treat price changes as elements in a 'dynamic' shift between two general equilibria. He regarded prices rather as empirical reflectors of specific circumstances and price changes as an *inter-related* series of changes in these 'signals', which produced a gradual adaptation in the entire price structure (and hence in the outputs of different commodities and services) to the constant, unpredictable changes in the real world. Pricing, in short, is seen as a continuous information-collecting and -disseminating process, but it is the institutional framework that determines both the extent to which, and the degree of success with which, prices are enabled to perform this potential signalling or allocative function.

This 'Austrian' analysis constitutes a substantial break with Classical economic theory from Adam Smith to J. S. Mill. It differs also both from the doctrines of the English economists after Mill and from the theoretical preoccupations of the Lausanne School with the conditions of general equilibrium.[20]

4 Is There a Price 'Level'?

In his first English work, the four lectures published as *Prices and Production*,[21] Hayek questioned the concept of a price 'level', i.e. a relationship between the total money stock and the total volume of production, variations in this 'level' being associated with variations in aggregate output. He argued that such a concept failed to show that there were specific influences of changes in the stream of money expenditure on the structure of relative prices, and hence on the structure of production.[22] These price and output changes, he maintained, occurred irrespective of changes in the price level. Hayek's analysis implied that if 'the' price 'level' is held 'stable' by offsetting monetary measures, under conditions where the relative price changes would result in a falling price 'level', the real dislocations would be the same as if prices were made to rise by monetary measures, if otherwise they might have remained 'stable'. In either case, the outcome is a painful correction of the preceding real misdirection, i.e. a 'depression'.

During the 1920s, the widespread theoretical and policy influence of the 'stabilisationists' meant that considerations of the kind sketched by Professor Hayek were not incorporated into either theoretical or policy analysis; consequently, the price 'level' 'stability' of the period was read as implying a lack of maladjustment in the underlying price structure. (This is an extremely over-simplified summary of a complex historical situation, the specific conditions of which were not uniform in all countries.)

Theoretically and practically, it may be argued that in conditions of 'depression' there is little choice save to augment the level of monetary expenditure to the highest possible degree. Hayekian analysis, while readily conceding that depressionary symptoms may thus be overlaid, would argue that the problems are then transformed into those arising out of a situation where every reappearance of recessionary symptoms has to be met by ever larger increases of monetary expenditure, eventually issuing in the 'stagflationist' dilemma.

This is not necessarily to say that the specific policies pursued in the 1920s and 1930s, or the economic and monetary framework of the time, represented an approximation to the Hayekian ideal. Hayek has said with regard to the period 1927–32:

> ... up to 1927, I should, indeed, have expected that because, during the preceding boom period, prices did not rise – but rather tended to fall – the subsequent depression would be very mild. But, as is well known, in that year an entirely unprecedented action was taken by the American monetary authorities, which makes it impossible to compare the effects of the boom on the subsequent depression with any previous experience. The authorities succeeded by means of an easy money policy, inaugurated as soon as the symptoms of an impending reaction were noticed, in prolonging the boom for two years beyond what would otherwise have been its natural end. And when the crisis finally occurred, for almost two more years deliberate attempts were made to prevent, by all conceivable means, the normal process of liquidation. It seems to me that these facts have had a far greater influence on the character of the depression than the developments up to 1927, which, from all we know, might instead have led to a comparatively mild depression in and after 1927.[23]

Shortly after the publication of the first edition of *Prices and Production*, Professor Hayek published (in *Economica*) the first part of a long, substantive review of Keynes's *Treatise on Money*.[24] This

provoked a reply from Keynes, followed by a rejoinder, before the publication of the second part of the review. Hayek criticised Keynes for
his neglect of the real structure of production, arguing that Keynes's
predilection for concentrating on the immediate and purely monetary
phenomena accompanying changes in money expenditure, together with
his penchant for aggregative macro concepts (*total* profits, *total* investment), had led him into contradictory or untenable conclusions. Keynes
apparently held that if there were no entrepreneurial profits or losses in
the aggregate, total output would be held constant. Hayek replied that
if profits in the 'lower' stages of production (nearer consumption) were
exactly counterbalanced by losses in the 'higher' stages, there would be
a contraction in the capital structure and a fall in output and employment – even though there were no aggregate profits or losses.

In his reply, Keynes failed to take up the numerous substantial criticisms made by Hayek. The main point of interest is his explicit statement
that '... in my view, saving and investment ... can get out of gear ...
there being no automatic mechanism in the economic system ... to keep
the two rates equal'. Hayek's reply to this was based on his analysis of
the relative price-structure:

> Mr Keynes's assertion that there is no automatic mechanism in the econ-
> omic system to keep the rate of saving and the rate of investing equal ...
> might with equal justification be extended to the more general contention
> that there is no automatic mechanism in the economic system to adapt
> production to any other shift in demand.

5 Further Implications of Hayekian Analysis

There are further implications of the Hayekian approach:

(a) If the current level of output and employment is made to depend
on inflation, a slowing-down in the pace of inflation will produce
recessionary symptoms. Moreover, as the economy becomes adjusted to
a particular rate of inflation, the rate must itself be continuously increased
if symptoms of a depression are to be avoided: to inflate is to have 'a
tiger by the tail'.

(b) To limit price or wage-rate increases by an incomes policy is to
freeze a particular set of price and wage-rate inter-relationships while
underlying circumstances of supply and demand are continually changing. This is like the 'stability' of a set of defective gauges perpetually

pointing to the same set of readings. It reinforces other institutional factors preventing the specific changes in relative prices and wage rates necessary to the maintenance of 'full' employment. Or, to put this same point from a different angle, if 'full' employment is to be maintained at union-determined wage rates (which are inflexible downwards), *all other* prices and wage rates must be adjusted to them: other prices and wage rates must be set at, or reach, levels consistent with this objective. *Even if* union-determined wage rates were held down to a maximum percentage increase, it still *does not* follow that the *same* percentage increase, or a lesser increase, in all other prices and wage rates would suffice to achieve 'full' employment. *This* is why it may be necessary for incomes to rise faster than output, even to secure that increase in output.[25]

(c) The major objection to an incomes policy approach is that it merely freezes a given array of prices and wage rates. It does nothing to bring about co-ordination or to introduce co-ordinative institutions into the labour sector. So long as the *dis*-co-ordinative potential of such non-market institutions as unions is not tackled, the problem will recur again and again. There may be no substitute for a very painful re-shaping of institutions or other means of bringing within the ambit of the pricing system wage rates made impervious to market forces.[26] The alternative is a *permanent* incomes policy: an all-round fixing of wage rates and prices, i.e. an effectively centrally-controlled economy (with all its problems), although we may, as it were, 'back into' this situation unintentionally. This is to say nothing about whether it is desirable politically.[27]

II The Misuse of Aggregates

6 Inflationism

In 1931 Professor Hayek believed that the naïve inflationist view – that every expansion of monetary expenditure produces expansion in output – had been superseded; but this view was revived in 1936 by the General Theory *which strengthened the 'subtler inflationism' against which he directed his attack.*

While the more naïve forms of inflationism are sufficiently discredited today not to do much harm in the near future, contemporary economic thought is so much permeated by an inflationism of a subtler kind that it is to be feared that for some time we shall still have to endure the consequences of a good deal of dangerous tampering with currency and credit. It is my belief that some even of those doctrines which are generally accepted in this field have no other basis than an uncritical application to the problems of society in general of the experience of the individual, that what he needs is more money.[28]

(Preface to first edition of *Prices and Production*, Routledge, 1931)

7 No Causal Connection Between Macro Totals and Micro Decisions

Professor Hayek emphasises the operational significance of individual specific price changes in the real world; he also emphasises the ex post nature of such statistical constructs as averages and aggregates.

... What I complain of is not only that [the quantity]theory in its various forms has unduly usurped the central place in monetary theory, but that the point of view from which it springs is a positive hindrance to further progress. Not the least harmful effect of this particular theory is the present isolation of the theory of money from the main body of general economic theory. For so long as we use different methods for the explanation of values as they are supposed to exist irrespective of any influence of money, and for the explanation of that influence of money on prices, it can never be otherwise. Yet we are doing nothing less than this if we try to establish *direct* causal connections between the *total* quantity of money, the *general level* of all prices and, perhaps, also the *total* amount of production. For none of these magnitudes *as such* ever exerts an influence on the decisions of individuals; yet it is on the assumption of a knowledge of the decisions of individuals that the main propositions of non-monetary economic theory are based. It is to this 'individualistic' method that we owe whatever understanding of economic phenomena we possess; that the modern 'subjective' theory has advanced beyond the classical school in its consistent use is probably its main advantage over their teaching.

If, therefore, monetary theory still attempts to establish causal relations between aggregates or general averages, this means that monetary theory lags behind the development of economics in general. In fact, neither aggregates nor averages do act upon one another, and it will never be possible to establish necessary connections of cause and effect between them as we can between individual phenomena, individual prices, etc. I would even go so far as to assert that, from the very nature of economic theory, averages can never form a link in its reasoning.

(Prices and Production, op. cit., pp. 3–5)

8 Fallacy of 'The' Price Level

Professor Hayek points out that the ex post *statistical construct of a price index, which we call 'the' price level, is* not *a representation of reality – in the sense in which, say, the 'observations' of the physical sciences are such a representation. (He also refers – in 1937 – to the serious monetary consequences of an attempt to offset by monetary policy downward inflexibility of prices and/or wage-rates.)*

It is clear that in this case the argument for a national monetary system cannot rest on any peculiarities of the national money. It must rest, and indeed it does rest, on the assumption that there is a particularly close connection between the prices – and particularly the wages – within the country which causes them to move to a considerable degree up and down together compared with prices outside the country. This is frequently regarded as sufficient reason why, in order to avoid the necessity that the 'country as a whole' should have to raise or lower its prices, the quantity of money in the country should be so adjusted as to keep the 'general price level' within the country stable. I do not want to consider this argument yet. I shall later argue that it rests largely on an illusion, based on the accident that the statistical measures of price movements are usually constructed for countries as such; and that in so far as there are genuine difficulties connected with general downward adjustments of many prices, and particularly wages, the proposed remedy would be worse than the disease.

(*Monetary Nationalism and International Stability*, Geneva, 1937, p. 7)

9 Economic Systems Overleap National Boundaries

In tracing through the effects of a change in demand that crosses an international political boundary Professor Hayek shows the series of interconnected price and income changes it produces, emphasising the

*basic point that it is these interlinked changes in relative prices that
constitute reality, rather than 'movements' in some statistical price-'level'.*

The important point in all this is that what wages and what prices will
have to be altered in consequence of the initial change will depend on
whether and to what extent the value of a particular factor or service,
directly or indirectly, depends on the particular change in demand which
has occurred, and not on whether it is inside or outside the same 'currency
area'. We can see this more clearly if we picture the series of successive
changes of money incomes, which will follow on the initial shift of
demand, as single chains, neglecting for the moment the successive
ramifications which will occur at every link. Such a chain may either
very soon lead to the other country or first run through a great many
links at home. But whether any particular individual in the country will
be affected will depend on whether he is a link in that particular chain,
that is whether he has more or less immediately been serving the individuals whose income has first been affected, and not simply on whether
he is in the same country or not. In fact this picture of the chain makes
it clear that it is not impossible that most of the people who ultimately
suffer a decrease of income in consequence of the initial transfer of
demand from A to B may be in B and not in A. This is often overlooked
because the whole process is presented as if the chain of effects came to
an end as soon as payments between the two countries balance. In fact,
however, each of the two chains – that started by the decrease of
somebody's income in A, and that started by the increase of another
person's income in B – may continue to run on for a long time after they
have passed into the other country, and may have even a greater number
of links in that country than in the one where they started. They will
come to an end only when they meet, not only in the same country but
in the same individual, so finally offsetting each other. This means that
the number of reductions of individual incomes and prices (not their
aggregate amount) which becomes necessary in consequence of a transfer
of money from A to B may actually be greater in B than in A.

Misleading concepts of prices and incomes

This picture is of course highly unrealistic because it leaves out of account
the infinite ramifications to which each of these chains of effects will
develop. But even so it should, I think, make it clear how superficial and
misleading the kind of argument is which runs in terms of *the* prices and

the incomes of the country, as if they would necessarily move in unison or even in the same direction. It will be prices and incomes of particular individuals and particular industries which will be affected and the effects will not be essentially different from those which will follow any shifts of demand between different industries or localities.

This whole question is of course the same as that which I discussed in my first lecture in connection with the problem of what constitutes one monetary system, namely the question of whether there exists a particularly close coherence between prices and incomes, and particularly wages, in any one country which tends to make them move as a whole relatively to the price structure outside. As I indicated then, I shall not be able to deal with it more completely until later on. But there are two points which, I think, will have become clear now and which are important for the understanding of the contrast between the working of the homogeneous international currency we are considering, and the mixed system to which I shall presently proceed.

In the first place it already appears very doubtful whether there is any sense in which the terms inflation and deflation can be appropriately applied to these inter-regional or international transfers of money. If, of course, we *define* inflation and deflation as changes in the quantity of money, or the price level, *within a particular territory*, then the term naturally applies. But it is by no means clear that the consequences which we can show will follow if the quantity of money in a closed system changes will also apply to such redistributions of money between areas. In particular there is no reason why the changes in the quantity of money within an area should bring about those merely temporary changes in relative prices which, in the case of a real inflation, lead to misdirections of production – misdirections because eventually the inherent mechanism of these inflations tends to reverse these changes in relative prices.

(*Monetary Nationalism and International Stability, op. cit.*, pp. 21–4)

10 Dangers of 'National' Stabilisation

This extract indicates the extent to which policies of national price-'level' 'stabilisation' may cumulatively produce international inflation. If prices in general are not permitted to fall in regions where a fall is necessitated by changes in circumstances, the only other method of securing such a relative decline is by a general rise in prices in all other regions.

Indeed, if we take a somewhat more realistic point of view, there can be little doubt what will happen. While, in the country where in consequence of the changes in international demand some prices will tend to fall the price level will be kept stable, it will certainly be allowed to rise in the country which has been benefited by the same shift in demand. It is not difficult to see what this implies if all countries in the world act on this principle. It means that prices would be stabilised only in that area where they tend to fall lowest relatively to the rest of the world, and that all further adjustments are brought about by proportionate increases of prices in all other countries. The possibilities of inflation which this offers if the world is split up into a sufficient number of very small separate currency areas seem indeed very considerable. And why, if this principle is once adopted, should it remain confined to average prices in particular national areas? Would it not be equally justified to argue that no price of any single commodity should ever be allowed to fall and that the quantity of money in the world should be so regulated that the price of that commodity which tends to fall lowest relatively to all others should be kept stable, and that the prices of all other commodities would be adjusted upwards in proportion? We only need to remember what happened, for instance, a few years ago to the price of rubber to see how such a policy would surpass the wishes of even the wildest inflationist. Perhaps this may be thought an extreme case. But, once the principle has been adopted, it is difficult to see how it could be confined to 'reasonable' limits, or indeed to say what 'reasonable' limits are.

But let us disregard the practical improbability that a policy of stabilisation will be followed in the countries where, with stable exchanges, the price level would rise, as well as in the countries where in this case it would have to fall. Let us assume that, in the countries which benefit from the increase of the demand, the prices of other goods are actually lowered to preserve stability of the national price level and that the opposite action will be taken in the countries from which demand has turned away. What is the justification and significance of such a policy of national stabilisation?

Theoretical case not argued

Now it is difficult to find the theoretical case for national stabilisation anywhere explicitly argued. It is usually just taken for granted that any sort of policy which appears desirable in a closed system must be equally beneficial if applied to a national area. It may therefore be desirable, before we go on to examine its analytical justification, to trace the historical causes which have brought this view to prominence. There can be little doubt that its ascendancy is closely connected with the peculiar difficulties of English monetary policy between 1925 and 1931. In the comparatively short space of the six years during which Great Britain was on a gold standard in the post-war period, it suffered from what is known as over-valuation of the pound. Against all the teaching of 'orthodox' economics – already a hundred years before Ricardo had expressly stated that he 'should never advise a government to restore a currency, which was depreciated 30 per cent, to par'[29] – in 1925 the British currency had been brought back to its former gold value. In consequence, to restore equilibrium, it was necessary to reduce *all* prices and costs in proportion as the value of the pound had been raised. This process, particularly because of the notorious difficulty of reducing money wages, proved to be very painful and prolonged. It deprived England of real participation in the boom which led up to the crisis of 1929, and, in the end, its results proved insufficient to secure the maintenance of the restored parity. But all this was not due to an initial shift in the conditions of demand or to any of the causes which may affect the condition of a particular country under stable exchanges. It was an *effect* of the change in the external value of the pound. It was not a case where with given exchange rates the national price or cost structure of a country as a whole had got out of equilibrium with the rest of the world, but rather that the change in the parities had suddenly upset the relations between all prices inside and outside the country.

Relative price and cost structures

Nevertheless this experience has created among many British economists a curious prepossession with the relations between national price- and cost- and particularly wage-levels, as if there were any reason to expect that as a rule there would arise a necessity that the price and cost structure of one country as a whole should change relatively to that of other countries. And this tendency has received considerable support from the fashionable pseudo-quantitative economics of averages with its argument running in terms of national 'price levels', 'purchasing power parities', 'terms of trade', the 'Multiplier', and what not.

The purely accidental fact that these averages are generally computed for prices in a national area is regarded as evidence that in some sense all prices of a country could be said to move together relatively to prices in other countries.[30] This has strengthened the belief that there is some peculiar difficulty about the case where 'the' price level of a country had to be changed relatively to its given cost level and that such adjustment had better be avoided by manipulations of the rate of exchange.

Now let me add immediately that of course I do not want to deny that there may be cases where some change in conditions might make fairly extensive reductions of money wages necessary in a particular area if exchange rates are to be maintained, and that under present conditions such wage reductions are at best a very painful and long drawn out process. At any rate in the case of countries whose exports consist largely of one or a few raw materials, a severe fall in the prices of these products might create such a situation. What I want to suggest, however, is that many of my English colleagues, because of the special experience of their country in recent times, have got the practical significance of this particular case altogether out of perspective: that they are mistaken in believing that by altering parities they can overcome many of the chief difficulties created by the rigidity of wages and, in particular, that by their fascination with the relation between 'the' price level and 'the' cost level in a particular area they are apt to overlook the much more important consequences of inflation and deflation.[31]

(*Monetary Nationalism and International Stability, op. cit.*, pp. 42–6)

11 Monetary Danger of Collective Bargaining

This extract is noteworthy for its prediction, in 1937, of the process of wage-inflation of the 1950s and 1960s.

While the whole idea of a monetary policy directed to adjust everything to a 'given' wage level appears to me misconceived on purely theoretical grounds, its consequences seem to me to be fantastic if we imagine it applied to the present world where this supposedly given wage level is at the same time the subject of political strife. It would mean that the whole mechanism of collective wage bargaining would in the future be used exclusively to raise wages, while any reduction – even if it were necessary only in one particular industry – would have to be brought about by monetary means. I doubt whether such a proposal could ever have been seriously entertained except in a country and in a period where labour has been for long on the defensive.[32] It is difficult to imagine how wage negotiations would be carried on if it became the recognised duty of the monetary authority to offset any unfavourable effect of a rise in wages on the competitive position of national industries on the world market. But of one thing we can probably be pretty certain: that the working class would not be slow to learn that an engineered rise of prices is no less a reduction of wages than a deliberate cut of money wages, and that in consequence the belief that it is easier to reduce by the round-about method of depreciation the wages of all workers in a country than directly to reduce the money wages of those who are affected by a given change, will soon prove illusory.

(*Monetary Nationalism and International Stability, op. cit.*, pp. 52–3)

III Neglect of Real for Monetary Aspects

12 Keynes's Neglect of Scarcity

Professor Hayek argues here that the Keynesian system rests implicitly on a denial of the existence of real scarcities, since it assumes that aggregate real output automatically changes in the same direction as total monetary expenditure – in other words, that every increase in money incomes automatically calls forth a corresponding supply of consumer goods and of investment goods.

Somewhat more careful consideration is needed of what exactly we mean here when we speak of an increase in investment. Strictly speaking, if we start from an initial equilibrium position where the existence of unused resources[33] is excluded by definition, an increase or decrease of investment should always mean a transfer of input from the production of consumers' goods for a nearer date to the production of consumers' goods for a more distant date, or vice versa. But where we assume that this diversion of input from one kind of production to another is accompanied, and in part brought about, by changes in total money expenditure, we cannot at the same time assume that prices will remain unchanged. It is, however, neither necessary nor advisable to adhere for our present purposes to so rigid a type of equilibrium assumption. At any rate, so far as concerns the impact effects of a rise in investment demand which we discussed in the last chapter, there is no reason why we should not assume that the additional input which is being invested has previously been unemployed, so that the increase in investment means a corresponding increase in the employment of all sorts of resources without any increase of prices and without a decrease in the production of consumers' goods. This assumption simply means that there are certain limited quantities of various resources available which have been offered but not bought at current prices, but which would be employed as soon as demand at existing prices rose. And since the amount of such resources will always be limited, the effect of making this assumption will be that we must distinguish between the effects which an increase of investments and income will have while there are unused resources of all kinds available and the effects which such an increase will have after the various resources become successively scarce and their prices begin to rise.

Investment demand and incomes

The initial change from which we started our discussion in the last chapter, an invention which gives rise to a new demand for capital, means that with given prices the margin between the cost of production and the price of the product produced with the new process will be higher than the ruling rate of profit, i.e. that the marginal rate of profit on the former volume of production will have risen. The first result of this, as we have seen, will be that investment will increase, the marginal rate of profit will fall, and the cash balances will decrease till the desire for holding the marginal units of the decreased cash balances is again just balanced by the higher profits which may be obtained by investing them. This new rate of profit will be somewhere between the old rate and the higher rate which would exist if investment had not increased. But since this additional investment has been financed by a release of money out of idle balances, incomes will have increased, and as a consequence the demand for consumers' goods will also increase, although probably not to the full extent, as some of the additional income is likely to be saved.

If we assume that there are unused resources available not only in the form of factors of production but also in the form of consumers' goods in all stages of completion, and so long as this is the case, the increase in the demand for consumers' goods will for some time lead merely to an increase in sales without an increase of prices. Such an increase of the quantity of output which can be sold at given prices will have the effect of raising the investment demand further, or, more exactly, of shifting our returns curve to the right without changing its shape. The amount that it will appear profitable to borrow and invest at any given rate of interest will accordingly increase; and this in turn will mean that, though some more money will be released from idle balances, the rate of interest and the rate of profit will be raised further. And since this process will have raised incomes still further, it will be repeated: that is, every further increase in the demand for consumers' goods will lead to some further increase of investment and some further increase of the rate of profit. But at every stage of this process some part of the additional income will be saved, and as rates of interest rise, any given increase in final demand will lead to proportionally less investment. (Or, what is really the same phenomenon, only seen from a different angle, successive increases of investment demand will lead to the release of decreasing amounts of money from idle balances.) So the process will gradually slow down and finally come to a stop.

Final position of rate of return

Where will the rate of interest be fixed in this final equilibrium? If we assume the quantity of money to have remained constant, it will evidently be above the rate which ruled before the initial change occurred and even above the somewhat higher impact rate which ruled immediately after the change occurred, since every revolution of the process we have been considering will have raised it a little further. But under our present assumptions there is no reason why, even when this process comes to an end, the rate of interest need have risen to the full extent to which it would have risen in the beginning had the supply of investible funds been entirely inelastic. Thus, under the conditions we have considered, the release of money from idle balances (and the same would of course be true of an increase in the quantity of money) may keep the rate of profit and interest lastingly below the figure to which it would have risen without any such monetary change.

Let us be quite clear, however, about which of our assumptions this somewhat surprising result is due to. We have assumed that not only the supply of pure input but also the supply of final and intermediate products and of instruments of all kinds was infinitely elastic, so that every increase in demand could be satisfied without any increase of price, or, in other words, that the increase of investment (or we should rather say output) was possible without society in the aggregate or even any single individual having to reduce consumption in order to provide an income for the additional people now employed. Or, in other words, we have been considering an economic system in which not only the

permanent resources but also all kinds of non-permanent resources, that
is, all forms of capital, were not scarce. There is indeed no reason why
the price of capital should rise if there are such unused reserves of capital
available, there is even no reason why capital should have a price at all
if it were abundant in all its forms. The existence of interest in such a
world would indeed be due merely to the scarcity of money, although
even money would not be scarce in any absolute sense; it would be scarce
only relatively to given prices on which people were assumed to insist.
By an appropriate adjustment of the quantity of money the rate of
interest could, in such a system, be reduced to practically any level.

Mr Keynes's economics of abundance

Now such a situation, in which abundant unused reserves of all kinds
of resources, including all intermediate products, exist, may occasionally
prevail in the depths of a depression. But it is certainly not a normal
position on which a theory claiming general applicability could be based.
Yet it is some such world as this which is treated in Mr Keynes's *The
General Theory of Employment, Interest and Money*, which in recent
years has created so much stir and confusion among economists and
even the wider public. Although the technocrats, and other believers in
the unbounded productive capacity of our economic system, do not yet
appear to have realised it, what he has given us is really that economics
of abundance for which they have been clamouring so long. Or rather,
he has given us a system of economics which is based on the assumption
that no real scarcity exists, and that the only scarcity with which we need
concern ourselves is the artificial scarcity created by the determination of
people not to sell their services and products below certain arbitrarily
fixed prices. These prices are in no way explained, but are simply assumed
to remain at their historically given level, except at rare intervals when
'full employment' is approached and the different goods begin successively to become scarce and to rise in price.

Now if there is a well-established fact which dominates economic life,
it is the incessant, even hourly, variation in the prices of most of the
important raw materials and of the wholesale prices of nearly all foodstuffs. But the reader of Mr Keynes's theory is left with the impression
that these fluctuations of prices are entirely unmotivated and irrelevant,
except towards the end of a boom, when the fact of scarcity is readmitted
into the analysis, as an apparent exception, under the designation of
'bottlenecks'.[34] And not only are the factors which determine the relative

prices of the various commodities systematically disregarded;[35] it is even explicitly argued that, apart from the purely monetary factors which are supposed to be the sole determinants of the rate of interest, the prices of the majority of goods would be indeterminate. Although this is expressly stated only for capital assets in the special narrow sense in which Mr Keynes uses this term, that is, for durable goods and securities, the same reasoning would apply to all factors of production. In so far as 'assets' in general are concerned the whole argument of the *General Theory* rests on the assumption that their yield only is determined by real factors (i.e. that it is determined by the given prices of their products), and that their price can be determined only by capitalising this yield at a given rate of interest determined solely by monetary factors.[36] This argument, if it were correct, would clearly have to be extended to the prices of all factors of production the price of which is not arbitrarily fixed by monopolists, for their prices would have to be equal to the value of their contribution to the product less interest for the interval for which the factors remained invested.[37] That is, the difference between costs and prices would not be a source of the demand for capital but would be unilaterally determined by a rate of interest which was entirely dependent on monetary influences.

Basic importance of scarcity

We need not follow this argument much further to see that it leads to contradictory conclusions. Even in the case we have considered before of an increase in the investment demand due to an invention, the mechanism which restores the equality between profits and interest would be inconceivable without an independent determinant of the prices of the factors of production, namely their scarcity. For, if the prices of the factors were directly dependent on the given rate of interest, no increase in profits could appear, and no expansion of investment would take place, since prices would be automatically marked to make the rate of profit equal to the given rate of interest. Or, if the initial prices were regarded as unchangeable and unlimited supplies of factors were assumed to be available at these prices, nothing could reduce the increased rate of profit to the level of the unchanged rate of interest. It is clear that, if we want to understand at all the mechanism which determines the relation between costs and prices, and therefore the rate of profit, it is to the relative scarcity of the various types of capital goods and of the other factors of production that we must direct our attention, for it is this scarcity which determines their prices. And although there may be, at most times, some goods an increase in demand for which may bring forth some increase in supply without an increase of their prices, it will on the whole be more useful and realistic to assume for the purposes of this investigation that most commodities are scarce, in the sense that any rise of demand will, *ceteris paribus*, lead to a rise in their prices. We must leave the consideration of the existence of unemployed resources of certain kinds to more specialised investigations of dynamic problems.

This critical excursion was unfortunately made necessary by the confusion which has reigned on this subject since the appearance of Mr Keynes's *General Theory*.

(*The Pure Theory of Capital*, Routledge, 1941, pp. 370–6)

13 Importance of Real Factors

The following passage is the concluding section of a long, intricate, and very closely argued exposition of the influence of price changes on the relative profitability of investment in the different stages of production; it demonstrates that it is the relative scarcities of types of goods in relation to the monetary expenditure on them that ultimately determine these prices and price changes. The whole discussion presents a sharp contrast to the 'en bloc' thinking of the macro-approach.

We will conclude the present treatment by once more stressing the fact that, though in the short run monetary influences may delay the tendencies inherent in the real factors from working themselves out, and temporarily may even reverse these tendencies, it will in the end be the scarcity of real resources relative to demand which will decide what kind of investment, and how much, is profitable. The fundamental fact which guides production, and in which the scarcity of capital expresses itself, is the price of input in terms of output, and this in turn depends on the proportion of income spent on consumers' goods compared with the proportion of income earned from the current production of consumers' goods. These proportions cannot be altered at will by adjustments in the money stream, since they depend on the one hand on the real quantities of the various types of goods in existence, and on the other hand on the way in which people will distribute their income between expenditure on consumers' goods and saving. Neither of these factors can be deliberately altered by monetary policy. As we have seen, any delay by monetary means of the adjustments made necessary by real changes can only have the effect of further accentuating these real changes, and any purely monetary change which in the first instance deflects interest rates in one direction is bound to set up forces which will ultimately change them in the opposite direction.

Significance of rate of saving

Ultimately, therefore, it is the rate of saving which sets the limits to the amount of investment that can be successfully carried through. But the effects of the rate of saving do not operate directly on the rate of interest or on the supply of investible funds, which will always be influenced largely by monetary factors. Its main influence is on the *demand* for investible funds, and here it operates in a direction opposite to that which is assumed by all the under-consumptionist theories. It will be via investment demand that a change in the rate of saving will affect the volume of investment. Similarly, it will be via investment demand that, if monetary influences should have caused investment to get out of step with saving, the balance will be restored. If throughout this discussion we have had little occasion to make explicit mention of the rate of saving, this is due to the fact that the effects considered will take place whatever the rate of saving, so long as this is a given magnitude and does not spontaneously change so as to restore the disrupted equilibrium. All that is required to make our analysis applicable is that, when incomes are increased by investment, the share of the additional income spent on consumers' goods during any period of time should be larger than the proportion by which the new investment adds to the output of consumers' goods during the same period of time. And there is of course no reason to expect that more than a fraction of the new income, and certainly not as much as has been newly invested, will be saved, because this would mean that practically all the income earned from the new investment would have to be saved.[38]

The relative prices of the various types of goods and services, and therefore the rate of profit to be earned in their production, will always be determined by the impact of the monetary demand for the various kinds of goods and the supplies of these goods. And unless we study the factors limiting the supplies of these various types of goods, and particularly if we assume, as Mr Keynes does, that they are all freely reproducible in practically unlimited quantities and without any appreciable lapse of time, we must remain in complete ignorance of the factors guiding production. In long-run equilibrium, the rate of profit and interest will depend on how much of their resources people want to use to satisfy their current needs, and how much they are willing to save and invest. But in the comparatively short run the quantities and kinds of consumers' goods and capital goods in existence must be regarded as fixed, and the rate of profit will depend not so much on the absolute quantity of real capital (however measured) in existence, or on the absolute height of the rate of saving, as on the relation between the proportion of the incomes spent on consumers' goods and the proportion of the resources available in the form of consumers' goods. For this reason it is quite possible that, after a period of great accumulation of capital and a high rate of saving, the rate of profit and the rate of interest may be higher than they were before – if the rate of saving is insufficient compared with the amount of capital which entrepreneurs have attempted to form, or if the demand for consumers' goods is too high compared with the supply. And for the same reason the rate of interest and profit may be higher in a rich community with much capital and a high rate of saving than in an otherwise similar community with little capital and a low rate of saving.

(*The Pure Theory of Capital, op. cit.*, pp. 393–96)

14 Dangers of the Short Run

This extract, the closing paragraphs of The Pure Theory of Capital, *concludes a long discussion of the interaction of real and monetary factors influencing interest-rate changes. Professor Hayek again stresses the superficiality of an analysis that confines itself to the immediate monetary impact of any policy and neglects its real long-term effects.*

The importance of the real factors are increasingly disregarded in contemporary discussion. But even without further continuing the discussion of the rôle money plays in this connection, we are certainly entitled to conclude from what we have already shown that the extent to which we can hope to shape events at will by controlling money is much more limited, that the scope of monetary policy is much more restricted, than is today widely believed. We cannot, as some writers seem to think, do more or less what we please with the economic system by playing on the monetary instrument. In every situation there will in fact always be only one monetary policy which will not have a disequilibrating effect and therefore eventually reverse its short-term influence. That it will always be exceedingly difficult, if not impossible, to know exactly what this policy is does not alter the fact that we cannot hope even to approach this ideal policy unless we understand not only the monetary but also, what are even more important, the real factors that are at work. There is little ground for believing that a system with the modern complex credit structure will ever work smoothly without some deliberate control of the monetary mechanism, since money by its very nature constitutes a kind of loose joint in the self-equilibrating apparatus of the price mechanism which is bound to impede its working – the more so the greater is the play in the loose joint. But the existence of such a loose joint is no justification for concentrating attention on that loose joint and disregarding the rest of the mechanism, and still less for making the greatest possible use of the short-lived freedom from economic necessity which the existence of this loose joint permits. On the contrary, the aim of any successful monetary policy must be to reduce as far as possible this slack in the self-correcting forces of the price mechanism, and to make adaptation more prompt so as to reduce the necessity for a later, more violent, reaction. For this, however, an understanding of the underlying real forces is even more important than an understanding of the monetary surface, just because this surface does not merely hide but often also disrupts the underlying mechanism in the most unexpected fashion. All this is not to deny that in the very short run the scope of monetary policy is very wide indeed. But the problem is not so much what we *can* do, but what we *ought* to do in the short run, and on this point a most harmful doctrine has gained ground in the last few years which can only be explained by a complete neglect – or complete lack of understanding – of the real forces at work. A policy has been advocated which at any moment aims at the maximum short-run effect of monetary policy, completely disregarding the fact that what is best in the short run may be extremely detrimental in the long run, because the indirect and slower effects of the short-run policy of the present shape the conditions, and limit the freedom, of the short-run policy of tomorrow and the day after.

Betrayal of economists' duty

I cannot help regarding the increasing concentration on short-run effects – which in this context amounts to the same thing as a concentration on purely monetary factors – not only as a serious and dangerous intellectual error, but as a betrayal of the main duty of the economist and a grave menace to our civilisation. To the understanding of the forces which determine the day-to-day changes of business, the economist has probably little to contribute that the man of affairs does not know better. It used, however, to be regarded as the duty and the privilege of the economist to study and to stress the long-run effects which are apt to be hidden to the untrained eye, and to leave the concern about the more immediate effects to the practical man, who in any event would see only the latter and nothing else. The aim and effect of two hundred years of continuous development of economic thought have essentially been to lead us away from, and 'behind', the more superficial monetary mechanism and to bring out the real forces which guide long-run development. I do not wish to deny that the preoccupation with the 'real' as distinguished from the monetary aspects of the problems may sometimes have gone too far. But this can be no excuse for the present tendencies which have already gone far towards taking us back to the pre-scientific stage of economics, when the whole working of the price mechanism was not yet understood, and only the problems of the impact of a varying money stream on a supply of goods and services with given prices aroused interest. It is not surprising that Mr Keynes finds his views anticipated by the mercantilist writers and gifted amateurs: concern with the surface phenomena has always marked the first stage of the scientific approach to our subject. But it is alarming to see that after we have once gone through the process of developing a systematic account of those forces which in the long run determine prices and production, we are now called upon to scrap it, in order to replace it by the short-sighted philosophy of the businessman raised to the dignity of a science. Are we not even told that, 'since in the long run we are all dead', policy should be guided entirely by short-run considerations? I fear that these believers in the principle of *après nous le déluge* may get what they have bargained for sooner than they wish.

(*The Pure Theory of Capital*, op. cit., pp. 407–10)

IV International versus National Policies

15 A Commodity Reserve Currency

In these two brief extracts Professor Hayek points to the advantages of an international economic system, and emphasises the necessity of an international monetary system for its proper functioning.

The gold standard as we knew it undoubtedly had some grave defects. But there is some danger that the sweeping condemnation of it which is now the fashion may obscure the fact that it also had some important virtues which most of the alternatives lack. A wisely and impartially controlled system of managed currency for the whole world might, indeed, be superior to it in all respects. But this is not a practical proposition for a long while yet. Compared, however, with the various schemes for monetary management on a national scale, the gold standard had three very important advantages: it created in effect an international currency without submitting national monetary policy to the decisions of an international authority; it made monetary policy in a great measure automatic and thereby predictable; and the changes in the supply of basic money which its mechanism secured were on the whole in the right direction.

The importance of these advantages should not be lightly under-estimated. The difficulties of a deliberate co-ordination of national policies are enormous, because our present knowledge gives us unambiguous guidance in only a few situations, and decisions in which nearly always some interests must be sacrificed to others will have to rest on subjective judgements. Unco-ordinated national policies, however, directed solely by the immediate interests of the individual countries, may in their aggregate effect on every country well be worse than the most imperfect international standard. Similarly, though the automatic operation of the gold standard is far from perfect, the mere fact that under the gold standard policy is guided by known rules, and that, in consequence, the action of the authorities can be foreseen, may well make the imperfect gold standard less disturbing than a more rational but less com-prehensible policy. The general principle that the production of gold is stimulated when its value begins to rise and discouraged when its value falls is right at least in the direction, if not in the way, in which it operates in practice.

An irrational but real prestige

It will be noticed that none of these points claimed in favour of the gold standard is directly connected with any property inherent to gold. Any internationally accepted standard based on a commodity whose value is regulated by its cost of production would possess essentially the same advantages. What in the past made gold the only substance on which in practice an international standard could be based was mainly the irrational, but no less real factor of its prestige – or, if you will, of the ruling superstitious prejudice in favour of gold, which made it universally more acceptable than anything else. So long as this belief prevailed it was possible to maintain an international currency based on gold without much design or deliberate organisation to support it. But if it was prejudice which made the international gold standard possible, the existence of such a prejudice at least made an international money possible at a time when any international system based on explicit agreement and systematic co-operation was out of the question. It is probably true to say that all the rational arguments which can be advanced in favour of the gold standard apply even more strongly to this proposal, which is at the same time free from most of the defects of the former. In judging the feasibility of the plan, it must, however, not be regarded solely as a scheme for currency reform. It must be borne in mind that the accumulation of commodity reserves is certain to remain part of national policy and that political considerations render it unlikely that the markets for raw commodities will in any future for which we can now plan be left entirely to themselves. All plans aiming at the direct control of the prices of particular commodities are, however, open to the most serious objections and certain to cause grave economic and political difficulties. Even apart from monetary consideration, the great need is for a system under which these controls are taken from the separate bodies which can but act in what is essentially an arbitrary and unpredictable manner and to make the controls instead subject to a mechanical and predictable rule. If this can be combined with the reconstruction of an international monetary system which would once more secure to the world stable international currency relations and a greater freedom in the movement of raw commodities, a great step would have been taken in the direction toward a more prosperous and stable world economy.

('A Commodity Reserve Currency', Economic Journal, 1943,
pp. 176–77, 184)

16 Keynes's Comment on Hayek

In a comment on Professor Hayek's article (section 15) Keynes argues that an international monetary system is incompatible with 'nationally determined' wage policies: i.e. the domestic restraint imposed by such an international system would be incompatible with the freedom of the organised trade union movement to determine wage-rates.

There are two complaints which it has been usual to lodge against a rigid gold standard as an instrument to secure stable prices. The first is that it does not provide the appropriate quantity of money. This is the familiar, old-fashioned criticism naturally put forward by adherents of the Quantity Theory. The way to meet it is, obviously, to devise a plan for varying appropriately the quantity of gold or its equivalent – for example, the tabular standard of Marshall 60 years ago, the compensated dollar of Irving Fisher 40 years ago, or the commodity standard of Professor Hayek expounded in the article printed above.

The peculiar merit of the Clearing Union as a means of remedying a chronic shortage of international money is that it operates through the velocity, rather than through the volume, of circulation. A *volume* of money is only required to satisfy hoarding, to provide reserves against contingencies, and to cover inevitable time-lags between buying and spending. If hoarding is discouraged and if reserves against contingencies are provided by facultative overdrafts, a very small amount of actually outstanding credit might be sufficient for clearing between well-organised central banks. The CU, if it were fully successful, would deal with the quantity of international money by making any significant quantity unnecessary. The system might be improved, of course, by further increasing the discouragements to hoarding.

Conditions for national price stability

On another view, however, each national price level is primarily determined by the relation of the national wage level to the national efficiency; or, more generally, by the relation of money costs to efficiency in terms of the national unit of currency. And if price-levels are determined by money costs, it follows that whilst an 'appropriate' quantity of money is a *necessary* condition of stable prices, it is not a *sufficient* condition.

For prices can only be stabilised by first stabilising the relation of money-wages (and other costs) to efficiency.

The second (and more modern) complaint against the gold standard is, therefore, that it attempts to confine the natural tendency of wages to rise beyond the limits set by the volume of money, but can only do so by the weapon of deliberately creating unemployment. This weapon the world, after a good try, has decided to discard. And this complaint may be just as valid against a new standard which aims at providing the quantity of money appropriate to stable prices, as it is against the old gold standard.

In the field of price stabilisation international currency projects have, therefore, as I conceive it, only a limited objective. They do not aim at stable prices as such. For international prices which are stable in terms of unitas or bancor cannot be translated into stable national price levels except by the old gold-standard methods of influencing the level of domestic money costs. And, failing this, there is not much point in an international price level providing stability in terms of an international unit which is not reflected in a corresponding stability of the actual price levels of member countries.

Different national policies needed

The primary aim of an international currency scheme should be, therefore, to prevent not only those evils which result from a chronic shortage of international money due to the draining of gold into creditor countries but also those which follow from countries failing to maintain stability of domestic efficiency-costs and moving out of step with one another in their national wage policies without having at their disposal any means of orderly adjustment. And if orderly adjustment is allowed, that is another way of saying that countries may be allowed by the scheme, which is not the case with the gold standard, to pursue, if they choose, different wage policies and, therefore, different price policies.

Thus the more difficult task of an international currency scheme, which will only be fully solved with the aid of experience, is to deal with the problem of members getting out of step in their domestic wage and credit policies. To meet this it can be provided that countries seriously out of step (whether too fast or too slow) may be asked in the first instance to reconsider their policies. But, if necessary (and it will be necessary, if efficiency wage rates move at materially different rates), exchange rates will have to be altered so as to reconcile a particular national policy to the average pace. If the initial exchange rates are fixed correctly, this is likely to be the only important dis-equilibrium for which a change in exchange rates is the appropriate remedy.

It follows that an international currency scheme can work to perfection within the field of maintaining exchange stability, and yet prices may move substantially. If wages and prices double everywhere alike, international exchange equilibrium is undisturbed. If efficiency wage rates in a particular country rise 10 per cent more than the norm, then it is that there is trouble which needs attention.

The fundamental reason for thus limiting the objectives of an international currency scheme is the impossibility, or at any rate the undesirability, of imposing stable price levels from without. The error of the gold standard lay in submitting national wage policies to outside dictation. It is wiser to regard stability (or otherwise) of internal prices as a matter of internal policy and politics. Commodity standards which try to impose this from without will break down just as surely as the rigid gold standard.

Some countries are likely to be more successful than others in preserving stability of internal prices and efficiency wages – and it is the offsetting of that inequality of success which will provide an international organisation with its worst headaches. A communist country is in a position to be very successful. Some people argue that a capitalist country is doomed to failure because it will be found impossible in conditions of full employment to prevent a progressive increase of wages. According to this view severe slumps and recurrent periods of unemployment have been hitherto the only effective means of holding efficiency wages within a reasonably stable range. Whether this is so remains to be seen. The more conscious we are of this problem, the likelier shall we be to surmount it.

('The Objective of International Price Stability', *Economic Journal*, 1943, pp. 185–87)

17 F. D. Graham's Criticism of Keynes

Professor F. D. Graham, in a comment on Keynes's criticism, indicated the full inflationary implications of Keynes's ideas: in the economic system Keynes envisaged, monetary policy would be subordinated to the wage-rate policies followed by the unions, so that the politically powerful were enabled to exploit the politically weak (since those who were unable

to raise their incomes along with the trade unionists would have to face
ever-increasing prices on static or more slowly rising incomes). Professor
Graham's essay is notable for its early exposition of this important
consideration.

The issues raised in Lord Keynes's reply to Professor F. A. Hayek's
article on a commodity reserve currency, in a recent issue of this *Journal*,
seem worthy of more extended discussion.[39]

It will perhaps do no great injustice to Professor Hayek's views to
assert that he brought the great weight of his authority to an all but
unqualified support of the proposal to give 'free coinage' to warehouse
receipts covering representative bales of the standard storable raw
materials of industry and trade.[40]

Professor Hayek believes that the defects of the gold standard lay not
in conception, but in adequacy to its task. The gold standard always
operated in the right direction, but not with sufficient power or speed.
Whenever the public showed an increasing preference for liquidity –
with a consequent fall in the price level – the mining of gold was
stimulated in compensation of the unemployment with which other
industries were then afflicted. But the relative unimportance of gold-
mining as an employer of labour, or its complete absence from many
economies, reduced this compensation to negligible importance everywhere but in South Africa. The gold standard also operated, at long last,
to check any secular trend in the price level through the increase in the
rate of gold supply which attended a rise in the real value of gold, and
the reduction in the rate of gold supply which occurred when the real
value of gold fell off. But, if the 19th century may be taken as a criterion,
the attendant 'cycle' takes something like a quarter of a century to run
its course.

Though the gold standard thus tended towards the maintenance of
full employment, and to the preservation of a stable price level, the
tendency in both cases was so faint as to be of no practical importance.
Professor Hayek, and other advocates of a commodity reserve standard,
assert that it would greatly ameliorate, if not completely cure, these
defects of adequacy in its gold counterpart.

The 'natural tendency of wages'

Lord Keynes, I take it, is not concerned to deny these asserted virtues of a commodity reserve standard, but says that it is open, along with the gold standard, to another, more modern and, one gathers, more important, objection, in that it would attempt 'to confine the natural tendency of wages to rise beyond the limits set by the volume of money', and that it could do so only by deliberately creating unemployment.

I do not know what Lord Keynes means by the 'natural' tendency of wages to rise beyond the limits set by the volume of money, unless it is that the wage-earner would always like to have higher money wages than he can currently earn on the basis of a stable price level, and that no one is in a position to prevent his getting them. This would certainly be news to Karl Marx, and if both Marx and Keynes were right in their day and generation, the proletariat has surely come into its own, and more, in a way that Marx never envisaged. The degree in which it is true that there is any 'natural' tendency towards an increase of money wages per unit of output is, of course, a matter of time, place, and circumstance, and what should be done about it, in any given case, is a political rather than an economic problem. The problem, that is, does not at all touch the question as to whether the commodity reserve standard is an economically good monetary standard, but is solely concerned with its reception by a politically potent group.

That Lord Keynes is under no illusions about the dangers of appeasement of such a group is shown by the fact that, in his concluding paragraph, he says that 'some people argue that a capitalist country is doomed to failure because it will be found impossible in conditions of full employment to prevent a progressive increase in wages' (beyond the point which can be sustained without a persistent rise in the price level). Disregarding the query as to whether a country so situated could be called 'capitalist', rather than under the domination of a not very enlightened proletariat, it may, perhaps, be at once conceded that there is much to be said for Lord Keynes's contention that, in dealing with the problem, it is essential that any given country have sovereignty over its own monetary arrangements. His opposition to an international stabilisation of prices, imposed from outside on all participating countries, applies, of course, to an international commodity reserve standard with fixed exchange rates. (It applies still more strongly to an international system of *unstable* prices, with fixed or viscous exchange-rate relationships, since the international price level might then fall rather than rise and would, in any case, inevitably fail to correspond with the varying shifts in independently determined efficiency-wage rates in the several countries.) Since Lord Keynes justifiably believes that the difficulty of securing the allegiance of the wage-earning group to a policy of stable national price levels would be greatly enhanced if it could be made to appear that such a policy was the result of an international convention, rather than of purely national interest, he looks askance at what he believes to be a proposal, through international action, to fasten stable price levels on all participating countries.

Gold standard 'dictation'

Lord Keynes, however, is, I think, not right in saying that 'the error of the gold standard lay in submitting national wage policies to outside dictation'. The original gold standard did not submit wage policies to *dictation*, by governing authority anywhere, but made them the resultant of impersonal forces issuing out of the disposition, and potentiality, of individuals to follow what they conceived to be their own interest. This system, as Professor Hayek points out, had many virtues, and we should be badly advised if we should throw away its virtues along with its imperfections. The automaticity of the gold standard was, *per se*, all to the good, and what we need is a similarly automatic system which will be free of the vices of the traditional gold standard. We should not forget that the once well-nigh universal adhesion to the gold standard was spontaneous rather than imposed, and that it was only *after* the gold standard had been subjected to varying national management, in an attempt to overcome the original objections against it, that it was abandoned by those countries that could not make their ideas on its management effective, that is, after (unstable) price levels had been imposed from without.

Lord Keynes's assertion, that a commodity reserve standard imposed from without (such as he supposes Professor Hayek to endorse) would break down just as surely as the rigid gold standard, is not obviously true, but I am not concerned to dispute it.[41] Professor Hayek, in his article, fails to state explicitly whether or not he posits fixed exchange rates of all national currencies against the international commodity standard and, therefore, against each other. But if, in line with Professor Hayek's suggestion, some international organisation, such as, e.g., the new 'Fund' or the Bank for International Settlements, should offer freely to exchange, both ways, an international currency unit against warehouse receipts covering a designated composite of raw materials, no monetary policy would thereby be *imposed* on any country. So far as any country chose to keep the exchange value of its own currency fixed, against the international unit and other currencies tied to it, it would automatically have a substantially stable price level. So far, however, as, for one reason or another, it preferred an unstabilised price level, the exchange value of its currency, *vis-à-vis* the international unit and the currencies of countries with stable exchange rates against that unit, would, as a result of commodity arbitrage, automatically shift in strictly appropriate correspondence with its shifting domestic purchasing power. It seems to me, therefore, that Lord Keynes's argument that an international commodity reserve currency would *impose*, from without, a price-level policy on any country, or would break down, is quite untenable.

There would seem to be no reason why an international monetary unit of this sort should not be the international currency around which the operations of a Clearing Union, on Lord Keynes's lines, or any international fund, could be centred. Through the concurrent free purchase and sale of gold, at a fixed price in the international currency, the gold value of the international unit could also be fixed, or, what is the same thing, the commodity value of gold would be stabilised. This would avoid all the controversy which would be involved in any proposal to deprive gold of its present, or traditional, functions.

Such a standard would represent a great advance over anything we have had in the past. Not only would it be of great value in connection with international investment, but it would furnish a *point d'appui* to which any country desirous of stable price levels, and of fixed exchange rates with other like-minded countries, could, by linking its own currency to the international unit through purchase and sale at fixed prices, repair.

Unanchored medium of exchange

When once a tie with any and every asset, or group of assets, is abandoned, and resort is had to a pure debt currency, one has, in my judgement, no *standard* at all, but merely a wholly unanchored medium of exchange and unit of account. Though I have the fullest sympathy with the wage-earner's getting the highest (real) wages possible, in the current state of the industrial arts, it seems to me that any monetary policy which does not confine such tendency as (money) wages may have to rise beyond the limits within which it is possible to preserve a stable price level, provides a very vicious 'standard'. If Lord Keynes takes the contrary view, he seems to me, in effect, to be plumping for a progressive inflation, wholly indefinite as to time and amount. Against any argument for such a currency I would assert that movements in the price *level* have no functional significance, or that, if they have, we cannot hope to run a satisfactory economic system with price as the regulating mechanism. In that case, the more quickly we go to some not very limited form of responsible totalitarianism the better it will be for all concerned. If we cannot have a distributorily neutral money, any group that can get control of the monetary system will have totalitarian power over the lives and fortunes of their fellows, without any clear recognition of responsibility.

In a perfectly free monetary system, there is, of course, no rate of money wages which would ever, of itself, bring unemployment, since there is nothing to prevent commodity prices from rising (under the stimulus of new issues of money) to whatever level is necessary to cover the stepped-up money cost of the labour factor of production. All of us, moreover, are impatient with the senseless unemployment with which we have so long been afflicted. But, if we refuse even to accept the threat of unemployment under any conditions whatever, we shall, under any 'natural' tendency of money wages to rise faster than efficiency, be forced to pay whatever money wages labourers may be pleased to demand and to jack up the price level unendingly to take care of the situation. The knowledge of what unlimited inflation can mean would seem to preclude the prevention, in this way, of a mote of unemployment.

A commodity reserve currency would operate to provide unlimited employment, through the unlimited demand for the commodities in the reserve, provided the workers did not seek to drive money wages above the figure which, at a stable price level, is warranted by their real productivity. They are entitled to so much – not less and not more – and, if we shrink from saying 'No' when they press their demands beyond this point, we shall no longer have an economic system, but merely a racket. One may contend, if he will, that to say 'No' is a deliberate induction of unemployment, but the answer is that employment will be available if the workers refrain from pushing what, in the circumstances, are quite impossible demands for higher (real) wages. Higher money wages, if granted in the circumstances, would do the workers no good as consumers, since such wages must be compensated by a higher price level, and, even if some slight unemployment were thus prevented, it would be at devastating cost in social freedom.

The real problem of unemployment

Our real problem of unemployment is not that people are denied the opportunity of work at whatever fancy wage they may desire, but that they are denied that opportunity at wages that they could readily earn under conditions of normal liquidity preference. It is the merit of commodity reserves that they would operate to keep the preference for liquidity from rising, or would sate the appetite for it, by offering it freely in such a way as not to interfere with production.

It is true, as Lord Keynes says, that 'prices can only be stabilised by first stabilising the relation of money wages (and other costs) to efficiency'. This is precisely the purpose of commodity reserve money, and I can see no reason for not pursuing it. As the efficiency of labour rises, money wages would tend to rise in correspondence – no more and no less – and there would be a steady tendency towards full employment without a trace of inflation.

It is also true that 'international prices which are stable in terms of unitas or bancor [the international unit] cannot be translated into stable national price-levels except by ... influencing the level of domestic money-costs'. Domestic money-costs would be so influenced, under fixed rates of exchange of a national currency against the international commodity unit, and I see no strong reason for objecting to this consequence. Whatever the objections, or lack of them, the influence would, in any case, not be present if, as pointed out above, the exchange rate of the national against the international unit were left free to move in correspondence with variations in the local currency price of the commodity composite relative to the fixed price in the international currency.[42] If one insists upon an unstabilised price level at home, there is nothing in a stabilised international unit to prevent it, or nothing to prevent other countries having stable price levels if they so desire. No country, therefore, would be any more inhibited in the presence of an international monetary unit of stable value than in the presence of an international unit without anchor, and a stable-value international unit would not interfere in any way with anything that Lord Keynes has proposed in his Clearing Union.

Professor Hayek's 'intransigence'

It is the intransigence of the attitude taken here, and by Professor Hayek, which is, I think, troubling Lord Keynes. To him it seems ruthless to accept, or provoke, unemployment as a means of enforcing adherence to pecuniary purity. How much otherwise avoidable unemployment, he asks, would you be willing to bring about for this purpose?[43] The query reflects not only Lord Keynes's humanitarian concern, but also his doubts as to political possibilities. He thinks that other, less punitive, means must be found if the desired end is to be attained. It would be churlish, and foolish, to deny the cogency of his objections on this point, and the answer, I think, lies in the adoption of a minimum wage policy with a normal yearly increase in the minimum equal to a generously computed expectation of enhancement in the general level of efficiency. Experience goes to show that wages above the minimum will respond, at least proportionately, to any increase in the lowest group, and if, at any time, the expectation of improvement in general efficiency were shown to be over-computed (by the fact or immediate threat of unemployment in the industries producing the goods in the commodity unit), the stated increase in the minimum wage should be temporarily suspended in accordance with appropriate provisions in the legislation. Some such measures as this would reduce the acerbity of disputes over the distribution of income and would promote adjustments in an orderly rather than a chaotic manner.

So long as our economic system deviates widely, and in certain respects progressively, from ideally free competition, there is bound to be some friction in the determination of who gets what, and why. So long, moreover, as we preserve anything whatever of the spirit of free contract, the enterpriser must be as free to reject the demands of workers as are the latter to reject the terms that the enterpriser may offer. Any unemployment that may result from this cause is an inevitable phase of freedom. It would be as fatal to freedom to insist that, to avoid any unemployment whatever, the enterpriser must pay whatever monetary wages organised workers may demand, and that the State must so shape its monetary policy as to make this possible, as it would be to insist, to the same end, that workers must accept whatever monetary wage a fascist group of employers might see fit to impose.

('Keynes *vs.* Hayek on a Commodity Reserve Currency',
Economic Journal, 1944, pp. 422–28)

18 Keynes's Reply to Graham

In his reply to F. D. Graham, Keynes failed to take up the major issue that had been raised: that of allowing monetary policy to be used as a supplement to union wage-rate fixing. Indeed, Keynes continued to assume that prices, as a normal course, would be adjusted to whatever wage-rates unions succeeded in obtaining, i.e. he assumed a continuous inflation.

Professor Graham's statement of my point of view is a very fair one. But in the note on which he comments I expressed myself much more briefly than the nature of the subject-matter really allowed. So, to diminish the chances of misunderstandings, there are one or two points I should like to re-state and emphasise.

I have no quarrel with a tabular standard as being intrinsically more sensible than gold. My own sympathies have always fallen that way. I hope the world will come to some version of it some time. But the opinion I was expressing was on the level of contemporary practical policy; and on that level I do not feel that this is the next urgent thing or that other measures should be risked or postponed for the sake of it. These are some of my reasons:

1   The immediate task is to discover some orderly, yet elastic, method of linking national currencies to an international currency, whatever the type of international currency may be. So long as national currencies change their values out of step with one another, I doubt if this task is made easier by substituting a tabular standard for gold. Indeed the task of getting an *elastic* procedure may be made more difficult, since a tabular standard might make rigidity seem more plausible. Perhaps unjustly, I was suspecting Professor Hayek of seeking a new way to satisfy a propensity towards a rigid system.

2   In particular, I doubt the political wisdom of appearing, more than is inevitable in any orderly system, to impose an external pressure on national standards and therefore on wage levels. Of course, I do not want to see money wages forever soaring upwards to a level to which real wages cannot follow. It is one of the chief tasks ahead of our statesmanship to find a way to prevent this. But we must solve it in our own domestic way, feeling that we are free men, free to be wise or foolish. The suggestion of *external* pressure will make the difficult

psychological and political problem of making good sense prevail still more difficult.

3   This does not strike me as an opportune moment to attack the vested interests of gold holders and gold producers. Why waste one's breath on what the Governments of the United States, Russia, Western Europe, and the British Commonwealth are bound to reject?

4   The right way to approach the tabular standard is to evolve a technique and to accustom men's minds to the idea through international buffer stocks. When we have thoroughly mastered the technique of these, which is sufficiently difficult without the further complications of the tabular standard and the oppositions and prejudices which this must overcome, it will be time enough to think again. On buffer stocks I can enthusiastically join forces with Professor Frank Graham and Mr Benjamin Graham. Though even here I am beginning to feel a slight reserve about whether just this moment, when many materials are scarce, is the right moment to start; they can so easily be turned into producers' ramps, and if they start that way the prospect of a brilliant improvement will have been prejudiced.

All this, I agree, is very low-level talk; for which I apologise. But it was in fact from a low level that I was, in the first instance, addressing Professor Hayek on his dolomite.

('Note by Lord Keynes', *Economic Journal*, 1944, pp. 429–30)

V Wage Rigidities and Inflation

19 Full Employment, Planning, and Inflation

Professor Hayek here develops one of his main themes. Save in the exceptional circumstances of the general unemployment of all factors of production, the 'unemployment' problem is one of securing the right distribution of labour; monetary expansion along Keynesian lines, by nullifying the effects of relative price movements, exacerbates the situation and makes it impossible to maintain any given volume of employment, except by continued inflation. Considerations such as these are not clearly grasped within the 'bloc' thinking of the macro-approach, which may thus serve to conceal important aspects of reality.

In the years that have elapsed since the war, central planning, 'full employment', and inflationary pressure have been the three features which have dominated economic policy in the greater part of the world. Of these only full employment can be regarded as desirable in itself. Central planning, direction, or government controls, however we care to call it, is at best a means which must be judged by the results. Inflation, even 'repressed inflation', is undoubtedly an evil, though some would say a necessary evil if other desirable aims are to be achieved. It is part of the price we pay for having committed ourselves to a policy of full employment and central planning.

The new fact which has brought about this situation is not a greater desire to avoid unemployment than existed before the war. It is the new belief that a higher level of employment can be permanently maintained by monetary pressure than would be possible without it. The pursuit of a policy based on these beliefs has somewhat unexpectedly shown that inflation and government controls are its necessary accompaniments – unexpected not by all, but by probably the majority of those who advocated those policies.

Full employment the main priority

Full employment policies as now understood are thus the dominant factor of which the other characteristic features of contemporary economic policy are mainly the consequence. Before we can further examine the manner in which central planning, full employment, and inflation interact, we must become clear about what precisely the full employment policies as now practised mean.

Full employment has come to mean that maximum of employment that can be brought about in the short run by monetary pressure. This may not be the original meaning of the theoretical concept, but it was inevitable that it should have come to mean this in practice. Once it was admitted that the momentary state of employment should form the main guide to monetary policy, it was inevitable that any degree of unemployment which might be removed by monetary pressure should be regarded as sufficient justification for applying such pressure. That in most situations employment can be temporarily increased by monetary expansion has long been known. If this possibility has not always been used, this was because it was thought that by such measures not only other dangers were created, but that long-term stability of employment itself might be endangered by them. What is new about present beliefs is that it is now widely held that so long as monetary expansion creates additional employment, it is innocuous or at least will cause more benefit than harm.

Yet while in practice full employment policies merely mean that in the short run employment is kept somewhat higher than it would otherwise be, it is at least doubtful whether over longer periods they will not in fact lower the level of employment which can be permanently maintained without progressive monetary expansion. These policies are, however, constantly represented as if the practical problem were not this, but as if the choice were between full employment thus defined and the lasting mass unemployment of the 1930s.

The habit of thinking in terms of an alternative between 'full employment' and a state of affairs in which there are unemployed factors of all kinds available is perhaps the most dangerous legacy which we owe to the great influence of the late Lord Keynes. That so long as a state of general unemployment prevails, in the sense that unused resources of *all* kinds exist, monetary expansion can be only beneficial, few people will deny. But such a state of general unemployment is something rather exceptional, and it is by no means evident that a policy which will be beneficial in such a state will also always and necessarily be so in the kind of intermediate position in which an economic system finds itself most of the time, when significant unemployment is confined to certain industries, occupations or localities.

Unemployment and inadequate demand

Of a system in a state of general unemployment it is roughly true that employment will fluctuate in proportion with money income, and that if we succeed in increasing money income we shall also in the same proportion increase employment. But it is just not true that all unemployment is in this manner due to an insufficiency of aggregate demand and can be lastingly cured by increasing demand. The causal connection between income and employment is not a simple one-way connection so that by raising income by a certain ratio we can always raise employment by the same ratio. It is all too naïve a way of thinking to believe that, since, if all workmen were employed at current wages, total income would reach such and such a figure, therefore, if we can bring income to that figure, we shall also necessarily have full employment. Where unemployment is not evenly spread, there is no certainty that additional expenditure will go where it will create additional employment. At least the amount of extra expenditure which would have to be incurred before the demand for the kind of services is raised which the unemployed offer may have to be of such a magnitude as to produce major inflationary effects before it substantially increases employment.

If expenditure is distributed between industries and occupations in a proportion different from that in which labour is distributed, a mere increase in expenditure need not increase employment. Unemployment can evidently be the consequence of the fact that the distribution of labour is different from the distribution of demand. In this case the low aggregate money income would have to be considered as a consequence rather than as a cause of unemployment. Even though, during the process of increasing incomes, enough expenditure may 'spill over' into the depressed sectors temporarily there to cure unemployment, as soon as the expansion comes to an end the discrepancy between the distribution of demand and the distribution of supply will again show itself. Where the cause of unemployment and of low aggregate incomes is such a discrepancy, only a re-allocation of labour can lastingly solve the problem in a free economy.

This raises one of the most crucial and most difficult problems in the whole field: is an inappropriate distribution of labour more likely to be corrected under more or less stable or under expanding monetary conditions? This involves in fact two separate problems: the first is whether demand conditions during a process of expansion are such that, if the distribution of labour adjusted itself to the then existing distribution of demand, this would create employment which would continue after expansion has stopped; the second problem is whether the distribution of labour is more likely to adapt itself promptly to any given distribution of demand under stable or under expansionary monetary conditions, or, in other words, whether labour is more mobile under expanding or under stable monetary conditions.

The answer to the first of these questions is fairly clear. During a process of expansion the direction of demand is to some extent necessarily different from what it will be after expansion has stopped. Labour will be attracted to the particular occupations on which the extra expenditure is made in the first instance. So long as expansion lasts, demand there will always run a step ahead of the consequential increases of demand elsewhere. And in so far as this temporary stimulus to demand in particular sectors leads to a movement of labour, it may well become the cause of unemployment as soon as the expansion comes to an end.

Main cause of recurrent unemployment

Some people may feel doubt about the importance of this phenomenon. To the present writer it seems the main cause of the recurrent waves of unemployment. That during every boom period a greater quantity of factors of production is drawn into the capital goods industries than can be permanently employed there, and that as a result we have normally a greater proportion of our resources specialised in the production of capital goods than corresponds to the share of income which, under full employment, will be saved and be available for investment, seems to him the cause of the collapse which has regularly followed a boom. Any attempt to create full employment by drawing labour into occupations where they will remain employed only so long as credit expansion continues creates the dilemma that either credit expansion must be continued indefinitely (which means inflation), or that, when it stops, unemployment will be greater than it would be if the temporary increase in employment had never taken place.

If the real cause of unemployment is that the distribution of labour does not correspond with the distribution of demand, the only way to create stable conditions of high employment which is not dependent on continued inflation (or physical controls) is to bring about a distribution of labour which matches the manner in which a stable money income will be spent. This depends of course not only on whether during the process of adaptation the distribution of demand is approximately what it will remain, but also on whether conditions in general are conducive to easy and rapid movements of labour.

This leads to the second and more difficult part of our question to which, perhaps, no certain answer can be given, though the probability seems to us to point clearly in one direction. This is the question whether workers will on the whole be more willing to move to new occupations or new localities when general demand is rising, or whether mobility is likely to be greater when total demand is approximately constant. The main difference between the two cases is that in the former the induce-ment to move will be the attraction of a higher wage elsewhere, while in the second case it will be the inability to earn the accustomed wages or to find any employment in the former occupation which will exercise a push. The former method is, of course, the more pleasant, and it is usually also represented as the more effective. It is this latter belief which I am inclined to question.

That the same wage differentials which in the long run would attract the necessary greater number of new recruits to one industry rather than another will not suffice to tempt workers already established in the latter to move is in itself not surprising. As a rule the movement from job to job involves expenditure and sacrifices which may not be justified by a mere increase in wages. So long as the worker can count on his accustomed money wage in his current job, he will be understandably reluctant to move. Even if, as would be inevitable under an expansionist policy which aimed at bringing about the adjustment entirely by raising some wages without allowing others to fall, the constant money wages meant a lower real wage, the habit of thinking in terms of money wages would deprive such a fall of real wages of most of its effectiveness. It is curious that those disciples of Lord Keynes who in other connections make such constant use of this consideration regularly fail to see its significance in this context.

To aim at securing to men who in the social interest ought to move elsewhere the continued receipt of their former wages can only delay movements which ultimately must take place. It should also not be forgotten that in order to give all the men formerly employed continued employment in a relatively declining industry, the general level of wages in that industry will have to fall more than would be necessary if some of the workers moved away from it.

What is so difficult here for the layman to understand is that to protect the individual against the loss of his job may not be a way to decrease unemployment but may over longer periods rather decrease the number which can be employed at given wages. If a policy is pursued over a long period which postpones and delays movements, which keeps people in their old jobs who ought to move elsewhere, the result must be that what ought to have been a gradual process of change becomes in the end a problem of the necessity of mass transfers within a short period. Continued monetary pressure which has helped people to earn an unchanged money wage in jobs which they ought to have left will have created accumulated arrears of necessary changes which, as soon as monetary pressure ceases, will have to be made up in a much shorter space of time and then result in a period of acute mass unemployment which might have been avoided.

Expansion may hinder adjustment

All this applies not only to those maldistributions of labour which arise in the course of ordinary industrial fluctuations, but even more to the task of large-scale re-allocations of labour such as arise after a great war or as a result of a major change in the channels of international trade. It seems highly doubtful whether the expansionist policies pursued since the war in most countries have helped and not rather hindered that adjustment to radically changed conditions of world trade which have become necessary. Especially in the case of Great Britain the low unemployment figures during recent years may be more a sign of a delay in necessary change than of true economic balance.

The great problem in all those instances is whether such a policy, once it has been pursued for years, can still be reversed without serious political and social disturbances. As a result of these policies, what not very long ago might merely have meant a slightly higher unemployment figure, might now, when the employment of large numbers has become dependent on the continuation of these policies, be indeed an experiment which politically is unbearable.

Full employment policies, as at present practised, attempt the quick and easy way of giving men employment where they happen to be, while the real problem is to bring about a distribution of labour which makes continuous high employment without artificial stimulus possible. What this distribution is we can never know beforehand. The only way to find out is to let the unhampered market act under conditions which will bring about a stable equilibrium between demand and supply. But the very full employment policies make it almost inevitable that we must constantly interfere with the free play of the forces of the market and that the prices which rule during such an expansionary policy, and to which supply will adapt itself, will not represent a lasting condition. These difficulties, as we have seen, arise from the fact that unemployment is never evenly spread throughout the economic system, but that, at the time when there may still be substantial unemployment in some sectors, there may exist acute scarcities in others. The purely fiscal and monetary measures on which current full employment policies rely are, however, by themselves indiscriminate in their effects on the different parts of the economic system. The same monetary pressure which in some parts of the system might merely reduce unemployment will in others produce definite inflationary effects. If not checked by other measures, such monetary pressure might well set up an inflationary spiral of prices and wages long before unemployment has disappeared, and – with present nation-wide wage bargaining – the rise of wages may threaten the results of the full employment policy even before it has been achieved.

As is regularly the case in such circumstances, the governments will then find themselves forced to take measures to counteract the effects of their own policy. The effects of the inflation have to be contained or 'repressed' by direct controls of prices and of quantities produced and sold: the rise of prices has to be prevented by imposing maximum prices and the resulting scarcities must be met by a system of rationing, priorities, and allocations.

The manner in which inflation leads a government into a system of overall controls and central planning is by now too well-known to need elaboration. It is usually a particularly pernicious kind of planning, because not thought out beforehand but applied piecemeal as the unwelcome results of inflation manifest themselves. A government which uses inflation as an instrument of policy but wants it to produce only the desired effects is soon driven to control ever increasing parts of the economy.

(*Studies in Philosophy, Politics and Economics*, Routledge, 1967, pp. 270–76)

20 Inflation Resulting from Downward Inflexibility of Wages

Professor Hayek reiterates the central rôle of wage rates in determining the volume of employment. Reasoning in terms of wage levels rather than in terms of the structure of wage rates obscures the inflationary implications of refusing to reduce wage rates where necessary. If union-determined wage rates are treated as the datum to which all other economic values must adjust themselves, the monetary consequences of such a course must be clearly recognised. If we wish to avoid the latter, trade unions must treat the flow of money incomes as the final datum to which they must adjust their wage rates. Professor Hayek here explicitly and unambiguously analyses the specific interactions of union wage policy and official monetary policy in creating one of the major dilemmas facing the developed economies.

Contrary to what is widely believed, the crucial result of the 'Keynesian Revolution' is the general acceptance of a factual assumption and, what is more, of an assumption which becomes true as a result of its being generally accepted. The Keynesian theory, as it has developed during the last 20 years, has become a formal apparatus which may or may not be more convenient to deal with the facts than classical monetary theory; this is not our concern here. The decisive assumption on which Keynes's original argument rested and which has since ruled policy is that it is impossible ever to reduce the money wages of a substantial group of workers without causing extensive unemployment. The conclusion which Lord Keynes drew from this, and which the whole of his theoretical system was intended to justify, was that since money wages can in practice not be lowered, the adjustment necessary, whenever wages have become too high to allow 'full employment', must be effected by the devious process of reducing the value of money. A society which accepts this is bound for a continuous process of inflation.

Importance of relative wages

This consequence is not at once apparent within the Keynesian system because Keynes and most of his followers are arguing in terms of a general wage level while the chief problem appears only if we think in terms of the relative wages of the different (sectional or regional) groups of workers. Relative wages of the different groups are bound to change substantially in the course of economic development. But if the money wage of no important group is to fall, the adjustment of the relative position must be brought about exclusively by raising all other money wages. The effect must be a continuous rise in the level of money wages greater than the rise of real wages, i.e. inflation. One need only consider the normal year-by-year dispersion of wage changes of the different groups in order to realise how important this factor must be.

The 12 years since the end of the war have in fact in the whole Western world been a period of more or less continuous inflation. It does not matter how far this was entirely the result of deliberate policy or the product of the exigencies of government finance. It certainly has been a very popular policy since it has been accompanied by great prosperity over a period of probably unprecedented length. The great problem is whether by the same means prosperity can be maintained indefinitely – or whether an attempt to do so is not bound sooner or later to produce other results which in the end must become unbearable.

The point which tends to be overlooked in current discussion is that inflation acts as a stimulus to business only in so far as it is unforeseen, or greater than expected. Rising prices by themselves, as has often been seen, are not necessarily a guarantee of prosperity. Prices must turn out to be higher than they were expected to be, in order to produce profits larger than normal. Once a further rise of prices is expected with certainty, competition for the factors of production will drive up costs in anticipation. If prices rise no more than expected there will be no extra profits, and if they rise less, the effect will be the same as if prices fell when they had been expected to be stable.

On the whole the post-war inflation has been unexpected or has lasted longer than expected. But the longer inflation lasts, the more it will be generally expected to continue; and the more people count on a continued rise of prices, the more must prices rise in order to secure adequate profits not only to those who would earn them without inflation but also to those who would not. Inflation greater than expected secures general prosperity only because those who without it would make no profit and be forced to turn to something else are enabled to continue with their present activities. A cumulative inflation at a progressive rate will probably secure prosperity for a fairly long time, but not inflation at a constant rate. We need hardly inquire why inflation at a progressive rate cannot be continued indefinitely: long before it becomes so fast as to make any reasonable calculation in the expanding currency impracticable and before it will be spontaneously replaced by some other medium of exchange, the inconvenience and injustice of the rapidly falling value of all fixed payments will produce irresistible demands for a halt – irresistible, at least, when people understand what is happening and realise that a government can always stop inflation. (The hyper-inflations after the First World War were tolerated only because people were deluded into believing that the increase of the quantity of money was not a cause but a necessary consequence of the rise of prices.)

We can therefore not expect inflation-borne prosperity to last indefinitely. We are bound to reach a point at which the source of prosperity which inflation now constitutes will no longer be available. Nobody can predict when this point will be reached, but come it will. Few things should give us greater concern than the need to secure an arrangement of our productive resources which we can hope to maintain at a reasonable level of activity and employment when the stimulus of inflation ceases to operate.

Inflation – a vicious circle

Yet the longer we have relied on inflationary expansion to secure prosperity, the more difficult that task will be. We shall be faced not only with an accumulated backlog of delayed adjustments – all those businesses which have been kept above water only by continued inflation. Inflation also becomes the active cause of new 'misdirections' of production, i.e. it induces new activities which will continue to be profitable only so long as inflation lasts. Especially when the additional money first becomes available for investment activities, these will be increased to a volume which cannot be maintained once only current savings are available to feed them.

The conception that we can maintain prosperity by keeping final demand always increasing a jump ahead of costs must sooner or later prove an illusion, because costs are not an independent magnitude but are in the long run determined by the expectations of what final demand will be. And to secure 'full employment' even an excess of 'aggregate demand' over 'aggregate costs' may not lastingly be sufficient, since the volume of employment depends largely on the magnitude of investment and beyond a certain point an excessive final demand may act as a deterrent rather than as a stimulus to investment.

I fear that those who believe that we have solved the problem of permanent full employment are in for a serious disillusionment. This is not to say that we need have a major depression. A transition to more stable monetary conditions by gradually slowing down inflation is probably still possible. But it will hardly be possible without a significant decrease of employment of some duration. The difficulty is that in the present state of opinion any noticeable increase of unemployment will at once be met by renewed inflation. Such attempts to cure unemployment by further doses of inflation will probably be temporarily successful and may even succeed several times if the inflationary pressure is massive enough. But this will merely postpone the problem and in the meantime aggravate the inherent instability of the situation.

In a short paper on the 20 years' outlook there is no space to consider the serious but essentially short-term problem of how to get out of a particular inflationary spell without producing a major depression. The long-term problem is how we are to stop the long-term and periodically accelerated inflationary trend which will again and again raise that problem. The essential point is that it must be once more realised that the employment problem is a wage problem and that the Keynesian device of lowering real wages by reducing the value of money when wages have become too high for full employment will work only so long as the workers let themselves be deceived by it. It was an attempt to get round what is called the 'rigidity' of wages which could work for a time but which in the long run has only made this obstacle to a stable monetary system greater than it had been. What is needed is that the responsibility for a wage level which is compatible with a high and stable level of employment should again be squarely placed where it belongs: with the trade unions. The present division of responsibility where each union is concerned only with obtaining the maximum rate of money wages without regard to the effect on employment, and the monetary authorities are expected to supply whatever increases of money income are required to secure full employment at the resulting wage level, must lead to continuous and progressive inflation. We are discovering that by refusing to face the wage problem and temporarily evading the consequences by monetary deception, we have merely made the whole problem much more difficult. The long-run problem remains the restoration of a labour market which will produce wages which are compatible with stable money. This means that the full and exclusive responsibility of the monetary authorities for inflation must once more be recognised. Though it is true that, so long as it is regarded as their duty to supply enough money to secure full employment at any wage level, they have no choice and their rôle becomes a purely passive one, it is this very conception which is bound to produce continuous inflation. Stable monetary conditions require that the stream of money expenditure is the fixed datum to which prices and wages have to adapt themselves, and not the other way round.

The state of public opinion

Such a change of policy as would be required to prevent progressive inflation, and the instability and recurrent crises it is bound to produce, presupposes, however, a change in the still predominant state of opinion. Though a 7 per cent bank rate in the country where they originated and were most consistently practised proclaims loudly the bankruptcy of Keynesian principles, there is yet little sign that they have lost their sway over the generation that grew up in their heyday. But quite apart from this intellectual power they still exercise, they have contributed so much to strengthen the position of one of the politically most powerful elements in the country, that their abandonment is not likely to come without a severe political struggle. The desire to avoid this will probably again and again lead politicians to put off the necessity by resorting once more to the temporary way out which inflation offers as the path of least resistance. It will probably be only when the dangers of this path have become much more obvious than they are now that the fundamental underlying problem of union power will really be faced.

(*Studies in Philosophy, Politics and Economics, op. cit.*, pp. 295–99)

21   Labour Unions and Employment

Professor Hayek makes two major points in this extract from the Con-
stitution of Liberty. First, it is unwarranted, he says, to identify the
interests of union members with the interests of the working class as a
whole, since unions are able to obtain higher wage rates for their
members only by limiting the supply of unionised labour and thus
increasing the supply of non-union labour, i.e. by reducing the wage
rates of non-union workers.

Secondly, the separate attempts of each union to raise real wages by
raising the money wages of its members would produce unemployment,
unless the monetary authorities inflated the flow of money incomes to
compensate for this disco-ordination; but such an inflation in turn leads
to even graver consequences.

Public policy concerning labour unions has, in little more than a century,
moved from one extreme to the other. From a state in which little the
unions could do was legal if they were not prohibited altogether, we
have now reached a state where they have become uniquely privileged
institutions to which the general rules of law do not apply. They have
become the only important instance in which governments signally fail
in their prime function – the prevention of coercion and violence.

This development has been greatly assisted by the fact that unions
were at first able to appeal to the general principles of liberty[44] and then
retain the support of the liberals long after all discrimination against
them had ceased and they had acquired exceptional privileges. In few
other areas are progressives so little willing to consider the reasonableness
of any particular measure but generally ask only whether it is 'for or
against unions' or, as it is usually put, 'for or against labour'.[45] Yet the
briefest glance at the history of the unions should suggest that the
reasonable position must lie somewhere between the extremes which
mark their evolution.

Changed character of the problem

Most people, however, have so little realisation of what has happened
that they still support the aspirations of the unions in the belief that they
are struggling for 'freedom of association', when this term has in fact
lost its meaning and the real issue has become the freedom of the

individual to join or not to join a union. The existing confusion is due in part to the rapidity with which the character of the problem has changed; in many countries voluntary associations of workers had only just become legal when they began to use coercion to force unwilling workers into membership and to keep non-members out of employment. Most people probably still believe that a 'labour dispute' normally means a disagreement about remuneration and the conditions of employment, while as often as not its sole cause is an attempt on the part of the unions to force unwilling workers to join.

The acquisition of privilege by the unions has nowhere been as spectacular as in Britain, where the Trade Disputes Act of 1906 conferred 'upon a trade union a freedom from civil liability for the commission of even the most heinous wrong by the union or its servant, and in short confer[red] upon every trade union a privilege and protection not possessed by any other person or body of persons, whether corporate or incorporate'.[46] Similar friendly legislation helped the unions in the United States, where first the Clayton Act of 1914 exempted them from the anti-monopoly provisions of the Sherman Act; the Norris–La Guardia Act of 1932 'went a long way to establish practically complete immunity of labour organisations for torts';[47] and, finally, the Supreme Court in a crucial decision sustained 'the claim of a union to the right to deny participation in the economic world to an employer'.[48] More or less the same situation had gradually come to exist in most European countries by the 1920s, 'less through explicit legislative permission than by the tacit toleration by authorities and courts'.[49] Everywhere the legalisation of unions was interpreted as a legalisation of their main purpose and as recognition of their right to do whatever seemed necessary to achieve this purpose – namely, monopoly. More and more they came to be treated not as a group which was pursuing a legitimate selfish aim and which, like every other interest, must be kept in check by competing interests possessed of equal rights, but as a group whose aim – the exhaustive and comprehensive organisation of all labour – must be supported for the good of the public.[50]

Although flagrant abuses of their powers by the unions have often shocked public opinion in recent times and uncritical pro-union sentiment is on the wane, the public has certainly not yet become aware that the existing legal position is fundamentally wrong and that the whole basis of our free society is gravely threatened by the powers arrogated by the unions. We shall not be concerned here with those criminal abuses of union power that have lately attracted much attention in the United States, although they are not entirely unconnected with the privileges that unions legally enjoy. Our concern will be solely with those powers that unions today generally possess, either with the explicit permission of the law or at least with the tacit toleration of the law-enforcing authorities. Our argument will not be directed against labour unions as such; nor will it be confined to the practices that are now widely recognised as abuses. But we shall direct our attention to some of their powers which are now widely accepted as legitimate, if not as their 'sacred rights'. The case against these is strengthened rather than weakened by the fact that unions have often shown much restraint in exercising them. It is precisely because, in the existing legal situation, unions could do infinitely more harm than they do, and because we owe it to the moderation and good sense of many union leaders that the situation is not much worse, that we cannot afford to allow the present state of affairs to continue.[51]

Union coercion of fellow workers

It cannot be stressed enough that the coercion which unions have been permitted to exercise contrary to all principles of freedom under the law is primarily the coercion of fellow workers. Whatever true coercive power unions may be able to wield over employers is a consequence of this primary power of coercing other workers; the coercion of employers would lose most of its objectionable character if unions were deprived of this power to exact unwilling support. Neither the right of voluntary agreement between workers nor even their right to withhold their services in concert is in question. It should be said, however, that the latter – the right to strike – though a normal right, can hardly be regarded as an inalienable right. There are good reasons why in certain employments it should be part of the terms of employment that the worker should renounce this right; i.e. such employments should involve long-term obligations on the part of the workers, and any concerted attempts to break such contracts should be illegal.

It is true that any union effectively controlling all potential workers of a firm or industry can exercise almost unlimited pressure on the employer and that, particularly where a great amount of capital has been invested in specialised equipment, such a union can practically expropriate the owner and command nearly the whole return of his enterprise.[52] The decisive point, however, is that this will never be in the interest of all workers – except in the unlikely case where the total gain from such action is equally shared among them, irrespective of whether they are employed or not – and that, therefore, the union can achieve this only by coercing some workers against their interest to support such a concerted move.

The reason for this is that workers can raise real wages above the level that would prevail on a free market only by limiting the supply, that is, by withholding part of labour. The interest of those who will get employment at the higher wage will therefore always be opposed to the interest of those who, in consequence, will find employment only in the less highly paid jobs or who will not be employed at all.

The fact that unions will ordinarily first make the employer agree to a certain wage and then see to it that nobody will be employed for less makes little difference. Wage fixing is quite as effective a means as any other of keeping out those who could be employed only at a lower wage. The essential point is that the employer will agree to the wage only when he knows that the union has the power to keep out others.[53] As a general rule, wage fixing (whether by unions or by authority) will make wages higher than they would otherwise be only if they are also higher than the wage at which all willing workers can be employed.

Wage increases at expense of others

Though unions may still often act on a contrary belief, there can now be no doubt that they cannot in the long run increase real wages for all wishing to work above the level that would establish itself in a free market – though they may well push up the level of money wages, with consequences that will occupy us later. Their success in raising real wages beyond that point, if it is to be more than temporary, can benefit only a particular group at the expense of others. It will therefore serve only a sectional interest even when it obtains the support of all. This means that strictly voluntary unions, because their wage policy would not be in the interest of all workers, could not long receive the support of all. Unions that had no power to coerce outsiders would thus not be strong enough to force up wages above the level at which all seeking work could be employed, that is, the level that would establish itself in a truly free market for labour in general.

But, while the real wages of all the employed can be raised by union action only at the price of unemployment, unions in particular industries or crafts may well raise the wages of their members by forcing others to stay in less-well-paid occupations. How great a distortion of the wage structure this in fact causes is difficult to say. If one remembers, however, that some unions find it expedient to use violence in order to prevent any influx into their trade and that others are able to charge high premiums for admission (or even to reserve jobs in the trade for children of present members), there can be little doubt that this distortion is considerable. It is important to note that such policies can be employed successfully only in relatively prosperous and highly paid occupations and that they will therefore result in the exploitation of the relatively poor by the better-off. Even though within the scope of any one union its actions may tend to reduce differences in remuneration, there can be little doubt that, so far as relative wages in major industries and trades are concerned, unions today are largely responsible for an inequality which has no function and is entirely the result of privilege.[54] This means that their activities necessarily reduce the productivity of labour all around and therefore also the general level of real wages; because, if union action succeeds in reducing the number of workers in the highly paid jobs and in increasing the number of those who have to stay in the less remunerative ones, the result must be that the over-all average will be lower. It is, in fact, more than likely that, in countries where unions are very strong, the general level of real wages is lower than it would otherwise be.[55] This is certainly true of most countries of Europe, where union policy is strengthened by the general use of restrictive practices of a 'make-work' character.

If many still accept as an obvious and undeniable fact that the general wage level has risen as fast as it has done because of the efforts of the unions, they do so in spite of these unambiguous conclusions of theoretical analysis – and in spite of empirical evidence to the contrary. Real wages have often risen much faster when unions were weak than when they were strong; furthermore, even the rise in particular trades or industries where labour was not organised has frequently been much faster than in highly organised and equally prosperous industries.[56] The common impression to the contrary is due partly to the fact that wage gains, which are today mostly obtained in union negotiations, are for that reason regarded as obtainable only in this manner[57] and even more to the fact that, as we shall presently see, union activity does in fact bring about a continuous rise in money wages exceeding the increase in real wages. Such increase in money wages is possible without producing general unemployment only because it is regularly made ineffective by inflation – indeed, it must be if full employment is to be maintained.

Harmful and dangerous activities

If unions have in fact achieved much less by their wage policy than is generally believed, their activities in this field are nevertheless economically very harmful and politically exceedingly dangerous. They are using their power in a manner which tends to make the market system ineffective and which, at the same time, gives them a control of the direction of economic activity that would be dangerous in the hands of government but is intolerable if exercised by a particular group. They do so through their influence on the relative wages of different groups of workers and through their constant upward pressure on the level of money wages, with its inevitable inflationary consequences.

The effect on relative wages is usually greater uniformity and rigidity of wages within any one union-controlled group and greater and non-functional differences in wages between different groups. This is accompanied by a restriction of the mobility of labour, of which the former is either an effect or a cause. We need say no more about the fact that this may benefit particular groups but can only lower the productivity and therefore the incomes of the workers in general. Nor need we stress here the fact that the greater stability of the wages of particular groups which unions may secure is likely to involve greater instability of employment. What is important is that the accidental differences in union power of the different trades and industries will produce not only gross inequalities in remuneration among the workers which have no economic justification but uneconomic disparities in the development of different industries. Socially important industries, such as building, will be greatly hampered in their development and will conspicuously fail to satisfy urgent needs simply because their character offers the unions special opportunities for coercive monopolistic practices.[58] Because unions are most powerful where capital investments are heaviest, they tend to become a deterrent to investment – at present probably second only to taxation. Finally, it is often union monopoly in collusion with enterprise that becomes one of the chief foundations of monopolistic control of the industry concerned.

The chief danger presented by the current development of unionism is that, by establishing effective monopolies in the supply of the different kinds of labour, the unions will prevent competition from acting as an effective regulator of the allocation of all resources. But if competition becomes ineffective as a means of such regulation, some other means will have to be adopted in its place. The only alternative to the market, however, is direction by authority. Such direction clearly cannot be left in the hands of particular unions with sectional interests, nor can it be adequately performed by a unified organisation of all labour, which would thereby become not merely the strongest power in the state but a power completely controlling the state. Unionism as it is now tends, however, to produce that very system of over-all socialist planning which few unions want and which, indeed, it is in their best interest to avoid.

Acting against members' interests

The unions cannot achieve their principal aims unless they obtain complete control of the supply of the type of labour with which they are concerned; and, since it is not in the interest of all workers to submit to such control, some of them must be induced to act against their own interest. This may be done to some extent through merely psychological and moral pressure, encouraging the erroneous belief that the unions benefit all workers. Where they succeed in creating a general feeling that every worker ought, in the interest of his class, to support union action, coercion comes to be accepted as a legitimate means of making a recalcitrant worker do his duty. Here the unions have relied on a most effective tool, namely, the myth that it is due to their efforts that the standard of living of the working class has risen as fast as it has done and that only through their continued efforts will wages continue to increase as fast as possible – a myth in the assiduous cultivation of which the unions have usually been actively assisted by their opponents. A departure from such a condition can only come from a truer insight into the facts, and whether this will be achieved depends on how effectively economists do their job of enlightening public opinion.

But though this kind of moral pressure exerted by the unions may be very powerful, it would scarcely be sufficient to give them the power to do real harm. Union leaders apparently agree with the students of this aspect of unionism that much stronger forms of coercion are needed if the unions are to achieve their aims. It is the techniques of coercion that unions have developed for the purpose of making membership in effect compulsory, what they call their 'organisational activities' (or, in the United States, 'union security' – a curious euphemism) that give them real power. Because the power of truly voluntary unions will be restricted to what are common interests of all workers, they have come to direct their chief efforts to the forcing of dissenters to obey their will.

They could never have been successful in this without the support of a misguided public opinion and the active aid of government. Unfortunately, they have to a large extent succeeded in persuading the public that complete unionisation is not only legitimate but important to public policy. To say that the workers have a right to form unions, however, is not to say that the unions have a right to exist independently of the will of the individual workers. Far from being a public calamity, it would indeed be a highly desirable state of affairs if the workers should not feel it necessary to form unions. Yet the fact that it is a natural aim of the unions to induce all workers to join them has been so interpreted as to mean that the unions ought to be entitled to do whatever seems necessary to achieve this aim. Similarly, the fact that it is legitimate for unions to try to secure higher wages has been interpreted to mean that they must also be allowed to do whatever seems necessary to succeed in their effort. In particular, because striking has been accepted as a legitimate weapon of unions, it has come to be believed that they must be allowed to do whatever seems necessary to make a strike successful. In general, the legalisation of unions has come to mean that whatever methods they regard as indispensable for their purposes are also to be treated as legal.

The present coercive powers of unions thus rest chiefly on the use of methods which would not be tolerated for any other purpose and which are opposed to the protection of the individual's private sphere. In the first place, the unions rely – to a much greater extent than is commonly recognised – on the use of the picket line as an instrument of intimidation. That even so-called 'peaceful' picketing in numbers is severely coercive and the condoning of it constitutes a privilege conceded because of its presumed legitimate aim is shown by the fact that it can be and is used by persons who themselves are not workers to force others to form a union which they will control, and that it can also be used for purely political purposes or to give vent to animosity against an unpopular person. The aura of legitimacy conferred upon it because the aims are often approved cannot alter the fact that it represents a kind of organised pressure upon individuals which in a free society no private agency should be permitted to exercise.

Next to the toleration of picketing, the chief factor which enables unions to coerce individual workers is the sanction by both legislation and jurisdiction of the closed or union shop and its varieties. These constitute contracts in restraint of trade, and only their exemption from the ordinary rules of law has made them legitimate objects of the 'organisational activities' of the unions. Legislation has frequently gone so far as to require not only that a contract concluded by the representatives of the majority of the workers of a plant or industry be available to any worker who wishes to take advantage of it, but that it apply to all employees, even if they should individually wish and be able to obtain a different combination of advantages.[59] We must also regard as inadmissible methods of coercion all secondary strikes and boycotts which are used not as an instrument of wage bargaining but solely as a means of forcing other workers to fall in with union policies.

Most of these coercive tactics of the unions can be practised, moreover, only because the law has exempted groups of workers from the ordinary responsibility of joint action, either by allowing them to avoid formal incorporation or by explicitly exempting their organisations from the general rules applying to corporate bodies. There is no need to consider separately various other aspects of contemporary union policies such as, to mention one, industry-wide or nation-wide bargaining. Their practicability rests on the practices already mentioned, and they would almost certainly disappear if the basic coercive power of the unions were removed.[60]

A non-coercive rôle

It can hardly be denied that raising wages by the use of coercion is today the main aim of unions. Even if this were their sole aim, legal prohibition of unions would, however, not be justifiable. In a free society much that is undesirable has to be tolerated if it cannot be prevented without discriminatory legislation. But the control of wages is even now not the only function of the unions; and they are undoubtedly capable of rendering services which are not only unobjectionable but definitely useful. If their only purpose were to force up wages by coercive action, they would probably disappear if deprived of coercive power. But unions have other useful functions to perform, and, though it would be contrary to all our principles even to consider the possibility of prohibiting them altogether, it is desirable to show explicitly why there is no economic ground for such action and why, as truly voluntary and non-coercive organisations, they may have important services to render. It is in fact more than probable that unions will fully develop their potential usefulness only after they have been diverted from their present anti-social aims by an effective prevention of the use of coercion.[61]

Unions without coercive powers would probably play a useful and important rôle even in the process of wage determination. In the first place, there is often a choice to be made between wage increases, on the one hand, and, on the other, alternative benefits which the employer could provide at the same cost but which he can provide only if all or most of the workers are willing to accept them in preference to additional pay. There is also the fact that the relative position of the individual on the wage scale is often nearly as important to him as his absolute position. In any hierarchical organisation it is important that the differentials between the remuneration for the different jobs and the rules of promotion are felt to be just by the majority.[62] The most effective way of securing consent is probably to have the general scheme agreed to in collective negotiations in which all the different interests are represented. Even from the employer's point of view it would be difficult to conceive of any other way of reconciling all the different considerations that in a large organisation have to be taken into account in arriving at a satisfactory wage structure. An agreed set of standard terms, available to all who wish to take advantage of them, though not excluding special arrangements in individual cases, seems to be required by the needs of large-scale organisations.

The same is true to an even greater extent of all the general problems relating to conditions of work other than individual remuneration, those problems which truly concern all employees and which, in the mutual interest of workers and employers, should be regulated in a manner that takes account of as many desires as possible. A large organisation must in a great measure be governed by rules, and such rules are likely to operate most effectively if drawn up with the participation of the workers.[63] Because a contract between employers and employees regulates not only relations between them but also relations between the various groups of employees, it is often expedient to give it the character of a multilateral agreement and to provide in certain respects, as in grievance procedure, for a degree of self-government among the employees.

There is, finally, the oldest and most beneficial activity of the unions, in which as 'friendly societies' they undertake to assist members in providing against the peculiar risks of their trade. This is a function which must in every respect be regarded as a highly desirable form of self-help, albeit one which is gradually being taken over by the State. We shall leave the question open, however, as to whether any of the above arguments justify unions of a larger scale than that of the plant or corporation.

An entirely different matter, which we can mention here only in passing, is the claim of unions to participation in the conduct of business. Under the name of 'industrial democracy' or, more recently, under that of 'co-determination', this has acquired considerable popularity, especially in Germany and to a lesser degree in Britain. It represents a curious recrudescence of the ideas of the syndicalist branch of 19th-century socialism, the least-thought-out and most impractical form of that doctrine. Though these ideas have a certain superficial appeal, they reveal inherent contradictions when examined. A plant or industry cannot be conducted in the interest of some permanent distinct body of workers if it is at the same time to serve the interests of the consumers. Moreover, effective participation in the direction of an enterprise is a full-time job, and anybody so engaged soon ceases to have the outlook and interest of an employee. It is not only from the point of view of the employers, therefore, that such a plan should be rejected; there are very good reasons why in the United States union leaders have emphatically refused to assume any responsibility in the conduct of business. For a fuller examination of this problem we must, however, refer the reader to the careful studies, now available, of all its implications.[64]

Minor changes in the law

Though it may be impossible to protect the individual against all union coercion so long as general opinion regards it as legitimate, most students of the subject agree that comparatively few and, as they may seem at first, minor changes in law and jurisdiction would suffice to produce far-reaching and probably decisive changes in the existing situation.[65] The mere withdrawal of the special privileges either explicitly granted to the unions or arrogated by them with the toleration of the courts would seem enough to deprive them of the more serious coercive powers which they now exercise and to channel their legitimate selfish interests so that they would be socially beneficial.

The essential requirement is that true freedom of association be assured and that coercion be treated as equally illegitimate whether employed for or against organisation, by the employer or by the employees. The principle that the end does not justify the means and that the aims of the unions do not justify their exemption from the general rules of law should be strictly applied. Today this means, in the first place, that all picketing in numbers should be prohibited, since it is not only the chief and regular cause of violence but even in its most peaceful forms is a means of coercion. Next, the unions should not be permitted to keep non-members out of any employment. This means that closed- and union-shop contracts (including such varieties as the 'maintenance of membership' and 'preferential hiring' clauses) must be treated as contracts in restraint of trade and denied the protection of the law. They differ in no respect from the 'yellow-dog contract' which prohibits the individual worker from joining a union and which is commonly prohibited by the law.

The invalidating of all such contracts would, by removing the chief objects of secondary strikes and boycotts, make these and similar forms of pressure largely ineffective. It would be necessary, however, also to rescind all legal provisions which make contracts concluded with the representatives of the majority of workers of a plant or industry binding on all employees and to deprive all organised groups of any right of concluding contracts binding on men who have not voluntarily delegated this authority to them.[66] Finally, the responsibility for organised and concerted action in conflict with contractual obligations or the general law must be firmly placed on those in whose hands the decision lies, irrespective of the particular form of organised action adopted.

It would not be a valid objection to maintain that any legislation making certain types of contracts invalid would be contrary to the principle of freedom of contract. We have seen before (in ch. 15) that this principle can never mean that all contracts will be legally binding and enforcible. It means merely that all contracts must be judged according to the same general rules and that no authority should be given discretionary power to allow or disallow particular contracts. Among the contracts to which the law ought to deny validity are contracts in restraint of trade. Closed- and union-shop contracts fall clearly into this category. If legislation, jurisdiction, and the tolerance of executive agencies had not created privileges for the unions, the need for special legislation concerning them would probably not have arisen in common-law countries. That there is such a need is a matter for regret, and the believer in liberty will regard any legislation of this kind with misgivings. But, once special privileges have become part of the law of the land, they can be removed only by special legislation. Though there ought to be no need for special 'right-to-work laws', it is difficult to deny that the situation created in the United States by legislation and by the decisions of the Supreme Court may make special legislation the only practicable way of restoring the principles of freedom.[67]

The specific measures which would be required in any given country to reinstate the principles of free association in the field of labour will depend on the situation created by its individual development. The situation in the United States is of special interest, for here legislation and the decisions of the Supreme Court have probably gone further than elsewhere[68] in legalising union coercion and very far in conferring discretionary and essentially irresponsible powers on administrative authority. But for further details we must refer the reader to the important study by Professor Petro on *The Labor Policy of the Free Society*,[69] in which the reforms required are fully described.

Though all the changes needed to restrain the harmful powers of the unions involve no more than that they be made to submit to the same general principles of law that apply to everybody else, there can be no doubt that the existing unions will resist them with all their power. They know that the achievement of what they at present desire depends on that very coercive power which will have to be restrained if a free society is to be preserved. Yet the situation is not hopeless. There are developments under way which sooner or later will prove to the unions that the existing state cannot last. They will find that, of the alternative courses of further development open to them, submitting to the general principle that prevents all coercion will be greatly preferable in the long run to continuing their present policy; for the latter is bound to lead to one of two unfortunate consequences.

Responsibility for unemployment

While labour unions cannot in the long run substantially alter the level of real wages that all workers can earn and are, in fact, more likely to lower than to raise them, the same is not true of the level of money wages. With respect to them, the effect of union action will depend on the principles governing monetary policy. What with the doctrines that are now widely accepted and the policies accordingly expected from the monetary authorities, there can be little doubt that current union policies must lead to continuous and progressive inflation. The chief reason for this is that the dominant 'full-employment' doctrines explicitly relieve the unions of the responsibility for any unemployment and place the duty of preserving full employment on the monetary and fiscal authorities. The only way in which the latter can prevent union policy from producing unemployment is, however, to counter through inflation whatever excessive rises in real wages unions tend to cause.

In order to understand the situation into which we have been led, it will be necessary to take a brief look at the intellectual sources of the full-employment policy of the 'Keynesian' type. The development of Lord Keynes's theories started from the correct insight that the regular cause of extensive unemployment is real wages that are too high. The next step consisted in the proposition that a direct lowering of money wages could be brought about only by a struggle so painful and prolonged that it could not be contemplated. Hence he concluded that real wages must be lowered by the process of lowering the value of money. This is really the reasoning underlying the whole 'full-employment' policy, now so widely accepted.[70] If labour insists on a level of money wages too high to allow of full employment, the supply of money must be so increased as to raise prices to a level where the real value of the prevailing money wages is no longer greater than the productivity of the workers seeking employment. In practice, this necessarily means that each separate union, in its attempt to overtake the value of money, will never cease to insist on further increases in money wages and that the aggregate effort of the unions will thus bring about progressive inflation.

This would follow even if individual unions did no more than prevent any reduction in the money wages of any particular group. Where unions make such wage reductions impracticable and wages have generally become, as the economists put it, 'rigid downward', all the changes in relative wages of the different groups made necessary by the constantly changing conditions must be brought about by raising all money wages except those of the group whose relative real wages must fall. Moreover, the general rise in money wages and the resulting increase in the cost of living will generally lead to attempts, even on the part of the latter group, to push up money wages, and several rounds of successive wage increases will be required before any readjustment of relative wages is produced. Since the need for adjustment of relative wages occurs all the time, this process alone produces the wage–price spiral that has prevailed since the Second World War, that is, since full-employment policies became generally accepted.[71]

The process is sometimes described as though wage increases directly produced inflation. This is not correct. If the supply of money and credit were not expanded, the wage increases would rapidly lead to unemployment. But under the influence of a doctrine that represents it as the duty of the monetary authorities to provide enough money to secure full employment at any given wage level, it is politically inevitable that each round of wage increases should lead to further inflation.[72] Or it is inevitable until the rise of prices becomes sufficiently marked and prolonged to cause serious public alarm. Efforts will then be made to apply the monetary brakes. But, because by that time the economy will have become geared to the expectation of further inflation and much of the existing employment will depend on continued monetary expansion, the attempt to stop it will rapidly produce substantial unemployment. This will bring a renewed and irresistible pressure for more inflation. And, with ever bigger doses of inflation, it may be possible for quite a long time to prevent the appearance of the unemployment which the wage pressure would otherwise cause. To the public at large it will seem as if progressive inflation were the direct consequence of union wage policy rather than of an attempt to cure its consequences.

Though this race between wages and inflation is likely to go on for some time, it cannot go on indefinitely without people coming to realise that it must somehow be stopped. A monetary policy that would break the coercive powers of the unions by producing extensive and protracted unemployment must be excluded, for it would be politically and socially fatal. But if we do not succeed in time in curbing union power at its source, the unions will soon be faced with a demand for measures that will be much more distasteful to the individual workers, if not the union leaders, than the submission of the unions to the rule of law: the clamour will soon be either for the fixing of wages by government or for the complete abolition of the unions.

Progression to central control

In the field of labour, as in any other field, the elimination of the market as a steering mechanism would necessitate the replacement of it by a system of administrative direction. In order to approach even remotely the ordering function of the market, such direction would have to co-ordinate the whole economy and therefore, in the last resort, have to come from a single central authority. And though such an authority might at first concern itself only with the allocation and remuneration of labour, its policy would necessarily lead to the transformation of the whole of society into a centrally planned and administered system, with all its economic and political consequences.

In those countries in which inflationary tendencies have operated for some time, we can observe increasingly frequent demands for an 'over-all wage policy'. In the countries where these tendencies have been most pronounced, notably in Great Britain, it appears to have become accepted doctrine among the intellectual leaders of the Left that wages should generally be determined by a 'unified policy', which ultimately means that government must do the determining.[73] If the market were thus irretrievably deprived of its function, there would be no efficient way of distributing labour throughout the industries, regions, and trades, other than having wages determined by authority. Step by step, through setting up an official conciliation and arbitration machinery with compulsory powers, and through the creation of wage boards, we are moving towards a situation in which wages will be determined by what must be essentially arbitrary decisions of authority.

All this is no more than the inevitable outcome of the present policies of labour unions, who are led by the desire to see wages determined by some conception of 'justice' rather than by the forces of the market. But in no workable system could any group of people be allowed to enforce by the threat of violence what it believes it should have. And when not merely a few privileged groups but most of the important sections of labour have become effectively organised for coercive action, to allow each to act independently would not only produce the opposite of justice but result in economic chaos. When we can no longer depend on the impersonal determination of wages by the market, the only way we can retain a viable economic system is to have them determined authoritatively by government. Such determination must be arbitrary, because there are no objective standards of justice that could be applied.[74] As is true of all other prices or services, the wage rates that are compatible with an open opportunity for all to seek employment do not correspond to any assessable merit or any independent standard of justice but must depend on conditions which nobody can control.

Once government undertakes to determine the whole wage structure and is thereby forced to control employment and production, there will be a far greater destruction of the present powers of the unions than their submission to the rule of equal law would involve. Under such a system the unions will have only the choice between becoming the willing instrument of governmental policy and being incorporated into the machinery of government, on the one hand, and being totally abolished, on the other. The former alternative is more likely to be chosen, since it would enable the existing union bureaucracy to retain their position and some of their personal power. But to the workers it would mean complete subjection to control by a corporative state. The situation in most countries leaves us no choice but to await some such outcome or to retrace our steps. The present position of the unions cannot last, for they can function only in a market economy which they are doing their best to destroy.

'Unassailable' union powers

The problem of labour unions constitutes both a good test of our principles and an instructive illustration of the consequences if they are infringed. Having failed in their duty of preventing private coercion, governments are now driven everywhere to exceed their proper function in order to correct the results of that failure and are thereby led into tasks which they can perform only by being as arbitrary as the unions. So long as the powers that the unions have been allowed to acquire are regarded as unassailable, there is no way to correct the harm done by them but to give the state even greater arbitrary power of coercion. We are indeed already experiencing a pronounced decline of the rule of law in the field of labour.[75] Yet all that is really needed to remedy the situation is a return to the principles of the rule of law and to their consistent application by legislative and executive authorities.

This path is still blocked, however, by the most fatuous of all fashionable arguments, namely, that 'we cannot turn the clock back'. One cannot help wondering whether those who habitually use this cliché are aware that it expresses the fatalistic belief that we cannot learn from our mistakes, the most abject admission that we are incapable of using our intelligence. I doubt whether anybody who takes a long-range view believes that there is another satisfactory solution which the majority would deliberately choose if they fully understood where the present developments were leading. There are some signs that far-sighted union leaders are also beginning to recognise that, unless we are to resign ourselves to the progressive extinction of freedom, we must reverse that trend and resolve to restore the rule of law and that, in order to save what is valuable in their movement, they must abandon the illusions which have guided it for so long.[76]

Nothing less than a re-dedication of current policy to principles already abandoned will enable us to avert the threatening danger to freedom. What is required is a change in economic policy, for in the present situation the tactical decisions which will seem to be required by the short-term needs of government in successive emergencies will merely lead us further into the thicket of arbitrary controls. The cumulative effects of those palliatives which the pursuit of contradictory aims makes necessary must prove strategically fatal. As is true of all problems of economic policy, the problem of labour unions cannot be satisfactorily solved by *ad hoc* decisions on particular questions but only by the consistent application of a principle that is uniformly adhered to in all fields. There is only one such principle that can preserve a free society: namely, the strict prevention of all coercion except in the enforcement of general abstract rules equally applicable to all.

(*The Constitution of Liberty*, Routledge, 1960; extracts from ch. 18)

22 (a) Inflation – a Short-term Expedient
    (b) Inflation – the Deceit is Short-lived

In the first of these two extracts, Professor Hayek points out that one effect of inflation in its initial stages is to keep afloat businesses that would otherwise suffer losses. But as inflation proceeds and comes to be expected, costs are bid up in anticipation, profits shrink back to non-inflationary levels (in real terms), and apparently deflationary symptoms begin to appear.

In the second extract he outlines a non-inflationary criterion for monetary stability in line with currently unchangeable historical circumstances, viz. maintaining the stability of a comprehensive price index. Given the change in union wage-rate policy outlined in earlier extracts, such a monetary policy would also produce stability in total employment.

Professor Hayek emphasises two social dangers of inflation. First, by destroying the value of savings and of fixed incomes it creates the problem of poverty in old age, as well as a dangerous gap between the wealthy minority and the property-less majority. Second, it reinforces the disinclination to take long-term effects into account when determining policy.

(a) Inflation – a Short-term Expedient

Although there are a few people who deliberately advocate a continuous upward movement of prices, the chief source of the existing inflationary bias is the general belief that deflation, the opposite of inflation, is so much more to be feared that, in order to keep on the safe side, a persistent error in the direction of inflation is preferable. But, as we do not know how to keep prices completely stable and can achieve stability only by correcting any small movement in either direction, the determination to avoid deflation at any cost must result in cumulative inflation. Also, the fact that inflation and deflation will often be local or sectional phenomena which must occur necessarily as part of the mechanism redistributing the resources of the economy means that attempts to prevent any deflation affecting a major area of the economy must result in over-all inflation.

Inflation similar to drug-taking

It is, however, rather doubtful whether, from a long-term point of view, deflation is really more harmful than inflation. Indeed, there is a sense in which inflation is infinitely more dangerous and needs to be more carefully guarded against. Of the two errors, it is the one much more likely to be committed. The reason for this is that moderate inflation is generally pleasant while it proceeds, whereas deflation is immediately and acutely painful.[77] There is little need to take precautions against any practice the bad effects of which will be immediately and strongly felt; but there is need for precautions wherever action which is immediately pleasant or relieves temporary difficulties involves much greater harm that will be felt only later. There is, indeed, more than a mere superficial similarity between inflation and drug-taking, a comparison which has often been made.

Inflation and deflation both produce their peculiar effects by causing unexpected price changes, and both are bound to disappoint expectations twice. The first time is when prices prove to be higher or lower than they were expected to be and the second when, as must sooner or later happen, these price changes come to be expected and cease to have the effect which their unforeseen occurrence had. The difference between inflation and deflation is that, with the former, the pleasant surprise comes first and the reaction later, while, with the latter, the first effect on business is depressing. The effects of both, however, are self-reversing. For a time the forces which bring about either tend to feed on themselves, and the period during which prices move faster than expected may thus be prolonged. But unless price movements continue in the same direction at an ever accelerating rate, expectations must catch up with them. As soon as this happens, the character of the effects changes.

Inflation at first merely produces conditions in which more people make profits and in which profits are generally larger than usual. Almost everything succeeds, there are hardly any failures. The fact that profits again and again prove to be greater than had been expected and that an unusual number of ventures turn out to be successful produces a general atmosphere favourable to risk-taking. Even those who would have been driven out of business without the windfalls caused by the unexpected general rise in prices are able to hold on and to keep their employees in the expectation that they will soon share in the general prosperity. This situation will last, however, only until people begin to expect prices to continue to rise at the same rate. Once they begin to count on prices being so many per cent higher in so many months' time, they will bid up the prices of the factors of production which determine the costs to a level corresponding to the future prices they expect. If prices then rise no more than had been expected, profits will return to normal, and the proportion of those making a profit also will fall and since, during the period of exceptionally large profits, many have held on who would otherwise have been forced to change the direction of their efforts, a higher proportion than usual will suffer losses.

The stimulating effect of inflation will thus operate only so long as it has not been foreseen; as soon as it comes to be foreseen, only its continuation at an increased rate will maintain the same degree of prosperity. If in such a situation prices rose less than expected, the effect would be the same as that of unforeseen deflation. Even if they rose only as much as was generally expected, this would no longer provide the exceptional stimulus but would lay bare the whole backlog of adjustments that had been postponed while the temporary stimulus lasted. In order for inflation to retain its initial stimulating effect, it would have to continue at a rate always faster than expected.

Accelerating inflation

We cannot consider here all the complications which make it impossible for adaptations to an expected change in prices ever to become perfect, and especially for long-term and short-term expectations to become equally adjusted; nor can we go into the different effects on current production and on investment which are so important in any full examination of industrial fluctuations. It is enough for our purpose to know that the stimulating effects of inflation must cease to operate unless its rate is progressively accelerated and that, as it proceeds, certain unfavourable consequences of the fact that complete adaptation is impossible become more and more serious. The most important of these is that the methods of accounting on which all business decisions rest make sense only so long as the value of money is tolerably stable. With prices rising at an accelerating rate, the techniques of capital and cost accounting that provide the basis for all business planning would soon lose all meaning. Real costs, profits, or income would soon cease to be ascertainable by any conventional or generally acceptable method. And, with the principles of taxation being what they are, more and more would be taken in taxes as profits that in fact should be re-invested merely to maintain capital.

Inflation thus can never be more than a temporary fillip, and even this beneficial effect can last only as long as somebody continues to be cheated and the expectations of some people unnecessarily disappointed. Its stimulus is due to the errors which it produces. It is particularly dangerous because the harmful after-effects of even small doses of inflation can be staved off only by larger doses of inflation. Once it has continued for some time, even the prevention of further acceleration will create a situation in which it will be very difficult to avoid a spontaneous deflation. Once certain activities that have become extended can be maintained only by continued inflation, their simultaneous discontinuation may well produce that vicious and rightly feared process in which the decline of some incomes leads to the decline of other incomes, and so forth. From what we know, it still seems probable that we should be able to prevent serious depressions by preventing the inflations which regularly precede them, but that there is little we can do to cure them, once they have set in. The time to worry about depressions is, unfortunately, when they are furthest from the minds of most people.

The path of least resistance

The manner in which inflation operates explains why it is so difficult to resist when policy mainly concerns itself with particular situations rather than with general conditions and with short-term rather than with long-term problems. It is usually the easy way out of any temporary difficulties for both government and private business – the path of least resistance and sometimes also the easiest way to help the economy get over all the obstacles that government policy has placed in its way.[78] It is the inevitable result of a policy which regards all the other decisions as data to which the supply of money must be adapted so that the damage done by other measures will be as little noticed as possible. In the long run, however, such a policy makes governments the captives of their own earlier decisions, which often force them to adopt measures that they know to be harmful. It is no accident that the author whose views, perhaps mistakenly interpreted, have given more encouragement to these inflationary propensities than any other man's is also responsible for the fundamentally anti-liberal aphorism, 'in the long run we are all dead'.[79] The inflationary bias of our day is largely the result of the prevalence of the short-term view, which in turn stems from the great difficulty of recognising the more remote consequences of current measures, and from the inevitable preoccupation of practical men, and particularly politicians, with the immediate problems and the achievement of near goals.

Because inflation is psychologically and politically so much more difficult to prevent than deflation and because it is, at the same time, technically so much more easily prevented, the economist should always stress the dangers of inflation. As soon as deflation makes itself felt, there will be immediate attempts to combat it – often when it is only a local and necessary process that should not be prevented. There is more danger in untimely fears of deflation than in the possibility of our not taking necessary counter-measures. While nobody is likely to mistake local or sectional prosperity for inflation, people often demand wholly inappropriate monetary counter-measures when there is a local or sectional depression.

These considerations would seem to suggest that, on balance, probably some mechanical rule which aims at what is desirable in the long run and ties the hands of authority in its short-term decisions is likely to produce a better monetary policy than principles which give to the authorities more power and discretion and thereby make them more subject to both political pressure and their own inclination to over-estimate the urgency of the circumstances of the moment. This, however, raises issues which we must approach more systematically.

(b) Inflation – the Deceit is Short-lived

I certainly have no wish to weaken the case for any arrangement that will force the authorities to do the right thing. The case for such a mechanism becomes stronger as the likelihood of the monetary policy's being affected by considerations of public finance becomes greater; but it would weaken, rather than strengthen, the argument if we exaggerated what can be achieved by it. It is probably undeniable that, though we can limit discretion in this field, we never can eliminate it; in consequence, what can be done within the unavoidable range of discretion not only is very important but is likely in practice to determine even whether or not the mechanism will ever be allowed to operate.

Limited central bank influence

There is one basic dilemma, which all central banks face, which makes it inevitable that their policy must involve much discretion. A central bank can exercise only an indirect and therefore limited control over all the circulating media. Its power is based chiefly on the threat of not supplying cash when it is needed. Yet at the same time it is considered to be its duty never to refuse to supply this cash at a price when needed. It is this problem, rather than the general effects of policy on prices or the value of money, that necessarily preoccupies the central banker in his day-to-day actions. It is a task which makes it necessary for the central bank constantly to forestall or counteract developments in the realm of credit, for which no simple rules can provide sufficient guidance.[80]

The same is nearly as true of the measures intended to affect prices and employment. They must be directed more at forestalling changes before they occur than at correcting them after they have occurred. If a central bank always waited until rule or mechanism forced it to take action, the resulting fluctuations would be much greater than they need be. And if, within the range of its discretion, it takes measures in a direction opposite to those which mechanism or rule will later impose upon it, it will probably create a situation in which the mechanism will not long be allowed to operate. In the last resort, therefore, even where the discretion of the authority is greatly restricted, the outcome is likely to depend on what the authority does within the limits of its discretion.

This means in practice that under present conditions we have little choice but to limit monetary policy by prescribing its goals rather than its specific actions. The concrete issue today is whether it ought to keep stable some level of employment or some level of prices. Reasonably interpreted and with due allowance made for the inevitability of minor fluctuations around a given level, these two aims are not necessarily in conflict, provided that the requirements for monetary stability are given first place and the rest of economic policy is adapted to them. A conflict arises, however, if 'full employment' is made the chief objective and this is interpreted, as it sometimes is, as that maximum of employment which can be produced by monetary means in the short run. That way lies progressive inflation.

The reasonable goal of a high and stable level of employment can probably be secured as well as we know how while aiming at the stability of some comprehensive price level. For practical purposes, it probably does not greatly matter precisely how this price level is defined, except that it should not refer exclusively to final products (for if it did, it might in times of rapid technological advance still produce a significant inflationary tendency), and that it should be based as much as possible on international rather than local prices. Such a policy, if pursued simultaneously by two or three of the major countries, should also be reconcilable with stability of exchange rates. The important point is that there will be definite known limits which the monetary authorities will not allow price movements to exceed – or even to approach to the point of making drastic reversals of policy necessary.

Weak opposition to inflation

Though there may be some people who explicitly advocate continuous inflation, it is certainly not because the majority wants it that we are likely to get it. Few people would be willing to accept it when it is pointed out that even such a seemingly moderate increase in prices as 3 per cent per annum means that the price level will double every $23\frac{1}{2}$ years and that it will nearly quadruple over the normal span of a man's working life. The danger that inflation will continue is not so much due to the strength of those who deliberately advocate it as to the weakness of the opposition. In order to prevent it, it is necessary for the public to become clearly aware of the things we can do and of the consequences of not doing them. Most competent students agree that the difficulty of preventing inflation is only political and not economic. Yet almost no one seems to believe that the monetary authorities have the power to prevent it and will exercise it. The greatest optimism about the short-term miracles that monetary policy will achieve is accompanied by a complete fatalism about what it will produce in the long run.

There are two points which cannot be stressed enough: first, it seems certain that we shall not stop the drift toward more and more state control unless we stop the inflationary trend; and, second, any continued rise in prices is dangerous because, once we begin to rely on its stimulating effect, we shall be committed to a course that will leave us no choice but that between more inflation, on the one hand, and paying for our mistake by a recession or depression, on the other. Even a very moderate degree of inflation is dangerous because it ties the hands of those responsible for policy by creating a situation in which, every time a problem arises, a little more inflation seems the only easy way out.

We have not had space to touch on the various ways in which the efforts of individuals to protect themselves against inflation, such as sliding-scale contracts, not only tend to make the process self-accelerating but also increase the rate of inflation necessary to maintain its stimulating effect. Let us simply note, then, that inflation makes it more and more impossible for people of moderate means to provide for their old age themselves; that it discourages saving and encourages running into debt; and that, by destroying the middle class, it creates that dangerous gap between the completely propertyless and the wealthy that is so characteristic of societies which have gone through prolonged inflations and which is the source of so much tension in those societies. Perhaps even more ominous is the wider psychological effect, the spreading among the population at large of that disregard of long-range views and exclusive concern with immediate advantages which already dominate public policy.

It is no accident that inflationary policies are generally advocated by those who want more government control – though, unfortunately, not by them alone. The increased dependence of the individual upon government which inflation produces and the demand for more govern-ment action to which this leads may for the socialist be an argument in its favour. Those who wish to preserve freedom should recognise, however, that inflation is probably the most important single factor in that vicious circle wherein one kind of government action makes more and more government control necessary. For this reason all those who wish to stop the drift toward increasing government control should concentrate their efforts on monetary policy. There is perhaps nothing more disheartening than the fact that there are still so many intelligent and informed people who in most other respects will defend freedom and yet are induced by the immediate benefits of an expansionist policy to support what, in the long run, must destroy the foundations of a free society.

(*The Constitution of Liberty, op. cit.*, pp. 330–33, 336–39)

VI Main Themes Restated

23 Personal Recollections of Keynes

Professor Hayek here brings together some of the major threads in his criticisms of Keynes and the macro approach. He points out that the Keynesian concept of what may be called 'full' unemployment assumes implicitly that all resources are freely available and that consequently any increase in money incomes will increase output, thus reviving the inflationist fallacies which in 1931 he had supposed to have been eradicated. Professor Hayek emphasises that the Keynesian mode of thinking systematically eliminates from consideration those price inter-relationships which operate in the real world; that the General Theory *was, in very large part, simply a tract for the times.*

Even to those who knew Keynes but could never bring themselves to accept his monetary theories, and at times thought his pronouncements somewhat irresponsible, the personal impression of the man remains unforgettable. And especially to my generation (he was my senior by 16 years) he was a hero long before he achieved real fame as an economic theorist. Was he not the man who had had the courage to protest against the economic clauses of the peace treaties of 1919? We admired the brilliantly written books for their outspokenness and independence of thought, even though some older and acuter thinkers at once pointed out certain theoretical flaws in his argument. And those of us who had the good fortune to meet him personally soon experienced the magnetism of the brilliant conversationalist with his wide range of interests and his bewitching voice.

I met him first in 1928 in London at some meeting of institutes of business cycle research, and though we had at once our first strong disagreement on some point of interest theory, we remained thereafter friends who had many interests in common, although we rarely could agree on economics. He had a somewhat intimidating manner in which he would try to ride roughshod over the objections of a younger man, but if one stood up to him he would respect him forever afterwards even if he disagreed. After I moved from Vienna to London in 1931 we had much occasion for discussion, both orally and by correspondence.

Keynes changes his mind

I had undertaken to review for *Economica* his *Treatise on Money* which had then just appeared, and I put a great deal of work into two long articles on it. To the first of these he replied by a counter-attack on my *Prices and Production*. I felt that I had largely demolished his theoretical scheme (essentially volume I), though I had great admiration for the many profound but unsystematical insights contained in volume II of the work. Great was my disappointment when all this effort seemed wasted because after the appearance of the second part of my article he told me that he had in the meantime changed his mind and no longer believed what he had said in that work.

This was one of the reasons why I did not return to the attack when he published his now famous *General Theory* – a fact for which I later much blamed myself. But I feared that before I had completed my analysis he would again have changed his mind. Though he had called it a 'general' theory, it was to me too obviously another tract for the times, conditioned by what he thought were the momentary needs of policy. But there was also another reason which I then only dimly felt but which in retrospect appears to me the decisive one: my disagreement with that book did not refer so much to any detail of the analysis as to the general approach followed in the whole work. The real issue was the validity of what we now call macro-analysis, and I feel now that in a long-run perspective the chief significance of the *General Theory* will appear that more than any other single work it decisively furthered the ascendancy of macro-economics and the temporary decline of micro-economic theory.

I shall later explain why I think that this development is fundamentally mistaken. But first I want to say that it is rather an irony of fate that Keynes should have become responsible for this swing to macro-theory, because he thought in fact rather little of the kind of econometrics which was just then becoming popular, and I do not think that he owed any stimulus to it. His ideas were rooted entirely in Marshallian economics, which was in fact the only economics he knew. Widely read as Keynes was in many fields, his education in economics was somewhat narrow. He did not read any foreign language except French – or, as he once said of himself, in German he could understand only what he knew already. It is a curious fact that before World War I he had reviewed L. von Mises's *Theory of Money* for the *Economic Journal* (just as A. C. Pigou had a little earlier reviewed Wicksell) without in any way profiting from it. I fear it must be admitted that before he started to develop his own theories, Keynes was not a highly trained or a very sophisticated economic theorist. He started from a rather elementary Marshallism economics, and what had been achieved by Walras and Pareto, the Austrians and the Swedes was very much a closed book to him. I have reason to doubt whether he ever fully mastered the theory of international trade; I don't think he had ever thought systematically on the theory of capital, and even in the theory of the value of money his starting-point – and later the object of his criticism – appears to have been a very simple, equation-of-exchange-type of the quantity theory rather than the much more sophisticated cash-balances approach of Alfred Marshall.

Thinking in aggregates

He certainly from the beginning was much given to thinking in aggregates and always had *faible* for the (sometimes very tenuous) global estimates. Already in discussion of the 1920s arising out of Great Britain's return to the Gold Standard his argument had been couched entirely in terms of price and wage levels in practically complete disregard of the structure of relative prices and wages, and later the belief that, because they were statistically measurable, such averages and the various aggregates were also causally of central importance, appears to have gained increasing hold upon him. His final conceptions rest entirely on the belief that there exist relatively simple and constant functional relationships between such 'measurable' aggregates as total demand, investment, or output, and that empirically established values of these presumed 'constants' would enable us to make valid predictions.

There seems to me, however, not only to exist no reason whatever to assume that these 'functions' will remain constant, but I believe that micro-theory had demonstrated long before Keynes that they cannot be constant but will change over time not only in quantity but even in sign. What these relationships will be, which all macro-economics must treat as quasi-constant, depends indeed on the micro-economic structure, especially on the relations between different prices which macro-economics systematically disregards. They may change very rapidly as a result of changes in the micro-economic structure, and conclusions based on the assumption that they are constant are bound to be very misleading.

Let me use as an illustration the relation between the demand for consumers' goods and the volume of investment. There are undoubtedly certain conditions in which an increase of the demand for consumers' goods *will* lead to an increase of investment. But Keynes assumes that this will always be the case. It can easily be demonstrated, however, that this cannot be so and that in some circumstances an increase of the demand for final products must lead to a *decrease* of investment. The first will generally be true only if, as Keynes generally assumes, there exist unemployed reserves of all factors of production and of the various kinds of commodities. In such circumstances it is possible at the same time to increase the production of consumers' goods and the production of capital goods.

The position is altogether different, however, if the economic system is in a state of full or nearly full employment. Then it is possible to increase the output of investment goods only by at least temporarily reducing the output of consumers' goods, because to increase the production of the former, factors will have to be shifted to it from the production of consumers' goods. And it will be some time before the additional investment helps to increase the flow of consumers' goods.

Full employment assumption

Keynes appears to have been misled here by a mistake opposite to that of which he accused the classical economists. He alleged, with only partial justification, that the classics had based their argument on the assumption of full employment, and he based his own argument on what may be called the assumption of full *un*employment, i.e. the assumption that there normally existed unused reserves of *all* factors and commodities. But the latter assumption is not only at least as unlikely to be true in fact as the former; it is also much more misleading. An analysis on the assumption of full employment, even if the assumption is only partially valid, at least helps us to understand the functioning of the price mechanism, the significance of the relations between different prices and of the factors which lead to a change in these relations. But the assumption that all goods and factors are available in excess makes the whole price system redundant, undetermined, and unintelligible. Indeed some of the most orthodox disciples of Keynes appear consistently to have thrown overboard all the traditional theory of price determination and of distribution, all that used to be the backbone of economic theory, and in consequence, in my opinion, to have ceased to understand any economics.

It is easy to see how such belief, according to which the creation of additional money will lead to the creation of a corresponding amount of goods, was bound to lead to a revival of the more naïve inflationist fallacies which we thought economics had once and for all exterminated. And I have little doubt that we owe much of the post-war inflation to the great influence of such over-simplified Keynesianism. Not that Keynes himself would have approved of this. Indeed, I am fairly certain that if he had lived he would in that period have been one of the most determined fighters against inflation. About the last time I saw him, a few weeks before his death, he more or less plainly told me so. As his remark on that occasion is illuminating in other respects, it is worth reporting. I had asked him whether he was not getting alarmed about the use to which some of his disciples were putting his theories. His reply was that these theories had been greatly needed in the 1930s, but if these theories should ever become harmful, I could be assured that he would quickly bring about a change in public opinion. What I blame him for is that he had called such a tract for the times the *General Theory*.

The fact is that, although he liked to pose as the Cassandra whose dire predictions were not listened to, he was really supremely confident of his powers of persuasion and believed that he could play on public opinion as a virtuoso plays on his instrument. He was, by gift and temperament, more an artist and politician than a scholar or student. Though endowed with supreme mental powers, his thinking was as much influenced by aesthetic and intuitive as by purely rational factors. Knowledge came easy to him and he possessed a remarkable memory. But the intuition which made him sure of the results before he had demonstrated them, and led him to justify the same policies in turn by very different theoretical arguments, made him rather impatient of the slow, painstaking intellectual work by which knowledge is normally advanced.

He was so many-sided that for his estimate as a man it seemed almost irrelevant that one thought his economics to be both false and dangerous. If one considers how small a share of his time and energy he gave to economics, his influence on economics and the fact that he will be remembered chiefly as an economist is both miraculous and tragic. He would be remembered as a great man by all who knew him even if he had never written on economics.

I cannot from personal knowledge speak of his services to his country during the last five or six years of his life when, already a sick man, he gave all his energy to public service. Yet it was during those years when I saw most of him and came to know him fairly well. The London School of Economics had at the outbreak of war been moved to Cambridge, and when it became necessary in 1940 for me to live wholly at Cambridge, he found quarters for me at his college. On the weekends for which, so far as possible, he sought the quiet of Cambridge, I then saw a fair amount of him and came to know him otherwise than merely pro-fessionally. Perhaps it was because he was seeking relief from his arduous duties, or because all that concerned his official work was secret, that all his other interests then came out most clearly. Though he had before the war reduced his business connections and given up the bursarships of his college, the interests and activities he still actively pursued besides his official duties would have taxed the whole strength of most other men. He kept as informed on artistic, literary, and scientific matters as in normal times, and always his strong personal likings and dislikings came through.

Wide intellectual interests

I remember particularly one occasion which now seems to me characteristic of many. The war was over and Keynes had just returned from an official mission to Washington on a matter of the greatest consequence which one would have assumed had absorbed all his energy. Yet he entertained a group of us for part of the evening with details about the state of the collection of Elizabethan books in the United States as if the study of this had been the sole purpose of his visit. He was himself a distinguished collector in this field, as of manuscripts of about the same period, and of modern paintings.

As I mentioned before, his intellectual interests were also largely determined by aesthetic predilections. This applied as much to literature and history as to other fields. Both the 16th and 17th centuries greatly appealed to him, and his knowledge, at least in selected parts, was that of an expert. But he much disliked the 19th century and would occasionally show a lack of knowledge of its economic history and even the history of its economics surprising in an economist.

I cannot in this short essay attempt even to sketch the general philosophy and outline on life which guided Keynes's thinking. It is a task which has yet to be attempted, because on this the otherwise brilliant and remarkably frank biography by Sir Roy Harrod is hardly sufficient – perhaps because he so completely shared and therefore took for granted the peculiar brand of rationalism which dominated Keynes's generation. Those who want to learn more about this I would strongly advise to read Keynes's own essay, 'My Early Beliefs', which was published in a little volume entitled *Two Memoirs*.

In conclusion I want to say a few words about the future of Keynesian theory. Perhaps it will be evident from what I have already said that I believe that this will be decided not by any future discussion of his special theorems but rather by the future development of views on the appropriate method of the social sciences. Keynes's theories will appear merely as the most prominent and influential instance of a general approach whose philosophical justification seems to be highly questionable. Though with its reliance on apparently measurable magnitudes it *appears* at first more scientific than the older micro-theory, it seems to me that it has achieved this pseudo-exactness at the price of disregarding the relationships which really govern the economic system. Even though the schemata of micro-economics do not claim to achieve those quantitative predictions at which the ambitions of macro-economics aim, I believe by learning to content ourselves with the more modest aims of the former, we shall gain more insight into at least the principle on which the complex order of economic life operates, than by the artificial simplification necessary for macro-theory which tends to conceal nearly all that really matters. I venture to predict that once this problem of method is settled, the 'Keynesian Revolution' will appear as an episode during which erroneous conceptions of the appropriate scientific method led to the temporary obliteration of many important insights which we had already achieved and which we shall then have painfully to regain.

('Personal Recollections of Keynes & the "Keynesian Revolution"',
The Oriental Economist, January 1966)

24 General and Relative Wages

Two major points are made in these two extracts (from a draft of an essay on Competition As A Discovery Procedure *– published later in a revised form in German).*

Professor Hayek first emphasises the rôle of the pricing system, and especially of price changes, as a means of adapting the economy to the unforeseeable changes that make up the real world. Without such continuous adaptations real income and the stock of real resources would necessarily be lower than they could *be with an optimal use of the pricing system. Professor Hayek here develops the concept of the pricing system as a transmitter of empirical knowledge, a concept first systematically propounded in his early essays on 'Economics and Knowledge' (1937), and 'The Use of Knowledge in Society' (1945).*

Applying this approach to the labour sector, Professor Hayek, in the second extract, shows the rôle of changes in relative wage rates in re-allocating labour between industries, thus facilitating the continuous adaptation to ever-changing circumstances necessary even for the maintenance of real income and wealth. Where such changes in wage rates are prevented by institutions, such as unions, the aggregate real income of the community is kept below the level it might have reached.

The inefficacy of non-market wage-rate fixing, *whether by trade unions or other bodies, as a method of raising the real incomes of all* members *of the working class is argued here.*

The consequences of this misinterpretation of the market as an economy that can and ought to satisfy different needs in a predetermined order of importance, are particularly evident in the efforts of policy to alter prices and incomes in the interest of what is called 'social justice'. Whatever meaning social philosophers have attached to this concept, in the practice of economic policy it has almost exclusively meant only one thing: the protection of groups against the necessity of a descent from the absolute or relative material positions that they have for some time occupied in society. Yet this is not a principle on which it is possible to act generally without destroying the whole foundation of the market order. Not only the continuous increase but in some circumstances even the maintenance of the present level of real income depends on adapting to unforeseen changes; such adaptation involves a reduction in the relative and perhaps even the absolute share of some, although they are in no way responsible for the situation.

Unpredictability and the price system

The point which we must constantly keep in mind is that *all* economic adjustment is made necessary by unforeseen changes; the whole point of employing the price mechanism is to inform individuals that what they have been doing or can do is now in greater or lesser demand for some reason which is no responsibility of theirs. Adaptation of the whole order of activities to changed circumstances rests on changes in the remuneration offered for different activities, without regard to the deserts or faults of those concerned.

The term 'incentives' is often used in this connection, with the some-what misleading connotation that the main problem is to induce people to exert themselves sufficiently. The main guidance which prices offer us is, however, not *how much* but *what* to do. In a continuously changing world even maintaining a given level of wealth requires continuous changes in the activities of some, that will be brought about only if the remuneration of some activities is increased and that of others decreased. These adjustments are needed merely to maintain the total income stream under relatively stable conditions; no 'surplus' will be achieved under them, which could be used to compensate those injured by changing prices. Only in a rapidly growing catallaxy can we hope to avoid absolute declines in the position of some.

Modern economists often seem to overlook that even the relative stability shown by many of those aggregates which macro-economics treats as data is itself the result of a micro-economic process of which changes in relative prices are an essential part. It is only thanks to the market mechanism that another is induced to step in and fill the gap caused by the failure of one to fulfil the expectations of his partners. In fact all those aggregate demand and supply curves with which we like to operate are not really objective given facts but results of the continuous processes of the market. Nor can we hope to learn from statistical information what alterations in prices or incomes are necessary to bring about adjustments to such inevitable changes. But the chief point is that in a democratic society it would be wholly impossible to bring changes about by commands which are not felt to be just and whose necessity can never be clearly demonstrated. Deliberate regulation in such a political system must always aim to secure prices which appear just, which in practice means preserving the traditional income and price structure. But an economic system in which each gets what the others think he 'deserves' would necessarily be highly inefficient – quite apart from also being an intolerably oppressive system. Every 'incomes policy' is therefore likely to prevent rather than facilitate those changes in the price and income structure that are required to adapt the system to changed conditions.

It is one of the paradoxes of the present world that the communist countries are probably freer than the 'capitalist' countries from the incubus of 'social justice' and more willing to let those suffer against whom developments turn. At least for some Western countries the position is so hopeless precisely because the ideology which at present dominates politics makes those changes well-nigh impossible that would be necessary in order to bring about that rapid further rise in the position of the working class which, in turn, would eclipse this ideology.

Wage rigidities

Market forces are relatively sturdy; they tend to reassert themselves in the most unexpected manner when we think we have driven them out. Nonetheless in the Western world we have succeeded in isolating the most ubiquitous factor of production from such forces. It is generally accepted that the most severe difficulties of contemporary economic policy are due to what is usually described as the rigidity of wages, which means in effect that both the wage structure and the level of money wages have increasingly become impervious to market forces. This rigidity is usually treated by economists as irreversible, so that we must adapt our policies to it. For 30 years the discussion of monetary policy has been concerned almost entirely with the search for expedients by which to circumvent it. I have long felt that these monetary devices

provide merely a *temporary* way out, and can but postpone the day
when we will have to face the central issue. They also make the real
solution, which cannot forever be avoided, more difficult because by
accepting these rigidities as unalterable we increase them and give the
sanction of legitimacy to what are anti-social and destructive practices.
I have largely lost interest in current discussions on monetary policy
because it seems to me that in its failure to face up to the central issue,
it passes the buck, in an irresponsible manner, on to our successors. We
are of course in this respect already reaping the harvest of the work of
the man who set this fashion since we are already in that long run in
which he knew we would be dead.

It is a great misfortune for the world that these theories were formed
as a result of an exceptional and unique situation in which it could be
properly argued that the problem of unemployment was largely a
problem of a too-high *level* of real wages, and in which the much more
crucial and general problem of the flexibility of the wage *structure* could
be neglected. As a result of Britain's return to gold in 1925 at the 1914
parity, a situation had been created in which it could be plausibly argued
that *all* real wages in Britain had become too high for her to achieve the
necessary volume of exports. I doubt whether the same has ever been
true of any other important country, and even whether it was entirely
true of the Britain of the 1920s. But of course Britain had then the oldest,
most firmly entrenched and most comprehensive trade union movement
in the world which by its wage policy had largely succeeded in establishing a wage structure determined much more by considerations of
'justice', which meant little else than the preservation of traditional wage
differentials, and which made those changes in relative wages demanded
by an adaptation to changed conditions 'politically impossible'. No
doubt the situation then meant that full employment required that some
real wages, perhaps those of many groups of workers, would have to be
reduced from the position to which they had been raised by deflation.
But nobody can say whether this would necessarily have meant a fall in
the general level of *all* real wages. The adjustment of the structure of
industry to the new condition adjustments in wages would have induced
might have made this unnecessary. But, unfortunately, the *fashionable*
macro-economic emphasis on the *average* level of wages prevented this
possibility from being seriously considered at the time.

Importance of relative wages

Let me put these conditions in a more general form. There can be little doubt that the productivity of labour, and hence the level of real wages, depends on its *distribution between* industries and occupations, and that the latter, in turn, depends on the structure of *relative* wages. If this wage structure has become more or less rigid, it will prevent or delay adjustments in industrial structure to changing conditions. It would seem probable that in a country in which the relations between different wage rates have long remained practically unchanged, the level of real wages at which full employment can be maintained would be considerably lower than it *could* be.

Indeed it would seem that without the rapid advance of technology and the relatively high level of capital formation to which we have become accustomed, a fully rigid wage structure would prevent most adaptations to changes in other conditions, including those necessary to maintain the initial level of incomes; wage-rate rigidities would thus lead to a gradual fall in the level of real wages at which full employment could be maintained. I know of no empirical studies of the relations between wage flexibility and growth but I should be inclined to expect that such a study would show a high positive correlation between the two magnitudes: not merely because growth will lead to changes in relative wages but even more because *such changes are essential* to adapt to the new conditions which growth requires.

But to return to what appears to me to be the crucial point: I have suggested that the level of real wages at which full employment can be maintained is dependent on the structure of relative wages, and that in consequence, if this structure is rigid and the relation between wages remains constant while conditions change, the level of real wages at which full employment can be maintained will tend to fall, or at least not rise as fast as it might because of the beneficial effects of other circumstances. This would mean that the manipulation of the level of real wages by monetary policy is not really a way out of the difficulties which the rigidity of the wage structure creates. Nor can we expect that any sort of 'incomes policy' or the like will offer a way out. In the end it will prove that the very rigidity in the wage structure which trade unions have created in the presumed interest of their members is one of the greatest obstacles to the advance of the real income of the working classes as a whole: real wages and other incomes will not rise as fast as they could if some real wages were allowed to fall, absolutely or at least relatively.

The classical aim, which, in the words of John Stuart Mill, was 'full employment at high wages', can therefore be achieved only by an efficient use of labour which requires the *free* movement of *relative* wage rates. That illustrious man, whose name for this reason I believe will go down to history as the grave-digger of the British economy, chose instead full employment at low wages. For this is the necessary result if the rigidity of relative wages is accepted as unalterable, and attempts made to correct its effects by lowering the general level of real wages by the round-about process of lowering the value of money. We see now clearly that this evasion of the central issue has offered only a temporary way out and that we have probably reached the point when we must face the evil at its source. We can no longer close our eyes to the fact that the interests of the working class as a whole demand that the power of particular labour unions to preserve the status of their members be *curbed*. The practical problem seems now to be, how we may assure the working class as a whole that if the status of particular groups is not protected, this policy will not only not endanger but indeed enhance the prospects of a rise in its real wages.

(From a draft paper referred to in the introductory note)

25   Caracas Conference Remarks

In this final extract Professor Hayek graphically illustrates the dilemma created by inflation, which leaves the economy, as he says, grasping a 'tiger by the tail'. Unless there is a continuous acceleration in the rate of increase of prices, recessionary symptoms begin to appear ... so that ultimately the choice is between a runaway inflation and an extensive depression and readjustment to a non-inflationary situation.

Twenty years ago I lost interest in monetary matters because of my disillusionment with Bretton Woods. I was wrong in my prediction that the arrangement would soon disappear. Its main innovation has been to impose the responsibility for restoring balance in international payments on the creditor nations. This was reasonable in the deflationary 1930s, but not in an inflationary period. Now we have an inflation-borne prosperity which depends for its continuation on continued inflation. If prices rise less than expected, then a depressing effect is exerted on the economy. I expected that 10 years would suffice to produce increasing difficulty; however, it has taken 25 years to reach the stage where to slow down inflation produces a recession. We now have a tiger by the tail: how long can this inflation continue? If the tiger [of inflation] is freed he will eat us up; yet if he runs faster and faster while we desperately hold on, we are *still* finished! I'm glad I won't be here to see the final outcome ...

(Notes of comments by F. A. Hayek on a paper presented to the Mont Pelerin Conference, Caracas, September 1969)

VII The Outlook for the 1970s: Open or Repressed Inflation?

In the last 40 years monetary policy has increasingly committed us to a development which has recurrently made necessary further measures that weakened the functioning of the market mechanism. We have now reached a point when it is widely proposed to combat the effects of our policy by further controls which would not only make the price mechanism wholly ineffective, but also make inevitable an ever-increasing central direction of all economic activity.

The development began with the acceptance of the given structure of money wages as not capable of being altered by the lowering of any wages, and the consequent demand that total money expenditure be raised sufficiently to take up the whole supply of labour at whatever wage rates prevailed. The result of this policy has been not only greatly to increase resistance to the lowering of *any* wage, but also to remove the main safeguard in the past to pushing wages above the point where the current supply of labour could be sold without further monetary expansion; i.e. to remove the acknowledged responsibility of the trade unions for the unemployment caused by their wage policies.

26 Long-run Vicious Circle

That it is always possible temporarily to reduce unemployment by a sufficient degree of monetary expansion was of course never doubted by anyone who had studied the major inflations of the past. If nevertheless the deliberate use of inflation to reduce unemployment was opposed by some economists, it was because of their belief that the employment thus created could be maintained only by continued and probably even progressive inflation. The reliance on what appears in the short run as the politically easy way out thus tends to preserve and intensify a disequilibrium position in which the maintenance of an adequate volume of employment would require ever more drastic doses of inflation.

These apprehensions have been fully confirmed by the developments since the war. A continuing moderate degree of monetary expansion has proved insufficient to secure lasting full employment. There are two important reasons for this failure. First, inflation tends not only to preserve but to increase the maldistribution of labour between industries, which must produce unemployment as soon as inflation ceases. Secondly, some of the stimulating effects of inflation are due to prices being for a time higher than expected, so that many undertakings are successful which would have failed if prices had not risen.

But a given rate of price increases comes to be expected after it has continued for some time, and the stimulating effect of inflation will therefore be maintained only if the rate of increase of prices accelerates and runs ahead of the expected rate of increase of prices. A continuing constant rate of increase of prices, on the other hand, must soon create a position in which future prices are correctly anticipated and present costs adapted to these expectations, with the result that the gains due to inflation disappear.

The magnitude of unemployment caused by a cessation of inflation will increase with the length of the period during which such policies are pursued. It not only becomes politically more and more difficult for policy to extricate itself from the train of events it has set up, but governments facing re-election find themselves recurrently forced to speed up inflation to whatever degree proves necessary to secure an acceptable level of employment.

While a mild degree of inflation is widely regarded as not too high a price for securing a high level of employment, the fact that inflation achieves this result only if it accelerates means that sooner or later the other effects of inflation will cause increasing discontent and a growing dislocation of economic processes. There are many harmful effects of inflation through which it endangers the efficiency, stability, and growth of production, but that which first tends to cause widespread discontent is the effect of rising prices for consumers' goods on those classes whose incomes, for one reason or another, do not keep pace with the rise of prices. It is the complaints of groups who find themselves poorer as a result of the increased costs of living that usually impel the first steps to combat inflation. They consist of attempts to prohibit or otherwise prevent the rise of prices caused by demand overtaking supply.

All measures of this kind do not of course remove the cause of the rise of prices but serve rather to make it possible for governments to continue with their inflationary policies without the effects manifesting themselves in the way in which they are most rapidly noticed. Because in a free market the general rise of prices is the most conspicuous sign of an excess of the stream of money expenditure over the stream of goods and services to be bought, people tend to think that if prices stop rising the evil of inflation has been conquered.

27 Repressed Inflation a Special Evil

It is probably no exaggeration to say that, although open inflation that manifests itself in a rise of prices is a great evil, it is less harmful than a repressed inflation, i.e. an increase of money which does not lead to a rise of prices because price increases are effectively prohibited. Such repressed inflation makes the price mechanism wholly inoperative and leads to its progressive replacement by central direction of all economic activity.

It is very doubtful, moreover, whether, after the imposition of price ceilings, the excess supply of money will still secure full employment. A significant part of the existing employment will have been based on the expectation of a further rise of prices which will now be disappointed. And in so far as the increase in the supply of money is reduced, those goods and services on which the additional money first impinged will suffer a reduction of demand. It is, however, unlikely that in such a situation the increase of the amount of money will stop. Since its immediate effects are rendered less obvious, it is likely to continue and to build up a further 'overhang' of excess money (i.e. cash holdings people would wish to spend if the commodities they wanted were available) which will make a removal of the imposed controls more and more difficult.

Preventing the rise of prices does not of course secure that everyone can buy more than they would if prices had risen. Instead of being certain to be able to buy goods and services at known though rising prices with the money they have to spend, buyers will be faced with shortages; who will get the available goods will be determined by accident or the favour of the sellers, and sooner or later inevitably by a more formal system of rationing.

The allocation of resources will at first still be determined by the structure of prices frozen after being distorted by inflation. These frozen relative prices will of course no longer be able to bring about the adjustment of production to changing conditions and needs. Consequently the direction of production will also have to be increasingly determined by decisions of government.

28   Central Control and 'Politically Impossible' Changes

This process by which attempts to control inflation by price ceilings lead to ever more comprehensive governmental controls, is self-accelerating also, because once production becomes dependent on rationing, licensing, permissions, and official allocations, a constant overhang of money becomes necessary to keep goods flowing. No centrally directed economy has yet been able to operate without relying on the effect of an excess supply of money to help overcome the obstacles it creates.

The ultimate transition to a centrally directed economy seems thus inevitable if inflation is allowed to continue while its effects are partly suppressed by a price stop. There seems little prospect that governments in such a situation will effectively prevent further inflation and not merely suppress its most visible consequences. As inflation becomes more rapid the demand for its discontinuance will also become more pressing, but the amount of unemployment caused by every slowing down of inflation will simultaneously increase. We can probably expect governments to make repeated further attempts to slow down inflation, only to abandon them when the unemployment they produce becomes politically unacceptable.

It is to be feared that we have already reached a stage in this process when to save the market economy will call for much more drastic changes in our institutions than most commentators are ready to contemplate or than will be thought by many to be 'politically possible'.[81] There seems little immediate prospect that we shall be able directly to eliminate that determination of wages by collective bargaining which is the ultimate cause of the inflationary trend,[82] or that we can reimpose upon trade unions the restraint which in the past stemmed from the fear of causing extensive unemployment. The only hope of escape from the vicious circle would seem to be to persuade the trade unions that it is in the interest of the workers in general to agree to an alternative method of wage determination which, while offering the workers as a whole a better chance of material advance, at the same time restores the flexibility of the relative wages of particular groups.

29 Profit-sharing a Solution?

The only solution of this problem I can conceive is that the workers be persuaded to accept part of their remuneration, not in the form of a fixed wage, but as a participation in the profits of the enterprise by which they are employed. Suppose that, instead of a fixed total, they could be induced to accept an assured sum equal to, say, 80 per cent of their past wages *plus* a share in profits which in otherwise unchanged conditions would give them on the average their former real income, but, in addition, a share in the growth of output of growing industries. In such a case the market mechanism would again be made to operate and at the same time one of the main obstacles to the growth of the social product would be removed.

This is not the place to develop in detail a suggestion which evidently raises many difficult problems. It is only mentioned to indicate that if we want to stop the process of cumulative inflation we shall have to consider much more radical changes in existing institutions than have yet been contemplated. If the dangers of present trends are clearly recognised, it may not be too late to extricate ourselves from a development in which we increasingly lose power over our fate. But unless we soon remedy the basic cause, we may find ourselves irrevocably committed to a path which leads to the destruction of far more than the material basis of our civilisation: not only economic progress but political and intellectual freedom would be threatened.

30 Basic Causes of Inflation

What is clear is that we must completely change the direction in which we have been endeavouring to reform the international monetary system during the last 25 years. Ever since Bretton Woods and the concern with the supposed lack of 'international liquidity', all efforts culminating in the creation of Special Drawing Rights have been aimed at enabling individual countries to inflate sufficiently to produce the maximum of employment which can be secured in the short run by monetary pressure. Now when it is becoming evident that employment is not simply a function of total demand, and that a rise in total money expenditure may indeed increase the part of employment dependent on a further rise in expenditure, it is crucially important that we turn our attention to the more fundamental factors governing employment: namely, the adjustment of the labour force and the structure of relative wages to the continuous changes in the direction of demand.

It should always have been obvious that whether a given total of money expenditure is sufficient to take off the market the amount of labour offered will depend on how this money expenditure is distributed between the different commodities and services relative to the distribution of labour devoted to their production. However much money may be spent on some part of total output, it will not secure the employment of those who produce more of other commodities than is demanded, certainly in the short run and not even in the long run.

The illusion that maladjustments in the allocation of resources and of *relative* prices can be cured by a manipulation of the *total* quantity of money is at the root of most of our difficulties. Such a use of monetary policy is more likely to aggravate than to reduce these maladjustments. Monetary policy can at most temporarily, but never in the long run, relieve us of the necessity to make changes in the use of resources required by changes in the real factors. It ought to aim at assisting this adjustment, not delaying it.

The fact that in the long run a market economy cannot operate effectively if relative wages are not determined by market forces has for a time been concealed by the effects of inflation. The time when this truth can be concealed by moderate inflation is probably past. And there clearly is a limit to the degree of inflation with which a market economy can operate. Combating inflation by price fixing makes the market inoperative even sooner.

If we want to preserve the market economy our aim must be to restore the effectiveness of the price mechanism. The chief obstacle to its functioning is trade union monopoly. It does not come from the side of money, and an exaggerated expectation of what can be achieved by monetary policy has diverted our attention from the chief causes. Though money may be one of them if it is mismanaged, monetary policy can do no more than prevent disturbances by *monetary* causes: it cannot remove those which come from other sources.

VIII Addendum 1978

31 Introduction

Professor Hayek's writings on inflation and monetary policy, during the six years since the publication of the first edition of *A Tiger by the Tail*, are contained in his other IEA publications: *Full Employment at Any Price?* (1975), *Choice in Currency* (1976), and *Denationalisation of Money* (1976 and 1978). This second edition has been enlarged by the addition of three early analyses of the Keynesian approach. These early articles are notable for Professor Hayek's anticipation of the kinds of difficulties now being encountered, after some 30-odd years of attempting to maintain full employment by increasing the level of spending.

At this juncture, I should like to add a few condensed reflections on the distinction between the average price-index approach to the analysis of the effects of inflation, and the 'relative' price structure approach on which the following extracts are based. This distinction derives from the difference between two alternative views of prices. One view sees them as components in some general equilibrium system. The other sees prices as empirical reflectors of specific circumstances. Such a distinction would appear to be important for the continuing debate on the nature of inflation.

Virtually all analyses of inflation are couched in terms of a movement in an index of prices. 'Keynesian' and 'Chicago-ite' may differ over whether or not the money supply is active or merely adjusts passively; but neither school goes beyond the impact (if any) on (or via) a price index.

The 'Austrian' would agree with the Chicago-ite on the 'active' rôle of the money supply. But he departs fundamentally thereafter. He emphasises that changes in a price index *cannot* encompass the major dislocating effect of increases in the supply of money. A price index is a statistical construct – it is an *ex post facto* compilation from *previous* changes in individual prices. An increase in the money supply does *not* affect all prices simultaneously and equi-proportionately – it affects some first and other prices afterwards; it affects different prices differently and at different times.

Economic decision-makers (individuals, firms, families) face not a price 'index' but specific *individual* prices. Different economic units face different prices. In an inflationary context, their problem is *not* to forecast the change in a price index as calculated in the future; it is rather to judge the specific changes made by a changing money supply at a specific time on the specific prices they deal with, as opposed to all the other influences also acting on these prices. The 'average' such change, as calculated some time *later*, is basically irrelevant – it provides no guide to the *individual* price changes that *precede* the calculation of the change in the price index. The knowledge that the money supply is increasing gives little help (if any) in *separating out* from all other components that component of individual price changes resulting from such an increase in the money supply.

Guiding rôle of individual price changes

It is individual price changes and price relationships that in practice guide production and employment. The *pattern* of output and employment is thus altered in accordance with a monetary change – the different lines of production and employment follow the same path as those particular price changes brought about by the change in the money supply. But these price changes now reflect increases in the supply of money. They do not tell us whether or not the underlying *real* influences have changed in the same direction. The alterations in the pattern of output and employment made in response to these price changes are thus *dis*-co-ordinated: the real changes brought about by the expansion cannot 'mesh' with changes that reflect *real* influences. As this lack of co-ordination becomes clear, resources have to be withdrawn from the former lines of output and employment and transferred into those lines that *do* correspond with the underlying pattern of relative real scarcities and preferences. Such transfers are not costless: higher capital and operating losses and higher unemployment are the necessary concomitants. Continuing monetary expansion implies a continuing and continuous *dis*-co-ordination, i.e. resources are rendered less productive than they might be.[83]

In this context, to reason in terms of any sort of general equilibrium model can be seriously misleading: such models must presuppose an 'evenly-rotating economy', in Professor Mises's graphic terminology.[84] The 'Austrian' position is that, in a world of continuous change, relative real scarcities and preferences themselves have to be rediscovered continuously.[85] Monetary expansion brings about price changes that are unco-ordinated: they do not reflect real scarcities and preferences. The resulting patterns of output and employment therefore cannot be sustained. A price index by its very mode of construction abstracts from these real *relative* changes in the process of pricing. 'Indexation' of money payments would add yet another random and unco-ordinated influence to an already unco-ordinated situation. It would not assist in the fundamental task of bringing about a better correspondence between the patterns of prices, available real resources, and preferences.

32 Good and Bad Unemployment Policies

In 1944 Professor Hayek emphasised that sustainable *employment depends on an appropriate* distribution *of labour among the different lines of production. This distribution must change as circumstances change.* Sustainable *employment thus depends on appropriate changes in* relative *real wage rates. If established producers – both unions and capitalists – prevent such relative changes from becoming effective, there follows an unnecessary rise in unemployment. Sustainable employment now depends on successfully tackling these established labour and capital monopolies.*

One of the obstacles to a successful employment policy is, paradoxically enough, that it is so comparatively easy quickly to reduce unemployment, or even almost to extinguish it, for the time being. There is always ready at hand a way of rapidly bringing large numbers of people back to the kind of employment they are used to, at no greater immediate cost than the printing and spending of a few extra millions. In countries with a disturbed monetary history this has long been known, but it has not made the remedy much more popular. In England the recent discovery of this drug has produced a somewhat intoxicating effect; and the present tendency to place exclusive reliance on its use is not without danger.

Though monetary expansion can afford quick relief, it can produce a lasting cure only to a limited extent. Few people will deny that monetary policy can successfully counteract the deflationary spiral into which every minor decline of activity tends to degenerate. This does not mean, however, that it is desirable that we should normally strain the instrument of monetary expansion to create the maximum amount of employment which it can produce in the short run. The trouble with such a policy is that it would be almost certain to aggravate the more fundamental or structural causes of unemployment and leave us in the end in a position worse than that from which we started.

Maladjustments

The main cause of this kind of unemployment is undoubtedly the dis-proportion between the distribution of labour among the different indus-tries and the rates at which the output of these industries could be continuously absorbed. At the end of this war we shall, of course, be faced with a particularly difficult problem of this character. In the past the best known disproportion of this kind and, because of its connection with periodical slumps the most important, was the chronic over-development of all the industries making equipment for use in further production.

It is more than likely that these industries, because of the intermittent way in which they operated, have always had a larger labour force than they could *continuously* employ. And while it is not difficult to create by means of monetary expansion in those industries another burst of feverish activity which will create temporarily conditions of 'full employ-ment', and even draw still more people into those industries, we are thereby making more difficult the task of maintaining even employment. A monetary policy aiming at a stable long-run position would indeed deliberately have to stop expansion *before* 'full employment' in those industries had been reached, in order to avoid a new maldirection of resources.

Though this is the most important single instance of structural mal-adjustments responsible for unemployment, the recurrent depression constitutes only part of our problem. The hard core of persistent unem-ployment is an even greater menace and is due largely to maldistributions of a different kind which monetary policy can do even less to cure. We must here face the fact that the problem of unemployment is in the last resort a wage problem – a fact which used to be well-understood but which a conspiracy of silence has recently relegated into oblivion.

Wages and mobility

Demand shifts constantly to new articles and industries, and the more rapidly we advance the more frequent such changes become. Though the increased speed of change will necessarily swell the numbers tem-porarily out of work while looking for a new job, it need not cause an increase of lasting unemployment, or a reduction in the demand for labour as a whole. If movement into the advancing industries were free, they should readily absorb those laid off elsewhere. The new development which more and more prevents this, and which has become the most serious cause of protracted unemployment, is the tendency of those established in the progressing industries to exclude newcomers. If the increase in demand in those industries leads, not to an increase of employment and output, but merely to an increase of the wages and profits of those already established, there will indeed be no new demand for labour to offset the decrease. If every gain of an industry is treated as the preserve of a closed group, to be taken out almost entirely in higher wages and profits, every shift of demand must add to the lasting unemployment.

The very special and almost unique experience of this country in the years after the pound was artificially raised to its former gold value has produced a fallacious preoccupation with the general wage level. Where such an artificial increase of the national wage level is the cause of unemployment, monetary manipulation is indeed the simplest way to cure it. Such a situation, however, is altogether exceptional and not likely to occur, except in consequence of currency fluctuations.

In normal times employment depends much more on the relation between wages in the different industries – or, rather, on the degree of mobility which the wage structure allows. There is little that monetary policy can positively achieve in this connection. Indeed, if Lord Keynes is right in emphasising that workers attach more importance to the nominal figure of their money wages than to real wages, any attempt to meet the problems of wage rigidity by monetary expansion can only increase the immobility which is the real trouble: if money wages are maintained in declining industries the workers will become even more hesitant to leave them in order to break the protective walls sheltering the privileged groups in the advancing industries.

The struggle against unemployment is in the last resort the same as the struggle against monopoly. Need it be added that on this fundamental issue we are *not* moving in the right direction? Or that it would be a poor service to the community to pretend that there is an easy way out which makes it unnecessary to face the basic difficulties?

Dangers ahead

It is easy to see how much more serious our problems must become if the present fashion should prevail and if it should become the accepted doctrine that it is the task of monetary policy to make good any harm done by monopolistic wage policies. Even apart from the effect on those responsible for wage policy, who are thus excused the responsibility for the effect of their action on employment, the one-sided emphasis on monetary policy may not only deprive our efforts of full results, but also produce effects as unlooked for as they are undesirable.

While it is true that an intelligent monetary policy is a *sine qua non* of the prevention of large-scale unemployment, it is equally certain that it is not enough. Short of universal compulsion we shall never lastingly conquer unemployment until we succeed in breaking the rigidities of our economic system which we have allowed the monopolies of capitalists and labour to create. To forget this and to trust solely to monetary policy is the more dangerous as it may succeed long enough to make it impossible to try anything else: the more we are induced to delay the more difficult adjustments, because for the time being we seem to be able to keep things going, the greater the sector of our economic system will grow which can be kept going only by the artificial stimulus of credit expansion and ever-increasing government investment.

It is a path which would force us into progressively increasing government control of all economic life, and eventually into the totalitarian State.

('Good and Bad Unemployment Policies', *Sunday Times*, 30 April 1944)

33 Full Employment Illusions

In this 1946 article Professor Hayek argues that even a continued increase in the demand for consumers' goods would not necessarily lead to a parallel increase in the demand for producers' goods. Continued increases in spending would not thus be sufficient to maintain 'full employment'. This happens because, as the boom continues, the rise in the demand for consumers' goods is met by switching from the use of fixed to circulating capital. Consequently, the demand for fixed capital eventually declines, as the demand for consumers' goods continues to rise. In these circumstances, to maintain or increase expenditure would not prevent a decline in the producers' goods industries.

The analysis Professor Hayek set out in 1946 thus predicted the appearance of 'stagflation' some 30 years before it emerged so unexpectedly.

It is a favourite trick of radical reformers to appropriate for a pet theory of their own some good word describing an attractive state of affairs, and then to accuse every one who is not prepared to swallow their proposals of callously disregarding the social good at which they aim. At the moment the most dangerous of these catchwords which seems to describe merely a desirable state of affairs, but in fact conceals a particular theory about the manner and extent to which it can be achieved, is, of course, 'full employment'. There is reason to believe that even many of those who originally gave currency to this phrase are becoming apprehensive about the way it is being used.

In the writings of the learned men who first systematically used the phrase, it did not mean what it was bound to come to mean in popular discussion: a guarantee to everyone of the kind of work and pay to which he thinks himself to be entitled. But this does not diminish the responsibility of those who in the first instance deliberately chose a popular catchword for a highly technical concept. It is more than likely that the belief they have created that full employment in the popular sense can be easily and painlessly achieved will prove the greatest obstacle to a rational policy which really would provide the maximum opportunity of employment which can be created in a free society.

Money expenditure and employment

It is an old story that in most situations an increase in total money expenditure will for a time produce an increase in employment. This has of old been the stock argument of all inflationists and soft money people. And any person who has lived through one of the great inflations can have little doubt that up to a point it is true. There is, however, a further lesson to be drawn from the experience of these inflations which ought not to be forgotten. They have not only shown that a sufficient increase of final demand will usually increase employment; they have also shown that in order to maintain the level of employment thus achieved, credit expansion has to go on at a certain progressive rate. This is shown particularly well by the great German inflation, during most of which the level of employment was very high. But as soon, and as often, as the rate was slowed down at which inflation progressed, unemployment at once reappeared, even though incomes and prices were still rising, yet at a somewhat slower rate than before.

An old argument in new form

But if the substance of the argument is not new, the new hold it has gained on our generation is due to the fact that it has been restated in an original and apparently much improved form. If in the way in which it is usually propounded, this new theory is highly technical, the essence of it is very simple. What it amounts to is little more than the following: if all people were employed at the jobs they are seeking, total money income would be so and so much. Therefore, it is argued, if we increased total money income to the figure it would reach if everyone were employed, everybody will be employed. Could anything be simpler? All we need to do is to spend sufficient money so that aggregate expenditure can take care of the aggregate supply of labour at the wage figure for which men will hold out.

It is useful at once to test this theory on a situation which has occurred often in recent times. Assume that in any country there has been a great shift of demand from one group of industries to another. It does not matter whether the causes of this are changes in tastes, technological progress, or shifts in the channels of international trade. The first result will be, as was the case in so many countries in recent times, that we shall have a group of depressed industries side by side with others which are fairly prosperous. If then, as is the rule rather than the exception at present, labour in the progressive industries prefers to take out the gain in the form of higher wages rather than in larger employment, what will happen? Clearly the consequence will be that those who lose their jobs in the declining industries will have nowhere to go and remain unemployed.

There is much indication that a great part of modern unemployment is due to this cause. How much can the measures of so-called 'fiscal' policy or any inflationary measures accomplish against this kind of unemployment? The problem is clearly not merely one of the total volume of expenditure but of its distribution, and of the prices and wages at which goods and services are offered. Before leaving this simplified illustration, let me underline a few important facts which it brings out clearly and which are commonly overlooked.

The shortcomings of fiscal policy

Firstly, it shows that the significant connection between wages and unemployment does not operate via changes in the general wage level. In the instance given it may well be that the general wage level will remain unchanged, and yet there can be no doubt that the unemployment is brought about by the rise of the wages of a certain group.

Secondly, this unemployment will not arise in the industries in which the wages are raised (which are the prosperous industries, in which the increase in wages merely prevents an expansion of employment and output), but in the depressed industries where wages will be either stationary or actually falling.

Thirdly, the illustration makes it easy to see how an attempt to cure this kind of unemployment by monetary expansion is bound to produce inflationary symptoms, and how the authority, if it persists in its attempt, will soon be forced to supplement its monetary policy by direct controls designed to conceal the symptoms of inflation. So long as the people insist on spending their extra income on the product of the industries where output is restricted by monopolistic policies of labour or capital, this will only tend to drive up wages and prices further but produce no significant effect on employment. If expansion is pressed further in the hope that ultimately enough of the extra income will spill over into the depressed industries, price control, rationing, or priorities will have to be applied to the prosperous industries. This is a very important point, and most of the expansionists make no bones about the fact that they mean to retain and even expand controls in order to prevent the extra money incomes which they propose to create, from going in 'undesirable' directions. There is little doubt that we shall see a good deal more of the same people on the one hand advocating more credit expansion, lower interest rates, etc., etc., and on the other demanding more controls in order to keep in check the inflation they are creating.

Cyclical unemployment

The illustration I have given may seem to refer mainly to long-run or technological unemployment, and the advocates of the fashionable type of full employment policy will perhaps reply that they are mainly concerned with cyclical unemployment. This would, of course, be an admission that their 'full employment' is not really *full* employment in the sense in which the term is now popularly understood, but at most a cure of part of the unemployment we used to have in the past. The more careful defenders of the new policy often admit this. The late Lord Keynes, for instance, shortly before this war, once stated that England had reached practically full employment though the unemployment figure was still well over one million. This is not what the public has now been taught full employment to mean. And it will be inevitable in the present state of opinion that so long as such a strong remnant of unemployment remains there will be intense pressure for more of the same medicine, even though on the full employment theorists' own views it can do only harm and no good in such a situation.

It is more than doubtful, however, whether even so far as cyclical unemployment is concerned, the fashionable 'full employment' proposals offer more than a palliative, and whether in the long run their application may not make matters worse. To the extent that they merely aim at mitigating the deflationary forces in a depression, there has of course never been any question that in such a situation an easy money policy may help a recession from degenerating into a major slump. But the hopes and ambitions of the present 'full employment' school go much further. Its adherents believe that by merely maintaining money incomes at the level reached at the top of the boom they can permanently keep employment and production at the maximum figure reached. This is probably not only an illusion but a certain way to perpetuate the underlying causes of the decline in investment activity.

In many ways the problems of smoothing out cyclical fluctuations are similar to those created by shifts in demand between industries. The main difference is that in the case of the business cycle we have to deal not with what may be called horizontal shifts in demand, from industries producing one sort of final goods to those producing another, but with changes in the relative demand for consumers' goods and capital goods respectively. The decline in the demand for consumers' goods, which occurs in the later phases of the depression, is a consequence of the decline of employment and incomes in the industries producing capital goods: and the basic problem is why in the latter, employment and production periodically decline, long before any decrease in the demand for consumers' goods occurs.

The current belief, which inspires all the popular full employment propaganda, is of course that investment expenditure is directly dependent upon, and moves with consumers' expenditure and that therefore the more we spend the richer we get. This argument has a certain specious plausibility because in times of all-round unemployment a mere revival of monetary demand may indeed lead to a proportional, or even more than proportional, increase in production. But it is utterly fallacious at other times and almost ridiculous if applied to the position which exists at the end of a boom and the onset of a depression. It is well worth while to examine its implications for a moment and to consider the paradox to which it leads if it is consistently followed.

Consumers' goods demand and investment activity

If it were true that an increase in the demand for consumers' goods always led to an increase of investment activity the consequences would indeed be astounding. It is important that at the top of the boom, or even at the early stages of an incipient depression, there are practically no unused resources available which would make it possible substantially to increase the output of investment goods without drawing labour and other resources away from the production of consumers' goods. In other words, if this curious theory were true it would mean that the result of people insistently demanding more consumers' goods would be that less consumers' goods would be produced for the time being. This in turn would undoubtedly lead to a rise in their prices and the profits made in their production, and according to the same theory this should lead to a still further stimulus to investment and therefore to another reduction in the current output of consumers' goods. This spiral would go on *ad infinitum*, presumably until a stage was reached when, because people so insistently demanded current consumers' goods, no consumers' goods at all would be currently produced and all energy devoted to creating facilities for an increased future output of such goods.

Purchasing power and prosperity

The economic system is, however, not quite as crazy as all that. There indeed exists a mechanism through which in conditions of fairly full employment an increase of final demand, far from stimulating investment, will actually discourage it. This mechanism is very important both as an explanation of the break of the boom and for our understanding of the reasons why an attempt to maintain prosperity merely by maintaining purchasing power is bound to fail.

Why the slump in capital goods industries?

The mechanism in question operates in a way which will be familiar to most business men: any given increase of prices will increase percentage profits on working capital by more than profits on fixed capital. This is so because the same difference between prices and costs will be earned as many times more often as the capital is turned over more frequently during a given period of time. If, then, in a situation where prices of consumers' goods tend to rise, the capital at the disposal of a given firm is limited; the need for working capital, as experience amply demonstrates, regularly has precedence over the need for fixed capital. In other words, the limited capital resources of the individual firm will be spent in the way in which output can be most rapidly increased and the largest aggregate amount of profit earned on the given resources, i.e. in the form of working capital, and outlay on fixed capital will for the time being actually be reduced to make funds available for an increase of working capital.

There are many ways in which this can be done rapidly: working in double or treble shifts, neglect of repair and upkeep, or replacement by cheaper machinery, etc. If the inducement of high profits and the scarcity of funds is strong enough, this will sooner or later lead to an absolute reduction of the outlay on fixed capital.

So far this explains only why firms will allocate their capital outlay differently, more for working capital and less for fixed capital, and not why their total outlay falls, which is what we have to explain if we are to account for the slump in the capital goods industries. But we are in fact very close to an answer to this question and only one further step is needed.

The answer lies in a special application of a principle long known to economists under the name of 'the acceleration principle of derived demand'. It shows why the effect of any change in final demand on the volume of production in the 'earlier stages' of the processes in question will be multiplied in proportion to the amount of capital required. In the case of an increase of final demand the additional capacity will have to be created by installing machinery, building up stocks, etc., and for a time outlay will increase very much more than output. Similarly, in the case of a decrease in final demand it will be possible for a time to decumulate stocks and machinery and outlay will be reduced more than output.

When we remember that this acceleration effect works both ways, positively and negatively, equally multiplying the effects of an increase or of a decrease of final demand many times insofar as the dependent investment demand is concerned, and that its strength depends on the amount of capital used per unit of output, it is easy to see what the results must be if outlay of the consumers' goods industries is shifted from fixed to circulating capital. Fixed capital means by definition a large amount of capital per unit of output and the decrease in the demand for fixed capital goods will therefore produce a very much greater decrease of production in the industries producing these capital goods. The simultaneous increase of the demand for circulating capital cannot compensate for this. Because, though the increased demand for circulating capital sets up a positive acceleration effect, this will be much less strong, since much less circulating capital is required per unit of final output. The net result of the initial shift in the outlay of the consumers' goods industries will therefore be a net decrease in the total demand for investment goods – caused ultimately by an excessive increase of final demand.

If this analysis is correct, it is clearly an illusion to expect investment demand to be maintained or revived by keeping up final demand. An increase of final demand may produce this kind of result at the bottom of a depression, when there are large reserves of unused resources in existence. But near the top of a boom it will have the contrary effect: investment will slacken further and it will seem as if there were an absolute lack of investment opportunities, which can be cured only by the government stepping in, while in fact it is the very policy intended to revive private investment which prevents its revival. Again we find that a policy of merely maintaining purchasing power cannot cure unemployment and that those who try to do so will be inevitably driven to control not only the amount of expenditure but also the way in which it is spent.

The worst of the popular illusion, that we can secure full employment by merely securing an adequate supply of expenditure, is, however, not that the hopes that it creates are bound to disappointment, but that it leads to a complete neglect of those measures which really could secure a stable and high level of employment. It will lead us further and further away from a free economy in which reasonable stability can be expected.
('Full Employment Illusions', *The Commercial and Financial Chronicle*,
Vol. 164, No. 4,508, New York, N.Y., 18 July 1946)

34 Full Employment in a Free Society

In this 1945 review of Full Employment in a Free Society *Professor Hayek highlights two major difficulties with the 'demand-deficiency' analysis of unemployment in the book. Firstly, there are extreme variations in the scale of unemployment from industry to industry and from area to area. These large variations must cast considerable doubt on whether a general lack of demand is the cause of widespread unemployment. Secondly, the book argues that the rise in the marginal propensity to save means that eventually consumer spending must fall short of the value of consumer goods output, thus producing a decline in total output. This argument overlooks the implications of changes in output. Since fluctuations in output in the capital goods industries are larger than fluctuations in the consumer goods industries, the marginal propensity to consume tends to be higher than the rate of increase in consumer goods output.*

If the present concern with full employment were the result of a belated recognition of the urgency of the problem, we should have much reason to be ashamed of the past and to congratulate ourselves on the new resolution. But this is not the position.

In England, in particular, unemployment has for nearly a generation been the burning problem that constantly occupied statesmen and economists. The reasons for the intensified agitation must be sought elsewhere. The fact is that the remedies proposed by the economists had been persistently disregarded because they were of a kind that hurt in the application.

Then Lord Keynes assured us that we had all been mistaken and that the cure could be painless and even pleasant: all that was needed to maintain employment permanently at a maximum was to secure an adequate volume of spending of some kind. The argument was not less effective because it was couched in highly technical language. It gave the support of the highest scientific authority to what had always been the popular belief, and the new view gained ground rapidly.

It is the great merit of democracy that the demand for the cure of a widely felt evil can find expression in an organised movement. That popular pressure might become canalised in support of particular theories that sound plausible to the ordinary man is one of its dangers. But it was almost inevitable that some gifted man should see the opportunity and try to ride into political power on the wave of support that could be created for some such scheme. This is what Sir William Beveridge is attempting. His *Full Employment in a Free Society* is as much a political manifesto as a handbook of economic policy. Its appearance coincides with the author's entry into Parliament, and together with his earlier report on social security constitutes his programme of action.

This is not to say that Sir William does not bring special qualifications to the task. But they are not mainly those of the economist. Himself a brilliant expositor who earned his spurs as a leader-writer on one of London's big dailies, a successful administrator with the essential skill of tapping other people's brains, and an acute student of unemployment statistics, he has called in the assistance of a group of younger economists for the more theoretical parts of the book. Its strength and its weakness reflect this origin. The clear exposition and the stress on some important facts that are not always recognised are Sir William at his best, and the great interest in changes in government machinery equally characteristic.

But the theoretical framework is that of Lord Keynes as seen by his younger disciples and familiar to American readers mainly through the writings of Professor A. H. Hansen. Only one of Sir William's collaborators, N. Kaldor, appears by name as the author of a highly ingenious appendix, which to the economist is the most interesting part of the book and supplies the foundation for much of it.

It is open to question whether the attempt to combine Sir William's characteristic views with the fashionable Keynesian doctrines has made the book more valuable, though it will certainly make it more acceptable to many of the younger economists. Although Sir William is confident that his own approach and 'the revolution of economic thought effected by J. M. Keynes' are 'not contradictory but complementary', the book leaves many inconsistencies unresolved. One of Sir William's most valuable contributions, e.g., is the emphasis on the extreme diversity of the extent of unemployment from industry to industry and from place to place, which certainly throws much doubt on the adequacy of an explanation in terms of a general deficiency of demand; yet he swallows the demand-deficiency theory lock, stock, and barrel.

Equally important is Sir William's stress on the close connection in Great Britain between unemployment and foreign trade. Yet his remedies are almost entirely of a domestic nature. Indeed, though he realises that hardly any of the imports of Great Britain before the war 'can be described as luxuries', he suggests as a way out 'the alternative of cutting down imports and becoming more independent' because 'the stability of international trade is as important as its scale'. The former champion of free trade has travelled far!

Perhaps most surprising of all is that, while Sir William admits that 'a policy of outlay for full employment, however vigorously it is pursued by the State, will fail to cure unemployment ... if, with peace, industrial demarcations with all the restrictive tendencies and customs of the past return in full force', these factors have no place in his diagnosis of the causes of unemployment. One wonders to what conclusions the author would have been led had they been given their proper place in the analysis and not merely added as an afterthought.

One of the main differences between Sir William's proposals and the British White Paper on employment policy is that Sir William refuses to accept the fact that private investment tends to fluctuate, and to confine himself to compensating measures. As an out-and-out planner, in the modern sense of the term, he proposes to deal with this difficulty by abolishing private investment as we knew it: that is, by subjecting all private investment to the direction of a National Investment Board. It is mainly here that apprehensions must arise against which the second half of the title of the book is meant to reassure us. Sir William endeavours to show that, despite all the control he wishes to impose, 'essential liberties' will be preserved. But private ownership of the means of production is, in his opinion, 'not an essential liberty in Britain, because it is not and never has been enjoyed by more than a very small proportion of the British people'.

It is surprising that he should not yet have learned that private ownership of the means of production is important to most people not because they hope to own such property, but because only such private ownership gives them the choice of competing employers and protects them from being at the mercy of the most complete monopolist ever conceived.

However interesting the points of detail on which Sir William differs from the current Keynes–Hansen theory, much the most important fact about his book is that he lends the weight of his prestige in support of this view. If all the conclusions he draws do not necessarily follow from it, they certainly stand and fall with the belief that a deficiency of final demand is the initial cause of cyclical unemployment.

This theory holds that as employment increases a progressively increasing share of the new income created will not be spent but will be saved. This, it is suggested, must sooner or later produce a situation in which final demand is insufficient to take the output of consumers' goods off the market at remunerative prices. One may grant the first statement and yet deny that the alleged consequences are at all likely to follow. The larger share that is saved out of the additional income would necessarily lead to an insufficiency of final demand only if the additional output contained as large a proportion of consumers' goods as total output.

This assumption seems highly implausible, however. Along with all other students of these matters Sir William stresses that unemployment during a depression is very much greater in the industries making capital goods than in the others. An approach to full employment therefore increases the output of capital goods proportionally much more than the output of consumers' goods. And if no larger proportion of the additional income were saved than was saved out of the smaller income, final demand would grow much faster than the supply of consumers' goods.

As a matter of fact, it seems highly unlikely that the share saved out of additional income during a recovery will be even as big as the share of the additional output that is in the form of capital goods. What then becomes of the case that depressions are brought on by over-saving and under-consumption? Of course, we can assume that the decline of investment in a slump *must* be due to an initial deficiency of final demand. This, however, is simply reasoning in a circle.

The cause of the decline of the demand for capital goods must, therefore, be sought elsewhere than in a deficiency of final demand, and may even be an excessive final demand. All the fashionable remedies, including Sir William's, not only fail to touch the root of the matter but may even aggravate the problem. Of course, once final demand shrinks on the scale that will occur as a result of extensive unemployment in the capital goods industries, this will start the vicious spiral of contraction. But the crucial question is: what causes the initial decline of the capital-goods industries?

If, as is more than likely, it is that they tend to overgrow during the boom, all attempts to maintain activity in them at the maximum will only perpetuate the causes of instability.

(Review of Sir William (later Lord) Beveridge's book, *Full Employment in a Free Society*, in *Fortune*, March 1945)

Notes

1   Cf. Axel Leijonhufvud, *On Keynesian Economics and the Economics of Keynes*, Oxford University Press, 1968; *Keynes and the Classics*, Occasional Paper 30, IEA, 1969; T. W. Hutchison, *Economics and Economic Policy in*

Britain, 1946–66, Allen & Unwin, 1968; H. Stein, *The Fiscal Revolution in America*, University of Chicago Press, 1969.

2   Cf. E. E. Hagen, 'The Classical Theory of Output and Employment', in M. G. Mueller (ed.), *Readings in Macroeconomics*, Holt, Rinehart and Winston, 1966; H. G. Johnson, 'Monetary Theory and Keynesian Economics' in *Money, Trade and Economic Growth*, Allen & Unwin, 1962; 'Introduction' in R. J. Ball and Peter Doyle (eds.), *Inflation*, Penguin Books, 1969.

3   Professor A. Smithies, in the *American Economic Review*, June 1945, p. 367. The symposium on employment policy, *American Economic Review*, May 1946, is also relevant.

4   The Congress declared it was '... the continuing policy and responsibility of the Federal Government to use all practicable means ... to co-ordinate and utilize all its plans, functions and resources for the purpose of creating and maintaining ... conditions under which there will be afforded useful employment for those able, willing and seeking work ...' (Quoted in Robert Lekachman, *The Age of Keynes*, Allen Lane, The Penguin Press, 1967, p. 144.)

5   'Full Employment at Whatever Cost?', *Quarterly Journal of Economics*, August 1950. Earlier Professor Viner said: '... it is a matter of serious concern whether under modern conditions, even in a socialist country if it adheres to democratic political procedures, employment can always be maintained at a high level without recourse to inflation, overt or disguised, or if maintained whether it will not itself induce an inflationary wage spiral through the operation of collective bargaining ...'

     Reviewing the *General Theory* in *Quarterly Journal of Economics*, 1936–7, he said: 'In a world organised in accordance with Keynes's specifications, there would be a constant race between the printing press and the business agents of the trade unions with the problem of unemployment largely solved if the printing press could maintain a constant lead ...'

6   *Economists and the Public*, Cape, 1936. Professor Hutt published a brief analysis of the central issues in his *Theory of Idle Resources*, Cape, 1939; his earlier work on the *Theory of Collective Bargaining*, 1930 (new edn, Glencoe, 1954; 2nd British edn published in *The Theory of Collective Bargaining 1930–1975*, Hobart Paperback No. 8, IEA, 1975) analysed the position of the Classical economists on the relation between unions and wage determination.

     There is also a collection of extracts from reviews and other early writings critical of the *General Theory*, edited by Henry Hazlitt: *The Critics of Keynesian Economics*, Princeton, 1960.

7   F. Machlup, 'Another view of cost push and demand pull inflation', *Review of Economics and Statistics*, 1960.

8   P. P. Streeten, 'Wages, prices and productivity', *Kyklos*, 1962.

9   D. J. Robertson, 'Guideposts and Norms: Contrasts in US and UK Wage

Policy', *Three Banks Review*, December 1966; D. C. Smith, 'Income Policy', in R. E. Caves and Associates (eds), *Britain's Economic Prospects*, Allen & Unwin, 1968.

10   W.H. Beveridge, *Full Employment in a Free Society*, Allen & Unwin, 1944, pp. 198–201, especially p. 201: 'Adoption by the State of a price policy is a natural and probably an inevitable consequence of a full employment policy'.

11   Lord Robbins, 'Inflation: The Position Now', *Financial Times*, 23 June 1971; J. E. Meade, *Wages and Prices in a Mixed Economy*, Occasional Paper 35, IEA for Wincott Foundation, 1971; F. W. Paish, *Rise and Fall of Incomes Policy*, Hobart Paper 47, IEA, second edn, 1971; S. Brittan, *Government and the Market Economy*, Hobart Paperback 2, IEA, 1971; E. Victor Morgan, 'Is Inflation Inevitable?', *Economic Journal*, March 1966.

12   T. Balogh, *Labour and Inflation*, Fabian Tract 403, Fabian Society, 1970; Streeten, *op. cit.*; R. G. Opie, 'Inflation' in P. D. Henderson (ed.), *Economic Growth in Britain*, Weidenfeld & Nicolson, 1966.

13   Robbins, 'Full Employment As An Objective', in *The Economist in the Twentieth Century*, Macmillan, 1954. (Italics in original.)

14   Robbins, *op. cit.*, pp. 35–6.

15   *Financial Times*, 23 June 1971.

16   E. V. Morgan, *op. cit.*, p. 14; F. W. Paish, *op. cit.*, Postscript; S. Weintraub, 'An Incomes Policy to Stop Inflation', *Lloyds Bank Review*, January 1971.

17   Brittan, *op. cit.*, pp. 48–56.

18   Professor W. B. Reddaway ('Wage Flexibility and the Distribution of Labour', *Lloyds Bank Review*, April 1959) has suggested, on empirical investigations, that relative wage-rate movements have little allocative significance today: labour reallocation among industries and firms is achieved by changes in job offers. Given union-determined wage-rate structure, this is perhaps to be expected; but it is not incompatible with the basic proposition that prices are *capable* of performing allocative functions – *if* the institutional framework is designed to this end.

Professor Reddaway has argued elsewhere ('Rising Prices Forever?', *Lloyds Bank Review*, July 1966) that rising prices are here to stay indefinitely. While advocating institutional restraints on price and wage increases, he recommends measures to raise productivity, arguing that, given such 'assured' increases in real income, even fairly high rates of price increase may be tolerated – the few hyper-inflations in history being special cases. To live with inflations of the Latin American type, as he seems to contemplate (p. 15), would imply not only very substantial changes in British economic institutions (which he might have made explicit); it would also imply the acquiescence or political impotence of groups whose incomes remained static or failed to rise as fast as prices.

19   Suggestions that wage increases be linked to productivity are clearly

attempts to offer some *co-ordinative* criterion, in this *dis*-co-ordinated situation.

20   F. A. Hayek, 'Economics and Knowledge', 'The Use of Knowledge in Society' and the three chapters on 'Socialist Calculation' in *Individualism and Economic Order*, Routledge, 1948.

21   Routledge and Kegan Paul, 1931 and 1933. A scheme which confines itself to contrasting 'the "Classical" model' (i.e. the conceptual framework used by the English economists contemporary with Keynes) and 'the Keynesian (and/or post-Keynesian) model' may therefore be incomplete. H. G. Johnson, *op. cit.*; Ball & Doyle (eds), *op. cit.*; and the 'Introduction' to R. W. Clower (ed.), *Monetary Theory* (Penguin Books, 1969) are instances of such schemes.

22   Professor Clower's stricture that 'at no stage in pre-Keynesian economics was any serious attempt made to build peculiarly monetary assumptions into the micro-foundations of economic analysis' (*op. cit.*, p. 19) is not accurate.

23   *Prices and Production*, Routledge, 2nd edn, 1935, pp. 161–2.

24   'Reflections on the Pure Theory of Money of Mr J. M. Keynes', *Economica*, August 1931 and February 1932; J. M. Keynes, 'The Pure Theory of Money – a Reply to Dr Hayek'; F. A. Hayek, 'A Rejoinder to Mr Keynes', *Economica*, November 1931.

25   Incomes policy advocates implicitly assume that 'full employment' relative price and wage interrelationships once established can be maintained indefinitely; their implicit 'model' is that of a rigid real structure of outputs and prices on which a varying monetary stream impinges (see especially Meade, *op. cit.*, pp. 11–12, E. V. Morgan, *op. cit.*, S. Brittan, *op. cit.*). Hayek has characterised such a mode of thinking as belonging essentially to the naïve early stages of economic thought. (*Pure Theory of Capital*, pp. 409–10; also see *Economica*, August 1931, p. 273.)

But if prices and wages are inflexible downwards, the 'full employment' level of expenditure may itself continually shift upwards, since the appropriate price changes can only be made by continually 'jacking up' the entire structure.

26   A similar view was put by Professors William Fellner and Friedrich Lutz in W. Fellner *et al.*, *The Problem of Rising Prices*, OEEC, 1961.

27   This stress on the labour side need *not* imply that established firms (in the Western economies or elsewhere) are *never* at present protected against actual or potential competition and against actual or potential losses, either by the institutional framework or by economic policy. The Hayekian approach implies that *no* incomes and assets – whether business or other – be protected against losses. (F. A. Hayek, ' "Free" Enterprise and Competitive Order' in *Individualism and Economic Order*, Routledge, 1949; and 'The Modern Corporation In A Democratic Society ...' in *Studies in Philosophy, Politics and Economics*, Routledge, 1967.)

28 This theme is elaborated in section 23 (below, pp. 76 *et seq.*).

29 In a letter to John Wheatley, dated 18 September 1821, reprinted in J. Bonar and J. Hollander (eds), *Letters of David Ricardo to Hutches Trower and Others*, Oxford, 1899, p. 160.

30 The fact that the averages of (more or less arbitrarily selected) groups of prices move differently in different countries does of course in no way prove that there is any tendency of the price structure of a country to move as a whole relatively to prices in other countries. It would however be a highly interesting subject for statistical investigation, if a suitable technique could be devised, to see whether, and to what extent, such a tendency existed. Such an investigation would of course involve a comparison not only of some mean value of the price changes in different countries, but of the whole frequency distribution of relative price changes in terms of some common standard. And it should be supplemented by similar investigations of the relative movements of the price structure of different parts of the same country.

31 The propensity of economists in the Anglo-Saxon countries to argue exclusively in terms of national price and wage levels is probably mainly due to the great influence which the writings of Professor Irving Fisher have exercised in these countries. Another typical instance of the dangers of this approach is the well-known controversy about the reparations problem, where it was left to Professor Ohlin to point out against his English opponents that what mainly mattered was not so much effects on total price levels but rather the effects on the position of particular industries.

32 It is interesting to note that those countries in Europe where up to 1929 wages had been rising relatively most rapidly were on the whole those most reluctant to experiment with exchange depreciation. The recent experience of France seems also to suggest that a working-class government may never be able to use exchange depreciation as an instrument to lower real wages.

33 This means unused resources which could be had at the ruling market price. There will of course always be further reserves which will be offered only if prices rise.

34 I should have thought that the abandonment of the sharp distinction between the 'freely reproducible goods' and goods of absolute scarcity and the substitution for this distinction of the concept of varying degrees of scarcity (according to the increasing costs of reproduction) was one of the major advances of modern economics. But Mr Keynes evidently wishes us to return to the older way of thinking. This at any rate seems to be what his use of the concept of 'bottlenecks' means; a concept which seems to me to belong essentially to a naïve early stage of economic thinking and the introduction of which into economic theory can hardly be regarded as an improvement.

35 It is characteristic that when at last, towards the end of his book, Mr Keynes comes to discuss prices, the 'Theory of Price' is to him merely 'the analysis

of the relations between changes in the quantity of money and changes in the price level' (*General Theory*, p. 296).

36 Cf. *General Theory*, p. 137: 'We must ascertain the rate of interest from some other source and only then can we value the asset by "capitalising" its prospective yield'.

37 The reason why Mr Keynes does not draw this conclusion, and the general explanation of his peculiar attitude towards the problem of the determination of relative prices, is presumably that under the influence of the 'real cost' doctrine which to the present day plays such a large rôle in the Cambridge tradition, he assumes that the prices of all goods except the more durable ones are even in the short run determined by costs. But whatever one may think about the usefulness of a cost explanation of relative prices in equilibrium analysis, it should be clear that it is altogether useless in any discussion of problems of the short period.

38 The rate at which a given amount of new investment will contribute during any given interval of time to the output of consumers' goods stands of course in a very simple relation to the proportion between any new demand and the amount of investment to which it gives rise: the latter is simply the reciprocal value of the former. For a fuller discussion of the relationship between this 'quotient' and the 'multiplier' with which the 'acceleration principle of derived demand' operates I must again refer to Hayek, 1939, pp. 48–52.

It cannot be objected to this argument that, since investment automatically creates an identical amount of saving, the situation contemplated here cannot arise. The irrelevant tautology, that *during any interval of time* the amount of income which has not been received from the sale of consumers' goods, and which therefore has been saved (namely, by those who spent that income), must have been spent on something other than consumers' goods (and therefore *ex definitione* must have been invested), is of little significance for this or for any other economic problem. What is relevant here is not the relation between one classification of money expenditure and another, but the relation of two streams of money expenditure to the streams of goods which they meet. We are interested in the amount of investment because it determines in what proportions (in terms of their relative costs) different kinds of goods will come into existence. And we are interested to know how these proportions between quantities of different kinds of goods are related to the proportions in which money expenditure will be distributed between the two kinds of goods, because it depends on the relation between these two proportions whether the production of either kind of good will become more or less profitable. It does not matter whether we put this question in the form of asking whether the distribution of income between expenditure on consumers' goods and saving corresponds to the proportion between the relative (replacement) *costs* of the total supply of consumers' goods and new investment goods, or whether the available resources are now distributed in the same proportion between the production of consumers' goods and the production of investment goods as those in which income earned from this production *will* be distributed between the two kinds of goods. Whichever of the two aspects of the question we prefer to stress, the essential thing, if we want to ask a meaningful question, is that we must always compare the result of investment embodied in concrete goods with the money expenditure on these goods. It is never the investment which is going on at the same time as the saving, but the result of *past* investment, that determines the supply of capital goods to which the monetary demand may or may not correspond. Playing about with the relationships between various classifications of total money expenditure during any given period will lead only to meaningless questions, and never to any result of the slightest relevance to any real problem.

I do not wish to suggest that the recent discussions of the various meanings of these concepts have been useless. They have helped us to make clear the conditions under which it is meaningful to talk about relations between saving and investment. But now that the obscurities and confusions connected with these concepts have been cleared up, the meaningless tautological use of these concepts ought clearly to disappear from scientific discussion. On the whole question, and the recent discussions about it, compare now the excellent exposition in the new chapter eight of the Second Edition of Professor Haberler's *Prosperity and Depression* (Geneva, 1939).

39 Professor Hayek's article, 'A Commodity Reserve Currency', was followed by Lord Keynes's reply, 'The Objective of International Price Stability', in the June–September 1943 issue (*Economic Journal*, Vol. LIII, Nos 210–11, pp. 176–87).

40 The proposal is elaborated by its initiator, Mr Benjamin Graham, in his book *Storage and Stability* (McGraw-Hill, New York, 1937), and is now so well known as not to require further exposition here.

41 The reason that it is not obviously true is that a policy of stable price levels would, I believe, prove to be much more generally acceptable than the caprices of the unmanaged gold standard or the arbitrariness of that standard in its managed form.

42 This whole matter is treated in detail in my brochure, *Fundamentals of International Monetary Policy*, International Finance Section, Department of Economics and Social Institutions, Princeton University, No. 2.

43 The question was raised in private correspondence with the author.

44 Including the most 'orthodox' political economists, who invariably supported freedom of association. See particularly the discussion in J. R. McCulloch, *Treatise on the Circumstances Which Determine the Rate of Wages and the Condition of the Labouring Classes* (London, 1851), pp. 79–89, with its stress on *voluntary* association. For a comprehensive statement of the classical liberal attitude toward the legal problems involved see

Ludwig Bamberger, *Die Arbeiterfrage unter dem Gesichtspunkte des Vereinsrechtes* (Stuttgart, 1873).

45 Characteristic is the description of the 'liberal' attitude to unions in C. W. Mills, *The New Men of Power* (New York, 1948), p. 21: 'In many liberal minds there seems to be an undercurrent that whispers: "I will not criticise the unions and their leaders. There I draw the line." This, they must feel, distinguishes them from the bulk of the Republican Party and the right-wing Democrats, this keeps them leftward and socially pure.'

46 A. V. Dicey, Introduction to the 2nd edition of his *Law and Opinion*, pp. xlv–xlvi. He continues to say that the law 'makes a trade union a privileged body exempted from the ordinary law of the land. No such privileged body has ever before been deliberately created by an English Parliament [and that] it stimulates among workmen the fatal delusion that workmen should aim at the attainment, not of equality, but of privilege.' Cf. also the comment on the same law 30 years later, by J. A. Schumpeter, *Capitalism, Socialism, and Democracy* (New York, 1942), p. 321: 'It is difficult, at the present time, to realise how this measure must have struck people who still believed in a state and in a legal system that centred in the institution of private property. For in relaxing the law of conspiracy in respect to peaceful picketing – which practically amounted to legalisation of trade-union action implying the threat of force – and in exempting trade-union funds from liability in action for damages *for torts* – which practically amounted to enacting that trade unions could do no wrong – this measure in fact resigned to the trade unions part of the authority of the state and granted to them a position of privilege which the formal extension of the exemption to employers' unions was powerless to affect.' Still more recently the Lord Chief Justice of Northern Ireland said of the same act (Lord MacDermott, *Protection from Power under English Law*, London, 1957, p. 174): 'In short, it put trade unionism in the same privileged position which the Crown enjoyed until ten years ago in respect of wrongful acts committed on its behalf'.

47 Roscoe Pound, *Legal Immunities of Labor Unions*, American Enterprise Association, Washington DC, 1957, p. 23; reprinted in E. H. Chamberlin *et al.*, *Labor Unions and Public Policy*, American Enterprise Association, Washington DC, 1958.

48 Justice Jackson dissenting in *Hunt* v. *Crumboch*, 325 US 831 (1946).

49 L. von Mises, *De Gemeinwirtschaft*, 2nd edn; Jena, 1932, p. 447.

50 Few liberal sympathisers of the trade unions would dare to express the obvious truth which a courageous woman from within the British labour movement frankly stated, namely, that 'it is in fact the business of a Union to be anti-social; the members would have a just grievance if their officials and committees ceased to put sectional interests first' (Barbara Wootton, *Freedom under Planning*, London, 1945, p. 97). On the flagrant abuses of union power in the United States, which I shall not further consider here,

see Sylvester Petro, *Power Unlimited: the Corruption of Union Leadership*, New York, 1959.

51   In this chapter, more than in almost any other, I shall be able to draw upon a body of opinion that is gradually forming among an increasing number of thoughtful students of these matters – men who in background and interest are at least as sympathetic to the true concerns of the workers as those who in the past have been championing the privileges of the unions. See particularly W. H. Hutt, *The Theory of Collective Bargaining*, London, 1930, and *Economists and the Public*, London, 1936; H. C. Simons, 'Some Reflections on Syndicalism', *Journal of Political Economy* LII, 1944, reprinted in *Economic Policy for a Free Society*; J. T. Dunlop, *Wage Determination under Trade Unions*, New York, 1944; *Economic Institute on Wage Determination and the Economics of Liberalism*, Chamber of Commerce of the United States, Washington DC, 1947 (especially the contributions by Jacob Viner and Fritz Machlup); Leo Wolman, *Industry-wide Bargaining*, Foundation for Economic Education, Irvington-on-Hudson, New York, 1948; C. E. Lindblom, *Unions and Capitalism*, Yale University Press, New Haven, 1949 (cf. the reviews of this book by A. Director, *University of Chicago Law Review* XVIII, 1950; by J. T. Dunlop in *American Economic Review* XL, 1950; and by Albert Rees in *Journal of Political Economy* LVIII, 1950); David McCord Wright (ed.), *The Impact of the Union*, New York, 1951 (especially the contributions by M. Friedman and G. Haberler); Fritz Machlup, *The Political Economy of Monopoly*, Johns Hopkins Press, Baltimore, 1952; D. R. Richberg, *Labor Union Monopoly*, Chicago, 1957; Sylvester Petro, *The Labor Policy of the Free Society*, New York, 1957; E.H. Chamberlin, *The Economic Analysis of Labor Power*, 1958, P. D. Bradley, *Involuntary Participation in Unionism*, 1956, and G. D. Reilley, *State Rights and the Law of Labor Relations*, 1955 – all three published by the American Enterprise Association (Washington, 1958) and reprinted together with the pamphlet by Roscoe Pound (above, note 47) in the volume quoted there; B. C. Roberts, *Trade Unions in a Free Society*, Institute of Economic Affairs, London, 1959; and John Davenport, 'Labor Unions in the Free Society', *Fortune*, April 1959, and 'Labor and the Law', *ibid.*, May 1959. On general wage theory and the limits of the powers of the unions see also J. R. Hicks, *The Theory of Wages*, London, 1932; R. Strigl, *Angewandte Lohntheorie*, Leipzig and Vienna, 1926; and J. T. Dunlop (ed.), *The Theory of Wage Determination*, London, 1957.

52   See particularly the works by H. C. Simons and W. H. Hutt cited in the preceding note. Whatever limited validity the old argument about the necessity of 'equalising bargaining power' by the formation of unions may ever have had, has certainly been destroyed by the modern development of the increasing size and specificity of the employers' investment, on the one hand, and the increasing mobility of labour (made possible by the automobile), on the other.

53   This must be emphasised especially against the argument of Lindblom in the work quoted above (note 51).

54   Chamberlin, *op. cit.*, pp. 4–5, rightly stresses that 'there can be no doubt that one effect of trade union policy ... is to diminish still further the real income of the really low income groups, including not only the low income wage receivers but also such other elements of society as "self-employed" and small business men.'

55   Cf. F. Machlup in the two studies quoted above (note 51).

56   A conspicuous example of this in recent times is the case of the notoriously unorganised domestic servants whose average annual wages (as pointed out by M. Friedman in D. Wright's *The Impact of the Union*, p. 224) in the United States in 1947 were 2.72 times as high as they had been in 1939, while at the end of the same period the wages of the comprehensively organised steel workers had risen only to 1.98 times the initial level.

57   Cf. Bradley, *op. cit.*

58   Cf. S. P. Sobotka, 'Union Influence on Wages: The Construction Industry', *Journal of Political Economy* LXI, 1953.

59   It would be difficult to exaggerate the extent to which unions prevent the experimentation with, and gradual introduction of, new arrangements that might be in the mutual interest of employers and employees. For example, it is not at all unlikely that in some industries it would be in the interest of both to agree on 'guaranteed annual wages' if unions permitted individuals to make a sacrifice in the amount of wages in return for a greater degree of security.

60   To illustrate the nature of much contemporary wage bargaining in the United States, E. H. Chamberlin, in the essay quoted above (note 51), uses an analogy which I cannot better: 'Some perspective may be had on what is involved by imagining an application of the techniques of the labour market in some other field. If A is bargaining with B over the sale of his house, and if A were given the privileges of a modern labour union, he would be able (1) to conspire with all other owners of houses not to make any alternative offers to B, using violence or the threat of violence if necessary to prevent them, (2) to deprive B himself of access to any alternative offers, (3) to surround the house of B and cut off all deliveries of food (except by parcel post), (4) to stop all movement from B's house, so that if he were for instance a doctor he could not sell his services and make a living, and (5) to institute a boycott of B's business. All of these privileges, if he were capable of carrying them out, would no doubt strengthen A's position. But they would not be regarded by anyone as part of "bargaining" – unless A were a labour union'.

61   Cf. Petro, *op. cit.*, p. 51: 'Unions can and do serve useful purposes, and they have only barely scratched the surface of their potential utility to employees. When they really get to work on the job of serving employees instead of making such bad names for themselves as they do in coercing and abusing employers, they will have much less difficulty than they pre-

sently have in securing and keeping new members. As matters now stand, union insistence upon the closed shop amounts to an admission that unions are really not performing their functions very well.'

62   Cf. C. I. Barnard, 'Functions and Pathology of Status Systems in Formal Organizations', in W. F. Whyte (ed.), *Industry and Society*, New York, 1946, reprinted in Barnard's *Organization and Management*, Harvard University Press, Cambridge, Mass., 1949.

63   Cf. Sumner Slichter, *Trade Unions in a Free Society*, Cambridge, Mass., 1947, p. 12, where it is argued that such rules 'introduce into industry the equivalent of civil rights, and they greatly enlarge the range of human activities which are governed by rule of law rather than by whim or caprice.' See also A. W. Gouldner, *Patterns of Industrial Bureaucracy*, Glencoe, Ill., 1954, especially the discussion of 'rule by rule'.

64   See particularly Franz Böhm, 'Das wirtschaftliche Mitbestimmungsrecht der Arbeiter im Betrieb', *Ordo* IV, 1951; and Goetz Briefs, *Zwischen Kapitalismus und Syndikalismus*, Bern, 1952.

65   See the essays by J. Viner, G. Haberler, M. Friedman, and the book by S. Petro cited above (note 51).

66   Such contracts binding on third parties are equally as objectionable in this field as is the forcing of price-maintenance agreements on non-signers by 'fair-trade' laws.

67   Such legislation, to be consistent with our principles, should not go beyond declaring certain contracts invalid, which is sufficient for removing all pretext for action to obtain them. It should not, as the title of the 'right-to-work laws' may suggest, give individuals a claim to a particular job, or even (as some of the laws in force in certain American states do) confer a right to damages for having been denied a particular job, when the denial is not illegal on other grounds. The objections against such provisions are the same as those which apply to 'fair employment practices' laws.

68   See A. Lenhoff, 'The Problem of Compulsory Unionism in Europe', *American Journal of Comparative Law* V, 1956.

69   See Petro, *op. cit.*, especially pp. 235ff and 282.

70   See the articles by G. Haberler and myself in Committee for Economic Development (ed.), *Problems of United States Economic Development*, Vol. I, New York, 1958.

71   Cf. Arthur J. Brown, *The Great Inflation, 1939–1951*, London, 1955.

72   See J. R. Hicks, 'Economic Foundations of Wage Policy', *Economic Journal* LXV, 1955, especially p. 391: 'The world we now live in is one in which the monetary system has become relatively elastic, so that it can accommodate itself to changes in wages, rather than the other way about. Instead of actual wages having to adjust themselves to an equilibrium level, monetary policy adjusts the equilibrium level of money wages so as to make it conform to the actual level. It is hardly an exaggeration to say that instead of being on a Gold Standard, we are on a Labour Standard.' But see also

the same author's later article, 'The Instability of Wages', *Three Banks Review*, No. 31, September 1956.

73   See W. Beveridge, *Full Employment in a Free Society*, London, 1944; M. Joseph and N. Kaldor, *Economic Reconstruction after the War* (handbooks published for the Association for Education in Citizenship [London, n.d.]); Barbara Wootton, *The Social Foundations of Wage Policy*, London, 1955; and, on the present state of the discussion, D. T. Jack, 'Is a Wage Policy Desirable and Practicable?', *Economic Journal* LXVII, 1957. It seems that some of the supporters of this development imagine that this wage policy will be conducted by 'labour', which presumably means by joint action of all unions. This seems neither a probable nor a practicable arrangement. Many groups of workers would rightly object to their relative wages being determined by a majority vote of all workers, and a government permitting such an arrangement would in effect transfer all control of economic policy to the labour unions.

74   See, e.g., Barbara Wootton, *Freedom under Planning*, p. 101: 'The continual use of terms like "fair", however, is quite subjective: no commonly accepted ethical pattern can be implied. The wretched arbitrator, who is charged with the duty of acting "fairly and impartially", is thus required to show these qualities in circumstances in which they have no meaning; for there can be no such thing as fairness or impartiality except in terms of an accepted code. No one can be impartial in a vacuum. One can only umpire at cricket because there are rules, or at a boxing match so long as certain blows, like those below the belt, are forbidden. Where, therefore, as in wage determinations, there are no rules and no code, the only possible interpretation of impartiality is conservatism.' Also Kenneth F. Walker, *Industrial Relations in Australia*, Harvard University Press, Cambridge, Mass., 1956, p. 362: 'Industrial tribunals, in contrast with ordinary courts, are called upon to decide issues upon which there is not only no defined law, but not even any commonly accepted standards of fairness or justice.' Cf. also Gertrud Williams (Lady Williams), 'The Myth of "Fair" Wages', *Economic Journal* LXVI, 1956.

75   See Petro, *op. cit.*, pp. 262ff, especially p. 264: 'I shall show in this chapter that the rule of law does not exist in labour relations; that there a man is entitled in only exceptional cases to a day in court, no matter how unlawfully he has been harmed'; and p. 272: 'Congress has given the NLRB [National Labor Relations Board] and its General Counsel arbitrary power to deny an injured person a hearing, Congress has closed the federal courts to persons injured by conduct forbidden under federal law. Congress did not, however, prevent unlawfully harmed persons from seeking whatever remedies they might find in state courts. That blow to the ideal that every man is entitled to his day in court was struck by the Supreme Court.'

76   The Chairman of the English Trade Union Congress, Mr Charles Geddes, was reported in 1955 to have said: 'I do not believe that the trade union

movement of Great Britain can live for very much longer on the basis of compulsion. Must people belong to us or starve, whether they like our policies or not? No. I believe the trade union card is an honour to be conferred, not a badge which signifies that you have got to do something, whether you like it or not. We want the right to exclude people from our union if necessary and we cannot do that on the basis of "Belong or starve".'

77   Cf. W. Roepke, *Welfare, Freedom and Inflation*, London, 1957.

78   Cf. my essay 'Full Employment, Planning, and Inflation', *Review of the Institute of Public Affairs* IV, Melbourne, Victoria, Australia, 1950; and the German version in A. Hunold (ed.), *Vollbeschäftigung, Inflation und Planwirtschaft*, Zurich, 1951; and F. A. Lutz, 'Inflationsgefahr und Konjunkturpolitik', *Schweizerische Zeitschrift für Volkswirtschaft und Statistik* XCIII, 1957, and 'Cost- and Demand-Induced Inflation', *Banca Nazionale de Lavoro Quarterly Review* XLIV, 1958.

79   J. M. Keynes, *A Tract on Monetary Reform*, p. 80.

80   See my essay, *Monetary Nationalism and International Stability*, *op. cit.*

81   See W. H. Hutt, *Politically Impossible . . .?*, Hobart Paperback 1, IEA, 1971.

82   Professor James E. Meade has proposed limits on trade union wage-bargaining power in *Wages and Prices in a Mixed Economy*, Wincott Memorial Lecture, published as Occasional Paper 35, IEA, 1971.

83   The above argument is highly condensed; a more extended statement is in G. P. O'Driscoll Jr. and Sudha R. Shenoy, 'Inflation, Recession, Stagflation', in E. G. Dolan (ed.), *Foundations of Modern Austrian Economics*, Sheed and Ward, Lawrence, Kansas, 1976; cf. F. A. Hayek, *Prices and Production*, Routledge and Kegan Paul, London, 1935, pp. 28–30.

84   Ludwig von Mises, *Human Action*, Regnery, Chicago, 1966, pp. 244–56.

85   F. A. Hayek, 'Competition as a Discovery Procedure', in *New Studies in Philosophy, Politics, Economics and the History of Ideas*, Routledge and Kegan Paul, 1978.

2

Denationalisation of Money – the Argument Refined

1 The Practical Proposal

The concrete proposal for the near future, and the occasion for the examination of a much more far-reaching scheme, is that:

> *The countries of the Common Market, preferably with the neutral countries of Europe (and possibly later the countries of North America), mutually bind themselves by formal treaty not to place any obstacles in the way of the free dealing throughout their territories in one another's currencies (including gold coins) or of a similar free exercise of the banking business by any institution legally established in any of their territories.*

This would mean in the first instance the abolition of any kind of exchange control or regulation of the movement of money between these countries, as well as the full freedom to use any of the currencies for contracts and accounting. Further, it would mean the opportunity for any bank located in these countries to open branches in any other on the same terms as established banks.

Free trade in money

The purpose of this scheme is to impose upon existing monetary and financial agencies a very much needed discipline by making it impossible for any of them, or for any length of time, to issue a kind of money

Published originally as *Hobart Paper Special* No. 70, 2nd (Extended) Edition, IEA (1978).

substantially less reliable and useful than the money of any other. As soon as the public became familiar with the new possibilities, any deviations from the straight path of providing an honest money would at once lead to the rapid displacement of the offending currency by others. And the individual countries, being deprived of the various dodges by which they are now able temporarily to conceal the effects of their actions by 'protecting' their currency, would be constrained to keep the value of their currencies tolerably stable.

Proposal more practicable than Utopian European currency

This seems to me both preferable and more practicable than the Utopian scheme of introducing a new European currency, which would ultimately only have the effect of more deeply entrenching the source and root of all monetary evil, the government monopoly of the issue and control of money. It would also seem that, if the countries were not prepared to adopt the more limited proposal advanced here, they would be even less willing to accept a common European currency. The idea of depriving government altogether of its age-old prerogative of monopolising money is still too unfamiliar and even alarming to most people to have any chance of being adopted in the near future. But people might learn to see the advantages if, at first at least, the currencies of the governments were allowed to compete for the favour of the public.

Though I strongly sympathise with the desire to complete the economic unification of Western Europe by completely freeing the flow of money between them, I have grave doubts about the desirability of doing so by creating a new European currency managed by any sort of supra-national authority. Quite apart from the extreme unlikelihood that the member countries would agree on the policy to be pursued in practice by a common monetary authority (and the practical inevitability of some countries getting a worse currency than they have now), it seems highly unlikely, even in the most favourable circumstances, that it would be administered better than the present national currencies. Moreover, in many respects a single international currency is not better but worse than a national currency if it is not better run. It would leave a country with a financially more sophisticated public not even the chance of escaping from the consequences of the crude prejudices governing the decisions of the others. The advantage of an international authority should be mainly to protect a member state from the harmful measures of others, not to force it to join in their follies.

Free trade in banking

The suggested extension of the free trade in money to free trade in banking is an absolutely essential part of the scheme if it is to achieve what is intended. First, bank deposits subject to cheque, and thus a sort of privately issued money, are today of course a part, and in most countries much the largest part, of the aggregate amount of generally accepted media of exchange. Secondly, the expansion and contraction of the separate national superstructures of bank credit are at present the chief excuse for national management of the basic money.

On the effects of the adoption of the proposal all I will add at this point is that it is of course intended to prevent national monetary and financial authorities from doing many things politically impossible to avoid so long as they have the power to do them. These are without exception harmful and against the long-run interest of the country doing them but politically inevitable as a temporary escape from acute difficulties. They include measures by which governments can most easily and quickly remove the causes of discontent of particular groups or sections but bound in the long run to disorganise and ultimately to destroy the market order.

Preventing government from concealing depreciation

The main advantage of the proposed scheme, in other words, is that it would prevent governments from 'protecting' the currencies they issue against the harmful consequences of their own measures, and therefore prevent them from further employing these harmful tools. They would become unable to conceal the depreciation of the money they issue, to prevent an outflow of money, capital, and other resources as a result of making their home use unfavourable, or to control prices – all measures which would, of course, tend to destroy the Common Market. The scheme would indeed seem to satisfy all the requirements of a common market better than a common currency without the need to establish a new international agency or to confer new powers on a supra-national authority.

The scheme would, to all intents and purposes, amount to a displacement of the national circulations only if the national monetary authorities misbehaved. Even then they could still ward off a complete displacement of the national currency by rapidly changing their ways. It is possible that in some very small countries with a good deal of international trade and tourism, the currency of one of the bigger countries might come to predominate, but, assuming a sensible policy, there is no reason why most of the existing currencies should not continue to be used for a long time. (It would, of course, be important that the parties did not enter into a tacit agreement not to supply so good a money that the citizens of the other nations would prefer it! And the presumption of guilt would of course always have to lie against the government whose money the public did not like!)

I do not think the scheme would prevent governments from doing anything they ought to do in the interest of a well-functioning economy, or which in the long run would benefit any substantial group. But this raises complex issues better discussed within the framework of the full development of the underlying principle.

2 The Generalisation of the Underlying Principle

If the use of several concurrent currencies is to be seriously considered for immediate application in a limited area, it is evidently desirable to investigate the consequences of a general application of the principle on which this proposal is based. If we are to contemplate abolishing the exclusive use within each national territory of a single national currency issued by the government, and to admit on equal footing the currencies issued by other governments, the question at once arises whether it would not be equally desirable to do away altogether with the monopoly of government supplying money and to allow private enterprise to supply the public with other media of exchange it may prefer.

The questions this reform raises are at present much more theoretical than the practical proposal because the more far-reaching suggestion is clearly not only much too strange and alien to the general public to be considered for present application. The problems it raises are evidently also still much too little understood even by the experts for anyone to make a confident prediction about the precise consequences of such a scheme. Yet it is clearly possible that there is no necessity or even advantage in the now unquestioned and universally accepted government prerogative of producing money. It may indeed prove to be harmful and its abolition a great gain, opening the way for very beneficial developments. Discussion therefore cannot begin early enough. Though its realisation may be wholly impracticable so long as the public is mentally unprepared for it and uncritically accepts the dogma of the necessary government prerogative, this should no longer be allowed to act as a bar to the intellectual exploration of the fascinating theoretical problems the scheme raises.

Competition in currency not discussed by economists

It is an extraordinary truth that competing currencies have until quite recently never been seriously examined.[1] There is no answer in the available literature to the question why a government monopoly of the provision of money is universally regarded as indispensable, or whether the belief is simply derived from the unexplained postulate that there must be within any given territory one single kind of money in circulation – which, so long as only gold and silver were seriously considered as possible kinds of money, might have appeared a definite convenience. Nor can we find an answer to the question of what would happen if that monopoly were abolished and the provision of money were thrown open to the competition of private concerns supplying different currencies. Most people seem to imagine that any proposal for private agencies to be allowed to issue money means that they should be allowed to issue the *same* money as anybody else (in token money this would, of course, simply amount to forgery) rather than *different* kinds of money clearly distinguishable by different denominations among which the public could choose freely.

Initial advantages of government monopoly in money

Perhaps when the money economy was only slowly spreading into the remoter regions, and one of the main problems was to teach large numbers the art of calculating in money (and that was not so very long ago), a single easily recognisable kind of money may have been of considerable assistance. And it may be argued that the exclusive use of such a single uniform sort of money greatly assisted comparison of prices and therefore the growth of competition and the market. Also, when the genuineness of metallic money could be ascertained only by a difficult process of assaying, for which the ordinary person had neither the skill nor the equipment, a strong case could be made for guaranteeing the fineness of the coins by the stamp of some generally recognised authority which, outside the great commercial centres, could be only the government. But today these initial advantages, which might have served as an excuse for governments to appropriate the exclusive right of issuing metallic money, certainly do not outweigh the disadvantages of this system. It has the defects of all monopolies: one must use their product even if it is unsatisfactory, and, above all, it prevents the discovery of better methods of satisfying a need for which a monopolist has no incentive.

If the public understood what price in periodic inflation and instability it pays for the convenience of having to deal with only one kind of money in ordinary transactions, and not occasionally to have to contemplate the advantage of using other money than the familiar kind, it would probably find it very excessive. For this convenience is much less import-ant than the opportunity to use a reliable money that will not periodically upset the smooth flow of the economy – an opportunity of which the public has been deprived by the government monopoly. But the people have never been given the opportunity to discover this advantage. Governments have at all times had a strong interest in persuading the public that the right to issue money belongs exclusively to them. And so long as, for all practical purposes, this meant the issue of gold, silver and copper coins, it did not matter so much as it does today, when we know that there are all kinds of other possible sorts of money, not least paper, which government is even less competent to handle and even more prone to abuse than metallic money.

3 The Origin of the Government Prerogative of Making Money

For more than 2,000 years the government prerogative or exclusive right of supplying money amounted in practice merely to the monopoly of minting coins of gold, silver or copper. It was during this period that this prerogative came to be accepted without question as an essential attribute of sovereignty – clothed with all the mystery which the sacred powers of the prince used to inspire. Perhaps this conception goes back to even before King Croesus of Lydia struck the first coins in the sixth century BC, to the time when it was usual merely to punch marks on the bars of metal to certify its fineness.

At any rate, the minting prerogative of the ruler was firmly established under the Roman emperors.[2] When, at the beginning of the modern era, Jean Bodin developed the concept of sovereignty, he treated the right of coinage as one of the most important and essential parts of it.[3] The *regalia*, as these royal prerogatives were called in Latin, of which coinage, mining, and custom duties were the most important, were during the Middle Ages the chief sources of revenue of the princes and were viewed solely from this angle. It is evident that, as coinage spread, governments everywhere soon discovered that the exclusive right of coinage was a most important instrument of power as well as an attractive source of gain. From the beginning the prerogative was neither claimed nor conceded on the ground that it was for the general good but simply as an essential element of governmental power.[4] The coins served, indeed, largely as the symbols of might, like the flag, through which the ruler asserted his sovereignty, and told his people who their master was whose image the coins carried to the remotest parts of his realm.

Government certificate of metal weight and purity

The task the government was understood to assume was of course initially not so much to make money as to certify the weight and fineness of the materials that universally served as money,[5] which after the earliest times were only the three metals, gold, silver, and copper. It was supposed to be a task rather like that of establishing and certifying uniform weights and measures.

The pieces of metal were regarded as proper money only if they carried the stamp of the appropriate authority, whose duty was thought to be to assure that the coins had the proper weight and purity to give them their value.

During the Middle Ages, however, the superstition arose that it was the act of government that conferred the value upon the money. Although experience always proved otherwise, this doctrine of the *valor impositus*[6] was largely taken over by legal doctrine and served to some extent as justification of the constant vain attempts of the princes to impose the same value on coins containing a smaller amount of the precious metal. (In the early years of this century the medieval doctrine was revived by the German Professor G. F. Knapp; his *State Theory of Money* still seems to exercise some influence on contemporary legal theory.)[7]

There is no reason to doubt that private enterprise would, if permitted, have been capable of providing as good and at least as trustworthy coins. Indeed occasionally it did, or was commissioned by government to do so. Yet so long as the technical task of providing uniform and recognisable coins still presented major difficulties, it was at least a useful task which government performed. Unfortunately, governments soon discovered that it was not only useful but could also be made very profitable, at least so long as people had no alternative but to use the money they provided. The seignorage, the fee charged to cover the cost of minting, proved a very attractive source of revenue, and was soon increased far beyond the cost of manufacturing the coin. And from retaining an excessive part of the metal brought to the government mint to be struck into new coins, it was only a step to the practice, increasingly common during the Middle Ages, of recalling the circulating coins in order to recoin the various denominations with a lower gold or silver content. We shall consider the effect of these debasements in the next section. But since the function of government in issuing money is no longer one of merely certifying the weight and fineness of a certain piece of metal, but involves a deliberate determination of the quantity of money to be issued, governments have become wholly inadequate for the task and, it can be said without qualifications, have incessantly and everywhere abused their trust to defraud the people.

The appearance of paper money

The government prerogative, which had originally referred only to the issue of coins because they were the only kind of money then used, was promptly extended to other kinds of money when they appeared on the scene. They arose originally when governments wanted money which they tried to raise by compulsory loans, for which they gave receipts that they ordered people to accept as money. The significance of the gradual appearance of government paper money, and soon of bank notes, is for our purposes complicated because for a long time the problem was not the appearance of new kinds of money with a different denomination, but the use as money of paper claims on the established kind of metallic money issued by government monopoly.

It is probably impossible for pieces of paper or other tokens of a material itself of no significant market value to come to be gradually accepted and held as money unless they represent a claim on some valuable object. To be accepted as money they must at first derive their value from another source, such as their convertibility into another kind of money. In consequence, gold and silver, or claims for them, remained for a long time the only kinds of money between which there could be any competition; and, since the sharp fall in its value in the 19th century, even silver ceased to be a serious competitor to gold. (The possibilities of bimetallism[8] are irrelevant for our present problems.)

Political and technical possibilities of controlling paper money

The position has become very different, however, since paper money established itself everywhere. The government monopoly of the issue of money was bad enough so long as metallic money predominated. But it became an unrelieved calamity since paper money (or other token money), which can provide the best and the worst money, came under political control. A money deliberately controlled in supply by an agency whose self-interest forced it to satisfy the wishes of the *users* might be the best. A money regulated to satisfy the demands of group interests is bound to be the worst possible (section 18).

The value of paper money obviously can be regulated according to a variety of principles – even if it is more than doubtful that any democratic government with unlimited powers can ever manage it satisfactorily. Though historical experience would at first seem to justify the belief that only gold can provide a stable currency, and that all paper money is bound to depreciate sooner or later, all our insight into the processes determining the value of money tells us that this prejudice, though understandable, is unfounded. The *political* impossibility that governments will achieve it does not mean there is reason to doubt that it is *technically* possible to control the quantity of any kind of token money so that its value will behave in a desired manner, and that it will for this reason retain its acceptability and its value. It would therefore now be possible, if it were permitted, to have a variety of essentially different monies. They could represent not merely different quantities of the same metal, but also different abstract units fluctuating in their value relatively to one another. In the same way, we could have currencies circulating concurrently throughout many countries and offering the people a choice. This possibility appears, until recently, never to have been contemplated seriously. Even the most radical advocates of free enterprise, such as the philosopher Herbert Spencer[9] or the French economist Joseph Garnier,[10] seem to have advocated only private coinage, while the free banking movement of the mid-19th century agitated merely for the right to issue notes in terms of the standard currency.[11]

Monopoly of money has buttressed government power

While, as we shall see presently, government's exclusive right to issue and regulate money has certainly not helped to give us a better money than we would otherwise have had, and probably a very much worse one, it has of course become a chief instrument for prevailing governmental policies and profoundly assisted the general growth of governmental power. Much of contemporary politics is based on the assumption that government has the power to create and make people accept any amount of additional money it wishes. Governments will for this reason strongly defend their traditional rights. But for the same reason it is also most important that they should be taken from them.

A government ought not, any more than a private person, to be able (at least in peace-time) to take whatever it wants, but be limited strictly to the use of the means placed at its disposal by the representatives of the people, and to be unable to extend its resources beyond what the people have agreed to let it have. The modern expansion of government was largely assisted by the possibility of covering deficits by issuing money – usually on the pretence that it was thereby creating employment. It is perhaps significant, however, that Adam Smith [54, p. 687] does not mention the control of the issue of money among the 'only three duties [which] according to the system of natural liberty, the sovereign has to attend to'.

4 The Persistent Abuse of the Government Prerogative

When one studies the history of money one cannot help wondering why people should have put up for so long with governments exercising an exclusive power over 2,000 years that was regularly used to exploit and defraud them. This can be explained only by the myth (that the government prerogative was necessary) becoming so firmly established that it did not occur even to the professional students of these matters (for a long time including the present writer[12]) ever to question it. But once the validity of the established doctrine is doubted its foundation is rapidly seen to be fragile.

We cannot trace the details of the nefarious activities of rulers in monopolising money beyond the time of the Greek philosopher Diogenes who is reported, as early as the fourth century BC, to have called money the politicians' game of dice. But from Roman times to the 17th century, when paper money in various forms begins to be significant, the history of coinage is an almost uninterrupted story of debasements or the continuous reduction of the metallic content of the coins and a corresponding increase in all commodity prices.

History is largely inflation engineered by government

Nobody has yet written a full history of these developments. It would indeed be all too monotonous and depressing a story, but I do not think it an exaggeration to say that history is largely a history of inflation, and usually of inflations engineered by governments and for the gain of governments – though the gold and silver discoveries in the 16th century had a similar effect. Historians have again and again attempted to justify inflation by claiming that it made possible the great periods of rapid economic progress. They have even produced a series of inflationist theories of history[13] which have, however, been clearly refuted by the evidence: prices in England and the Unites States were at the end of the period of their most rapid development almost exactly at the same level as 200 years earlier. But their recurring rediscoverers are usually ignorant of the earlier discussions.

Early Middle Ages' deflation: local or temporary

The early Middle Ages may have been a period of deflation that con-tributed to the economic decline of the whole of Europe. But even this is not certain. It would seem that on the whole the shrinking of trade led to the reduction of the amount of money in circulation, not the other way round. We find too many complaints about the dearness of commodities and the deterioration of the coin to accept deflation as more than a local phenomenon in regions where wars and migrations had destroyed the market and the money economy shrank as people buried their treasure. But where, as in Northern Italy, trade revived early, we find at once all the little princes vying with one another in diminishing the coin – a process which, in spite of some unsuccess-ful attempts of private merchants to provide a better medium of exchange, lasted throughout the following centuries until Italy came to be described as the country with the worst money and the best writers on money.

But though theologians and jurists joined in condemning these prac-tices, they never ceased until the introduction of paper money provided governments with an even cheaper method of defrauding the people. Governments could not, of course, pursue the practices by which they forced bad money upon the people without the cruellest measures. As

one legal treatise on the law of money sums up the history of punishment
for merely refusing to accept the legal money:

> From Marco Polo we learn that, in the 13th century, Chinese law made
> the rejection of imperial paper money punishable by death, and twenty
> years in chains or, in some cases death, was the penalty provided for the
> refusal to accept French *assignats*. Early English law punished repudiation
> as *lese-majesty*. At the time of the American revolution, non-acceptance
> of Continental notes was treated as an enemy act and sometimes worked
> a forfeiture of the debt.[14]

Absolutism suppressed merchants' attempts to create stable money

Some of the early foundations of banks at Amsterdam and elsewhere
arose from attempts by merchants to secure for themselves a stable
money, but rising absolutism soon suppressed all such efforts to create
a non-governmental currency. Instead, it protected the rise of banks
issuing notes in terms of the official government money. Even less than
in the history of metallic money can we here sketch how this development
opened the doors to new abuses of policy.

It is said that the Chinese had been driven by their experience with
paper money to try to prohibit it for all time (of course unsuccessfully)
before the Europeans ever invented it.[15] Certainly European governments,
once they knew about this possibility, began to exploit it ruthlessly, not
to provide people with good money, but to gain as much as possible
from it for their revenue. Ever since the British Government in 1694 sold
the Bank of England a limited monopoly of the issue of bank notes, the
chief concern of governments has been not to let slip from their hands
the power over money, formerly based on the prerogative of coinage,
to really independent banks. For a time the ascendancy of the gold
standard and the consequent belief that to maintain it was an important
matter of prestige, and to be driven off it a national disgrace, put an
effective restraint on this power. It gave the world the one long period –
200 years or more – of relative stability during which modern indus-
trialism could develop, albeit suffering from periodic crises. But as soon
as it was widely understood some 50 years ago that the convertibility
into gold was merely a method of controlling the *amount* of a currency,
which was the real factor determining its value, governments became
only too anxious to escape that discipline, and money became more than

ever before the plaything of politics. Only a few of the great powers preserved for a time tolerable monetary stability, and they brought it also to their colonial empires. But Eastern Europe and South America never knew a prolonged period of monetary stability.

But, while governments have never used their power to provide a decent money for any length of time, and have refrained from grossly abusing it only when they were under such a discipline as the gold standard imposed, the reason that should make us refuse any longer to tolerate this irresponsibility of government is that we know today that it is possible to control the quantity of a currency so as to prevent significant fluctuations in its purchasing power. Moreover, though there is every reason to mistrust government if not tied to the gold standard or the like, there is no reason to doubt that private enterprise whose business depended on succeeding in the attempt could keep stable the value of a money it issued.

Before we can proceed to show how such a system would work we must clear out of the way two prejudices that will probably give rise to unfounded objections against the proposal.

5 The Mystique of Legal Tender

The first misconception concerns the concept of 'legal tender'. It is not of much significance for our purposes, but is widely believed to explain or justify government monopoly in the issue of money. The first shocked response to the proposal here discussed is usually 'But there must be a legal tender', as if this notion proved the necessity for a single government-issued money believed indispensable for the daily conduct of business.

In its strictly legal meaning, 'legal tender' signifies no more than a kind of money a creditor cannot refuse in discharge of a debt due to him in the money issued by government.[16] Even so, it is significant that the term has no authoritative definition in English statute law.[17] Elsewhere it simply refers to the means of discharging a debt contracted in terms of the money issued by government or due under an order of a court. In so far as government possesses the monopoly of issuing money and uses it to establish one kind of money, it must probably also have power to say by what kind of objects debts expressed in its currency can be discharged. But that means neither that all money need be legal tender, nor even that all objects given by the law the attribute of legal tender need to be money. (There are historical instances in which creditors have been compelled by courts to accept commodities such as tobacco, which could hardly be called money, in discharge of their claims for money.[18])

The superstition disproved by spontaneous money

The term 'legal tender' has, however, in popular imagination come to be surrounded by a penumbra of vague ideas about the supposed necessity for the state to provide money. This is a survival of the medieval idea that it is the state which somehow confers value on money it otherwise would not possess. And this, in turn, is true only to the very limited extent that government can force us to accept whatever it wishes in place of what we have contracted for; in this sense it can give the substitute the same value for the debtor as the original object of the contract. But the superstition that it is necessary for government (usually called the 'State' to make it sound better) to declare what is to be money, as if it had created the money which could not exist without it, probably originated in the naïve belief that such a tool as money must have been 'invented' and given to us by some original inventor. This belief has been wholly displaced by our understanding of the spontaneous generation of such undesigned institutions by a process of social evolution of which money has since become the prime paradigm (law, language and morals being the other main instances). When the medieval doctrine of the *valor impositus* was in this century revived by the much admired German Professor Knapp it prepared the way for a policy which in 1923 carried the German Mark down to 1/1,000,000,000,000 of its former value!

Private money preferred

There certainly can be and has been money, even very satisfactory money, without government doing anything about it, though it has rarely been allowed to exist for long.[19] But a lesson is to be learned from the report of a Dutch author about China a hundred years ago who observed of the paper money then current in that part of the world that '*because it is not legal tender* and because it is no concern of the State it is generally accepted as money'.[20] We owe it to governments that within given national territories today in general only one kind of money is universally accepted. But whether this is desirable, or whether people could not, if they understood the advantage, get a much better kind of money without all the to-do about legal tender, is an open question. Moreover, a 'legal means of payment' (*gesetzliches Zahlungsmittel*) need not be specifically designated by a law. It is sufficient if the law enables the judge to decide in what sort of money a particular debt can be discharged.

The commonsense of the matter was put very clearly 80 years ago by a distinguished defender of a liberal economic policy, the lawyer, statistician and high civil servant Lord Farrer. In a paper written in 1895[21] he contended that if nations

> ... make nothing else but the standard unit [of value they have adopted] legal tender, there is no need and no room for the operation of any special law of legal tender. The ordinary law of contract does all that is necessary without any law giving special function to particular forms of currency. We have adopted a gold sovereign as our unit, or standard of value. If I promised to pay 100 sovereigns, it needs no special currency law of legal tender to say that I am bound to pay 100 sovereigns, and that, if required to pay the 100 sovereigns, I cannot discharge the obligation by anything else.

And he concludes, after examining typical applications of the legal tender conception, that

> *Looking to the above cases of the use or abuse of the law of legal tender other than the last* [i.e. that of subsidiary coins] *we see that they possess one character in common – viz. that the law in all of them enables a debtor to pay and requires a creditor to receive something different from that which their contract contemplated.* In fact it is a forced and unnatural construction put upon the dealings of men by arbitrary power.[22]

To this he adds a few lines later that 'any Law of Legal Tender is in its own nature "suspect".'[23]

Legal tender creates uncertainty

The truth is indeed that legal tender is simply a legal device to force people to accept in fulfilment of a contract something they never intended when they made the contract. It becomes thus, in certain circumstances, a factor that intensifies the uncertainty of dealings and consists, as Lord Farrer also remarked in the same context,

> in substituting for the free operation of voluntary contract, and a law

which simply enforces the performance of such contracts, an artificial construction of contracts such as would never occur to the parties unless forced upon them by an arbitrary law.

All this is well illustrated by the historical occasion when the expression 'legal tender' became widely known and treated as a definition of money. In the notorious 'legal tender cases', fought before the Supreme Court of the United States after the Civil War, the issue was whether creditors must accept at par current dollars in settlement of their claims for money they had lent when the dollar had a much higher value.[24] The same problem arose even more acutely at the end of the great European inflations after the First World War when, even in the extreme case of the German Mark, the principle 'Mark is Mark' was enforced until the end – although later some efforts were made to offer limited compensation to the worst sufferers.[25]

Taxes and contracts

A government must of course be free to determine in what currency taxes are to be paid and to make contracts in any currency it chooses (in this way it can support a currency it issues or wants to favour), but there is no reason why it should not accept other units of accounting as the basis of the assessment of taxes. In non-contractual payments such as damages or compensations for torts, the courts would have to decide the currency in which they have to be paid, and might for this purpose have to develop new rules; but there should be no need for special legislation.

There is a real difficulty if a government-issued currency is replaced by another because the government has disappeared as a result of conquest, revolution, or the break-up of a nation. In that event the government taking over will usually make legal provisions about the treatment of private contracts expressed in terms of the vanished currency. If a private issuing bank ceased to operate and was unable to redeem its issue, this currency would presumably become valueless and the holders would have no enforceable claim for compensation. But the courts may decide that in such a case contracts between third parties in terms of that currency, concluded when there was reason to expect it to be stable, would have to be fulfilled in some other currency that came to the nearest presumed intention of the parties to the contract.

6 The Confusion About Gresham's Law

It is a misunderstanding of what is called Gresham's law to believe that the tendency for bad money to drive out good money makes a government monopoly necessary. The distinguished economist, W. S. Jevons, emphatically stated the law in the form that better money cannot drive out worse precisely to prove this. It is true he argued then against a proposal of the philosopher, Herbert Spencer, to throw the coinage of gold open to free competition, at a time when the only different currencies contemplated were coins of gold and silver. Perhaps Jevons, who had been led to economics by his experience as assayer at a mint, even more than his contemporaries in general, did not seriously contemplate the possibility of any other kind of currency. Nevertheless his indignation about what he described as Spencer's proposal

> ... that, as we trust the grocer to furnish us with pounds of tea, and the baker to send us loaves of bread, so we might trust Heaton and Sons, or some of the other enterprising firms of Birmingham, to supply us with sovereigns and shillings at their own risk and profit,[26]

led him to the categorical declaration that generally, in his opinion, 'there is nothing less fit to be left to the action of competition than money'.[27]

It is perhaps characteristic that even Herbert Spencer had contemplated no more than that private enterprise should be allowed to produce the same sort of money as government then did, namely gold and silver coins. He appears to have thought them the only kind of money that could reasonably be contemplated, and in consequence that there would necessarily be fixed rates of exchange (namely of 1 : 1 if of the same weight and fineness) between the government and private money. In that event, indeed, Gresham's law would operate if any producer supplied shoddier ware. That this was in Jevons's mind is clear because he justified his condemnation of the proposal on the ground that

> ... while in all other matters everybody is led by self-interest to choose the better and reject the worse; but in the case of money, it would seem as if they paradoxically retain the worse and get rid of the better.[28]

What Jevons, as so many others, seems to have overlooked, or regarded as irrelevant, is that Gresham's law will apply *only* to different kinds of money between which a fixed rate of exchange is enforced *by law*.[29] If the law makes two kinds of money perfect substitutes for the payment of debts and forces creditors to accept a coin of a smaller content of gold in the place of one with a larger content, debtors will, of course, pay only in the former and find a more profitable use for the substance of the latter.

With variable exchange rates, however, the inferior quality money would be valued at a lower rate and, particularly if it threatened to fall further in value, people would try to get rid of it as quickly as possible. The selection process would go on towards whatever they regarded as the best sort of money among those issued by the various agencies, and it would rapidly drive out money found inconvenient or worthless.[30] Indeed, whenever inflation got really rapid, all sorts of objects of a more stable value, from potatoes to cigarettes and bottles of brandy to eggs and foreign currencies like dollar bills, have come to be increasingly used as money,[31] so that at the end of the great German inflation it was contended that Gresham's law was false and the opposite true. It is not false, but it applies only if a *fixed rate of exchange* between the different forms of money is enforced.

7 The Limited Experience with Parallel Currencies and Trade Coins

So long as coins of the precious metals were the only practicable and generally acceptable kinds of money, with all close substitutes at least redeemable in them (copper having been reduced comparatively early to subsidiary token money), the only different kinds of money which appeared side by side were coins of gold and silver.

The multiplicity of coins with which the old money-changers had to deal consisted ultimately only of these two kinds, and their respective value within each group was determined by their content of either metal (which the expert but not the layman could ascertain). Most princes had tried to establish a fixed legal rate of exchange between gold and silver coins, thereby creating what came to be called a bimetallic system. But since, in spite of very early suggestions that this rate be fixed by an international treaty,[32] governments established different exchange rates, each country tended to lose all the coins of the metal it under-valued relatively to the rates prevailing in other countries. The system was for that reason more correctly described as an alternative standard, the value of a currency depending on the metal which for the time being was over-valued. Shortly before it was finally abandoned in the second half of the 19th century, a last effort was made to establish internationally a uniform rate of exchange of $15\frac{1}{2}$ between gold and silver. That attempt might have succeeded so long as there were no big changes in production. The comparatively large share of the total stocks of either metal that were in monetary use meant that, by an inflow or outflow into or from that use, their relative values could probably have been adjusted to the rate at which they were legally exchangeable as money.

Parallel currencies

In some countries, however, gold and silver had also been current for long periods side by side, their relative value fluctuating with changing conditions. This situation prevailed, for example, in England from 1663 to 1695 when, at last, by decreeing a rate of exchange between gold and silver coins at which gold was over-valued, England inadvertently established a gold standard.[33] The simultaneous circulation of coins of the two metals without a fixed rate of exchange between them was later called, by a scholar from Hanover where such a system existed until 1857, parallel currencies (*Parallelwährung*), to distinguish it from bimetallism.[34]

This is the only form in which parallel currencies were ever widely used, but it proved singularly inconvenient for a special reason. Since for most of the time gold was by weight more than 15 times as valuable as silver, it was evidently necessary to use the former for large and silver for the smaller (and copper for the still smaller) units. But, with variable values for the different kinds of coins, the smaller units were not constant fractions of the larger ones. In other words, the gold and the silver coins were parts of different systems without smaller or larger coins respectively of the same system being available.[35] This made any change from large to small units a problem, and nobody was able, even for his own purposes, to stick to one unit of account.

Except for a few instances in the Far East in recent times,[36] there seem to have been very few instances of concurrent circulation of currencies, and the memory of the parallel circulation of gold and silver coins has given the system rather a bad name. It is still interesting because it is the only important historical instance in which some of the problems arose that are generally raised by concurrent currencies. Not the least of them is that the concept of *the* quantity of money of a country of territory has strictly no meaning in such a system, since we can add the quantities of

the different monies in circulation only after we know the relative value
of the different units.

Trade coins

Nor are the somewhat different but more complex instances of the use
of various trade coins[37] of much more help: the Maria Theresa Thaler
in the regions around the Red Sea and the Mexican Dollar in the Far
East, or the simultaneous circulation of two or more national currencies
in some frontier districts or tourist centres. Indeed, our experience is so
limited that we can do no better than fall back upon the usual procedure
of Classical economic theory and try to put together, from what we
know from our common experience of the conduct of men in relevant
situations, a sort of mental model (or thought experiment) of what is
likely to happen if many men are exposed to new alternatives.

8 Putting Private Token Money into Circulation

I shall assume for the rest of this discussion that it will be possible to
establish a number of institutions in various parts of the world which
are free to issue notes in competition and similarly to carry cheque
accounts in their individual denominations. I shall call these institutions
simply 'banks', or 'issue banks' when necessary to distinguish them from
other banks that do not choose to issue notes. I shall further assume that
the name or denomination a bank chooses for its issue will be protected
like a brand name or trade mark against unauthorised use, and that there
will be the same protection against forgery as against that of any other
document. These banks will then be vying for the use of their issue by
the public by making them as convenient to use as possible.

The private Swiss 'ducat'

Since readers will probably at once ask how such issues can come to be
generally accepted as money, the best way to begin is probably to describe
how I would proceed if I were in charge of, say, one of the major Swiss
joint-stock banks. Assuming it to be legally possible (which I have not
examined), I would announce the issue of non-interest bearing certificates

or notes, and the readiness to open current cheque accounts, in terms of a unit with a distinct registered trade name such as 'ducat'. The only legal obligation I would assume would be to redeem these notes and deposits on demand with, at the option of the holder, either 5 Swiss francs or 5 D-marks or 2 dollars per ducat. This redemption value would, however, be intended only as a floor below which the value of the unit could not fall, because I would announce at the same time my intention to regulate the quantity of the ducats so as to keep their (precisely defined) purchasing power as nearly as possible constant. I would also explain to the public that I was fully aware I could hope to keep these ducats in circulation only if I fulfilled the expectation that their real value would be kept approximately constant. And I would announce that I proposed from time to time to state the precise commodity equivalent in terms of which I intended to keep the value of the ducat constant, but that I reserved the right, after announcement, to alter the composition of the commodity standard as experience and the revealed preferences of the public suggested.

It would, however, clearly be necessary that, though it seems neither necessary nor desirable that the issuing bank legally commits itself to maintain the value of its unit, it should in its loan contracts specify that any loan could be repaid either at the nominal figure in its own currency, or by corresponding amounts of any other currency or currencies sufficient to buy in the market the commodity equivalent which at the time of making the loan it had used as its standard. Since the bank would have to issue its currency largely through lending, intending borrowers might well be deterred by the formal possibility of the bank arbitrarily raising the value of its currency, that they may well have to be explicitly reassured against such a possibility.

These certificates or notes, and the equivalent book credits, would be made available to the public by short-term loans or sale against other currencies. The units would presumably, because of the option they offered, sell from the outset at a premium above the value of any one of the currencies in which they were redeemable. And, as these governmental currencies continued to depreciate in real terms, this premium would increase. The real value at the price at which the ducats were first sold would serve as the standard the issuer would have to try to keep constant. If the existing currencies continued to depreciate (and the availability of a stable alternative might indeed accelerate the process) the demand for the stable currency would rapidly increase and competing enterprises offering similar but differently named units would soon emerge.

The sale (over the counter or by auction) would initially be the chief form of issue of the new currency. After a regular market had established itself, it would normally be issued only in the course of ordinary banking business, i.e. through short-term loans.

Constant but not fixed value

It might be expedient that the issuing institution should from the outset announce precisely the collection of commodities in terms of which it would aim to keep the value of the 'ducat' constant. But it would be neither necessary nor desirable that it tie itself legally to a particular standard. Experience of the response of the public to competing offers would gradually show which combination of commodities constituted the most desired standard at any time and place. Changes in the importance of the commodities, the volume in which they were traded, and the relative stability or sensitivity of their prices (especially the degree to which they were determined competitively or not) might suggest alterations to make the currency more popular. On the whole I would expect that, for reasons to be explained later (section 13), a collection of raw material prices, such as has been suggested as the basis of a commodity reserve standard,[38] would seem most appropriate, both from the point of view of the issuing bank and from that of the effects of the stability of the economic process as a whole.

Control of value by competition

In most respects, indeed, the proposed system should prove a more practicable method of achieving all that was hoped from a commodity reserve standard or some other form of 'tabular standard'. At the same time it would remove the necessity of making it fully automatic by taking the control from a monopolistic authority and entrusting it to private concerns. The threat of the speedy loss of their whole business if they failed to meet expectations (and how any government organisation would be certain to abuse the opportunity to play with raw material prices!) would provide a much stronger safeguard than any that could be devised against a government monopoly. Competition would certainly prove a more effective constraint, forcing the issuing institutions to keep the value of their currency constant (in terms of a stated collection of commodities), than would any obligation to redeem the currency in those commodities (or in gold). And it would be an infinitely cheaper method than the accumulation and the storing of valuable materials.

The kind of trust on which private money would rest would not be very different from the trust on which today all private banking rests (or in the United States rested before the governmental deposit insurance scheme!). People today trust that a bank, to preserve its business, will arrange its affairs so that it will at all times be able to exchange demand deposits for cash, although they know that banks do not have enough cash to do so if everyone exercised his right to demand instant payment at the same time. Similarly, under the proposed scheme, the managers of the bank would learn that its business depended on the unshaken confidence that it would continue to regulate its issue of ducats (etc.) so that their purchasing power remained approximately constant.

Is the risk in the venture therefore too big to justify entry by men with the kind of conservative temper its successful conduct probably requires?[39] It is not to be denied that, once announced and undertaken, the decision on how large the commitment was to grow would be taken out of the hands of the issuing institution. To achieve its announced aim of maintaining the purchasing power of its currency constant, the amount would have to be promptly adapted to any change of demand, whether increase or decrease. Indeed, so long as the bank succeeded in keeping the value of its currency constant, there would be little reason to fear a sudden large reduction of the demand for it (though successful competitors might well make considerable inroads on its circulation). The most embarrassing development might be a rapid growth of demand beyond the limits a private institution likes to handle. But we can be fairly sure that, in the event of such success, new competition would soon relieve a bank of this anxiety.

The issuing bank could, at first, at no prohibitive cost keep in cash a 100 per cent reserve of the currencies in terms of which it had undertaken to redeem its issue and still treat the premiums received as freely available for general business. But once these other currencies had, as the result of further inflation, substantially depreciated relative to the ducat, the bank would have to be prepared, in order to maintain the value of the ducat, to buy back substantial amounts of ducats at the prevailing higher rate of exchange. This means that it would have to be able rapidly to liquidate investments of very large amounts indeed. These investments would therefore have to be chosen very carefully if a temporary rush of demand for its currency were not to lead to later embarrassment when the institution that had initiated the development had to share the market with imitators. Incidentally, the difficulty of finding investments of an assured stable value to match similar obligations would not be anything like as difficult for such a bank as we are considering as present-day bankers seem to find it: all the loans made in its own currency would of course represent such stable assets. The curious fact that such an issuing bank would have claims and obligations in terms of a unit the value of which it determined itself, though it could not do so arbitrarily or capriciously without destroying the basis of its business, may at first appear disturbing but should not create real difficulties. What may at first appear somewhat puzzling accounting problems largely disappear when it is remembered that such a bank would of course keep its accounts in terms of its own currency. The outstanding notes and deposits of such a bank are not claims on it in terms of some other unit of value; it determines itself the value of the unit in terms of which it has debts and claims and keeps its books. This will cease to seem shocking when we remember that this is precisely what practically all central banks have been doing for nearly half a century – their notes were of course redeemable in precisely nothing. But notes which may appreciate relatively to most other capital assets may indeed present to accountants problems with which they never before had to deal. Initially the issuing bank would of course be under a legal obligation to redeem its currency in terms of the other currencies against which it was at first issued. But after it has existed for some time their value may have shrunk to very little or they may have altogether disappeared.[40]

9 Competition Between Banks Issuing Different Currencies

It has for so long been treated as a self-evident proposition that the supply of money cannot be left to competition that probably few people could explain why. As we have seen, the explanation appears to be that it has always been assumed that there must be only *one* uniform kind of currency in a country, and that competition meant that its amount was to be determined by several agencies issuing it independently. It is, however, clearly not practicable to allow tokens with the same name and readily exchangeable against each other to be issued competitively, since nobody would be in a position to control their quantity and therefore be responsible for their value. The question we have to consider is whether competition between the issuers of clearly distinguishable kinds of currency consisting of *different* units would not give us a better kind of money than we have ever had, far outweighing the inconvenience of encountering (but for most people not even having to handle) more than one kind.

In this condition the value of the currency issued by one bank would not necessarily be affected by the supplies of other currencies by different institutions (private or governmental). And it should be in the power of each issuer of a distinct currency to regulate its quantity so as to make it most acceptable to the public – and competition would force him to do so. Indeed, he would know that the penalty for failing to fulfil the expectations raised would be the prompt loss of the business. Successful entry into it would evidently be a very profitable venture, and success would depend on establishing the credibility and trust that the bank was able and determined to carry out its declared intentions. It would seem that in this situation sheer desire for gain would produce a better money than government has ever produced.[41]

Effects of competition

It seems to me to be fairly certain that:

1   A money generally expected to preserve its purchasing power approximately constant would be in continuous demand so long as the people were free to use it.
2   With such a continuing demand depending on success in keeping the value of the currency constant one could trust the issuing banks to make every effort to achieve this better than would any monopolist who runs no risk by depreciating his money.
3   The issuing institution could achieve this result by regulating the quantity of its issue.
4   Such a regulation of the quantity of each currency would constitute the best of all practicable methods of regulating the quantity of media of exchange for all possible purposes.

Clearly a number of competing issuers of different currencies would have to compete in the quality of the currencies they offered for loan or sale. Once the competing issuers had credibly demonstrated that they provided currencies more suitable to the needs of the public than government has ever provided, there would be no obstacle to their becoming generally accepted in preference to the governmental currencies – at least in countries in which government had removed all obstacles to their use. The appearance and increasing use of the new currencies would, of course, decrease the demand for the existing national ones and, unless their volume was rapidly reduced, would lead to their depreciation. This is the process by which the unreliable currencies would gradually all be eliminated. The condition required in order that this displacement of the government money should terminate before it had entirely disappeared would be that government reformed and saw to it that the issue of its currency was regulated on the same principles as those of the competing private institutions. It is not very likely that it would succeed, because to prevent an accelerating depreciation of its currency it would have to respond to the new currencies by a rapid contraction of its own issue.

'A thousand hounds': the vigilant Press

The competition between the issuing banks would be made very acute by the close scrutiny of their conduct by the Press and at the currency exchange. For a decision so important for business as which currency to use in contracts and accounts, all possible information would be supplied daily in the financial press, and have to be provided by the issuing banks themselves for the information of the public. Indeed, a thousand hounds would be after the unfortunate banker who failed in the prompt responses required to ensure the safeguarding of the value of the currency he issues. The papers would probably print a table daily, not only of the current rates of exchange between the currencies but also of the current value, and the deviation of each of the currencies likely to be used by their readers from the announced standard of value in terms of commodities. These tables might look something like table 1 (with the initials of the issuing institution given after the name of the currency it issues).

Nothing would be more feared by the bankers than to see the quotation of their currency in heavy type to indicate that the real value had fallen below the standard of tolerance set by the paper publishing the table.

Three questions

This sketch of the competition between several private issuing institutions presupposes answers to a number of questions we shall have to examine in more detail in succeeding sections.

● The first is whether a competing institution issuing its distinctive currency will always be able to regulate its value by controlling its

Table 1   *Illustration of possible currency price deviations*

Currency	Deviation from	
	Announced Standard (%)	Our Test Standard (%)
Ducats (SGB)	− 0.04	− 0.04
Florins (FNB)	+ 0.02	+ 0.03
Mengers (WK)	+ 0.10	+ 0.10
Piasters (DBS)	− 0.06	− 0.12
Reals (CNB)	**− 1.02**	**− 1.01**
Shekels (ORT)	− 0.45	− 0.45
Talents (ATBC)	+ 0.26	+ 0.02

quantity so as to make it more attractive to people than other currencies, and how far other issuers of currencies can by their policy interfere with these efforts.

● The second is which value (or other attribute of a currency) the public will prefer if different banks announce that it is their intention (and demonstrate their ability) to keep announced values of their currency constant.

● A third and no less important question is whether the kind of money most people will individually prefer to use will also best serve the aims of all. Though one might at first think that this must necessarily be so, it is not inevitably true. It is conceivable that the success of people's efforts will depend not only on the money they themselves use but also on the effects of the money others use, and the benefits they derive for themselves from using a particular kind of money may conceivably be more than offset by the disturbances caused by its general use. I do not believe this to be the case in the present instance, but the question certainly requires explicit consideration.

Before we can discuss further the interaction between currencies it will be expedient to devote a section to precisely what we mean by money or currency and its different kinds, and the various ways in which they may differ from one another.

10   A Digression on the Definition of Money

Money is usually defined as *the* generally acceptable medium of exchange,[42] but there is no reason why within a given community there should be only one kind of money that is generally (or at least widely) accepted. In the Austrian border town in which I have been living for the past few years, shopkeepers and most other business people will usually accept D-Marks as readily as Austrian schillings, and only the law prevents German banks in Salzburg from doing their business in D-Marks in the same manner as they do 10 miles away on the German side of the border. The same is true of hundreds of other tourist centres in Austria frequented mainly by Germans. In most of them dollars will also be accepted nearly as readily as D-Marks. I believe the situation is not very different on both sides of long stretches of the border between the United States and Canada or Mexico, and probably along many other frontiers.

But though in such regions everybody may be ready to accept several currencies at the current rate of exchange, individuals may use different kinds of money to hold (as liquidity reserves), to make contracts for deferred payments, or to keep their accounts in, and the community may respond in the same manner to changes in the amounts of the different currencies.

By referring to different kinds of money we have in mind units of different denomination whose relative values may fluctuate against one another. These fluctuating values must be emphasised because they are not the only way in which media of exchange may differ from one another. They may also, even when expressed in terms of the same unit, differ widely in their degree of acceptability (or liquidity, i.e. in the very quality which makes them money), or the groups of people that readily accept them. This means that different kinds of money can differ from one another in more than one dimension.

No clear distinction between money and non-money

It also means that, although we usually assume there is a sharp line of distinction between what is money and what is not – and the law generally tries to make such a distinction – so far as the causal effects of monetary events are concerned, there is no such clear difference. What we find is rather a continuum in which objects of various degrees of liquidity, or with values which can fluctuate independently of each other, shade into each other in the degree to which they function as money.[43]

I have always found it useful to explain to students that it has been rather a misfortune that we describe money by a noun, and that it would be more helpful for the explanation of monetary phenomena if 'money' were an adjective describing a property which different things could possess to varying *degrees*.[44] 'Currency' is, for this reason, more appropriate, since objects can 'have currency' to varying degrees and through different regions or sectors of the population.

Pseudo-exactness, statistical measurement, and scientific truth

Here we encounter a difficulty we frequently meet in our efforts to explain the ill-defined phenomena of economic life. In order to simplify our exposition of what are very complex interconnections that otherwise would become difficult to follow, we introduce sharp distinctions where in real life different attributes of the objects shade into each other. A similar situation arises where we try to draw sharp distinctions between such objects as commodities and services, consumers' goods and capital goods, durable and perishable, reproducible and non-reproducible, specific and versatile, or substitutable and non-substitutable goods. All are very important distinctions but they can become very misleading if, in the popular striving for pseudo-exactness, we treat these classes as measurable quantities. This involves a simplification which is perhaps sometimes necessary but always dangerous and has led to many errors in economics. Though the differences are significant, this does not mean we can neatly and unambiguously divide these things into two, or any other number of, distinct classes. We often do, and perhaps often must talk as if this division were true, but the usage can be very deceptive and produce wholly erroneous conclusions.[45]

Legal fictions and defective economic theory

Similarly, the legal fiction that there is one clearly defined thing called 'money' that can be sharply distinguished from other things, a fiction introduced to satisfy the work of the lawyer or judge, was never true so far as things are to be referred to which have the characteristic effects of events on the side of money. Yet it has done much harm through leading to the demand that, for certain purposes, only 'money' issued by government may be used, or that there must always be some single kind of object which can be referred to as *the* 'money' of the country. It has also, as we shall see, led to the development in economic theory of an explanation of the value of units of money which, though under its simplified assumptions it gives some useful approximations, is of no help for the kind of problems we have to examine here.

For what follows it will be important to keep in mind that different kinds of money can differ from one another in two distinct although not wholly unrelated dimensions: acceptability (or liquidity) and the expected behaviour (stability or variability) of its value. The expectation of stability will evidently affect the liquidity of a particular kind of money, but it may be that in the short run liquidity may sometimes be more important than stability, or that the acceptability of a more stable money may for some reason be confined to rather limited circles.

Meanings and definitions

This is perhaps the most convenient place to add explicit statements concerning the meanings in which we shall use other frequently recurring terms. It will have become clear that in the present connection it is rather more expedient to speak of 'currencies' than 'monies', not only because it is easier to use the former term in the plural but also because, as we have seen, 'currency' emphasises a certain attribute. We shall also use 'currency', perhaps somewhat in conflict with the original meaning of the term, to include not only pieces of paper and other sorts of 'hand-to-hand money', but also bank balances subject to cheque and other media of exchange that can be used for most of the purposes for which cheques are used. There is, however, as we have just pointed out, no need for a very sharp distinction between what is and what is not money. The reader will do best if he remains aware that we have to deal with a *range* of objects of varying degrees of acceptability which imperceptibly shade at the lower end into objects that are clearly not money.

Although we shall frequently refer to the agencies issuing currency simply as 'banks', this is not meant to imply that all banks will be issuing money. The term 'rate of exchange' will be used throughout for rates of exchange between currencies, and the term 'currency exchange' (analogous to stock exchange) for the organised currency market. Occasionally we shall also speak of 'money substitutes' when we have to consider borderline cases in the scale of liquidity – such as travellers' cheques, credit cards, and overdrafts – where it would be quite arbitrary to assert that they either are or are not part of the circulation of currency.

11 The Possibility of Controlling the Value of a Competitive Currency

The chief attraction the issuer of a competitive currency has to offer to his customers is the assurance that its value will be kept stable (or otherwise be made to behave in a predictable manner). We shall leave for section 12 the question of precisely what kind of stability the public will probably prefer. For the moment we shall concentrate on whether an issuing bank in competition with other issuers of similar currencies will have the power to control the quantity of its distinctive issue so as to determine the value it will command in the market.

The expected value of a currency will, of course, not be the only consideration that will lead the public to borrow or buy it. But the expected value will be the decisive factor determining how much of it the public will wish to hold, and the issuing bank will soon discover that the desire of the public to *hold* its currency will be the essential circumstance on which its value depends. At first it might perhaps seem obvious that the exclusive issuer of a currency, who as such has complete control over its supply, will be able to determine its price so long as there is anyone who wants it at that price. If, as we shall provisionally assume, the aim of the issuing bank is to keep constant the aggregate price in terms of its currency of a particular collection of commodities it would, by regulating the amount of the currency in circulation, have to counteract any tendency of that aggregate price to rise or fall.

Control by selling/buying currency and (short-term) lending

The issuing bank will have two methods of altering the volume of its currency in circulation: it can sell or buy its currency against other currencies (or securities and possibly some commodities); and it can contract or expand its lending activities. In order to retain control over its outstanding circulation, it will on the whole have to confine its lending to relatively short-time contracts so that, by reducing or temporarily stopping new lending, current repayments of outstanding loans would bring about a rapid reduction of its total issue.

To assure the constancy of the value of its currency the main consideration would have to be never to increase it beyond the total the public is prepared to hold without increasing expenditure in it so as to drive up prices of commodities in terms of it; it must also never reduce its supply below the total the public is prepared to hold without reducing expenditure in it and driving prices down. In practice, many or even most of the commodities in terms of which the currency is to be kept stable would be currently traded and quoted chiefly in terms of some other competing currencies (especially if, as we suggest in section 13, it will be mainly prices of raw materials or wholesale prices of foodstuffs). The bank would therefore have to look to the effect of changes in its circulation, not so much directly on the prices of other *commodities*, but on the rates of exchange with the *currencies* against which they are chiefly traded. Though the task of ascertaining the appropriate rates of exchange (considering the given rates of exchange between the different currencies) would be complex, computers would help with almost instantaneous calculation, so the bank would know hour by hour whether to increase or decrease the amounts of its currency to be offered as loans or for sale. Quick and immediate action would have to be taken by buying or selling on the currency exchange, but a lasting effect would be achieved only by altering the lending policy.

Current issuing policy

Perhaps I ought to spell out here in more detail how an issuing bank would have to proceed in order to keep the chosen value of its currency constant. The basis of the daily decisions on its lending policy (and its sales and purchases of currencies on the currency exchange) would have to be the result of a constant calculation provided by a computer into which the latest information about commodity prices and rates of exchange would be constantly fed as it arrived. The character of this calculation can be illustrated by the following abridged table (table 2). (I am neglecting here the question how far the costs of transport from the chief market to some common centre, or perhaps separate items representing the costs of different forms of transport, should be considered or not.)

The essential information would be the guide number at the lower right-hand corner, resulting either from the quantities of the different commodities being so chosen that at the base date their aggregate price in Ducats was 1,000, or 1,000 was used as the base of an index number. This figure and its current changes would serve as a signal telling all

Table 2   *Illustration of a currency stabilisation scheme*

Commodity	Quantity	Currency in which quoted	Price in that currency	Rate of exchange	Price in own currency
Aluminium	x tons	$	.	.	.
Beef	.	£	.	.	.
Camphor	.	Ducats	—	—	.
Cocoa	.	.	.	.	.
Coffee	.	.	.	.	.
Coal	.	.	.	.	.
Coke	.	.	.	.	.
Copper	.	.	.	.	.
Copra	.	.	.	.	.
Corn	.	Ducats	—	—	.
etc.	.	.	.	.	.
				Total 1,000	

executive officers of the bank what to do. A 1,002 appearing on the screen would tell them to contract or tighten controls, i.e. restrict loans by making them dearer or being more selective, and selling other currencies more freely; 997 would tell them that they could slightly relax and expand. (A special write-out of the computer in the chairman's office would currently inform him which of his officers did promptly respond to these instructions.) The effect of this contraction or expansion on commodity prices would be chiefly indirect through the rates of exchange with the currencies in which these commodities were chiefly traded, and direct only with regard to commodities traded chiefly in ducats.

The same signal would appear on the currency exchange and, if the bank was known for taking prompt and effective measures to correct any deviation, would lead to its efforts being assisted by more of its currency being demanded when it was expected to appreciate because its value was below normal (the guide number showing 1,002), and less being demanded when it was expected slightly to depreciate (because the guide number had fallen to 997). It is difficult to see how such a policy consistently pursued would not result in the fluctuations of the value of the currency around the chosen commodity standard being reduced to a very small range indeed.

The crucial factor: demand for currency to hold

But, whether directly or indirectly via the price of other currencies, it would seem clear that, if an institution acts in the knowledge that the public preparedness to hold its currency, and therefore its business, depends on maintaining the currency value, it will be both able and compelled to assure this result by appropriate continuous adjustments of the quantity in circulation. The crucial point it must keep in mind will be that, to keep a large and growing amount of its currency in circulation, it will be not the demand for *borrowing* it but the willingness of the public to *hold* it that will be decisive. An incautious increase of the current issue may therefore make the flow back to the bank grow faster than the public demand to hold it.

The Press, as pointed out, would closely watch the results of the efforts of each issuing bank and daily quote how much the various currencies deviate from the self-set standards. From the point of view of the issuing banks it would probably be desirable to allow a small, previously announced, tolerance or standard of deviation in either direction. For in that event, and so long as a bank demonstrated its power and resolution to bring rates of exchange (or commodity prices in terms of its currency) promptly back to its standard, speculation would come to its aid and relieve it of the necessity to take precipitate steps to assure absolute stability.

So long as the bank had succeeded in keeping the value of its currency at the desired level, it is difficult to see that it should for this purpose have to contract its circulation so rapidly as to be embarrassed. The usual cause of such developments in the past was circumstances which increased the demand for liquid 'cash', but the bank would have to reduce the aggregate amount outstanding only to adjust it to a shrunken total demand for both forms of its currency. If it had lent mainly on short term, the normal repayment of loans would have brought this result fairly rapidly. The whole matter appears to be very simple and straightforward so long as we assume that all the competing banks try to control their currencies with the aim of keeping their values in some sense constant.

Would competition disrupt the system?

What, however, would be the consequences if one competitor attempted to gain in this competition by offering other advantages such as a low rate of interest, or if it granted book credits or perhaps even issued notes (in other words, incurred debts payable on demand) in terms of the currency issued by another bank? Would either practice seriously interfere with the control the issuing banks can exercise over the value of their currencies?

There will of course always be a strong temptation for any bank to try and expand the circulation of its currency by lending cheaper than competing banks; but it would soon discover that, insofar as the additional lending is not based on a corresponding increase of saving, such attempts would inevitably rebound and hurt the bank that over-issued. While people will no doubt be very eager to *borrow* a currency offered at a lower rate of interest, they will not want to *hold* a larger proportion of their liquid assets in a currency of the increased issue of which they would soon learn from various reports and symptoms.

It is true that, so long as the currencies are almost instantaneously exchangeable against one another at a known rate of exchange, the relative prices of commodities in terms of them will also remain the same. Even on the commodity markets the prices of those commodities (or, in regions where a high proportion of the demand is expressed in terms of the increased currency, prices in terms of all currencies) will tend to rise compared with other prices. But the decisive events will take place on the currency exchange. At the prevailing rate of exchange the currency that has increased in supply will constitute a larger proportion of the total of all currencies than people have habitually held. Above all, everybody indebted in the currencies for which a higher rate of interest has to be paid will try to borrow cheap in order to acquire currencies in which he can repay the more burdensome loans. And all the banks that have not reduced their lending rate will promptly return to the bank that lends more cheaply all of its currency they receive. The result must be the appearance on the currency exchange of an excess supply of the over-issued currency, which will quickly bring about a fall in the rate at which it can be exchanged into the others. And it will be at this new rate that commodity prices normally quoted in other currencies will be translated into the offending currency; while, as a result of its over-issue, prices normally quoted in it will be immediately driven up. The fall in the market quotation and the rise of commodity prices in terms of the offending currency would soon induce habitual holders to shift to another currency. The consequent reduction in the demand for it would probably soon more than offset the temporary gain obtained by lending it more cheaply. If the issuing bank nevertheless pursued cheap lending, a general flight from the currency would set in; and continued cheap lending would mean that larger and larger amounts would be dumped on the currency exchange. We can confidently conclude that it would not be possible for a bank to pull down the real value of other currencies by over-issue of its currency – certainly not if their issuers are prepared, so far as necessary, to counter such an attempt by temporarily curtailing their issues.

Would parasitic currencies prevent control of currency value?

A more difficult question, the answer to which is perhaps not so clear, is how far the unavoidable appearance of what one may call parasitic currencies, i.e. the pyramiding of a superstructure of circulating credit through other banks carrying cheque accounts and perhaps even issuing notes in the denomination of the currency of the original issuer, would interfere with the issuer's control over the value of his own currency. So long as such parasitic issues were clearly labelled as debts to be paid in the currency of the issuer it is difficult to see how this could be or should be prevented by law.

Clearly not all banks would wish to issue, or probably could issue, a currency of their own. Those that did not would have no choice but to accept deposits and grant credits in terms of some other currency, and would prefer to do so in the best currency available. Nor would the original issuer wish altogether to prevent this, although he might dislike the issue of notes more than the mere running of accounts subject to cheque in terms of his currency. Notes issued by a secondary issuer would, of course, have to show clearly that they were not the original ducats issued by the bank that owned that trade mark, but merely claims for ducats, since otherwise they would simply be a forgery. Yet I do not see how the ordinary legal protection of brand names or trade marks could prevent the issue of such claims in the form of notes, and very much doubt whether it would be desirable to prevent it by law, especially in view of the essential similarity between such notes and deposits subject to cheque which even the issuing banks would hardly wish to prevent.

What the original issuer of such a currency could do and would have to do is not to repeat the mistakes governments have made, as a result of which control of these secondary or parasitic issues has slipped from their hands. It must make clear that it would not be prepared to bail out secondary issuers by supplying the 'cash' (i.e. the original notes) they will need to redeem their obligations. We shall see later (section 16) how governments were led into this trap and allowed their monopoly of the issue of money to be watered down in the most undesirable manner. (They shared the responsibility for control of the total amount of the standard denomination, yielding to the constant pressure for cheap money that was supposed to be met by the rapid spread of banks which they assisted by securing their liquidity; and in the end nobody had full power over the total quantity of money.)

The answer to the most serious problem arising from the scheme seems to me that, though private issuers will have to tolerate the appearance of parasitic circulations of deposits and notes of the same denomination, they ought not to assist but rather restrain it by making it clear in advance that they would not be prepared to provide the notes needed to redeem parasitic issues except against 'hard cash', i.e. by sale against some other reliable currency. By adhering strictly to this principle they would force the secondary issuer to practise something very close to '100 per cent banking'. So far as there would still be limited fiduciary parasitic issues they would have to be kept in circulation by a policy which assured that their value was never questioned. Though this policy might limit the circulation and thus the profit of the original issuer, it should not seriously impair his ability to keep the value of his currency constant.

To achieve this the original issuer of a currency with a certain label would have to anticipate the effects of the over-issue of such a parasitic currency (or any other currency claiming to maintain a value equal to its own) and ruthlessly to refuse to buy it at par even before the expected depreciation manifests itself in the rise of some commodity prices in terms of that other currency. The dealings of an issue bank in other currencies would therefore never be a purely mechanical affair (buying and selling at constant prices) guided only by the observed changes in the purchasing power of the other currencies; nor could such a bank undertake to buy any other currency at a rate corresponding to its current buying power over the standard batch of commodities; but it would require a good deal of judgement effectively to defend the short-run stability of one's own currency, and the business would have to be guided in some measure by prediction of the future development of the value of other currencies.

12   Which Sort of Currency Would the Public Select?

Since it is my thesis that the public would select from a number of competing private currencies a better money than governments provide, I must now examine the process and the criteria by which such a selection would take place.

This is a question on which we have little empirical knowledge. It would be of little use to try asking the people (perhaps by an opinion poll). Never having been in such a position, most people have never thought or formed an opinion about what they would do. We can merely attempt to derive the probable character of individual decisions from our general knowledge of the purpose for which people want money, and the manner in which they act in similar situations. This is, after all, the procedure by which most of economic theory has been built up and has arrived at conclusions usually confirmed by later experience. We must not, of course, assume that people will at once act rationally in a new situation. But, if not by insight, they would soon learn by experience and imitation of the most successful what conduct best serves their interests.[46] A major change like the one considered here might at first cause much uncertainty and confusion. Yet I do not think there is much reason to doubt that people would soon discover what rational consideration could have told them at once. Whether in practice the process would be fast or slow may differ from country to country.[47]

Four uses of money

There are four kinds of uses of money that would chiefly affect the choice among available kinds of currency: its use, first, for cash purchases of commodities and services, second, for holding reserves for future needs, third, in contracts for deferred payments, and, finally, as a unit of account, especially in keeping books. To treat these uses as different 'functions' of money is common but not really expedient. They are in effect simply consequences of the basic function of money as a medium of exchange, and will only in exceptional conditions, such as a rapid depreciation of the medium of exchange, come to be separated from it. They are also interdependent in such a way that, although at first different attributes of money may seem desirable for its different uses, money renders one service, namely that as a unit of account, which makes stability of value the most desirable of all. Although at first convenience in daily purchases might be thought decisive in the selection, I believe it would prove that suitability as a unit of account would rule the roost.

Cash purchases   To the great mass of wage- and salary-earners the chief interest will probably be that they can make their daily purchases in the currency in which they are paid, and that they find prices everywhere indicated in the currency they use. Shopkeepers, on the other hand, so long as they know they can instantaneously exchange any currency at a known rate of exchange against any other, would be only too willing to accept any currency at an appropriate price. Electronic cash registers would probably be developed rapidly, not only to show instantaneously the equivalent of any price in any currency desired, but also to be connected through the computer with banks so that firms would immediately be credited with the equivalent in the currency in which they kept their accounts. (Cash balances in the currencies would be collected every evening.) On the other hand, shopkeepers would find it expedient, if two or three currencies were in common local use, to mark their wares in an easily distinguishable manner, for example in different colours for each currency, so as to ease price comparisons between shops and currencies.

Holding reserves for future payments   Beyond the desire to use his regular receipts for his ordinary expenditure, the wage- and salary-earner would probably be interested chiefly in stability. And although in his mortgage and instalment payments he might for a while profit from a depreciating currency, his wage or salary contract would incline his wishes towards an appreciating currency.

All holders of cash, that is, everybody, would prefer an appreciating currency and for this reason there might be a substantial demand for such money; but it would clearly not be to the advantage of borrowers to borrow in it, or for banks to have to maintain a value higher than that at which they issued a currency. It is conceivable that a limited amount of notes of such an appreciating currency might be issued and used for special purposes, but it would seem most unlikely that they would become generally used. The chief demand for holding would probably be for the currency in which people expected to have to pay debts.

Standard of deferred payments   When we come to the third use, as a standard of deferred payments, the primary interests of the parties to the contract would of course be precisely opposite: lenders preferring an appreciating and borrowers a depreciating currency. But each group would be of a very mixed composition, the creditors including all wage- and salary-earners as well as the owners of capital, and the debtors including the banks as well as enterprises and farmers. It therefore seems unlikely that market forces would produce a predominant bias in one direction. And, though they would all in the short run either lose or gain from changes in the value of the currency on their borrowing or lending business, they would probably all soon discover that these losses or gains were merely temporary and tended to disappear as soon as interest rates adapted themselves to expected price movements.

A reliable unit of account   It seems to me that the decisive factor that would create a general preference for a currency stable in value would be that only in such a currency is a realistic calculation possible, and therefore in the long run a successful choice between alternative currencies for use in production and trade. In particular, the chief task of accounting, to ensure that the stock of capital of the business is not eaten into and only true net gains shown as profits available for disposal by the shareholders, can be realised only if the value of the unit of account is approximately stable.

An attempt to explain further why successful economic calculation is possible only with a stable value of money raises the question of what precisely we mean by 'the value of money' and the various respects in which it may be kept stable. This we must leave to section 13. For the present we content ourselves with the empirical fact that effective capital maintenance and cost control is possible only if accounts are kept in a unit that in some sense remains tolerably stable. So we will provisionally leave the present subject with the conclusion that, in the long run at least, the effective choice between competitive offers of currencies will be the usual one of competition. The currency that will prevail will be the one preferred by the people who are helped to succeed and who in consequence will be imitated by others.

13   Which Value of Money?

Strictly speaking, in a scientific sense, there is no such thing as a perfectly stable value of money – or of anything else. Value is a relationship, a rate of equivalence, or, as W. S. Jevons said, 'an indirect mode of expressing a ratio',[48] which can be stated only by naming the quantity of one object that is valued equally with the 'equivalent' quantity of another object. Two objects may keep a constant relative value in terms of each other, but unless we specify the other, the statement that the value of something is unchanged has no definite meaning.

What we mean when we habitually but carelessly use such expressions as 'Beer is more stable in value than beetroot' (and this is the most we can ever assert with any meaning) is that the relative value of beer, or its rate of exchange, tends to remain more stable with a larger number of other goods or over longer periods, than is true of beetroot and many other goods. For ordinary goods or services we have in mind in the first instance usually their relation to money. When we apply the term 'value' to money itself what is meant is that the price of most commodities will not tend to change predominantly in one direction, or will change only little, over short periods.

'A stable value of money'

But some prices always change on a free market. We will sometimes feel that the value of money has remained approximately constant although many prices have changed, and at other times that the value of money has definitely decreased or increased, although the prices of only a few important commodities have changed but all in the same direction. What then do we call, in a world of constantly changing individual prices, a stable value of money?

In a rough sense it is of course fairly obvious that the command over commodities in general conferred by a sum of money has decreased if it brings a smaller amount of most of them and more of only a few of them. It is then sensible to say that the command over commodities has remained about the same if these two changes in command over commodities just balance. But for our purposes we need, of course, a more precise definition of 'a stable value of money' and a more exact definition of the benefits we expect from it.

Balancing errors

As we have seen, the chief disturbances which changes in the value of money will cause operate through the effects on contracts for deferred payments and on the use of money units as the basis of calculation and accounting. Decisions in both have to cope with the unalterable truth that for the individual the future movement of most prices is unpredictable (because they serve as signals of events of most of which he cannot know). The resulting risk can best be reduced by basing calculations on expectations of future prices from which current prices are quite as likely to deviate in the one direction as in the other by any given percentage. This median value of probable future changes will be correctly estimated only if it is zero and thus coincides with the probable behaviour of the large number of prices that are fairly rigid or sluggish (chiefly public utility rates but also the prices of most branded articles, goods sold by mail order houses, and the like).

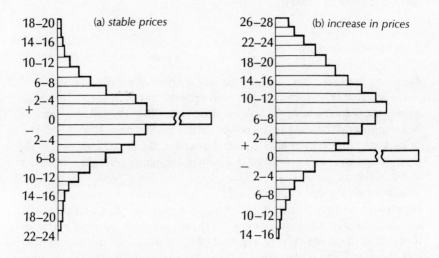

Figure 1   *Aggregate price of commodities sold at prices changed (against previous period) by percentage indicated.*

The position is best illustrated by two diagrams. If the value of money is so regulated that an appropriate average of prices is kept constant, the probabilities of future price movements with which all planning of future activities will have to cope can be represented as in figure 1(a). Though in this case the unpredictability of particular future prices, inevitable in a functioning market economy, remains, the fairly high long-run chances are that for people in general the effects of the unforeseen price changes will just about cancel out. They will at least not cause a general error of expectations in one direction but on the whole make fairly successful calculations based on the assumption of the continuance of prices (where no better information is available).

Where the divergent movement of individual prices results in a *rise* in the average of all prices, it will look somewhat as in figure 1(b).

Since the individual enterprise will have as little foundation for correctly foreseeing the median of all the movements as for predicting the movements of individual prices, it could also not base its calculations and decisions on a known median from which individual movements of prices were as likely to diverge in the one direction as in the other. Successful calculations, or effective capital and cost accounting, would then become impossible. People would more and more wish for a unit of account whose value moved more closely together with the general trend, and might even be driven to use as the unit of account something that could not be used as a medium of exchange.[49]

Criteria of choice

These skewed shifts of the distribution of price changes to one side of constancy which changes in the quantity of money may cause, and the resulting difficulty of foresight, calculation and accounting, must not be confused with the merely temporary changes in the structure of relative prices the same process also brings about which will cause misdirections of production. We shall have to consider (section 17) how a stabilisation of the value of money will also substantially prevent those misdirections of production which later inevitably lead to reversals of the process of growth, the loss of much investment, and periods of unemployment. We shall argue that this would be one of the chief benefits of a stable currency. But it is hardly possible to argue that the users of money will for this reason select a currency with a stable value. This is an effect they are not likely to perceive and take into account in their individual decision of what money to use – although the observation of the smooth course of business in regions using a stable currency may induce the people of other regions to prefer a similar currency. The individual also could not protect himself against this effect by himself using a stable currency, because the structure of relative prices will be the same in terms of the different concurrent currencies and those distortions cannot therefore be avoided so long as side by side with stable currencies fluctuating currencies are used to a significant extent.

The reason why people will tend to prefer a currency with a value stable in terms of commodities will thus be that it will help them to minimise the effects of the unavoidable uncertainty about price movements because the effect of errors in opposite directions will tend to cancel each other out. This cancelling will not take place if the median around which the deviation of individual prices clusters is not zero but some unknown magnitude. Even if we agree that the stable money people will prefer to use will be such that they expect the individual prices in which they are chiefly interested to be as likely to increase in terms of it as to decrease, this does not yet tell us which price level most people will want to see constant. Different people or enterprises will evidently be interested in the prices of different commodities. And the aggregate prices of different collections of commodities would of course move differently.

Effectiveness for accounting again decisive

While one probably is at first again inclined to think in terms of retail prices or cost of living, and even most individual consumers might prefer a money stable in these terms, it is not likely that an extensive circulation could be built up for a currency so regulated. The cost of living differs from place to place and is apt to change at varying rates. Business would certainly prefer a money acceptable over wide regions. What would be most important for calculation and accounting in each enterprise (and therefore for the efficient use of resources), relying on the general stability of prices rather than its specialised knowledge of a particular market, would be the prices of widely traded products such as raw materials, agricultural foodstuffs and certain standardised semi-finished industrial products. They have the further advantage that they are traded on regular markets, their prices are promptly reported and, at least with raw materials, are particularly sensitive and would therefore make it possible by early action to forestall tendencies towards general price movements (which often show themselves in such commodities first).

Indeed it may well be that a regulation of the issue which directly aimed at stabilising raw material prices might result in a greater stability even of the prices of consumers' goods than a management which aimed directly at the latter object. The considerable lag which experience has shown to prevail between changes in the quantity of money and changes in the price level of consumers' goods may indeed mean that, if adjustment of circulation were postponed until the effects of an excess or shortage of the issue showed itself in changes in the prices of consumers' goods, quite noticeable changes in their prices could not be avoided; while, in the case of raw materials, where this lag seems to be shorter, an earlier warning would make prompter precautionary measures possible.

Wage- and salary-earners would probably also discover that it was advantageous to conclude collective bargains in average raw material prices or a similar magnitude, which would secure for earners of fixed incomes an automatic share in an increase of industrial productivity. (The underdeveloped countries would also prefer an international currency that gave raw materials in general an increasing purchasing power over industrial products – though they are likely to spoil the possibility by insisting on the stabilisation of individual raw material prices.) I hope, at any rate, that this will be the predominant choice because a currency stable in terms of raw material prices is probably also the nearest approach we can hope to achieve to one conducive to stability of general economic activity.

Wholesale commodity prices as standard of value for currencies over international regions

My expectation would be that, at least for large regions much exceeding present national territories, people would agree on a standard set of wholesale prices of commodities to treat as the standard of value in which they would prefer to have their currencies kept constant. A few banks that had established wide circulation by accommodating this preference, and issued currencies of different denominations but with roughly constant rates of exchange with one another, might continue to try and refine the precise composition of the standard 'basket' of commodities whose price they tried to keep constant in their currency.[50] But this practice would not cause substantial fluctuations in the relative values of the chief currencies circulating in the region. Regions with different compositions of the currencies in circulation would, of course, overlap, and currencies whose value was based chiefly on commodities important for one way of life, or for one group of predominant industries, might fluctuate relatively more against others but yet retain their distinct clientele among people with particular occupations and habits.

14 The Uselessness of the Quantity Theory for Our Purposes

The usual assumptions of monetary theory, that there is only one kind of currency, *the* money, and that there is no sharp distinction between full money and mere money substitutes, thus disappear. So does the applicability of what is called the quantity theory of the value of money – even as a rough approximation to a theoretically more satisfactory explanation of the determination of the value of money, which is all that it can ever be.[51]

The quantity theory presupposes, of course, that there is only one kind of money in circulation within a given territory, the quantity of which can be ascertained by counting its homogeneous (or near-homogeneous) units. But if the different currencies in circulation within a region have no constant relative value, the aggregate amount in circulation can only be derived from the relative value of the currencies and has no meaning apart from it. A theory which is of use only in a particular situation, even if it happened to prevail during a long period, evidently suffers from a serious defect. Though we are apt to take it for granted, it is by no means of the essence of money that within a given territory there should exist only one kind, and it is usually true only because governments have prevented the use of other kinds. Even so, it is never fully true because there are always significant differences in the demand for different forms of money and money substitutes of varying degrees of liquidity. But if we assume that issuers of currency continually compete with one another for additional users of their currency, we cannot also assume, as the quantity theory can assume with some justification with respect to a currency of a single denomination, that there exists a fairly constant demand for money in the sense that the aggregate value of the total stock will tend to be approximately constant (or change in a predictable manner with the size of the population, the gross national product, or similar magnitudes).

The cash balance approach ...

For the problems discussed in this *Paper* we certainly require a more generally applicable tool. It is fortunately available in the form of a theory which is more satisfactory even for dealing with the simpler situations: the cash balance approach deriving from Carl Menger, Leon

Walras, and Alfred Marshall. It enables us not merely to explain the ultimate effect of changes in 'the quantity of money' on 'the' general price level, but also to account for the process by which changes in the supplies of various kinds of money will successively affect different prices. It makes possible an analysis which admittedly cannot pretend to the pseudo-exactness of the quantity theory, but which has a much wider reach and can take account of the preferences of individuals for different kinds of money.

The decisive consideration to keep in mind for our present purpose is that in a multi-currency system there is no such thing as *the* magnitude of the demand for money. There will be different demands for the different kinds of currency; but since these different currencies will not be perfect substitutes, these distinct demands cannot be added up into a single sum. There may be little demand for (but large supply of) depreciating currencies, there will, we hope, be an equality of demand and supply for stable currencies (which is what will keep their values stable), and a large demand for (but little supply of) appreciating currencies. Though, so long as there exists a free market for currencies, people will be prepared to *sell* (at some price) for any currency, they will not be prepared to *hold* any currency; and the character of the available substitutes would affect the demand for any particular currency. There would therefore be no single quantity the magnitude of which could be said to be decisive for the value of money.

... and the velocity of circulation

It can be maintained that the analyses in terms of the demand for cash balances and the use of the concept of velocity of circulation by the quantity theory are formally equivalent. The difference is important. The cash balance approach directs attention to the crucial causal factor, the individuals' desire for holding stocks of money. The velocity of circulation refers to a resultant statistical magnitude which experience may show to be fairly constant over the fairly long periods for which we have useful data – thus providing some justification for claiming a simple connection between 'the' quantity of money and 'the' price level – but which is often misleading because it becomes so easily associated with the erroneous belief that monetary changes affect only the *general* level of prices. They are then often regarded as harmful chiefly for this reason, as if they raised or lowered all prices *simultaneously* and by the *same* percentage. Yet the real harm they do is due to the *differential* effect on different prices, which change successively in a very irregular order and to a very different degree, so that as a result the whole structure of relative prices becomes distorted and misguides production into wrong directions.

Unfortunately, Lord Keynes made practically no use of this most important contribution to monetary theory of the Cambridge tradition deriving from Marshall. Though criticising the alleged tendency of all contemporary monetary theory to argue as if prices all changed simultaneously, he moved almost entirely within the framework of (or argued against) the Irving Fisher type of quantity theory. It is one of the chief damages the Keynesian flood has done to the understanding of the economic process that the comprehension of the factors determining both the value of money and the effects of monetary events on the value of particular commodities has been largely lost. I cannot attempt here even a concentrated restatement of this central chapter of monetary theory but must content myself with recommending economists who have had the misfortune to study monetary theory at institutions wholly dominated by Keynesian views but who still wish to understand the theory of the value of money to fill this gap by first working through the two volumes of A. W. Marget's *Theory of Prices* [42] and then skip most of the literature of the next 25 years until Professor Axel Leijonhufvud's recent book [37],[52] which will guide them to works of the interval they ought not to miss.

A note on 'monetarism'

It has become usual, since the reaction against the dominance of the 'Keynesian' dogma set in, to lump together as 'monetarists' all who regard as mistaken Keynes's denial 'that an inflationary or deflationary movement was normally caused or necessarily accompanied' by 'changes in the quantity of money and velocity of its circulation'.[53] This 'monetarism' is of course a view held before Keynes by almost all economists except a very few dissenters and cranks, including in particular those Continental economists who by their advice on policy became responsible for the great inflations of the 1920s. I agree with these 'monetarists' in particular on what is now probably regarded as their defining characteristic, namely that they believe that all inflation is what is now called 'demand-pull' inflation, and that there is, so far as the economic mechanism is concerned, no such thing as a 'cost-push' inflation – unless one treats as part of the economic causation the political decision to increase the quantity of money in response to a rise of wages which otherwise would cause unemployment.[54]

Where I differ from the majority of other 'monetarists' and in particular from the leading representative of the school, Professor Milton Friedman, is that I regard the simple quantity theory of money, even for situations where in a given territory only one kind of money is employed, as no more than a useful rough approximation to a really adequate explanation, which, however, becomes wholly useless where several concurrent distinct kinds of money are simultaneously in use in the same territory. Though this defect becomes serious only with the multiplicity of concurrent currencies which we are considering here, the phenomenon of substitution of things not counted as money by the theory for what is counted as money by it always impairs the strict validity of its conclusions.

Its chief defect in any situation seems to me to be that by its stress on the effects of changes in the quantity of money on the general level of prices it directs all-too exclusive attention to the harmful effects of inflation and deflation on the creditor–debtor relationship, but disregards the even more important and harmful effects of the injections and withdrawals of amounts of money from circulation on the structure of relative prices and the consequent misallocation of resources and particularly the misdirection of investments which it causes.

This is not an appropriate place for a full discussion of the fine points of theory on which there exist considerable differences within the 'monetarist' school, though they are of great importance for the evaluation of the effects of the present proposals. My fundamental objection to the adequacy of the pure quantity theory of money is that, even with a single currency in circulation within a territory, there is, strictly speaking, no such thing as *the* quantity of money, and that any attempt to delimit certain groups of the media of exchange expressed in terms of a single unit as if they were homogeneous or perfect substitutes is misleading even for the usual situation. This objection becomes of decisive importance, of course, when we contemplate different concurrent currencies.

A stable price level and a high and stable level of employment do not require or permit the total quantity of money to be kept constant or to change at a constant rate. It demands something similar yet still significantly different, namely that the quantity of money (or rather the aggregate value of all the most liquid assets) be kept such that people will not reduce or increase their outlay for the purpose of adapting their balances to their altered liquidity preferences. Keeping the quantity of money constant does not assure that the money stream will remain constant, and in order to make the volume of the money stream behave in a desired manner the supply of money must possess considerable elasticity.

Monetary management cannot aim at a particular predetermined volume of circulation, not even in the case of a territorial monopolist of issue, and still less in the case of competing issues, but only at finding out what quantity will keep prices constant. No authority can beforehand ascertain, and only the market can discover, the 'optimal quantity of money'. It can be provided only by selling and buying at a fixed price the collection of commodities the aggregate price of which we wish to keep stable.

As regards Professor Friedman's proposal of a legal limit on the rate at which a monopolistic issuer of money was to be allowed to increase the quantity in circulation, I can only say that I would not like to see what would happen if under such a provision it ever became known that the amount of cash in circulation was approaching the upper limit and that therefore a need for increased liquidity could not be met.[55]

Why indexation is not a substitute for a stable currency

The usual emphasis on the most generally perceived and most painfully felt harm done by inflation, its effect on debtor–creditor relations and in particular on the receivers of fixed incomes, has led to the suggestion that these effects be mitigated by stipulating long-term obligations in terms of a 'tabular standard', the nominal sum of the debt being continuously corrected according to the changes in an index number of prices. It is, of course, correct that such a practice would eliminate the most glaring injustices caused by inflation and would remove the most severe suffering visibly due to it. But these are far from being the most severe damage which inflation causes, and the adoption of such a partial remedy for some of the symptoms would probably weaken the resistance against inflation, thus prolonging and increasing it, and in the long run considerably magnify the damage it causes and particularly the suffering it produces by bringing about unemployment.

Everybody knows of course that inflation does not affect all prices at the same time but makes different prices rise in succession, and that it therefore changes the relation between prices – although the familiar statistics of *average* price movements tend to conceal this movement in *relative* prices. The effect on relative incomes is only one, though to the superficial observer the most conspicuous, effect of the distortion of the whole structure of relative prices. What is in the long run even more damaging to the functioning of the economy and eventually tends to make a free market system unworkable is the effect of this distorted price structure in misdirecting the use of resources and drawing labour and other factors of production (especially the investment of capital) into uses which remain profitable only so long as inflation accelerates. It is this effect which produces the major waves of unemployment,[56] but which the economists using a macro-economic approach to the problem usually neglect or underrate.

This crucial damage done by inflation would in no way be eliminated by indexation. Indeed, government measures of this sort, which make it easier to live with inflation, must in the long run make things worse. They would certainly not make it easier to fight inflation, because people would be less aware that their suffering was due to inflation. There is no justification for Professor Friedman's suggestion that

> ... by removing distortions in relative prices produced by inflation, wide-spread escalator clauses would make it easier for the public to recognise changes in the rate of inflation, would thereby reduce the time-lag in adapting to such changes, and thus make the nominal price level more sensitive and variable.[57]

Such inflation, with some of its visible effect mitigated, would clearly be less resisted and last correspondingly longer.

It is true that Professor Friedman explicitly disclaims any suggestion that indexation is a substitute for stable money,[58] but he attempts to make it more tolerable in the short run and I regard any such endeavour as exceedingly dangerous. In spite of his denial it seems to me that to some degree it would even speed up inflation. It would certainly strengthen the claims of groups of workers whose real wages ought to fall (because their kind of work has become less valuable) to have their real wages kept constant. But that means that all relative increases of any wages relatively to any others would have to find expression in an increase of the nominal wages of all except those workers whose wages were the lowest, and this itself would make continuous inflation necessary.

It seems to me, in other words, like any other attempts to accept wage and price rigidities as inevitable and to adjust monetary policy to them, the attitude from which 'Keynesian' economics took its origin, to be one of those steps apparently dictated by practical necessity but bound in the long run to make the whole wage structure more and more rigid and thereby lead to the destruction of the market economy. But the present political necessity ought to be no concern of the economic scientist. His task ought to be, as I will not cease repeating, to make politically possible what today may be politically impossible. To decide what can be done at the moment is the task of the politician, not of the economist, who must continue to point out that to persist in this direction will lead to disaster.

I am in complete agreement with Professor Friedman on the inevitability of inflation under the existing political and financial institutions. But I believe that it will lead to the destruction of our civilisation unless we change the political framework. In this sense I will admit that my radical proposal concerning money will probably be practicable only as part of a much more far-reaching change in our political institutions, but an essential part of such a reform which will be recognised as necessary before long. The two distinct reforms which I am proposing in the economic and the political order[59] are indeed complementary: the sort of monetary system I propose may be possible only under a limited government such as we do not have, and a limitation of government may require that it be deprived of the monopoly of issuing money. Indeed the latter should necessarily follow from the former.

The historical evidence

Professor Friedman has since[60] more fully explained his doubts about the efficacy of my proposal and claimed that

> ... we have ample empirical and historical evidence that suggests that [my] hopes would not in fact be realised – that private currencies which offer purchasing power security would not drive out governmental currencies.

I can find no such evidence that anything like a currency of which the public has learnt to understand that the issuer can continue his business only if he maintains its currency constant, for which all the usual banking facilities are provided and which is legally recognised as an instrument for contracts, accounting and calculation has not been preferred to a deteriorating official currency, simply because such a situation seems never to have existed. It may well be that in many countries the issue of such a currency is not actually prohibited, but the other conditions are rarely if ever satisfied. And everybody knows that if such a private experiment promised to succeed, governments would at once step in to prevent it.

If we want historical evidence of what people will do where they have free choice of the currency they prefer to use, the displacement of sterling as the general unit of international trade since it began continuously to depreciate seems to me strongly to confirm my expectations. What we know about the behaviour of individuals having to cope with a bad national money, and in the face of government using every means at its disposal to force them to use it, all points to the probable success of any money which has the properties the public wants if people are not artificially deterred from using it. Americans may be fortunate in never having experienced a time when everybody in their country regarded some national currency other than their own as safer. But on the European Continent there were many occasions in which, if people had only been permitted, they would have used dollars rather than their national currencies. They did in fact do so to a much larger extent than was legally permitted, and the most severe penalties had to be threatened to prevent this habit from spreading rapidly – witness the billions of unaccounted-for dollar notes undoubtedly held in private hands all over the world.

I have never doubted that the public at large would be slow in recognising the advantages of such a new currency and have even suggested that at first, if given the opportunity, the masses would turn to gold rather than any form of other paper money. But as always the success of the few who soon recognise the advantages of a really stable currency would in the end induce the others to imitate them.

I must confess, however, that I am somewhat surprised that Professor Friedman of all people should have so little faith that competition will make the better instrument prevail when he seems to have no ground to believe that monopoly will ever provide a better one and merely fears the indolence produced by old habits.

15 The Desirable Behaviour of the Supply of Currency

We have so far provisionally assumed that the kind of money individuals will prefer to use will also be most conducive to the smooth functioning of the market process as a whole. Although this is plausible and, as we shall see, approximately true in practice, it is not self-evident. We have still to examine the validity of this belief. It is at least conceivable that the use of one particular kind of currency might be most convenient for each separate individual but that each might be better off if all the others used a different kind.

We have seen (section 13) that successful economic action (or the fulfilment of the expectations which prompted it) depends largely on the approximately correct prediction of future prices. These predictions will be based on current prices and the estimation of their trend, but future prices must always be to some degree uncertain because the circumstances which determine them will be unknown to most individuals. Indeed, the function of prices is precisely to communicate, as rapidly as possible, signals of changes of which the individual cannot know but to which his plans must be adjusted. This system works because on the whole current prices are fairly reliable indications of what future prices will probably be, subject only to those 'accidental' deviations which, as we have seen, if average prices remain constant, are likely to offset each other. We have also seen how such an offsetting of opposite disappointments becomes impossible if a substantial general movement of prices in one direction takes place.

But the current prices of particular commodities or groups of commodities can also be positively misleading if they are caused by non-recurring events, such as temporary inflows or outflows of money to the system. For such apparent changes in demand from a particular direction are in a peculiar manner self-reversing: they systematically channel productive efforts into directions where they cannot be maintained. The most important recurrent misdirections of the use of resources of this sort occur when, by the creation (or withdrawal) of amounts of money, the funds available for investment are increased substantially above (or decreased substantially below) the amounts currently transferred from consumption to investment, or saved.

Although this is the mechanism by which recurrent crises and depressions are caused, it is not a specific effect of a particular kind of currency which the users are likely to be aware of and which might therefore lead them to switch to another. We can expect the selection of the currency they use to be influenced only by such attributes as recognisably affect their actions, but not by indirect effects of changes of its amount which will operate largely through their effects on the decisions of others.

*The supply of currency, stable prices, and the equivalence
of investment and saving*

While the modern author who first drew attention to the crucial importance of these divergences between investment and saving, Knut Wicksell,
believed that they would disappear if the value of money were kept
constant, this has unfortunately proved to be not strictly correct. It is
now generally recognised that even those additions to the quantity of
money that in a growing economy are necessary to secure a *stable* price
level may cause an excess of investment over saving. But though I was
among those who early pointed out this difficulty,[61] I am inclined to
believe that it is a problem of minor practical significance. If increases
or decreases of the quantity of money never exceeded the amount necessary to keep average prices approximately constant, we would come as
close to a condition in which investment approximately corresponded
to saving as we are likely to do by any conceivable method. Compared,
anyhow, with the divergences between investment and saving which
necessarily accompany the major swings in the price level, those which
would still occur under a stable price level would probably be of an
order of magnitude about which we need not worry.

'Neutral money' fictitious

My impression is that economists have become somewhat over-ambitious
concerning the degree of stability that is either achievable or even desirable under any conceivable economic order, and that they have unfortunately encouraged political demands concerning the certainty of
employment at a hoped-for wage which in the long run no government
can satisfy. That perfect matching or correspondence of the individual
plans, which the theoretical model of a perfect market equilibrium
derives on the assumption that the money required to make indirect
exchange possible has no influence on relative prices, is a wholly fictitious
picture to which nothing in the real world can ever correspond. Although
I have myself given currency to the expression 'neutral money' (which,
as I discovered later, I had unconsciously borrowed from Wicksell), it
was intended to describe this almost universally made assumption of
theoretical analysis and to raise the question whether any real money
could ever possess this property, and not as a model to be aimed at by
monetary policy.[62] I have long since come to the conclusion that no real
money can ever be neutral in this sense, and that we must be content

with a system that rapidly corrects the inevitable errors. The nearest approach to such a condition which we can hope to achieve would appear to me to be one in which the average prices of the 'original factors of production' were kept constant. But as the average price of land and labour is hardly something for which we can find a statistical measure, the nearest practicable approximation would seem to be precisely that stability of raw material and perhaps other wholesale prices which we could hope competitively issued currencies would secure.

I will readily admit that such a provisional solution (on which the experimentation of competition might gradually improve), though giving us an infinitely better money and much more general economic stability than we have ever had, leaves open various questions to which I have no ready answer. But it seems to meet the most urgent needs much better than any prospects that seemed to exist while one did not contemplate the abolition of the monopoly of the issue of money and the free admission of competition into the business of providing currency.

Increased demand for liquidity

To dispel one kind of doubt which I myself at one stage entertained about the possibility of maintaining a stable price level, we may briefly consider here what would happen if at one time most members of a community wished to keep a much larger proportion of their assets in a highly liquid form than they did before. Would this not justify, and even require, that the value of the most liquid assets, that is, of all money, should rise compared with that of commodities?

The answer is that such needs of all individuals could be met not only by increasing the *value* of the existing liquid assets, money, but also by increasing the *amounts* they can hold. The wish of each individual to have a larger share of his resources in a very liquid form can be taken care of by additions to the total stock of money. This, paradoxically, increases the sum of the value to the individuals of all existing assets and thereby also the share of them that is highly liquid. Nothing, of course, can increase the liquidity of a closed community as a whole, if that concept has any meaning whatsoever, except, perhaps, if one wishes to extend its meaning to a shift from the production of highly specific to very versatile goods which would increase the ease of adaptation to unforeseen events.

There is no need to be afraid of spurious demands for more money on the ground that more money is needed to secure adequate liquidity.

The amount required of any currency will always be that which can be issued or kept in circulation without causing an increase or decrease of the aggregate (direct or indirect) price of the 'basket' of commodities supposed to remain constant. This rule will satisfy all legitimate demands that the variable 'needs of trade' be satisfied. And this will be true in so far as the stated collection of goods can be bought or sold at the stated aggregate price, and the absorption or release of currency from cash balances does not interfere with this condition.

It remains true, however, that so long as good and bad currencies circulate side by side, the individual cannot wholly protect himself from the harmful effects of the bad currencies by using only the good ones in his own transactions. Since the relative prices of the different commodities must be the same in terms of the different concurrent currencies, the user of a stable currency cannot escape the effects of the distortion of the price structure by the inflation (or deflation) of a widely used competing currency. The benefit of a stable course of the economic activities which, we shall argue, the use of a stable money would produce, would therefore be achieved only if the great majority of transactions were effected in stable currencies. Such a displacement of most bad money by good would, I believe, come about fairly soon, but occasional disturbances of the whole price structure and in consequence of general economic activity cannot be wholly excluded until the public has learnt rapidly to reject tempting offers of cheap money.

16 Free Banking

Some of the problems we are encountering were discussed extensively in the course of a great debate on 'free banking' during the middle of the last century, mainly in France and Germany.[63] This debate turned on the question whether commercial banks should have the right to issue bank notes redeemable in the established national gold or silver currency. Bank notes were then very much more important than the scarcely yet developed use of chequing accounts which became important only after (and in part perhaps because) the commercial banks were in the end definitely denied the right to issue bank notes. This outcome of the debate resulted in the establishment in all European countries of a single bank privileged by government to issue notes. (The United States followed only in 1914.)

A single national currency, not several competing currencies

It should be specially observed that the demand for free banking at that time was wholly a demand that the commercial banks should be allowed to issue notes in terms of the single established national currency. So far as I am aware, the possibility of competing banks issuing *different* currencies was never contemplated. That was of course a consequence of the view that only bank notes redeemable in gold or silver were practicable, and therefore that notes for other than the standard quantity of precious metal would seem to be merely inconvenient and not serve any useful purpose.

The older legitimate argument for freedom of the note issue by banks became, however, invalid once the notes they issued were no longer to be redeemed in gold or silver, for the supply of which each individual bank of issue was fully responsible, but in terms of a legal tender money provided by a privileged central bank of issue, which then was in effect under the necessity of supplying the cash needed for the redemption of the notes of the private banks of issue. That would have been a wholly indefensible system which was prevented (at least so far as the issue of notes, though not the issue of cheque deposits, was concerned) by the prohibition of private note issue.

The demands for free banking (i.e. for the free issue of bank notes) were mostly based on the ground that banks would thereby be enabled to provide more and cheaper credit. They were for the same reason resisted by those who recognised that the effect would be inflationary – although at least one advocate of the freedom of note issue had supported it on the ground that

> what is called freedom of banking would result in the total suppression of bank notes in France. I want to give everybody the right to issue bank notes so that nobody should take any bank notes any longer.[64]

The idea was, of course, that the inevitable abuse of this right, i.e. the issue of an amount of notes which the banks could not redeem from their own reserves, would lead to their failure.

The ultimate victory of the advocates of the centralisation of the national note issue was, however, in effect softened by a concession to those who were mainly interested in the banks being able to provide cheap credit. It consisted in the acknowledgement of a duty of the privileged bank of issue to supply the commercial banks with any notes they needed in order to redeem their demand deposits – rapidly growing in importance. This decision, or rather recognition of a practice into which central banks had drifted, produced a most unfortunate hybrid system in which responsibility for the total quantity of money was divided in a fatal manner so that nobody was in a position to control it effectively.

Demand deposits are like bank notes or cheques

This unfortunate development came about because for a long time it was not generally understood that deposits subject to cheque played very much the same rôle, and could be created by the commercial banks in exactly the same manner, as bank notes. The consequent dilution of what was still believed to be a government monopoly of the issue of all money resulted in the control of the total circulation of money being divided between a central bank and a large number of commercial banks whose creation of credit it could influence only indirectly. Not till much later did it come to be understood that the 'inherent instability of credit'[65] under that system was a necessary outcome of this feature; that liquid means was mostly supplied by institutions which themselves had to keep liquid in terms of another form of money, so that they had to *reduce* their outstanding obligations precisely when everybody else also desired to be *more* liquid. By that time this kind of structure had become so firmly established that, in spite of the 'perverse elasticity of the supply of credit'[66] it produced, it came to be regarded as unalterable. Walter Bagehot had clearly seen this dilemma a hundred years ago but despaired of the possibility of remedying this defect of the firmly established banking structure.[67] And Wicksell and later von Mises made it clear that this arrangement must lead to violent recurring fluctuations of business activity – the so-called 'trade-cycle'.

New controls over currencies; new banking practices

Not the least advantage of the proposed abolition of the government monopoly of the issue of money is that it would provide an opportunity to extricate ourselves from the *impasse* into which this development had led. It would create the conditions in which responsibility for the control of the quantity of the currency is placed on agencies whose self-interest would make them control it in such a manner as to make it most acceptable to the users.

This also shows that the proposed reform requires a complete change in the practices not only of the banks which take up the business of issuing currency but also of those which do not. For the latter could no longer rely on being bailed out by a central bank if they could not meet from their own reserves their customers' demands for cash – not even if they chose to keep their accounts in terms of the currency issued by a still existing governmental central bank which, to maintain its circulation, would have to adopt the practices of the other issuing banks with which it competed.

Opposition to new system from established bankers ...

This necessity of all banks to develop wholly new practices will undoubtedly be the cause of strong opposition to the abolition of the government monopoly. It is unlikely that most of the older bankers, brought up in the prevailing routine of banking, will be capable of coping with those problems. I am certain that many of the present leaders of the profession will not be able to conceive how it could possibly work and therefore will describe the whole system as impracticable and impossible.

Especially in countries where competition among banks has for generations been restricted by cartel arrangements, usually tolerated and even encouraged by governments, the older generation of bankers would probably be completely unable even to imagine how the new system would operate and therefore be practically unanimous in rejecting it. But this foreseeable opposition of the established practitioners ought not to deter us. I am also convinced that if a new generation of young bankers were given the opportunity they would rapidly develop techniques to make the new forms of banking not only safe and profitable but also much more beneficial to the whole community than the existing one.

... and from banking cranks

Another curious source of opposition, at least once they had discovered that the effects of 'free banking' would be exactly the opposite of those they expected, would be all the numerous cranks who had advocated 'free banking' from inflationist motives.[68] Once the public had an alternative, it would become impossible to induce it to hold cheap money, and the desire to get rid of currency that threatened to depreciate would indeed rapidly turn it into a dwindling money. The inflationists would protest because in the end only very 'hard' money would remain. *Money is the one thing competition would not make cheap, because its attractiveness rests on it preserving its 'dearness'.*

The problem of a 'dear' (stable) money

A competition the chief merit of which is that it keeps the products of the competitors dear raises various interesting questions. In what will the suppliers compete once they have established somewhat similar reputations and trust for keeping their currencies stable? The profits from the issuing business (which amounts to borrowing at zero interest) will be very large and it does not seem probable that very many firms can succeed in it. For this reason services to the enterprises basing their accounting on a bank's currency would be likely to become the chief weapon of competition, and I should not be surprised if the banks were practically to take over the accounting for their customers.

Though even very large profits of the successfully established issuers of currency would not be too high a price for a good money, they would inevitably create great political difficulties. Quite apart from the inevitable outcry against the profits of the money monopoly, the real threat to the system would be the cupidity of Ministers of Finance who would soon claim a share in them for the permission to allow a currency to circulate in their country, which would of course spoil everything. It might indeed prove to be nearly as impossible for a democratic government not to interfere with money as to regulate it sensibly.

The real danger is thus that, while today the people submissively put up with almost any abuse of the money prerogative by government, as soon as it will be possible to say that money is issued by 'rich financial institutions', the complaint about their abuse of the alleged monopoly will become incessant. To wring from the money power their alleged privilege will become the constant demand of demagogues. I trust the banks would be wise enough not to desire even a distant approach to a monopoly position, but to limit the volume of their business may become one of their most delicate problems.

17   No More General Inflation or Deflation?

Neither a *general* increase nor a *general* decrease of prices appears to be possible in normal circumstances so long as several issuers of different currencies are allowed freely to compete without the interference of government. There will always be one or more issuers who find it to their advantage to regulate the supply of their currency so as to keep its value constant in step with the aggregate price of a bundle of widely used commodities. This would soon force any less provident issuers of competing currencies to put a stop to a slide in the value of their currency in either direction if they did not wish to lose the issue business altogether or to find the value of their currency falling to zero.

No such thing as oil-price (or any other) cost-push inflation

It is, of course, taken for granted here that the average prices in terms of a currency can always be controlled by appropriate adjustments of its quantity. Theoretical analysis and experience seem to me alike to confirm this proposition. We need therefore pay no attention to the views always advanced in periods of prolonged inflation in attempts to exculpate governments by contending that the continued rise in prices is not the fault of policy but the result of an initial rise in costs. To this claim it must be replied emphatically that, in the strict sense, there is simply no such thing as a 'cost-push' inflation. Neither higher wages nor higher prices of oil, or perhaps of imports generally, can drive up the aggregate price of all goods *unless the purchasers are given more money to buy them.* What is called a cost-push inflation is merely the effect of increases in the quantity of money which governments feel forced to provide in order to prevent the unemployment resulting from a rise in wages (or other costs), which preceded it and which was conceded in the expectation that government would increase the quantity of money. They mean thereby to make it possible for all the workers to find employment through a rise in the demand for their products. If government did not increase the quantity of money such a rise in the wages of a group of workers would not lead to a rise in the general price level but simply to a reduction in sales and therefore to unemployment.

It is, however, worth considering a little more fully what would happen if a cartel or other monopolistic organisation, such as a trade union, did succeed in substantially raising the price of an important raw material or the wages of a large group of workers, fixing them in terms of a currency which the issuer .endeavours to keep stable. In such circumstances the stability of the price level in terms of this currency could be achieved only by the reduction of a number of other prices. If people have to pay a larger amount of money for the oil or the books and printed papers they consume, they will have to consume less of some other things.

The problem of rigid prices and wages

No currency, of course, can remove the rigidity of some prices which has developed. But it can make impossible the policies which have assisted this development by making it necessary for those who hold prices rigid in the face of a reduced demand to accept the consequent loss of sales.

The whole difference of approach between the dominant 'Keynesian' school and the view underlying the present exposition rests in the last resort on the position taken with regard to the phenomenon of rigid prices and wages. Keynes was largely led to his views by his belief that the increasing rigidity of wages was an unalterable fact which had to be accepted and the effect of which could be mitigated only by accommodating the rate of money expenditure to the given rate of wages. (This opinion was in some measure justified in the British position in the 1920s, when, as a result of an injudicious attempt to raise the external value of the pound, most British wages had become out of line with international commodity prices.) I have maintained ever since that such an adaptation of the quantity of money to the rigidity of some prices and particularly wages would greatly extend the range of such rigidities and must therefore, in the long run, entirely destroy the functioning of the market.

The error of the 'beneficial mild inflation'

All inflation is so very dangerous precisely because many people, including many economists, regard a mild inflation as harmless and even beneficial. But there are few mistakes of policy with regard to which it is more important to heed the old maxim *principiis obsta*.[69] Apparently, and surprisingly, the self-accelerating mechanism of all engineered inflation is not yet understood even by some economists. The initial general stimulus which an increase of the quantity of money provides is chiefly due to the fact that prices and therefore profits turn out to be higher than expected. Every venture succeeds, including even some which ought to fail. But this can last only so long as the continuous rise of prices is not generally expected. Once people learn to count on it, even a continued rise of prices at the same rate will no longer exert the stimulus that it gave at first.

Monetary policy is then faced with an unpleasant dilemma. In order to maintain the degree of activity it created by mild inflation, it will have to accelerate the rate of inflation, and will have to do so again and again at an ever increasing rate every time the prevailing rate of inflation comes to be expected. If it fails to do so and either stops accelerating or ceases to inflate altogether, the economy will be in a much worse position than when the process started. Not only has inflation allowed the ordinary errors of judgement to accumulate which are normally promptly eliminated and will now all have to be liquidated at the same time. It will in addition have caused misdirection of production and drawn labour and other resources into activities which could be maintained only if the additional investment financed by the increase in the quantity of money could be maintained.

Since it has become generally understood that whoever controls the total supply of money of a country has thereby power to give in most situations almost instantaneous relief to unemployment, even if only at the price of much unemployment later, the political pressure on such an agency must become irresistible. The threat of that possibility has always been understood by some economists, who for this reason have ever been anxious to restrain the monetary authorities by barriers they could not break. But since the betrayal, or ignorance, of this insight by a school of theorists which thereby bought themselves temporary popularity, political control of the supply of money has become too dangerous to the preservation of the market order to be any longer tolerated. However much political pressure might be brought on the most important private banks of issue to make them relax their credit conditions and extend their circulation, if a *non-monopolistic* institution gave in to such pressure it would soon cease to be one of the most important issuers.

The 'money illusion', i.e. the belief that money represents a constant value, could arise only because it was useless to worry about changes in the value of money so long as one could not do anything about it. Once people have a choice they will become very much aware of the different changes of the value of the different currencies accessible to them. It would, as it should, become common knowledge that money needs to be watched, and would be regarded as a praiseworthy action rather than as an unpatriotic deed to warn people that a particular currency was suspect.

Responsibility for unemployment would be traced back to trade unions

Depriving government of the power of thus counteracting the effects of monopolistically enforced increases in wages or prices by increasing the quantity of money would place the responsibility for the full use of resources back to where it belongs: where the causally effective decisions are taken – the monopolists who negotiate the wages or prices. We ought to understand by now that the attempt to combat by inflation the unemployment caused by the monopolistic actions of trade unions will merely postpone the effects on employment to the time when the rate of inflation required to maintain employment by continually increasing the quantity of money becomes unbearable. The sooner we can make impossible such harmful measures, probably unavoidable so long as government has the monetary power to take them, the better for all concerned.

The scheme proposed here would, indeed, do somewhat more than prevent only inflations and deflations in the strict sense of these terms. Not all changes in the general level of prices are caused by changes in the quantity of money, or its failure to adapt itself to changes in the demand for holding money; and only those brought about in this manner can properly be called inflation or deflation. It is true that there are nowadays unlikely to be large simultaneous changes in the supply of many of the most important goods, as happened when variations in harvests could cause dearths or gluts of most of the main foodstuffs and clothing materials. And, even today, perhaps in wartime in a country surrounded by enemies or on an island, an acute scarcity (or glut) of the products in which the country has specialised is perhaps conceivable. At least if the index number of commodity prices that guided the issue of the currency in the country were based chiefly on national prices, such a rule might lead to changes in the supply of currency designed to counteract price movements not caused by monetary factors.

Preventing general deflation

The reader may not yet feel fully reassured that, in the kind of competitive money system we are here contemplating, a general deflation will be as impossible as a general inflation. Experience seems indeed to have shown that, in conditions of severe uncertainty or alarm about the future, even very low rates of interest cannot prevent a shrinking of a bank's outstanding loans. What could a bank issuing its own distinct currency do when it finds itself in such a situation, and commodity prices in terms of its currency threaten to fall? And how strong would be its interest in stopping such a fall of prices if the same circumstances affected the competing institutions in the same way?

There would of course be no difficulty in placing additional money at a time when people in general want to keep very liquid. The issuing bank, on the other hand, would not wish to incur an obligation to maintain by redemption a value of its currency higher than that at which it had issued it. To maintain profitable investments, the bank would presumably be driven to buy interest-bearing securities and thereby put cash into the hands of people looking for other investments as well as bring down the long-term rates of interest, with a similar effect. An institution with a very large circulation of currency might even find it expedient to buy for storage quantities of commodities represented in the index that tended to fall particularly strongly in price.

This would probably be sufficient to counteract any downward tendency of general prices produced by the economic process itself, and if it achieved this effect it is probably as much as can be accomplished by any management of money. But it is of course not to be wholly excluded that some events may cause such a general state of discouragement and lethargy that nothing could induce people to resume investment and thereby stop an impending fall of prices. So far as this were due to extraneous events, such as the fear of an impending world catastrophe or of the imminent advent of communism, or in some region the desire to convert all private possessions into cash to be prepared for flight, probably nothing could prevent a general fall in the prices of possessions that are not easily portable. But so long as the general conditions for the effective conduct of capitalist enterprise persisted, competition would provide a money that caused as little disturbance to its working as possible. And this is probably all we can hope.[70]

18 Monetary Policy Neither Desirable Nor Possible

It is true that under the proposed arrangements monetary policy as we now know it could not exist. It is not to be denied that, with the existing sort of division of responsibility between the issues of the basic money and those of a parasitic circulation based on it, central banks must, to prevent matters from getting completely out of hand, try deliberately to forestall developments they can only influence but not directly control. But the central banking system, which only 50 years ago was regarded as the crowning achievement of financial wisdom, has largely discredited itself. This is even more true since, with the abandonment of the gold standard and fixed exchange rates, the central banks have acquired fuller discretionary powers than when they were still trying to act on firm rules. And this is true no less where the aim of policy is still a reasonable degree of stability, as in countries overwhelmed by inflation.

Government the major source of instability

We have it on the testimony of a competent authority who was by no means unsympathetic to those modern aspirations that, during the recent decade 1962 to 1972 when the believers in a 'fine tuning' of monetary policy had an influence which we must hope they will never have again, the larger part of the fluctuations were a consequence of budgetary and monetary policy.[71] And it is certainly impossible to claim that the period since the abandonment of the semi-automatic regulation of the quantity of money has *generally* been more stable or free from monetary disturbances than the periods of the gold standard or fixed rates of exchange.

We indeed begin to see how completely different an economic landscape the free issue of competitive currencies would produce when we realise that under such a system what is known today as monetary policy would neither be needed nor even possible. The issuing banks, guided solely by their striving for gain, would thereby serve the public interest better than any institution has ever done or could do that supposedly aimed at it. There neither would exist a definable quantity of money of a nation or region, nor would it be desirable that the individual issuers of the several currencies should aim at anything but to make as large as possible the aggregate value of their currency that the public was prepared to hold at the given value of the unit. If we are right that, being able to choose, the public would prefer a currency whose purchasing power it could expect to be stable, this would provide a better currency and secure more stable business conditions than have ever existed before.

The supposed chief weakness of the market order, the recurrence of periods of mass unemployment, is always pointed out by socialists and other critics as an inseparable and unpardonable defect of capitalism.[72] It proves in fact wholly to be the result of government preventing private enterprise from working freely and providing itself with a money that would secure stability. We have seen that there can be no doubt that free enterprise would have been both able to provide a money securing stability and that striving for individual gain would have driven private financial institutions to do so if they had been permitted. I am not sure that private enterprise would adopt the manner of performing the task I have suggested, but I am inclined to think that, by its habitual procedure of selecting the most successful, it would in time throw up better solutions to these problems than anyone can foresee today.

Monetary policy a cause of depressions

What we should have learned is that monetary policy is much more likely to be a cause than a cure of depressions, because it is much easier, by giving in to the clamour for cheap money, to cause those misdirections of production that make a later reaction inevitable, than to assist the economy in extricating itself from the consequences of overdeveloping in particular directions. *The past instability of the market economy is the consequence of the exclusion of the most important regulator of the market mechanism, money, from itself being regulated by the market process.*

A single monopolistic governmental agency can neither possess the information which should govern the supply of money nor would it, if it knew what it ought to do in the general interest, usually be in a position to act in that manner. Indeed, if, as I am convinced, the main advantage of the market order is that prices will convey to the acting individuals the relevant information, only the constant observation of the course of current prices of particular commodities can provide information on the direction in which more or less money ought to be spent. Money is not a tool of policy that can achieve particular foreseeable results by control of its quantity. But it should be part of the self-steering mechanism by which individuals are constantly induced to adjust their activities to circumstances on which they have information only through the abstract signals of prices. It should be a serviceable link in the process that communicates the effects of events never wholly known to anybody and that is required to maintain an order in which the plans of participating persons match.

Government cannot act in the general interest

Yet even if we assumed that government could know what should be done about the supply of money in the general interest, it is highly unlikely that it would be able to act in that manner. As Professor Eckstein, in the article quoted above, concludes from his experience in advising governments:

> Governments are not able to live by the rules even if they were to adopt the philosophy [of providing a stable framework].[73]

Once governments are given the power to benefit particular groups or sections of the population, the mechanism of majority government forces them to use it to gain the support of a sufficient number of them to command a majority. The constant temptation to meet local or sectional dissatisfaction by manipulating the quantity of money so that more can be spent on services for those clamouring for assistance will often be irresistible. Such expenditure is not an appropriate remedy but necessarily upsets the proper functioning of the market.

In a true emergency such as war, governments would of course still be able to force upon people bonds or other pieces of paper for unavoidable payments which cannot be made from current revenues. Compulsory loans and the like would probably be more compatible with the required rapid readjustments of industry to radically changed circumstances than an inflation that suspends the effective working of the price mechanism.

No more balance-of-payment problems

With the disappearance of distinct territorial currencies there would of course also disappear the so-called 'balance-of-payment problems' believed to cause intense difficulties to present-day monetary policy. There would, necessarily, be continuous redistributions of the relative and absolute quantities of currency in different regions as some grew relatively richer and others relatively poorer. But this would create no more difficulties than the same process causes today within any large

country. People who grew richer would have more money and those
who grew poorer would have less. That would be all. The special
difficulties caused by the fact that under existing arrangements the
reduction of the distinct cash basis of one country requires a contraction
of the whole separate superstructure of credit erected on it would no
longer exist.

Similarly, the closer connections of the structure of the prices prevailing within any one country as against prices in neighbouring
countries, and with it the statistical illusion of the relative movement of
distinct national price levels, would largely disappear. Indeed it would
be discovered that 'balance-of-payment problems' are a quite unnecessary effect of the existence of distinct national currencies, which is the
cause of the wholly undesirable closer coherence of national prices
than of international prices. From the angle of a desirable international
economic order the 'balance-of-payment problem' is a pseudo-problem
about which nobody need worry but a monopolist of the issue of money
for a given territory. And not the least advantage of the disappearance
of distinct national currencies would be that we could return to the
happy days of statistical innocence in which nobody could know what
the balance of payment of his country or region was and thus nobody
could worry or would have to care about it.

The addictive drug of cheap money

The belief that cheap money is always desirable and beneficial makes
inevitable and irresistible the pressure on any political authority or
monopolist known to be capable of making money cheap by issuing
more of it. Yet loanable funds made artificially cheap by creating more
money for lending them, not only help those to whom they are lent,
though at the expense of others, but for a while have a general stimulating
effect on business activity. That at the same time such issues have the
effect of destroying the steering mechanism of the market is not so easily
seen. But supplies of such funds for additional purchases of goods
produce a distortion of the structure of relative prices which draws
resources into activities that cannot be lastingly maintained and thereby
become the cause of an inevitable later reaction. These indirect and slow
effects are, however, in their nature very much more difficult to recognise
or understand than the immediate pleasant effects and particularly the
benefits to those to whom the additional money goes in the first instance.

To provide a medium of exchange for people who want to hold it until they wish to buy an equivalent for what they have supplied to others is a useful service like producing any other good. If an increase in the demand for such cash balances is met by an increase of the quantity of money (or a reduction of the balances people want to hold by a corresponding decrease of the total amount of money), it does not disturb the correspondence between demand and supply of all other commodities or services. But it is really a crime like theft to enable some people to buy more than they have earned by more than the amount which other people have at the same time foregone to claim.

When committed by a monopolistic issuer of money, and especially by government, it is however a very lucrative crime which is generally tolerated and remains unpunished because its consequences are not understood. But for the issuer of a currency which has to compete with other currencies, it would be a suicidal act, because it would destroy the service for which people did want to hold his currency.

Because of a lack of general understanding, the crime of over-issue by a monopolist is still not only tolerated but even applauded. That is one of the chief reasons why the smooth working of the market is so frequently upset. But today almost any statesman who tries to do good in this field, and certainly anyone forced to do what the large organised interests think good, is therefore likely to do much more harm than good. On the other hand, anyone who merely knows that the success of his business of issuing money rests wholly on his ability to keep the buying power of his currency constant, will do more for the public good by aiming solely at large profits for himself than by any conscious concern about the more remote effects of his actions.

The abolition of central banks

Perhaps a word should be explicitly inserted here about the obvious corollary that the abolition of the government monopoly of the issue of money should involve also the disappearance of central banks as we know them, both because one might conceive of some private bank assuming the function of a central bank and because it might be thought that, even without a government monopoly of issue, some of the classic functions of central banks, such as that of acting as 'lender of last resort' or of 'holder of the ultimate reserve', [74] might still be required.

The need for such an institution is, however, entirely due to the commercial banks incurring liabilities payable on demand in a unit of currency which some other bank has the sole right to issue, thus in effect creating money redeemable in terms of another money. This, as we shall have still to consider, is indeed the chief cause of the instability of the existing credit system, and through it of the wide fluctuations in all economic activity. Without the central bank's (or the government's) monopoly of issuing money, and the legal tender provisions of the law, there would be no justification whatever for the banks to rely for their solvency on the cash to be provided by another body. The 'one reserve system', as Walter Bagehot called it, is an inseparable accompaniment of the monopoly of issue but unnecessary and undesirable without it.

It might still be argued that central banks are necessary to secure the required 'elasticity' of the circulation. And though this expression has probably in the past been more abused than any other to disguise inflationist demands, we must not overlook its valid kernel. The manner in which elasticity of supply and stability of value of the money can be reconciled is a genuine problem, and it will be solved only if the issuer of a given currency is aware that his business depends on so regulating the quantity of his currency that the value of its unit remains stable (in terms of commodities). If an addition to the quantity would lead to a rise of prices, it would clearly not be justified, however urgently some may feel that they need additional cash – which then will be cash to spend and not to add to their liquidity reserves. What makes a currency a universally acceptable, that is really liquid, asset will be precisely that it is preferred to other assets because its buying power is expected to remain constant.

What is necessarily scarce is not liquidity but buying power – the command over goods for consumption or use in further production, and this is limited because there is no more than a given amount of these things to buy. So far as people want more liquid assets solely to hold them but not to spend them, they can be manufactured without thereby depreciating their value. But if people want more liquid assets in order to spend them on goods, the value of such credits will melt between their fingers.

No fixing of rates of interest

With the central banks and the monopoly of the issue of money would, of course, disappear also the possibility of deliberately determining the rate of interest. The disappearance of what is called 'interest policy' is wholly desirable. The rate of interest, like any other price, ought to record the aggregate effects of thousands of circumstances affecting the demand for and supply of loans which cannot possibly be known to any one agency. The effects of most price changes are unpleasant to some, and, like other price changes, changes in the rate of interest convey to all concerned that an aggregate of circumstances which nobody knows has made them necessary. The whole idea that the rate of interest ought to be used as an instrument of policy is entirely mistaken, since only competition in a free market can take account of all the circumstances which ought to be taken account of in the determination of the rate of interest.

So long as each separate issue bank in its lending activity aimed at regulating the volume of its outstanding currency so as to keep its buying power constant, the rate of interest at which it could do so would be determined for it by the market. And, on the whole, the lending for investment purposes of all the banks together, if it was not to drive up the price level, could not exceed the current volume of savings (and conversely, if it was not to depress the price level, must not fall short of the current volume of savings) by more than was required to increase aggregate demand in step with a growing volume of output. The rate of interest would then be determined by balancing the demand for money for spending purposes with the supply required for keeping the price level constant. I believe this would assure as close an agreement between saving and investment as we can hope to achieve, leaving a balance of change in the quantity of money to take account of changes in the demand for money caused by changes in the balances people want to hold.

Of course, government would still affect this market rate of interest by the net volume of its borrowing. But it could no longer practise those most pernicious manipulations of the rate of interest which are intended to enable it to borrow cheaply – a practice which has done so much harm in the past that this effect alone would seem an adequate reason why government should be kept away from the tap.

19 A Better Discipline than Fixed Rates of Exchange

Readers who know of my consistent support over more than 40 years of fixed rates of exchange between national currencies, and of my critique of a system of flexible rates of foreign exchange,[75] even after most of my fellow defenders of a free market had become converts to this system, will probably feel at first that my present position is in conflict with, or even represents a complete reversal of, my former views. This is not so. In two respects my present proposal is a result of the further development of the considerations which determined my former position.

In the first instance, I have always regarded it as thoroughly undesirable that the structure of the prices of commodities and services in one country should be lifted and lowered as a whole relatively to the price structure of other countries in order to correct some alteration in the supply of or demand for a particular commodity. This was erroneously thought to be necessary chiefly because the availability of statistical information in the form of index numbers of the *average* movement of prices in one country gave the misleading impression that 'the internal value' of one currency as such had to be changed relatively to the value of other currencies, while what was required were primarily changes of the relations between particular prices in all the countries concerned. So far as the assumed necessity of changes in relation between general prices in the countries was true, this was an artificial and undesirable effect of the imperfection of the international monetary system which the gold standard with a superstructure of deposit money produced. We will consider these questions further in the next section.

Remove protection of official currency from competition

Secondly, I had regarded fixed rates of exchange as necessary for the same reason for which I now plead for completely free markets for all kinds of currency, namely that it was required to impose a very necessary discipline or restraint on the agencies issuing money. Neither I, nor apparently anybody else, then thought of the much more effective discipline that would operate if the providers of money were deprived of the power of shielding the money they issued against the rivalry of *competing currencies*.

The compulsion to maintain a fixed rate of redemption in terms of gold or other currencies has in the past provided the only discipline that effectively prevented monetary authorities from giving in to the demands of the ever-present pressure for cheap money. The gold standard, fixed rates of exchange, or any other form of obligatory conversion at a fixed rate, served no other purpose than to impose upon the issuers of money such a discipline and, by making its regulation automatic, to deprive them of the power arbitrarily to change the quantity of money. It is a discipline that has proved too weak to prevent governments from breaking it. Yet, though the regulations achieved by those automatic controls were far from ideal or even tolerably satisfactory, so long as currencies were thus regulated they were much more satisfactory than anything the discretionary powers of governmental monopolies have ever achieved for any length of time. Nothing short of the belief that it would be a national disgrace for a country not to live up to its obligations has ever sufficed adequately to strengthen the resistance of monetary authorities against pressures for cheap money. I should never have wanted to deny that a very wise and politically independent monetary authority might do better than it is compelled to do in order to preserve a fixed parity with gold or another currency. But I can see no hope of monetary authorities in the real world prevailing for any length of time in their good intentions.

Better even than gold – the 'wobbly anchor'

It ought by now of course to be generally understood that the value of a currency redeemable in gold (or in another currency) is not *derived* from the value of that gold, but merely kept at the same value through the automatic regulation of its quantity. The superstition dies only slowly, but even under a gold standard it is no more (or perhaps even less) true that the value of the currency is determined by the value in other uses of the gold it contains (or by its costs of production) than is the converse, that the value of gold is determined by the value of the currencies into which it can be converted. Historically it is true that all the money that preserved its value for any length of time was metallic (or money convertible into metal – gold or silver); and governments sooner or later used to debase even metallic money, so that all the kinds of paper money of which we have experience were so much worse. Most people therefore now believe that relief can come only from returning to a metallic (or other commodity) standard. But not only is a metallic money also exposed to the risks of fraud by government; even at its best it would never be as good a money as one issued by an agency whose whole business rested on its success in providing a money the public preferred to other kinds. Though gold is an anchor – and any anchor is better than a money left to the discretion of government – it is a very wobbly anchor. It certainly could not bear the strain if the majority of countries tried to run their own gold standard. There just is not enough gold about. An international gold standard could today mean only that a few countries maintained a real gold standard while the others hung on to them through a gold exchange standard.

Competition would provide better money than would government

I believe we can do much better than gold ever made possible. Governments cannot do better. Free enterprise, i.e. the institutions that would emerge from a process of competition in providing good money, no doubt would. There would in that event also be no need to encumber the money supply with the complicated and expensive provision for convertibility which was necessary to secure the automatic operation of the gold standard and which made it appear as at least more practicable than what would ideally seem much more suitable – a commodity reserve standard. A very attractive scheme for storing a large variety of raw materials and other standard commodities had been worked out for such a standard to ensure the redeemability of the currency unit by a fixed combination of such commodities and thereby the stability of the currency. Storage would however be so expensive, and practicable only for such a small collection of commodities, as to reduce the value of the proposal.[76] But some such precaution to force the issuer to regulate the amount of his currency appears necessary or desirable only so long as his interest would be to increase or decrease its value above or below the standard. Convertibility is a safeguard necessary to impose upon a *monopolist*, but unnecessary with *competing* suppliers who cannot maintain themselves in the business unless they provide money at least as advantageous to the user as anybody else.

Government monopoly of money unnecessary

Not so very long ago, in 1960, I myself argued that it is not only impracticable but probably undesirable even if possible to deprive governments of their control over monetary policy.[77] This view was still based on the common tacit assumption that there must be in each country a single uniform kind of money. I did not then even consider the possibility of true competition between currencies within any given country or region. If only one kind of money is permitted, it is probably true that the monopoly of its issue must be under the control of government. The concurrent circulation of several currencies might at times be slightly inconvenient, but careful analysis of its effects indicates that the advantages appear to be so very much greater than the inconveniences that they hardly count in comparison, though unfamiliarity with the new situation makes them appear much bigger than they probably would be.

Difference between voluntarily accepted and enforced paper money

Much as all historical experience appears to justify the deep mistrust most people harbour against paper money, it is well founded only with regard to money issued by *government*. Frequently the term 'fiat money' is used as if it applied to all paper money, but the expression refers of course only to money which has been given currency by the arbitrary decree or other act of authority. Money which is current only because people have been forced to accept it is wholly different from money that has come to be accepted because people trust the issuer to keep it stable. Voluntarily accepted paper money therefore ought not to suffer from the evil reputation governments have given paper money.

Money is valued because, and in so far as, it is known to be scarce, and is for this reason likely to be accepted at the going value by others. And any money which is voluntarily used only because it is trusted to be kept scarce by the issuer, and which will be held by people only so long as the issuer justifies that trust, will increasingly confirm its acceptability at the established value. People will know that the risk they run in holding it will be smaller than the risk they run in holding any other good on which they do not possess special information. Their willingness to hold it will rest on the experience that other people will be ready to accept it at an approximately known range of prices because they also have learnt to hold the same expectation, and so on. This is a state of affairs that can continue indefinitely and will even tend to stabilise itself more and more as confirmed expectations increase the trust.

Some people apparently find it difficult to believe that a mere token money which did not give the holder a legal claim for redemption in terms of some object possessing an intrinsic value (equal to its current value) could ever be generally accepted for any length of time or preserve its value. They seem to forget that for the past 40 years in the whole Western world there has been no other money than such irredeemable tokens. The various paper currencies we have had to use have preserved a value which for some time was only slowly decreasing not because of any hope of ultimate redemption, but only because the monopolistic agencies authorised to issue the exclusive kind of currency of a particular country did in some inadequate degree restrict its amount. But the clause on a pound-note saying 'I promise to pay to the bearer on demand the sum of one pound', or whatever the figure be, signed for the Governor and Company of the Bank of England by their Chief Cashier, means of course no more than that they promise to exchange that piece of paper for other pieces of paper.

It is entirely at the discretion of these institutions or governments to regulate the total amount of their issues in circulation by exchanging some of the notes for other kinds of money or for securities. This sort of redemption is just a method of regulating the quantity of money in the hands of the public, and, so long as public opinion was not misguided by specious theories, it has always been taken as a matter of course that, e.g. 'the value of [greenbacks] changes as the government chooses to enlarge or to contract the issue'.[78]

History certainly disproves the suggestion that in this respect government, which only profits from excessive issues, can be trusted more than a private issuer whose whole business depends on his not abusing that trust. Does anyone really believe that in the industrial countries of the West, after the experience of the last half-century, anybody trusts the value of government-sponsored money more than he would trust money issued by a private agency whose business was understood to depend wholly on its issuing good money?

20 Should There be Separate Currency Areas?

We are so used to the existence in each country of a distinct currency in which practically all internal transactions are conducted that we tend to regard it also as natural and necessary for the whole structure of internal prices to move together relatively to the price structure of other countries. This is by no means a necessary or in any sense natural or desirable state of affairs.

National currencies not inevitable or desirable

At least without tariffs or other obstructions to the free movement of goods and men across frontiers, the tendency of national prices to move in unison is an *effect* of, rather than a justification for, maintaining separate national currency systems. And it has led to the growth of national institutions, such as nation-wide collective bargaining, which have intensified these differences. The reason for this development is that the control over the supply of money gives national governments more power over actions which are wholly undesirable from the point of view of international order and stability. It is the kind of arrangement of which only *étatists* of various complexions can approve but which is wholly inimical to frictionless international relations.

There is indeed little reason why, apart from the effects of monopolies made possible by national protection, territories that happen to be under the same government should form distinct national economic areas which would benefit by having a common currency distinct from that of other areas. In an order largely dependent on international exchange, it was rather absurd to treat the often accidental agglomeration of different regions under the same government as a distinct economic area. The recognition of this truth has, however, only recently led a few economists to ask what would be desirable currency areas – a question they found rather difficult to answer.[79]

While historically distinct national currencies were simply an instrument to enhance the power of national governments, the modern argument for monetary nationalism favours an arrangement under which *all* prices in a region can simultaneously be raised or lowered *relatively* to *all* prices in other regions. This is regarded as an advantage because it avoids the necessity to lower a group of particular prices, especially wages, when foreign demand for the products concerned has fallen and shifted to some other national region. But it is a political makeshift; in practice it means that, instead of lowering the *few* prices immediately affected, a very much *larger* number of prices will have to be raised to restore international equilibrium after the international price of the local currency has been reduced. The original motive for the agitation for flexible rates of exchange between national currencies was therefore purely inflationist, although a foolish attempt was made to place the burden of adjustment on the surplus countries. But it was later also taken up in countries which wanted to protect themselves against the effects of the inflationist policies of others.

There is no better case for preventing the decrease of the quantity of money circulating in a region or sector of a larger community than there is for governmental measures to prevent a decrease of the money incomes of particular individuals or groups – even though such measures might temporarily relieve the hardships of the groups living there. It is even essential for honest government that nobody should have the power of relieving groups from the necessity of having to adapt themselves to unforeseen changes, because, if government can do so, it will be forced by political necessity to do so all the time.

Rigidity of wage rates: raising national price structure is no solution

Experience has shown that what was believed to be the easy way out from the difficulties created by the rigidity of wages, namely, raising the *whole* national price level, is merely making matters worse, since in effect it relieves trade unions of the responsibility for the unemployment their wage demands would otherwise cause and creates an irresistible pressure on governments to mitigate these effects by inflation. I remain therefore as opposed to monetary nationalism[80] or flexible rates of exchange between national currencies as ever. But I prefer now abolishing monetary frontiers altogether to merely making national currencies convertible into each other at a fixed rate. The whole conception of cutting out a particular sector from the international structure of prices and lifting or lowering it, as it were, bodily against all the other prices of the same commodities still seems to me an idea that could be conceived only in the brains of men who have come to think exclusively in terms of national ('macro') price levels, not of individual ('micro') prices. They seem to have thought of national price levels as the acting determinants of human action and to have ceased to understand the function of relative prices.

Stable national price level could disrupt economic activity

There is really no reason why we should want the price level of a region interconnected by a large number of commodity streams with the rest of the world economy to have a stable price level. To keep this price level stable in spite of shifts of demand towards or away from the region only disturbs and does not assist the functioning of the market. The relation between regions or localities is in this respect not essentially different from the relations between countries. The transfer of demand for airplanes from Seattle to Los Angeles will indeed lead to a loss of jobs and a decline of incomes and probably of retail prices in Seattle; and if there is a fall in wages in Seattle, it will probably attract other industries. But nothing would be gained, except perhaps for the moment, by increasing the quantity of money in Seattle or the State of Washington. And it would not ease the problem if the whole North West of the United States had a currency of its own which it could keep constant or even increase to meet such a misfortune for some of its inhabitants.

But while we have no foundations for desiring particular areas to have their individual currencies, it is of course an altogether different question whether the free issue of competitive currencies in each area would lead to the formation of currency areas – or rather of areas where different currencies were predominant, although others could be used. As we have seen (section 12), there might develop different preferences as regards the commodity equivalent of the currency that should be kept constant. In a primitive country where people used little but rice, fish, pork, cotton and timber, they would be chiefly concerned about different prices – though local tendencies of this sort would probably be offset by those of the users to be guided in their preferences by the greater trust they had in an internationally reputed issuer of money than in one who adapted his currency specially to local circumstances. Nor would I be surprised to find that in large areas only one currency was generally used in ordinary dealings, so long as potential competition made its issuer keep it stable. As everywhere else, so long as it does not come to trying out innovations or improvements, competition *in posse*[81] is likely to be nearly as effective as competition *in esse*.[81] And the ready convertibility of the generally used currency would make all those who had any traffic beyond the region change their holdings quickly enough into another currency if their suspicions about the commonly accepted one were aroused.

Such areas in which one currency predominates would however not have sharp or fixed boundaries but would largely overlap, and their dividing lines would fluctuate. But once the principle were generally accepted in the economically leading countries, it would probably spread rapidly to wherever people could choose their institutions. No doubt there would remain enclaves under dictators who did not wish to let go their power over money – even after the absence of exchange control had become the mark of a civilised and honest country.

21 The Effects on Government Finance and Expenditure

The two goals of public finance and of the regulation of a satisfactory currency are entirely different from, and largely in conflict with, each other. To place both tasks in the hands of the same agency has in consequence always led to confusion and in recent years has had disastrous consequences. It has not only made money the chief cause of economic fluctuations but has also greatly facilitated an uncontrollable growth of public expenditure. If we are to preserve a functioning market economy (and with it individual freedom), *nothing can be more urgent than that we dissolve the unholy marriage between monetary and fiscal policy,* long clandestine but formally consecrated with the victory of 'Keynesian' economics.

We need not say much more about the unfortunate effects of the 'needs' of finance on the supply of money. Not only have all major inflations until recently been the result of governments covering their financial 'needs' by the printing press. Even during relatively stable periods the regular necessity for central banks to accommodate the financial 'needs' of government by keeping interest rates low has been a constant embarrassment: it has interfered with the banks' efforts to secure stability and has given their policies an inflationist bias that was usually checked only belatedly by the mechanism of the gold standard.

Good national money impossible under democratic government dependent on special interests

I do not think it an exaggeration to say that it is wholly impossible for a central bank subject to political control, or even exposed to serious political pressure, to regulate the quantity of money in a way conducive to a smoothly functioning market order. A good money, like good law, must operate without regard to the effects that decisions of the issuer will have on known groups or individuals. A benevolent dictator might conceivably disregard these effects; no democratic government dependent on a number of special interests can possibly do so. But to use the control of the supply of money as an instrument for achieving particular ends destroys the equilibrating operation of the price mechanism, which is required to maintain the continuing process of ordering the market that gives individuals a good chance of having their expectations fulfilled.

Government monopoly of money and government expenditure

But we have probably said enough about the harm that monetary policy guided by financial considerations is likely to do. What we must still consider is the effect that power over the supply of money has had on financial policy. Just as the absence of competition has prevented the monopolist supplier of money from being subject to a salutary discipline, the power over money has also relieved governments of the necessity to keep their expenditure within their revenue. It is largely for this reason that 'Keynesian' economics has become so rapidly popular among socialist economists. Indeed, since ministers of finance were told by economists that running a deficit was a meritorious act, and even that, so long as there were unemployed resources, extra government expenditure cost the people nothing, any effective bar to a rapid increase in government expenditure was destroyed.

There can be little doubt that the spectacular increase in government expenditure over the last 30 years, with governments in some Western countries claiming up to half or more of the national income for collective purposes, was made possible by government control of the issue of money. On the one hand, inflation has constantly pushed people with a given real income into much higher tax brackets than they anticipated when they approved the rates, and thus raised government revenue more rapidly than they had intended. On the other, the habitual large deficits, and the comparative ease with which budgeted figures could be exceeded, still further increased the share of the real output governments were able to claim for their purposes.

Government money and unbalanced budgets

In a sense it is arbitrary to require governments to balance their budget for the calendar year. But the alternations of the seasons and the firmly established business practices of accounting provide a good reason; and the practice of business, where receipts and expenditure are regularly balanced over a period with known fluctuations, further supports the usage. If major economic fluctuations can be prevented by other arrangements, the conventional annual budget is still the best term for requiring such balancing. Assuming it to be true that the regulation of the supply of money by competition between private currencies would secure not only a stable value of money but also stable business conditions, the argument that government deficits are necessary to reduce unemployment amounts to the contention that a government control of money is needed to cure what it is itself causing. There is no reason why, with a stable money, it should ever be desirable to allow government to spend more than it has. And it is certainly more important that government expenditure does not become a cause of general instability than that the clumsy apparatus of government should (in the most unlikely event that it acts in time) be available to mitigate any slackening of economic activity.

The ease with which a minister of finance can today both budget for an excess of expenditure over revenue and exceed that expenditure has created a wholly new style of finance compared with the careful housekeeping of the past. And since the ease with which one demand after another is conceded evokes ever new expectations of further bounty, the process is a self-accelerating one which even men who genuinely wish to avoid it find it impossible to stop. Anyone who knows the difficulty of restraining a bureaucratic apparatus not controlled by profit-and-loss calculations from constantly expanding also knows that without the rigid barrier of strictly limited funds there is nothing to stop an indefinite growth of government expenditure.

Unless we restore a situation in which governments (and other public authorities) find that if they overspend they will, like everybody else, be unable to meet their obligations, there will be no halt to this growth which, by substituting collective for private activity, threatens to suffoc-ate individual initiative. Under the prevailing form of unlimited democ-racy, in which government has power to confer special material benefits on groups, it is forced to buy the support of sufficient numbers to add up to a majority. Even with the best will in the world, no government can resist this pressure unless it can point to a firm barrier it cannot cross. While governments will of course occasionally be forced to borrow from the public to meet unforeseen requirements, or choose to finance some investments in that manner, it is highly undesirable in any cir-cumstances that these funds should be provided by the creation of additional money. Nor is it desirable that those additions to the total quantity of money which are required in a growing economy to equip the suppliers of additional factors of production with the needed cash balances should be introduced into circulation in this manner.

Government power over money facilitates centralisation

There can be little doubt also that the ability of central governments to resort to this kind of finance is one of the contributory causes of the advance in the most undesirable centralisation of government. Nothing can be more welcome than depriving government of its power over money and so stopping the apparently irresistible trend towards an accelerating increase of the share of the national income it is able to claim. If allowed to continue, this trend would in a few years bring us to a state in which governments would claim 100 per cent (in Sweden and Britain it already exceeds 60 per cent) of all resources – and would in consequence become literally 'totalitarian'.[82] The more completely public finance can be separated from the regulation of the monetary circulation, the better it will be. It is a power which always has been harmful. Its use for financial purposes is always an abuse. And government has neither the *interest* nor the *capacity* to exercise it in the manner required to secure the smooth flow of economic effort.

The suggestion of depriving government of the monopoly of issuing money and of its power of making any money 'legal tender' for all existing debts has been made here in the first instance because governments have invariably and inevitably grossly abused that power throughout the whole of history and thereby gravely disturbed the self-steering mechanism of the market. But it may turn out that cutting off government from the tap which supplies it with additional money for its use may prove as important in order to stop the inherent tendency of unlimited government to grow indefinitely, which is becoming as menacing a danger to the future of civilisation as the badness of the money it has supplied. Only if people are made to perceive that they must pay in undisguised taxes (or voluntarily lend) all the money government can spend can the process of buying majority support by granting special benefits to ever-increasing numbers with particular interests be brought to a stop.

22 Problems of Transition

For the vast majority of people the appearance of several concurrent currencies would merely offer them alternatives; it would not make necessary any change in their habitual use of money. Experience would gradually teach them how to improve their position by switching to other kinds of money. Retail merchants would soon be offered by the banks the appropriate calculating equipment which would relieve them of any initial difficulties in management or accounting. Since the issuer of the money they used would be interested in supplying assistance, they would probably discover they were better served than before. In manufacture, trade and the service industries, learning to take full advantage of the new opportunities might take a little longer, but there would be no important necessary changes in the conduct of business or unavoidably difficult adaptations.

Preventing rapid depreciation of formerly exclusive currency

The two activities that would be most profoundly affected, and in which an almost complete change of habitual practices and routines would be required, are public finance and the whole range of private finance, including banking, insurance, building societies, saving and mortgage banks as well. For government, apart from the changes in financial policy mentioned in section 21, the chief task would be to guard against a rapid displacement and consequent accelerating depreciation of the currency issued by the existing central bank. This could probably be achieved only by instantly giving it complete freedom and independence, putting it thus on the same footing with all other issue banks, foreign or newly created at home, coupled with a simultaneous return to a policy of balanced budgets, limited only by the possibility of borrowing on an open loan market which they could not manipulate. The urgency of these steps derives from the fact that, once the displacement of the hitherto exclusive currency by new currencies had commenced, it would be rapidly speeded up by an accelerating depreciation that would be practically impossible to stop by any of the ordinary methods of contracting the circulation. Neither the government nor the former central banks would possess the reserves of other currencies or of gold to redeem all the old money the public would want to get rid of as soon as it could change from a rapidly depreciating currency to one it had reason to believe would remain stable. It could be brought to trust such a currency only if the bank issuing it demonstrated a capacity to regulate it in precisely the same manner as the new issue banks competing with it.

Introduce new currencies at once, not gradually

The other important requirement of government action, if the transition to the new order is to be successful, is that all the required liberties be conceded at once, and no tentative and timid attempt be made to introduce the new order gradually, or to reserve powers of control 'in case anything goes wrong'. The possibility of free competition between a multiplicity of issuing institutions and the complete freedom of all movements of currency and capital across frontiers are equally essential to the success of the scheme. Any hesitant approach by a *gradual* relaxation of the existing monopoly of issue would be certain to make it fail. People would learn to trust the new money only if they were confident it was completely exempt from any government control. Only because they were under the sharp control of competition could the private banks be trusted to keep their money stable. Only because people could freely choose which currency to use for their different purposes would the process of selection lead to the good money prevailing. Only because there was active trading on the currency exchange would the issuing banks be warned to take the required action in time. Only because the frontiers were open to the movement of currency and capital would there be assurance of no collusion between local institutions to mis-manage the local currency. And only because there were free commodity markets would stable average prices mean that the process of adapting supply to demand was functioning.

Commercial bank change in policy

If the government succeeded in handing over the business of supplying money to private institutions without the existing currency collapsing, the chief problem for the individual commercial banks would be to decide whether to try and establish their own currency, or to select the other currency or currencies in which they would in future conduct their business. The great majority clearly would have to be content to do their business in other currencies. They would thus (sections 11 and 12) have to practise a kind of '100 per cent banking', and keep a full reserve against all their obligations payable on demand.

This necessity would probably prove the most far-reaching change in business practice required by competing currencies. Since these banks presumably would have to charge substantially for running chequing accounts, they would lose that business largely to the issuing banks and be reduced to the administration of less liquid kinds of capital assets.

So long as this change could be effected by a deliberate transition to the use of a currency of their choice, it might prove somewhat painful but not raise unmanageable problems. And to do away with banks which, in effect, created currency without bearing any responsibility for the results has been for more than a hundred years the *desideratum* of economists who perceived the inherent instability of the mechanism into which we had drifted but who usually saw no hope of ever getting out of it. An institution which has proved as harmful as fractional reserve banking without responsibility of the individual bank for the money (i.e. cheque deposits) it created cannot complain if the support by a government monopoly that has made its existence possible is withdrawn.

There will certainly also have to develop generally a much sharper distinction between pure banking and the investment business, or between what used to be regarded as the English and the Continental types of banks (*Depositenbanken* and *Spekulationsbanken*, as these types were once described in German). I expect that it will soon be discovered that the business of creating money does not go along well with the control of large investment portfolios or even control of large parts of industry.

A wholly different set of difficulties would of course arise if the government or its privileged bank did not succeed in preventing a collapse of its currency. This would be a possibility which the banks not able to issue their own currency would rightly fear, since a large part of their assets, namely all their loans, would dwindle away with most of their liabilities. But this would merely mean that the danger of a high inflation, of the kind that now always threatens and that others might avoid by shifting to other currencies, would for them become particularly threatening. But banks have usually claimed that they have more or less succeeded in bringing their assets through even a galloping inflation. Bankers who do not know how to do it might perhaps consult their colleagues in Chile and elsewhere where they have had plenty of experience with this problem. At any rate, to get rid of the present unstable structure is too important a task for it to be sacrificed to the interests of some special groups.

23 Protection Against the State

Though under the proposed arrangement the normal provision of money would be entirely a function of private enterprise, the chief danger to its smooth working would still be interference by the state.[83] If the international character of the issuing business should largely protect the issuing banks against direct political pressure (though it would certainly invite attacks by demagogues), the trust in any one institution would still largely depend on the trust in the government under which it was established. To obviate the suspicion of serving the political interests of the country in which they were established, it would clearly be important that banks with headquarters in different countries should compete with one another. The greatest confidence, at least so long as peace was regarded as assured, would probably be placed in institutions established in small wealthy countries for which international business was an important source of income and that would therefore be expected to be particularly careful of their reputation for financial soundness.

Pressures for return to national monetary monopolies

Many countries would probably try, by subsidies or similar measures, to preserve a locally established bank issuing a distinct national currency that would be available side by side with the international currencies, even if they were only moderately successful. There would then be some danger that the nationalist and socialist forces active in a silly agitation against multinational corporations would lead governments, by advantages conceded to the national institution, to bring about a gradual return to the present system of privileged national issuers of currency.

Recurring governmental control of currency and capital movements

The chief danger, however, would threaten from renewed attempts by governments to control the international movements of currency and capital. It is a power which at present is the most serious threat not only to a working international economy but also to personal freedom; and it will remain a threat so long as governments have the physical power to enforce such controls. It is to be hoped that people will gradually recognise this threat to their personal freedom and that they will make the complete prohibition of such measures an entrenched constitutional provision. The ultimate protection against the tyranny of government is that at least a large number of able people can emigrate when they can no longer stand it. I fear that few Englishmen, most of whom thought the statement which I now repeat unduly alarmist and exaggerated when I published it more than 30 years ago, will still feel so:

> The extent of the control over all life that economic control confers is nowhere better illustrated than in the field of foreign exchanges. Nothing would at first seem to affect private life less than a state control of the dealings in foreign exchange, and most people will regard its introduction with complete indifference. Yet the experience of most continental countries has taught thoughtful people to regard this step as the decisive advance on the path to totalitarianism and the suppression of individual liberty. It is in fact the complete delivery of the individual to the tyranny of the state, the final suppression of all means of escape – not merely for the rich, but for everybody. Once the individual is no longer free to travel,

no longer free to buy foreign books or journals, once all means of foreign contact can be restricted to those whom official opinion approves or for whom it is regarded as necessary, the effective control of opinion is much greater than that ever exercised by any of the absolutist governments of the seventeenth and eighteenth centuries.[84]

Next to the barrier to the excessive growth of government expenditure, the second fundamental contribution to the protection of individual freedom which the abolition of the government monopoly of issuing money would secure would probably be the intertwining of international affairs, which would make it more and more impossible for government to control international movements, and thus safeguard the ability of dissidents to escape the oppression of a government with which they profoundly disagreed.

24 The Long-run Prospects

A hope one may cherish is that, as competition usually does, it will lead to the discovery of yet unknown possibilities in currency. This makes any attempt at prediction of the long-run effects of the proposed reform exceedingly hazardous, but we will attempt to summarise briefly what would appear to be the probable long-run developments if it were adopted.

I believe that, once the system had fully established itself and competition had eliminated a number of unsuccessful ventures, there would remain in the free world several extensively used and very similar currencies. In various large regions one or two of them would be dominant, but these regions would have no sharp or constant boundaries, and the use of the currencies dominant in them would overlap in broad and fluctuating border districts. Most of these currencies, based on similar collections of commodities, would in the short run fluctuate very little in terms of one another, probably much less than the currencies of the most stable countries today, yet somewhat more than currencies based on a true gold standard. If the composition of the commodity basket on which they are based were adapted to the conditions of the region in which they are mainly used, they might slowly drift apart. But most of them would thus *concur*, not only in the sense of running side by side, but also in the sense of agreeing with one another in the movement of their values.

After the experimental process of finding the most favoured collection of commodities to the price of which the currency was to be tied, further changes would probably be rare and minor. Competition between the issuing banks would concentrate on the avoidance of even minor fluctuations of their value in terms of these commodities, the degree of information provided about their activities, and various additional services (such as assistance in accounting) offered to their customers. The currencies issued by any surviving government banks would often themselves be driven more and more to accept and even to seek payment in currencies other than those issued by a favoured national institution.

The possibility of a multiplicity of similar currencies

There exists, however, a possibility or even probability I did not consider in the First Edition. After certain currencies based on a particular batch of commodities have become widely accepted, many other banks might, under different names, issue currencies the value of which was based on the same collection of commodities as the one successful first, either in the same or smaller or larger units. In other words, competition might lead to the extensive use of the same commodity base by a large number of issue banks that would still compete for the favour of the public through the constancy of the value of their issues or other services they offered. The public might then learn to accept a considerable number of such monies with different names (but all described as, say, of 'Zurich Standard') at constant rates of exchange; and shops might post lists of all the currencies which they were prepared to accept as representing that standard. So long as the Press properly exercised its supervisory function and warned the public in time of any dereliction of duty on the part of some issuers, such a system might satisfactorily serve for a long time.

Considerations of convenience would probably also lead to the adoption of a standard unit, i.e. based not only on the same collection of commodities but also of the same magnitude. In this case most banks could issue, under distinct names, notes for these standard units which would be readily accepted locally as far as the reputation of the individual bank extended.

*The preservation of a standard of long-term debts even while currencies
may lose their value*

With the availability of at least some stable currencies the absurd practice
of making 'legal tender' a mere token which may become valueless but
still remain effective for the discharge of debts contracted in what had
been an object of a certain value is bound to disappear. It was solely the
power of government to force upon people what they had not meant in
their contracts which produced this absurdity. With the abolition of the
government monopoly of issuing money the courts will soon understand,
and, I trust, statute law recognise, that justice requires debts to be paid
in terms of the units of value which the parties to the contracts intended
and not in what government says is a substitute for them. (The exception
is where the contract explicitly provides for a stated number of tokens
rather than for a value expressed in terms of an amount of tokens.)

After the development of a widely preferred common standard of
value the courts would in most cases have no difficulty in determining
the approximate magnitude of the abstract value intended by the parties
to a contract for the value of such and such an amount of a widely
accepted unit of currency. If one currency in terms of the value of which
a contract had been concluded seriously depreciated beyond a reasonable
range of fluctuation, a court would not allow the parties to gain or lose
from the malpractice of the third party that issued the currency. They
would without difficulty be able to determine the amount of some other
currency or currencies with which the debtor was entitled and obliged
to discharge his obligation.

As a result, even the complete collapse of one currency would not
have the disastrous far-reaching consequences which a similar event has
today. Though the holders of cash, either in the form of notes or of
demand deposits in a particular currency, might lose their whole value,
this would be a relatively minor disturbance compared with the general
shrinkage or wiping out of all claims to third persons expressed in that
currency. The whole structure of long-term contracts would remain
unaffected, and people would preserve their investments in bonds, mort-
gages and similar forms of claims even though they might lose all their
cash if they were unfortunate to use the currency of a bank that failed.
A portfolio of bonds and other long-term claims might still be a very
safe investment even if it happened that some issuers of currency became
insolvent and their notes and deposits valueless. Completely liquid assets
would still involve a risk – but who wants, except perhaps temporarily,
to keep all his assets in a very liquid form? There could never occur that

complete disappearance of any common standard of debts or such a wiping out of all monetary obligations as has been the final effect of all major inflations. Long before this could happen, everybody would have deserted the depreciated unit and no old obligation could be discharged in terms of it.

New legal framework for banking

While governments should not interfere in this development by any conscious attempts at control (i.e. any acts of intervention in the strict sense of the term), it may be found that new rules of law are needed to provide an appropriate legal framework within which the new banking practices could successfully develop. It would, however, seem rather doubtful whether it would assist developments if such rules were at once made generally applicable by international treaties and experimentation with alternative arrangements thereby prevented.

How long it would take for some countries no longer to desire to have a currency of their own for purely nationalistic or prestige reasons, and for governments to stop misleading the public by complaining about an undue restriction of their sovereign power, is difficult to say.[85] The whole system is of course wholly irreconcilable with any striving for totalitarian powers of any sort.

25 Conclusions

The abolition of the government monopoly of money was conceived to prevent the bouts of acute inflation and deflation which have plagued the world for the past 60 years. It proves on examination to be also the much needed cure for a more deep-seated disease: the recurrent waves of depression and unemployment that have been represented as an inherent and deadly defect of capitalism.

Gold standard not the solution

One might hope to prevent the violent fluctuations in the value of money in recent years by returning to the gold standard or some régime of fixed exchanges. I still believe that, *so long as the management of money is in the hands of government*, the gold standard with all its imperfections is the only tolerably safe system. But we certainly can do better than that, though not through government. Quite apart from the undeniable truth that the gold standard also has serious defects, the opponents of such a move can properly point out that a central direction of the quantity of money is in the present circumstances necessary to counteract the inherent instability of the existing credit system. But once it is recognised that this inherent instability of credit is itself the effect of the structure of deposit banking determined by the monopolistic control of the supply of the hand-to-hand money in which the deposits must be redeemed, these objections fall to the ground. If we want free enterprise and a market economy to survive (as even the supporters of a so-called 'mixed economy' presumably also wish), we have no choice but to replace the governmental currency monopoly and national currency systems by free competition between private banks of issue. We have never had the control of money in the hands of agencies whose *sole* and *exclusive* concern was to give the public what currency it liked best among several kinds offered, and which at the same time staked their existence on fulfilling the expectations they had created.

It may be that, with free competition between different kinds of money, gold coins might at first prove to be the most popular. But this very fact, the increasing demand for gold, would probably lead to such a rise (and perhaps also violent fluctuations) of the price of gold that, though it might still be widely used for hoarding, it would soon cease to be convenient as the unit for business transactions and accounting. There should certainly be the same freedom for its use, but I should not expect this to lead to its victory over other forms of privately issued money, the demand for which rested on its quantity being successfully regulated so as to keep its purchasing power constant.

The very same fact which at present makes gold more trusted than government-controlled paper money, namely that its total quantity cannot be manipulated at will in the service of political aims, would in the long run make it appear inferior to token money used by competing institutions whose business rested on successfully so regulating the quantity of their issues as to keep the value of the units approximately constant.

Good money can come only from self-interest, not from benevolence

We have always had bad money because private enterprise was not permitted to give us a better one. In a world governed by the pressure of organised interests, the important truth to keep in mind is that we cannot count on intelligence or understanding but only on sheer self-interest to give us the institutions we need. Blessed indeed will be the day when it will no longer be from the benevolence of the government that we expect good money but from the regard of the banks for their own interest.

> It is in this manner that we obtain from one another the far greater part of those good offices we stand in need of.[86]

– but unfortunately not yet a money that we can rely upon.

It was not 'capitalism' but government intervention which has been responsible for the recurrent crises of the past.[87] Government has prevented enterprise from equipping itself with the instruments that it required to protect itself against its efforts being misdirected by an unreliable money and that it would be both profitable for the supplier and beneficial to all others to develop. The recognition of this truth makes it clear that the reform proposed is not a minor technicality of finance but a crucial issue which may decide the fate of free civilisation. What is proposed here seems to me the only discernible way of completing the market order and freeing it from its main defect and the cause of the chief reproaches directed against it.

Is competitive paper currency practicable?

We cannot, of course, hope for such a reform before the public understands what is at stake and what it has to gain. But those who think the whole proposal wholly impracticable and Utopian should remember that 200 years ago in *The Wealth of Nations* Adam Smith wrote that

> to expect, indeed, that the freedom of trade should ever be entirely restored in Great Britain, is as absurd as to expect that an Oceana or Utopia should ever be established in it.[88]

It took nearly 90 years from the publication of his work in 1776 until Great Britain became the first country to establish complete free trade in 1860. But the idea caught on rapidly; and if it had not been for the political reaction caused by the French Revolution and the Napoleonic Wars no doubt it would have taken effect sooner. It was not until 1819 that an effective movement to educate the general public on these matters started and it was in the end due to the devoted efforts of a few men who dedicated themselves to spread the message by an organised Free Trade Movement that what Smith had called 'the insolent outrage of furious and disappointed monopolists' was overcome.[89,90]

I fear that since 'Keynesian' propaganda has filtered through to the masses, has made inflation respectable and provided agitators with arguments which the professional politicians are unable to refute, the only way to avoid being driven by continuing inflation into a controlled and directed economy, and therefore ultimately in order to save civilisation, will be to deprive governments of their power over the supply of money.[91]

'Free Money Movement'

What we now need is a Free Money Movement comparable to the Free Trade Movement of the 19th century, demonstrating not merely the harm caused by acute inflation, which could justifiably be argued to be avoidable even with present institutions, but the deeper effects of producing periods of stagnation that are indeed inherent in the present monetary arrangements.

The alarm about current inflation is, as I can observe as I write, only too quickly dispelled whenever the rate of inflation slows down only a little. I have not much doubt that, by the time these lines appear in print, there will be ample cause for a renewal of this alarm (unless, which would be even worse, the resumed inflation is concealed by price controls). Probably even the new inflationary boom already initiated will again have collapsed. But it will need deeper insight into the superficially invisible effects of inflation to produce the result required to achieve the abolition of the harmful powers of government on the control of money. There is thus an immense educational task ahead before we can hope to free ourselves from the gravest threat to social peace and continued prosperity inherent in existing monetary institutions.

It will be necessary that the problem and the urgent need of reform come to be widely understood. The issue is not one which, as may at first appear to the layman, concerns a minor technicality of the financial system which he has never quite understood. It refers to the one way in

which we may still hope to stop the continuous progress of all government towards totalitarianism which already appears to many acute
observers as inevitable. I wish I could advise that we proceed slowly.
But the time may be short. What is now urgently required is not the
construction of a new system but the prompt removal of all the legal
obstacles which have for two thousand years blocked the way for an
evolution which is bound to throw up beneficial results which we cannot
now foresee.

Notes

1   But, though I had independently arrived at the realisation of the advantages
    possessed by independent competing currencies, I must now concede intel-
    lectual priority to Professor Benjamin Klein, who, in a paper written in
    1970 and published in 1975 [35], until recently unknown to me, had clearly
    explained the chief advantage of competition among currencies.
2   W. Endemann [15], Vol. II, p. 171.
3   J. Bodin [5], p. 176. Bodin, who understood more about money than most
    of his contemporaries, may well have hoped that the governments of large
    states would be more responsible than the thousands of minor princelings
    and cities who, during the later part of the Middle Ages, had acquired the
    minting privilege and sometimes abused it even more than the richer princes
    of large territories.
4   The same applies to the postal monopoly which everywhere appears to
    provide a steadily deteriorating service and of which in Great Britain
    (according to *The Times*, 25 May 1976) the General Secretary of the Union
    of Post Office Workers (!) said recently that 'Governments of both political
    complexions have reduced a once great public service to the level of a
    music-hall joke'. *Politically* the broadcasting monopoly may be even more
    dangerous, but *economically* I doubt whether any other monopoly has done
    as much damage as that of issuing money.
5   Cf. Adam Smith [54, p. 40]: '. . . those public offices called mints: institutions
    exactly of the same nature with those of the aulnagers and stampmasters
    of woollen and linen cloth'.
6   Endemann [15], p. 172.
7   Knapp [36], and compare Mann [41].
8   Section 7 below, pp. 142–4.
9   Herbert Spencer [57].
10 Joseph Garnier [21].
11 Vera C. Smith [55].

12   F.A. Hayek [29], pp. 324 *et seq.*
13   Especially Werner Sombart [56] and before him Archibald Alison [1] and others. Cf. on them Paul Barth [4], who has a whole chapter on 'History as a function of the value of money', and Marianne von Herzfeld [32].
14   A. Nussbaum [50], p. 53.
15   On the Chinese events, see W. Vissering [61] and G. Tullock [58], who does not, however, allude to the often recounted story of the 'final prohibition'.
16   Nussbaum [50], Mann [41], and Breckinridge [6].
17   Mann [41], p. 38. On the other hand, the refusal until recently of English Courts to give judgement for paying in any other currency than the pound sterling has made this aspect of legal tender particularly influential in England. But this is likely to change after a recent decision (Miliangos v. George Frank Textiles Ltd [1975]) established that an English Court can give judgement in a foreign currency on a money claim in a foreign currency, so that, for instance, it is now possible in England to enforce a claim from a sale in Swiss francs. (*Financial Times*, 6 November 1975: the report is reproduced in F. A. Hayek [31], pp. 45–6).
18   Nussbaum [50], pp. 54–5.
19   Occasional attempts by the authorities of commercial cities to provide a money of at least a constant metallic content, such as the establishment of the Bank of Amsterdam, were for long periods fairly successful and their money used far beyond the national boundaries. But even in these cases the authorities sooner or later abused their quasi-monopoly positions. The Bank of Amsterdam was a state agency which people had to use for certain purposes and its money even as exclusive legal tender for payments above a certain amount. Nor was it available for ordinary small transactions or local business beyond the city limits. The same is roughly true of the similar experiments of Venice, Genoa, Hamburg and Nuremberg.
20   Willem Vissering [61].
21   Lord Farrer [17], p. 43.
22   *Ibid.*, p. 45. The *locus classicus* on this subject from which I undoubtedly derived my views on it, though I had forgotten this when I wrote the First Edition of this *Paper*, is Carl Menger's discussion in 1892 [43a] of legal tender under the even more appropriate equivalent German term *Zwangskurs*. See pp. 98–106 of the reprint, especially p. 101, where the *Zwangskurs* is described as 'eine Massregel, die in der überwiegenden Zahl der Fälle den Zweck hat, gegen den Willen der Bevölkerung, zumindest durch einen Missbrauch der Münzhoheit oder des Notenregals entstandene pathologische (also exceptionelle[?]) Formen von Umlaufsmitteln, durch einen Missbrauch der Justizhoheit dem Verkehr aufzudrängen oder in demselben zu erhalten'; and p. 104 where Menger describes it as 'ein auf die Forderungsberechtigten geübter gesetzlicher Zwang, bei Summenschulden (bisweilen auch bei Schulden anderer Art) solche Geldsorten als Zahlung anzunehmen, welche dem ausdrücklich oder stillschweigend vereinbarten

Inhalte der Forderungen nicht entsprechen, oder dieselben sich zu einem Wert aufdrangen zu lassen, der ihrem Wert im freien Verkehr nicht entspricht'. Especially interesting also is the first footnote on p. 102 in which Menger points out that there had been fairly general agreement on this among the liberal economists of the first half of the 19th century, while during the second half of that century, through the influence of the (presumably German) lawyers, the economists were led erroneously to regard legal tender as an attribute of perfect money.

23 *Ibid.*, p. 47.

24 Cf. Nussbaum [50], pp. 586–92.

25 In Austria after 1922 the name 'Schumpeter' had become almost a curse word among ordinary people, referring to the principle that 'Krone is Krone', because the economist J. A. Schumpeter, during his short tenure as Minister of Finance, had put his name to an order of council, merely spelling out what was undoubtedly valid law, namely that debts incurred in crowns when they had a higher value could be repaid in depreciated crowns, ultimately worth only a 15,000th part of their original value.

26 W. S. Jevons [34], p. 64, as against Herbert Spencer [57].

27 Jevons, *ibid.*, p. 65. An earlier characteristic attempt to justify making banking and note issue an exception from a general advocacy of free competition is to be found in 1837 in the writings of S. J. Loyd (later Lord Overstone) [38], p. 49: 'The ordinary advantages to the community arising from competition are that it tends to excite the ingenuity and exertion of the producers, and thus to secure to the public the best supply and quantity of the commodity at the lowest price, while all the evils arising from errors or miscalculations on the part of the producers will fall on themselves, and not on the public. With respect to a paper currency, however, the interest of the public is of a very different kind; a steady and equable regulation of its amount by fixed law is the end to be sought and the evil consequence of any error or miscalculation upon this point falls in a much greater proportion upon the public than upon the issuer.' It is obvious that Loyd thought only of the possibility of different agencies issuing the *same* currency, not of currencies of *different* denominations competing with one another.

28 Jevons, *ibid.*, p. 82. Jevons's phrase is rather unfortunately chosen, because in the literal sense Gresham's law of course operates by people getting rid of the worse and retaining the better for other purposes.

29 Cf. Hayek [30] and Fetter [17a].

30 If, as he is sometimes quoted, Gresham maintained that better money quite generally could not drive out worse, he was simply wrong, until we add his probably tacit presumption that a *fixed* rate of exchange was enforced.

31 Cf. Bresciani-Turroni [7], p. 174: 'In monetary conditions characterised by a great distrust in the national currency, the principle of Gresham's law is reversed and *good money drives out bad*, and the value of the latter

continually depreciates.' But even he does not point out that the critical difference is not the 'great distrust' but the presence or absence of effectively enforced fixed rates of exchange.

32   In 1582 by G. Scaruffi [57].

33   A. E. Feaveryear [16], p. 142.

34   H. Grote [23].

35   For a time during the Middle Ages gold coins issued by the great commercial republics of Italy were used extensively in international trade and maintained over fairly long periods at a constant gold content, while at the same time the petty coins, mostly of silver, used in local retail trade suffered the regular fate of progressive debasement. (Cipolla [11], pp. 34 ff.)

36   G. Tullock [58] and [59]; compare B. Klein [35].

37   A convenient summary of information on trade coins is in Nussbaum [50], p. 315.

38   Cf. Hayek [30], pp. 318–20.

39   On the question of its attractiveness the discussion by S. Fischer [18] of the notorious reluctance of enterprise to issue indexed bonds is somewhat relevant. It is true that a gradual increase of the value of the notes issued by a bank in terms of other concurrent currencies might produce a situation in which the aggregate value of its outstanding notes (*plus* its liabilities from other sources) would exceed its assets. The bank would of course not be legally liable to redeem its notes at this value, but it could preserve this business only if it did in fact promptly buy at the current rate any of its notes offered to it. So long as it succeeded in maintaining the real value of its notes, it would never be called upon to buy back more than a fraction of the outstanding circulation. Probably no one would doubt that an art dealer who owns the plates of the engravings of a famous artist could, so long as his works remained in fashion, maintain the market value of these engravings by judiciously selling and buying, even though he could never buy up all the existing prints. Similarly, a bank could certainly maintain the value of its notes even though it could never buy back all the outstanding ones.

40   A real difficulty could arise if a sudden large increase in the demand for such a stable currency, perhaps due to some acute economic crisis, had to be met by selling large amounts of it against other currencies. The bank would of course have to prevent such a rise in the value and could do so only by increasing its supply. But selling against other currencies would give it assets likely to depreciate in terms of its own currency. It probably could not increase its short-term lending very rapidly, even if it offered to lend at a very low rate of interest – even though in such a situation it would be safer to lend even at a small negative rate of interest than to sell against other currencies. And it would probably be possible to grant long-term loans at very low rates of interest against negotiable securities (in terms of its own currency) which it should be easy to sell if the sudden increase of

demand for its currency should be as rapidly reversed.

41   Apart from notes and cheque deposits in its distinctive currency, an issuing bank would clearly also have to provide fractional coins; and the availability of convenient fractional coins in that currency might well be an important factor in making it popular. It would also probably be the habitual use of one sort of fractional coins (especially in slot machines, fares, tips, etc.) which would secure the predominance of one currency in the retail trade of one locality. The effective competition between different currencies would probably be largely confined to inter-business use, with retail trade following the decisions about the currency in which wages and salaries were to be paid.

Certain special problems would arise where present sales practices are based on the general use of uniform coins of a few relatively small standard units, as, e.g., in vending machines, transportation or telephones. Probably even in localities in which several different currencies were in general use, one set of small coins would come to dominate. If, as seems probable, most of these competing currencies were kept at practically the same value, the technical problem of the use of coins might be solved in any one of various ways. One might be that one institution, e.g. an association of retailers, specialised in the issue of uniform coins at slightly fluctuating market prices. Tradesmen and transport and communication undertakings of a locality might join to sell, at market prices and probably through the banks, a common set of tokens for all automats in the locality. We can certainly expect commercial inventiveness rapidly to solve such minor difficulties. Another possible development would be the replacement of the present coins by plastic or similar tokens with electronic markings which every cash register and slot machine would be able to sort out, and the 'signature' of which would be legally protected against forgery as any other document of value.

42   This definition was established by Carl Menger [43], whose work also ought to have finally disposed of the medieval conception that money, or the value of money, was a creation of the state. Vissering [61], p. 9, reports that in early times the Chinese expressed their notions of money by a term meaning literally 'current merchandise'. The now more widely used expression that money is the most liquid asset comes, of course (as Carlile [8] pointed out as early as 1901), to the same thing. To serve as a widely accepted medium of exchange is the only function which an object must perform to qualify as money, though a generally accepted medium of exchange will generally acquire also the further functions of unit of account, store of value, standard of deferred payment, etc. The definition of money as 'means of payment' is, however, purely circular, since this concept presupposed debts incurred in terms of money. (Cf. L. von Mises [45], pp. 34 ff.)

The definition of money as the generally acceptable medium of exchange does not, of course, necessarily mean that even within one national territory there must be a single kind of money which is more acceptable than all others; there may be several equally acceptable kinds of money (which we may more conveniently call currencies), particularly if one kind can be quickly exchanged into the others at a known, though not fixed, rate.

43   Cf. J. R. Hicks [33].

44   Machlup for this reason speaks occasionally, e.g. [39], p. 225, of 'moneyness' and 'near-moneyness'.

45   It is a practice particularly congenial to statisticians, the applicability of whose techniques frequently depends on using it. Though the popular tendency in economics to accept only *statistically* testable theories has given us some useful gross approximations to the truth, such as the quantity theory of the value of money, they have acquired a quite undeserved reputation. The idea discussed in the text makes most quantitative formulations of economic theory inadequate in practice. To introduce sharp distinctions which do not exist in the real world in order to make a subject susceptible to mathematical treatment is not to make it more scientific but rather less so.

46   Cf. C. Menger [43], p. 261: 'There is no better way in which men can become more enlightened about their economic interests than by observation of the economic success of those who employ the correct means of achieving their ends.'

47   We must not entirely overlook the possibility that the practices and expectations of business men based on past experience, and particularly the experience of the last 50 years or so, are so much adjusted to the probability of a continuous upward trend of prices, that the realisation that average prices in future are likely to remain constant may at first have a discouraging effect. This may even make some business men prefer to deal and keep accounts in a slowly depreciating currency. I believe, however, that in the end those who have chosen a stable currency will prove more successful.

48   W. S. Jevons [34], p. 11. Cf. also *ibid.*, p. 68: 'value merely expresses the essentially variable ratio in which two commodities exchange, so that there is no reason to suppose that any substance does for two days together retain the same value.'

49   The curve representing the dispersion of price changes by showing the percentage of all sales effected at one period at prices increased or decreased compared with an earlier period would, of course, if drawn on a logarithmic scale, have the same shape whether we used money or any commodity as the measure of price. If we used as standard the commodity whose price had fallen more than that of any other, all price changes would merely appear as increases, but an increase of the relative price compared with that of another would still be shown as, say, a 50 per cent increase, whatever measure we used. We would probably obtain a curve of the general shape of a normal (Gaussian) curve of error – the, so far as we could have predicted, accidental deviations from the mode on either side just offsetting

each other and becoming less numerous as the deviations increase. (Most price changes will be due to a shifting of demand with corresponding falls of some prices and rises of others; and relatively small transfers of this kind seem likely to be more frequent than large ones.) In terms of a money with stable value in this sense, the price of the commodities represented by the mode would then be unchanged, while the amount of transactions taking place at prices increased or decreased by a certain percentage would just balance each other. This will minimise errors, not necessarily of particular individuals, but in the aggregate. And though no practicable index number can fully achieve what we have assumed, a close approximation to the effect ought to be possible.

50   Indeed emulation would probably lead them to refine the technique for maintaining maximum stability to a point far beyond any practical advantage.

51   But, as I wrote 45 years ago [24], p. 3, and would still maintain, '. . . from a practical point of view, it would be one of the worst things which could befall us if the general public should ever again cease to believe in the elementary propositions of the quantity theory'.

52   [A short guide to Professor Leijonhufvud's book is his *Keynes and the Classics*, Occasional Paper 30, IEA, 1969 (7th impression, 1981). – ED.]

53   R. F. Harrod [23a], p. 513.

54   In another sense I stand, however, outside the Keynes–monetarists controversy: both are macro-economic approaches to the problem, while I believe that monetary theory neither needs nor ought to employ such an approach, even if it can hardly wholly dispense with such an essentially macro-economic concept. Macro-economics and micro-economics are alternative methods of dealing with the difficulty that, in the case of such a complex phenomenon as the market, we never command all the factual information which we would need to provide a full explanation. Macro-economics attempts to overcome this difficulty by referring to such magnitudes as aggregates or averages which are statistically available. This gives us a useful approximation to the facts, but as a theoretical explanation of causal connections is unsatisfactory and sometimes misleading, because it asserts empirically observed correlations with no justification for the belief that they will always occur.

The alternative micro-economic approach which I prefer relies on the construction of models which cope with the problem raised by our inescapable ignorance of all the relevant facts by 'reducing the scale' by diminishing the number of independent variables to the minimum required to form a structure which is capable of producing all the *kinds* of movements or changes of which a market system is capable. It is, as I have tried to explain more fully elsewhere [30], a technique which produces merely what I have called 'pattern' predictions but is incapable of producing those predictions of specific events which macro-economics claims, as I believe mistakenly, to be able to produce.

55   To such a situation the classic account of Walter Bagehot [3, penultimate paragraph] would apply: 'In a sensitive state of the English money market the near approach to the legal limit of reserve would be a sure incentive to panic; if one-third were fixed by law, the moment the banks were close to one-third, alarm would begin and would run like magic.'

56   A remarkable recognition of this fundamental truth occurs in the opening paragraphs of the final communique of the Downing Street 'summit' meeting of 8 May 1977, chaired by the Prime Minister of the UK and attended by the President of the USA, the Chancellor of West Germany, the President of France, the Prime Minister of Japan and the Prime Minister of Italy. The first few lines said: 'Inflation is not a remedy for unemployment, but is one of its major causes'. This is an insight for which I have been fighting, almost single-handed, for more than 40 years. Unfortunately, however, that statement over-simplified the issue. In many circumstances inflation indeed leads to a *temporary* reduction of unemployment, but only at the price of causing much more unemployment later. This is exactly what makes inflation so seductive and politically almost irresistible, but for that reason particularly insidious.

57   M. Friedman [20b], p. 31.

58   *Ibid.*, p. 28.

59   F. A. Hayek [31a], vol. III.

60   In an interview given to *Reason* magazine, IX: 34, New York, August 1977, p. 28.

61   Hayek [25], pp. 114 ff.

62   Hayek [26].

63   A good survey of this discussion will be found in V. C. Smith [55].

64   H. Cernuschi [9], as quoted by L. von Mises [47], p. 446; also V. C. Smith [55], p. 91.

65   The expression was originally coined by R. G. Hawtrey.

66   Cf. L. Currie [12].

67   W. Bagehot [3], p. 160: 'I have tediously insisted that the natural system of banking is that of many banks keeping their own reserves, with the penalty of failure before them if they neglect it. I have shown that our system is that of a single bank keeping the whole reserve under no effectual penalty of failure. And yet I propose to retain that system and only attempt to mend and palliate it ... because I am quite sure that it is of no manner of use proposing to alter it ... there is no force to be found adequate to so vast a reconstruction, and so vast a destruction, and therefore it is useless proposing them.' That was almost certainly true so long as the prevailing system worked tolerably, but not after it had broken down.

68   The list is very long and, apart from the well-known writers whose works are noted under numbers [13], [22], [44] and [51] in the Bibliography (pp.

232, 233, 234 and 235), the series of studies by Edward Clarence Riegel (1879–1953) published between 1929 and 1944 deserves special mention as an instance of how the results of acute insights and long reflection which seem to have gained the attention of an economist of the rank of Irving Fisher may be completely invalidated by an ignorance of elementary economics. A posthumous volume by Riegel, entitled *Flight from Inflation. The Monetary Alternative*, has been announced by the Hecther Foundation, San Pedro, California.

69   ['Resist beginnings' (or, colloquially, 'nip it in the bud'): Ovid, *Remedia Amoris*, 91, trans. Showerman, *Oxford Dictionary of Quotations*, OUP. – ED.]

70   The remaining doubt concerns the question whether in such circumstances the holders of cash might wish to switch towards an appreciating currency, but such a currency would then probably not be available.

71   O. Eckstein [14], especially p. 19: 'Traditionally, stabilisation theory has viewed private, capitalist economy as a mechanism which produces fluctuations. ... There is no question that government is a major source of instability.' And p. 25: 'The rate of inflation [in the US between 1962 and 1972] would have been substantially less, real growth would have been smoother, the total amount of unemployment experienced would have been little changed but the variations would have been milder, and the terminal conditions at the end of the period would have made it possible to avoid the wage and price controls.'

72   The long depression of the 1930s, which led to the revival of Marxism (which would probably have been dead today without it), was wholly due to the mismanagement of money by government – before as well as after the crisis of 1929.

73   O. Eckstein [14], p. 26.

74   The standard description of this function and of how it arose is still W. Bagehot, who could rightly speak [3], p. 142 of 'a natural state of banking, that in which all the principal banks kept their own reserve'.

75   The first systematic exposition of my position will be found in my 1937 Geneva lectures on *Monetary Nationalism and International Stability* [27]. It contains a series of lectures hastily and badly written on a topic to which I had earlier committed myself but which I had to write when I was preoccupied with other problems. I still believe that it contains important arguments against flexible exchange rates between national currencies which have never been adequately answered, but I am not surprised that few people appear ever to have read it.

76   Cf. Friedman [19].

77   Hayek [29], pp. 324 *et seq.*

78   W. Bagehot [3], p. 12.

79   McKinnon [40] and Mundell [49].

80   The historical origin of the preoccupation with national price levels as well

as the other aspects of *Monetary Nationalism* were discussed in my book
with that title [27], especially p. 43.

81   [*In posse*, potential; *in esse*, in being. – ED.]

82   One alarming feature, the threat of which is not yet sufficiently appreciated,
is the spreading tendency to regard a government pension as the *only*
trustworthy provision for one's old age, because experience seems to demonstrate that political expediency will force governments to maintain or
even to increase its real value.

83   I use here for once the term 'state' because it is the expression which in the
context would be commonly used by most people who would wish to
emphasise the probability of the beneficial nature of these public activities.
Most people rapidly become aware of the idealistic and unrealistic nature
of their argument if it is pointed out to them that the agent who acts is
never an abstract state but always a very concrete government with all the
defects necessarily inherent in this kind of political institution.

84   Hayek [28], p. 69, note.

85   Indeed it would be the day of final triumph of the new system when
governments began to prefer to receive taxes in currencies other than those
they issue!

86   Adam Smith [54], p. 26.

87   A theme repeatedly argued by the late Ludwig von Mises [45–47].

88   [54], p. 471. The whole paragraph beginning with the sentence quoted and
concluding with the phrase cited further on is well worth reading in the
present connection.

89   As a reviewer of the First Edition of this essay (John Porteous, *New
Statesman*, 14 January 1977) sensibly observed: 'It would have seemed
unthinkable 400 years ago that governments would ever relinquish control
over religious belief.'

90   It has been said that my suggestion to 'construct' wholly new monetary
institutions is in conflict with my general philosophical attitude. But nothing
is further from my thoughts than any wish to design new institutions. What
I propose is simply to remove the existing obstacles which for ages have
prevented the evolution of desirable institutions in money. Our monetary
and banking system is the product of harmful restrictions imposed by
governments to increase their powers. They are certainly not institutions
of which it can be said they have been tried and found good, since the
people were not allowed to try any alternative.

To justify the demand for freedom of development in this field it was
necessary to explain what consequences would probably result from granting such freedom. But what it is possible to foresee is necessarily limited.
It is one of the great merits of freedom that it encourages new inventions,
and they are in their very nature unpredictable. I expect evolution to be
much more inventive than I can possibly be. Though it is always the new
ideas of comparatively few which shape social evolution, the difference

between a free and a regulated system is precisely that in the former it is people who have the better ideas who will determine developments because they will be imitated, while in the latter only the ideas and desires of those in power are allowed to shape evolution. Freedom always creates some new risks. All I can say is that if I were responsible for the fate of a country dear to me I would gladly take that risk in the field I have been considering here.

91   Recent experience also suggests that in future governments may find themselves exposed to international pressure to pursue monetary policies which, while harmful to their own citizens, are supposed to help some other country, and will be able to escape such pressure only by divesting themselves both of the power and the responsibility of controlling the supply of money. We have already reached a stage in which countries which have succeeded in reducing the annual rate of *inflation* to 5 per cent are exhorted by others who lustily continue to inflate at 15 per cent per annum to assist them by 'reflation'.

Bibliography

(Including some relevant works not explicitly referred to in the text.)

For reprints or translations, square brackets show the year of original publication, but page references are to the later publication quoted in full.

[1]   Archibald Alison, *History of Europe*, vol. I, London, 1833.

[2]   Joseph Aschheim and Y. S. Park, *Artificial Currency Units: The Formation of Functional Currency Areas*, Essays in International Finance, No. 114, Princeton, 1976.

[3]   Walter Bagehot, *Lombard Street* [1873], Kegan Paul, London, 1906.

[4]   Paul Barth, *Die Philosophie der Geschichte als Soziologie*, 2nd edn, Leipzig, 1915.

[5]   Jean Bodin, *The Six Books of a Commonweale* [1576], London, 1606.

[5a]   Fernand Braudel, *Capitalism and the Material Life 1400–1800* [1967], London, 1973.

[6]   S. P. Breckinridge, *Legal Tender*, University of Chicago Press, Chicago, 1903.

[7]   C. Bresciani-Turroni, *The Economics of Inflation* [1931], Allen & Unwin, London, 1937.

[7a]   Henry Phelps Brown and Sheila V. Hopkins, 'Seven Centuries of the Prices of Consumables, compared with Builders' Wage-rates', *Economica*, November 1956.

[7b] Henry Phelps Brown and Sheila V. Hopkins, 'Builders' Wage-rates, Prices and Population: Some Further Evidence', *Economica*, February 1959.

[8]   W. W. Carlile, *The Evolution of Modern Money*, Macmillan, London, 1901.

[9]   H. Cernuschi, *Mecanique de l'echange*, Paris, 1865.

[10] H. Cernuschi, *Contre le billet de banques*, Paris, 1866.

[11] Carlo M. Cipolla, *Money, Prices and Civilization in the Mediterranean World: Fifth to Seventeenth Century*, Gordian Press, New York, 1967.

[12] Lauchlin Currie, *The Supply and Control of Money in the United States*, Harvard University Press, Cambridge, Mass., 1934.

[12a] Raymond de Roover, *Gresham on Foreign Exchanges*, Cambridge, Mass., 1949.

[13] C. H. Douglas, *Social Credit* [1924], Omnie Publications, Hawthorn, Calif., 1966.

[14] Otto Eckstein, 'Instability in the Private and Public Sector', *Swedish Journal of Economics*, 75/1, 1973.

[15] Wilhelm Endemann, *Studien in der Romanisch-kanonistischen Rechtslehre*, vol. II, Berlin, 1887.

[16] A. E. Feaveryear, *The Pound Sterling*, Oxford University Press, London, 1931.

[17] Lord Farrer, *Studies in Currency*, London, 1898.

[17a] F. W. Fetter, 'Some Neglected Aspects of Gresham's Law', *Quarterly Journal of Economics*, XLVI, 1931/2.

[18] Stanley Fischer, 'The Demand for Index Bonds', *Journal of Political Economy*, 83/3, 1975.

[18a] Ferdinand Friedensburg, *Münzkunde und Geldgeschichte des Mittelalters und der Neuzeit*, Munich and Berlin, 1926.

[19] Milton Friedman, 'Commodity Reserve Currency' [1951], in *Essays in Positive Economics*, University of Chicago Press, Chicago, 1953.

[20] Milton Friedman, *A Program for Monetary Stability*, Fordham University Press, New York, 1960.

[20a] Milton Friedman, 'The Quantity Theory of Money: A Restatement', in *Studies in the Quantity Theory of Money*, Chicago, 1956.

[20b] Milton Friedman, *Monetary Correction*, Occasional Paper 41, Institute of Economic Affairs, London, 1974.

[21] Josef Garnier, *Traité théorique et pratique du change et des operations de banque*, Paris, 1841.

[21a] Richard Gaettens, *Inflationen, Das Drama der Geldentwertungen vom Altertum bis zur Gegenwart*, Munich, 1955.

[22] Silvio Gesell, *The Natural Economic Order* [1916], Rev. Edn., Peter Owen, London, 1958.

[22a] Herbert Giersch, 'On the Desirable Degree of Flexibility of Exchange Rates', *Weltwirtschaftliches Archiv*, CIX, 1973.

[23] H. Grote, *Die Geldlehre*, Leipzig, 1865.

[23a] R. F. Harrod, *The Life of John Maynard Keynes*, London, 1951.

[24] F. A. Hayek, *Prices and Production*, Routledge, London, 1931.

[25] F. A. Hayek, *Monetary Theory and the Trade Cycle* [1929], Jonathan Cape, London, 1933.

[26] F. A. Hayek, 'Über "Neutrales Geld" ', *Zeitschrift für Nationalökonomie*, 4/5, 1933.

[27] F. A. Hayek, *Monetary Nationalism and International Stability*, The Graduate School of International Studies, Geneva, 1937.

[28] F. A. Hayek, *The Road to Serfdom*, Routledge, London and Chicago, 1944.

[29] F. A. Hayek, *The Constitution of Liberty*, Routledge & Kegan Paul, London and Chicago, 1960.

[30] F. A. Hayek, *Studies in Philosophy, Politics and Economics*, Routledge & Kegan Paul, London and Chicago, 1967.

[31] F. A. Hayek, *Choice in Currency*, Occasional Paper 48, Institute of Economic Affairs, London, 1976.

[31a] F. A. Hayek, *Law, Legislation and Liberty*, Routledge & Kegan Paul and the University of Chicago Press, London and Chicago, vol. I, 1973, vol. II, 1976, vol. III, 1979.

[31b] Karl Helfferich, 'Die geschichtliche Entwicklung der Münzsysteme', *Jahrbücher für Nationalökonomie*, 3.f. IX (LXIV), 1895.

[32] Marianne von Herzfeld, 'Die Geschichte als Funktion der Geldwertbewegungen', *Archiv für Sozialwissenschaft und Sozialpolitik*, 56/3, 1926.

[33] J. R. Hicks, 'A Suggestion for Simplifying the Theory of Money', *Economica*, February 1935.

[34] W. S. Jevons, *Money and the Mechanism of Exchange*, Kegan Paul, London, 1875.

[34a] H. G. Johnson, *Essays in Monetary Economics* [1967], Second Edition, London, 1969.

[34b] H. G. Johnson, *Further Essays in Monetary Economics*, London, 1972.

[34c] H. G. Johnson and A. K. Swoboda (eds.), *The Economics of Common Currencies*, London, 1973.

[34d] Robert A. Jones, 'The Origin and Development of Media of Exchange', *Journal of Political Economy*, LXXXIV, 1976.

[35] Benjamin Klein, 'The Competitive Supply of Money', *Journal of Money, Credit and Banking*, VI, November 1975.

[35a] Benjamin Klein, 'Competing Moneys: Comment', *Journal of Money, Credit and Banking*, 1975.

[36] G. F. Knapp, *The State Theory of Money* [1905], Macmillan, London, 1924.

[37] Axel Leijonhufvud, *On Keynesian Economics and the Economics of Keynes*, Oxford University Press, New York and London, 1968.

[37a] Wilhelm Lexis, 'Bermerkungen über Paralellgeld und Sortengeld', *Jahrbücher für Nationalökonomie*, 3.f.IX (LXIV), 1895.

[37b] Thelma Liesner & Mervyn A. King (eds.), *Indexing for Inflation*, London, 1975.

[37c] R. G. Lipsey, 'Does Money Always Depreciate?', *Lloyds Bank Review*, 58, October 1960.

[38]   S. J. Loyd (later Lord Overstone), *Further Reflections on the State of the Currency and the Action of the Bank of England*, London, 1837.

[39]   Fritz Machlup, 'Euro-Dollar Creation: A Mystery Story', *Banca Nazionale del Lavoro Quarterly Review*, 94, 1970, reprinted Princeton, December 1970.

[40]   R. I. McKinnon, 'Optimum Currency Areas', *American Economic Review*, 53/4, 1963.

[41]   F. A. Mann, *The Legal Aspects of Money*, 3rd Edition, Oxford University Press, London, 1971.

[42]   Arthur W. Marget, *The Theory of Prices*, 2 vols., Prentice-Hall, New York and London, 1938 and 1942.

[42a] A. James Meigs, *Money Matters*, Harper & Row, New York, 1972.

[43]   Carl Menger, *Principles of Economics* [1871], The Free Press, Glencoe, Ill., 1950.

[43a] Carl Menger, 'Geld' [1892], *Collected Works of Carl Menger*, ed. by the London School of Economics, London, 1934.

[44]   Henry Meulen, *Free Banking*, 2nd Edition, Macmillan, London, 1934.

[44a] Fritz W. Meyer and Alfred Schüller, *Spontane Ordnungen in der Geldwirtschaft und das Inflationsproblem*, Tübingen, 1976.

[45]   Ludwig von Mises, *The Theory of Money and Credit* [1912], New Edition, Jonathan Cape, London, 1952.

[46]   Ludwig von Mises, *Geldwertstabilisierung und Konjunkturpolitik*, Jena, 1928.

[47]   Ludwig von Mises, *Human Action*, William Hodge, Edinburgh, 1949; Henry Regnery, Chicago, 1966.

[47a] E. Victor Morgan, *A History of Money* [1965], Penguin Books, Harmondsworth, Rev. Edition, 1969.

[48]   Robert A. Mundell, 'The International Equilibrium', *Kyklos*, 14, 1961.

[49]   Robert A. Mundell, 'A Theory of Optimum Currency Areas', *American Economic Review*, 51, September 1963.

[49a] W. T. Newlyn, 'The Supply of Money and Its Content', *Economic Journal*, LXXIV, 1964.

[50]   Arthur Nussbaum, *Money in the Law, National and International*, Foundation Press, Brooklyn, 1950.

[50a] Karl Olivecrona, *The Problem of the Monetary Unit*, Stockholm, 1957.

[50b] Franz Pick and René Sédillot, *All the Moneys of the World. A Chronicle of Currency Values*, Pick Publishing Corporation, New York, 1971.

[50c] Henri Pirenne, *La civilisation occidentale au Moyen Âge du Milieu du XVe siècle*, Paris, 1933.

[51]   H. Rittershausen, *Der Neubau des deutschen Kredit-Systems*, Berlin, 1932.

[51a] Herbert Rittmann, *Deutsche Geldgeschichte 1484–1914*, Munich, 1974.

[52] Murray N. Rothbard, *What has Government Done to Our Money?*, New Rev. Edition, Rampart College Publications, Santa Anna, Calif., 1974.

[53] Gasparo Scaruffi, *L'Alitinonfo per far ragione e concordandanza d'oro e d'argento*, Reggio, 1582.

[53a] W. A. Shaw, *The History of Currency 1252–1894*, London, 1894.

[54] Adam Smith, *An Inquiry into the Nature and Causes of the Wealth of Nations* [1776], Glasgow edition, Oxford University Press, London, 1976.

[55] Vera C. Smith, *Rationale of Central Banking*, P. S. King, London, 1936.

[56] Werner Sombart, *Der moderne Kapitalismus*, vol. II, 2nd Edition, Munich and Leipzig, 1916/17.

[57] Herbert Spencer, *Social Statics* [1850], Abridged and Rev. Edition, Williams & Norgate, London, 1902.

[58] Wolfgang Stützel, *Über unsere Währungsverfassung*, Tübingen, 1975.

[58a] Brian Summers, 'Private Coinage in America', *The Freeman*, July 1976.

[58b] Earl A. Thompson, 'The Theory of Money and Income Consistent with Orthodox Value Theory', in P. A. Samuelson and G. Horwich (eds.), *Trade, Stability and Macro-economics. Essays in Honor of Lloyd Metzler*, Academic Press, New York and London, 1974.

[59] Gordon Tullock, 'Paper Money – A Cycle in Cathay', *Economic History Review*, IX/3, 1956.

[60] Gordon Tullock, 'Competing Moneys', *Money, Credit and Banking*, 1976.

[61] Roland Vaubel, 'Plans for a European Parallel Currency and SDR Reform', *Weltwirtschaftliches Archiv*, 110/2, 1974.

[61a] Roland Vaubel, 'Freier Wettbewerb zwischen Währungen', *Wirtschaftsdienst*, August 1976.

[62] Willem Vissering, *On Chinese Currency. Coin and Paper Money*, Leiden, 1877.

[63] Knut Wicksell, *Geldzins und Güterpreise*, Jena, 1898.

[64] Knut Wicksell, *Vorlesungen über Nationalökonomie* [1922], English Edition, *Lectures on Political Economy*, vol. II: *Money*, Routledge, 1935.

[64a] Leland B. Yeager, 'Essential Properties of the Medium of Exchange', *Kyklos*, 21, 1968.

3

Market Standards for Money

The power of governments to debauch currencies for political ends has long been condemned by market economists. Monetarists have argued that the government should restrain its production of money; Professor Hayek contended in 1976 that monetary continence would succumb to political pressures and argued for national currencies to be replaced by competing private monies. Here he refines this thinking and suggests that a private 'store of value' – the Standard – would be more likely to overcome the political obstruction to the wholesale denationalisation of currencies, but would be immune from use as a political tool by the state.

Most of the institutions that make it possible to maintain something like 200 times as many human beings alive than could exist on this earth 6,000 years ago are the outcome of a process of competitive evolution. Yet people have never been allowed to experiment in order to find out what would make a really good money. As soon as money came to be widely adopted in exchange, all governments claimed the exclusive right to provide the only kind of money people were allowed to use. In consequence, neither economists nor any other analysts really know yet what kind of money would make the market process work in a truly satisfactory manner.

However inadequate the metallic standards that governments endeavoured to maintain, the gold standard, while it lasted, provided at least a relative degree of stability far more reliable than anything we have had in the last 50 years, during which the purchasing power of the pound sterling has fallen to less than 4 per cent of its value in the 1930s.

Published originally as a contribution to *Economic Affairs*, April–May 1986.

The destruction of the gold standard was itself a consequence of a fundamental change of attitude which occurred a little more than 60 years ago, when a wholly new conception of what came to be regarded as monetary policy emerged with Keynes and replaced efforts directed solely at maintaining the value of the monetary unit at a fixed standard. At about the same time the idea that the powers of central banks should be used to stabilise general economic activity – and employment in particular – was made popular by Keynes's *Tract on Monetary Reform*[1] and by a highly influential Annual Report of the still young US central banking authority, the Federal Reserve Board. Their conceptions of the more ambitious aim of monetary policy were then received with enthusiasm by most young economists, including me.

1 Politics versus Money

These high hopes of what could be expected from political control of the supply of money have been bitterly disappointed. They were indeed bound to fail, because of an elementary truth which by now appears to me to have been demonstrated beyond reasonable doubt: namely, that, because an increase of money in the short run has an undeniably beneficial effect on employment but in the long run must lead to a mis-direction of employment and through it large-scale long-run unemployment, no government can resist the pressure for measures which must eventually prove exceedingly harmful. It cannot be otherwise for one very simple reason: *unchecked party politics and stable money are inherently incompatible.* The beneficial effect on employment of the expansion of credit can last only as long as this expansion is increased at a progressively rising rate; it must therefore ultimately lead to severe economic crises and lasting unemployment.

If present conditions continue, there is no prospect that Britain will ever again have a reliable money that will make it possible for the market economy to reveal its full potential to create wealth. I am wholly convinced that the illusion still held by some economists that Western economies can settle down to a constant mild rate of inflation will soon be recognised as unachievable. The probable developments which economists must expect – unless the system is altered – are alternating periods of inflationary expansion and recurrent depression, with a tend-ency to an upward trend in unemployment. For this instability the market order will be blamed, and its replacement by a planned system more and more urgently demanded. But the fault cannot be blamed on the market order; on the contrary, it occurs precisely because it has never been given the opportunity to develop an effective system of supplying a stabilising medium of exchange.[2]

2 Stable Commodity Prices Preferred

So far as is known at present, the most favourable monetary condition for the working of the market order would secure approximate constancy of the average commodity prices. The reason is that under such a condition individual traders, insofar as they possessed no special information about the factors affecting the prices of particular commodities, would be able to act successfully on the assumption that it was equally probable that any particular commodity would rise or fall in price by a specific percentage; they could therefore also assume that any change of the money price of a good would indicate a similar change in its real price compared with other goods.

The gold standard did secure some limited approach to such a condition, and its abandonment has certainly much reduced the degree of stability which we can expect from the currencies which are now used.

3 Gold Standard: 200 Years of Stability

It is inevitable that any condition in which government, by political pressure, is responsible for monetary policy will lead to recurrent periods of inflation with the ultimate necessity to break them, causing a severe depression. The history of money indicates that, so long as there was a gold standard, fluctuations were short, because the expansion of credit would be braked in time before it had gone very far. On the whole, the gold standard meant that for about 200 years, from the beginning of the 18th century, average prices had been the same, occasionally rising by about 30 per cent and falling by about 30 per cent, but fluctuating around this figure.

Contrast that stability with what has happened in the last 50 years. So long as government is in charge of monetary policy, inflation is bound to continue. The present illusion that government has achieved control over prices will last only so long as 3 per cent inflation is still sufficient to maintain employment. We may find that next year it is no longer sufficient. We shall be told 'You will require at least 5 per cent'; then it will be 10 per cent – and we shall be back to the same instability. The urgency of finding an alternative is as intense as it ever was.

But a return to the gold standard is, unfortunately, impracticable, because any attempt to do so would cause such fluctuations in the value of gold as to produce an even more unstable monetary unit.

4 Denationalisation of Money

A denationalisation of the government monies that are now used and their replacement by competing private currencies, as I suggested some years ago,[3] would still seem to me desirable yet apparently wholly Utopian since no government is likely to permit such a development in the foreseeable future. But in present circumstances it is no longer necessary for this purpose to introduce a new circulating medium. The availability of current accounts, credit cards, and similar devices makes it possible to offer a stable unit available for most current transactions without issuing it in the form of circulating pieces of metal or paper. The offer of current accounts in a stable unit – redeemable on demand in such amounts of the currencies generally used as are required to buy a 'basket' of raw materials and foodstuffs at spot prices determined at the international commodity exchanges, and measured by a weighted index – would achieve the same result. Ideally, such a standard ought to be based on the prices of all the different original factors of production, including land and labour. But as there cannot be a common physical unit for any of these which would be able to fetch an ascertainable market price, we are restricted for a practicable international unit to the commodities traded on international commodity exchanges.

The weighted index number of wholesale prices used would have to be based on a large number – some 30 or 40 – of different quotations of internationally traded raw materials and foodstuffs, weighted according to the approximate volume of their turnover at the commodity exchanges. The weights on which the index number was based would vary with changes in the relative volume of these transactions, on condition that any such change must substitute a 'basket' of the same aggregate value as that which it replaced.

5 'The Standard'

The ideal name for the new unit of account, clearly making its function universally intelligible, would be the proverbial term *Standard*, a rather obvious name which, however, has so far never been used as the designation of a particular monetary unit. Any first user of it for such a purpose who was able to obtain international trade-mark protection would therefore gain an immense advantage over any competitors.

Deposits received by 'Standard Accounts Limited' in whatever current monies it decided to accept, and credit with an equivalent amount of Standards, would have to be invested either in highly liquid securities or other assets bringing net real returns or in loans expressed in Standards.

The chief problem (and risk) of the establishment of 'Standard Accounts Limited' would be that, in order to meet its commitments, it would have to be prepared, and enabled, to meet any growth of the volume of its business, however rapid, if it were to maintain the market value of its Standard as it had been fixed: that is, it would have to be able at any time to accept deposits of any amount of the number of currencies stated. It would similarly have to be able to redeem on demand any amount likely to be requested in the currencies that would be needed to buy at the commodity exchanges the quantities of the different commodities stated in the definition of the Standard. The only acceptable restriction on this requirement would be a constant small premium on the selling price of the Standard over its redemption value.

The crucial question is, of course, how such a 'Standard Accounts Limited' could invest the unpredictable amounts of circulating money it must be prepared to accept in order to be able to redeem them on demand with a presumably larger (possibly very much larger) amount of the same kind of currency. If it is at all possible to earn any real return on assets which must be kept wholly liquid, this obstacle should not be insurmountable; but it clearly raises various difficulties.

If and so long as the institution is fully trusted, most of the balances it holds would soon be used chiefly for transfers from account to account, and only a small part ever would have to be repaid in cash (i.e. the currently circulating money). Yet this may create a dangerous temptation rather than provide a real answer to the difficulty.

6 Reaction of Existing Banks

These aspects can be adequately examined only at length, but the practical conclusion we probably must draw is that such an institution will depend for its functioning on the active help of the existing banks. Yet to these banks it is likely to appear not only as an unwelcome competitor but also as something so wholly different from, and foreign to, traditional banking routine as to be scarcely comprehensible.

But while the common opposition of the banks at one financial centre might well produce a fatal obstacle to the creation of such an institution, the potential gain for the centre at which such an institution is first established may be incalculable. For London, in particular, it might well provide a unique opportunity to regain its position as a financial centre of the world of even more importance than in the past.

Whether it would be possible to secure international legal protection for the exclusive use of the symbolic name 'The Standard' for the new unit of account appears doubtful. Perhaps it might even be preferable if several competitive institutions could use it with some distinguishing byword, perhaps without possessing a monopoly even in their particular country, so long as they agreed on a common composition of the standard index number (and on its occasional modification).

It seems probable that for a long time the use of such a common international unit of exchange would, at least, be used chiefly in wholesale or other large-scale transactions (although including also much expenditure on travel). I do not contemplate that the Standard will be used as pricing in retail trade. For local business, coins and notes, and even some cheques or credit cards, a local currency may well remain indefinitely preferred. But I would anticipate that once such a unit exists it will become increasingly the unit of long-term business contracts. Contracts will begin to be made in Standards, the future value of which is calculable. I suggested in *Denationalisation of Money* that gradually the courts would come to interpret all contracts as intended to be expressed in a stable monetary unit, so that the difficulty of uncertain value of contracts disappears.

But the absurd conception of a 'national currency', with the eternal temptation for politicians to abuse it, will vanish – sooner or later.

Notes

1 First published in 1923; republished by Macmillan, London, 1971.
2 The European Currency Unit (ECU) of the European Monetary System is
   merely a device to measure and co-ordinate the average rate of inflation of
   the several national currencies in the European Community.
3 *Denationalisation of Money: The Argument Refined*, Hobart Paper 70, IEA,
   1976; second edition, 1978; third edition, 1990 (see ch. 2 above). References
   to early discussions of these aspects and some recent contributions will be
   found in Pascal Salin (ed.), *Currency Competition and Monetary Union*,
   Martinus Nijhoff, The Hague, 1984, which also deals with the related but
   distinct problem of free banking.

4

Choice in Currency: a Way to Stop Inflation

1 Money, Keynes and History[1]

The chief root of our present monetary troubles is, of course, the sanction of scientific authority which Lord Keynes and his disciples have given to the age-old superstition that by increasing the aggregate of money expenditure we can lastingly ensure prosperity and full employment. It is a superstition against which economists before Keynes had struggled with some success for at least two centuries.[2] It had governed most of earlier history. This history, indeed, has been largely a history of inflation; significantly, it was only during the rise of the prosperous modern industrial systems and during the rule of the gold standard, that over a period of about two hundred years (in Britain from about 1714 to 1914, and in the United States from about 1749 to 1939) prices were at the end about where they had been at the beginning. During this unique period of monetary stability the gold standard had imposed upon monetary authorities a discipline which prevented them from abusing their powers, as they have done at nearly all other times. Experience in other parts of the world does not seem to have been very different: I have been told that a Chinese law attempted to prohibit paper money for all times (of course, ineffectively), long before the Europeans ever invented it!

Published originally as IEA Occasional Paper No. 48 (1976). The first part of this chapter is based on an address entitled 'International Money', delivered to the Geneva Gold and Monetary Conference on 25 September 1975, at Lausanne, Switzerland.

Keynesian rehabilitation

It was John Maynard Keynes, a man of great intellect but limited knowledge of economic theory, who ultimately succeeded in rehabilitating a view long the preserve of cranks with whom he openly sympathised. He had attempted by a succession of new theories to justify the same, superficially persuasive, intuitive belief that had been held by many practical men before, but that will not withstand rigorous analysis of the price mechanism: just as there cannot be a uniform price for all kinds of labour, an equality of demand and supply for labour in general cannot be secured by managing *aggregate* demand. The volume of employment depends on the correspondence of demand and supply *in each sector* of the economy, and therefore on the wage structure and the distribution of demand between the sectors. The consequence is that over a longer period the Keynesian remedy does not cure unemployment but makes it worse.

The claim of an eminent public figure and brilliant polemicist to provide a cheap and easy means of permanently preventing serious unemployment conquered public opinion and, after his death, professional opinion too. Sir John Hicks has even proposed that we call the third quarter of this century, 1950 to 1975, the age of Keynes, as the second quarter was the age of Hitler.[3] I do not feel that the harm Keynes did is really so much as to justify *that* description. But it is true that, so long as his prescriptions seemed to work, they operated as an orthodoxy which it appeared useless to oppose.

Personal confession

I have often blamed myself for having given up the struggle after I had spent much time and energy criticising the first version of Keynes's theoretical framework. Only after the second part of my critique had appeared did he tell me he had changed his mind and no longer believed what he had said in the *Treatise on Money* of 1930 (somewhat unjustly towards himself, as it seems to me, since I still believe that volume II of the *Treatise* contains some of the best work he ever did). At any rate, I felt it then to be useless to return to the charge, because he seemed so likely to change his views again. When it proved that this new version – the *General Theory* of 1936 – conquered most of the professional opinion, and when in the end even some of the colleagues I most respected supported the wholly Keynesian Bretton Woods agreement, I largely withdrew from the debate, since to proclaim my dissent from the near-unanimous views of the orthodox phalanx would merely have deprived me of a hearing on other matters about which I was more concerned at the time. (I believe, however, that, so far as some of the best British economists were concerned, their support of Bretton Woods was determined more by a misguided patriotism – the hope that it would benefit Britain in her post-war difficulties – than by a belief that it would provide a satisfactory international monetary order.)

2 The Manufacture of Unemployment

I wrote 36 years ago on the crucial point of difference:

> It may perhaps be pointed out that it has, of course, never been denied that employment can be rapidly increased, and a position of 'full employment' achieved in the shortest possible time, by means of monetary expansion – least of all by those economists whose outlook has been influenced by the experience of a major inflation. All that has been contended is that the kind of full employment which can be created in this way is inherently unstable, and that to create employment by these means is to perpetuate fluctuations. There may be desperate situations in which it may indeed be necessary to increase employment at all costs, even if it be only for a short period – perhaps the situation in which Dr Brüning found himself in Germany in 1932 was such a situation in which desperate means would have been justified. But the economist should not conceal the fact that to aim at the maximum of employment which can be achieved in the short run by means of monetary policy is essentially the policy of the desperado who has nothing to lose and everything to gain from a short breathing space.[4]

To this I would now like to add, in reply to the constant deliberate misrepresentation of my views by politicians, who like to picture me as a sort of bogey whose influence makes conservative parties dangerous, what I regularly emphasise and stated nine months ago in my Nobel Memorial Prize Lecture at Stockholm in the following words:

> The truth is that by a mistaken theoretical view we have been led into a precarious position in which we cannot prevent substantial unemployment from re-appearing: not because, as my view is sometimes misrepresented, this unemployment is deliberately brought about as a means to combat

inflation, but because it is now bound to appear as a deeply regrettable but *inescapable* consequence of the mistaken policies of the past as soon as inflation ceases to accelerate.[5]

Unemployment via 'full employment policies'

This manufacture of unemployment by what are called 'full employment policies' is a complex process. In essence it operates by temporary changes in the distribution of demand, drawing both unemployed and already employed workers into jobs which will disappear with the end of inflation. In the periodically recurrent crises of the pre-1914 years the expansion of credit during the preceding boom served largely to finance industrial investment, and the over-development and subsequent unemployment occurred mainly in the industries producing capital equipment. In the engineered inflation of the last decades things were more complex.

What will happen during a major inflation is illustrated by an observation from the early 1920s which many of my Viennese contemporaries will confirm: in the city many of the famous coffee houses were driven from the best corner sites by new bank offices and returned after the 'stabilisation crisis', when the banks had contracted or collapsed and thousands of bank clerks swelled the ranks of the unemployed.

The lost generation

The whole theory underlying the full employment policies has by now of course been thoroughly discredited by the experience of the last few years. In consequence the economists are also beginning to discover its fatal intellectual defects which they ought to have seen all along. Yet I fear the theory will still give us a lot of trouble: it has left us with a lost generation of economists who have learnt nothing else. One of our chief problems will be to protect our money against those economists who will continue to offer their quack remedies, the short-term effectiveness of which will continue to ensure them popularity. It will survive among blind doctrinaires who have always been convinced that they have the key to salvation.

The 1863 penny

In consequence, though the rapid descent of Keynesian doctrine from intellectual respectability can be denied no longer, it still gravely threatens the chances of a sensible monetary policy. Nor have people yet fully realised how much irreparable damage it has already done, particularly in Britain, the country of its origin. The sense of financial respectability which once guided British monetary policy has rapidly disappeared. From a model to be imitated Britain has in a few years descended to be a warning example for the rest of the world. This decay was recently brought home to me by a curious incident: I found in a drawer of my desk a British penny dated 1863 which a short 12 years ago, that is, when it was exactly a hundred years old, I had received as change from a London bus conductor and had taken back to Germany to show to my students what long-run monetary stability meant. I believe they were duly impressed. But they would laugh in my face if I now mentioned Britain as an instance of monetary stability.

3 The Weakness of Political Control of Money

A wise man should perhaps have foreseen that less than 30 years after the nationalisation of the Bank of England the purchasing power of the pound sterling would have been reduced to less than one-quarter of what it had been at that date. As has sooner or later happened everywhere, government control of the quantity of money has once again proved fatal. I do not want to question that a very intelligent and wholly independent national or international monetary authority *might* do better than an international gold standard, or any other sort of automatic system. But I see not the slightest hope that any government, or any institution subject to political pressure, will ever be able to act in such a manner.

Group interests harmful

I never had much illusion in this respect, but I must confess that in the course of a long life my opinion of governments has steadily worsened: the more intelligently they try to act (as distinguished from simply following an established rule), the more harm they seem to do – because once they are known to aim at particular goals (rather than merely maintaining a self-correcting spontaneous order) the less they can avoid serving sectional interests. And the demands of all organised group interests are almost invariably harmful – except only when they protest against restrictions imposed upon them for the benefit of other group interests. I am by no means re-assured by the fact that, at least in some countries, the civil servants who run affairs are mostly intelligent, well-meaning, and honest men. The point is that, if governments are to remain in office in the prevailing political order, they have no choice but to use their powers for the benefit of particular groups – and one strong interest is always to get additional money for extra expenditure. However harmful inflation is in general seen to be, there are always substantial groups of people, including some for whose support collectivist-inclined governments primarily look, which in the short run greatly gain by it – even if only by staving off for some time the loss of an income which it is human nature to believe will be only temporary if they can tide over the emergency.

Rebuilding the resistances to inflation

The pressure for more and cheaper money is an ever-present political force which monetary authorities have never been able to resist, unless they were in a position credibly to point to an absolute obstacle which made it impossible for them to meet such demands. And it will become even more irresistible when these interests can appeal to an increasingly unrecognisable image of St Maynard. There will be no more urgent need than to erect new defences against the onslaughts of popular forms of Keynesianism; that is, to replace or restore those restraints which, under the influence of his theory, have been systematically dismantled. It was the main function of the gold standard, of balanced budgets, of the necessity for deficit countries to contract their circulation, and of the limitation of the supply of 'international liquidity', to make it impossible for the monetary authorities to capitulate to the pressure for more money. And it was exactly for that reason that all these safeguards against inflation, which had made it possible for representative governments to resist the demands of powerful pressure groups for more money, have been removed at the instigation of economists who imagined that, if governments were released from the shackles of mechanical rules, they would be able to act wisely for the general benefit.

I do not believe we can now remedy this position by *constructing* some new international monetary order, whether a new international monetary authority or institution, or even an international agreement to adopt a particular mechanism or system of policy, such as the classical gold standard. I am fairly convinced that any attempt now to re-instate the gold standard by international agreement would break down within a short time and merely discredit the ideal of an international gold standard for even longer. Without the conviction of the public at large that certain immediately painful measures are occasionally necessary to preserve reasonable stability, we cannot hope that any authority which has power to determine the quantity of money will long resist the pressure for, or the seduction of, cheap money.

Protecting money from politics

The politician, acting on a modified Keynesian maxim that in the long run we are all out of office, does not care if his successful cure of unemployment is bound to produce more unemployment in the future. The politicians who will be blamed for it will not be those who created the inflation but those who stopped it. No worse trap could have been set for a democratic system in which the government is forced to act on the beliefs that the people think to be true. Our only hope for a stable money is indeed now to find a way to protect money from politics.

With the exception only of the 200-year period of the gold standard, practically all governments of history have used their exclusive power to issue money in order to defraud and plunder the people. There is less ground than ever for hoping that, so long as the people have no choice but to use the money their government provides, governments will become more trustworthy. Under the prevailing systems of government, which are supposed to be guided by the opinion of the majority but under which in practice any sizeable group may create a 'political necessity' for the government by threatening to withhold the votes it needs to claim majority support, we cannot entrust dangerous instruments to it. Fortunately we need not yet fear, I hope, that governments will start a war to please some indispensable group of supporters, but money is certainly too dangerous an instrument to leave to the fortuitous expediency of politicians – or, it seems, economists.

A dangerous monopoly

What is so dangerous and ought to be done away with is not governments' right to issue money but the *exclusive* right to do so and their power to force people to use it and to accept it at a particular price. This monopoly of government, like the postal monopoly, has its origin not in any benefit it secures for the people but solely in the desire to enhance the coercive powers of government. I doubt whether it has ever done any good except to the rulers and their favourites. All history contradicts the belief that governments have given us a safer money than we would have had without their claiming an exclusive right to issue it.

4 Choice of Money for Payment in Contracts

But why should we not let people choose freely what money they want to use? By 'people' I mean the individuals who ought to have the right to decide whether they want to buy or sell for francs, pounds, dollars, D-marks, or ounces of gold. I have no objection to governments issuing money, but I believe their claim to a *monopoly*, or their power to *limit* the kinds of money in which contracts may be concluded within their territory, or to determine the *rates* at which monies can be exchanged, to be wholly harmful.

At this moment it seems that the best thing we could wish governments to do is for, say, all the members of the European Economic Community, or, better still, all the governments of the Atlantic Community, to bind themselves mutually not to place any restrictions on the free use within their territories of one another's – or any other – currencies, including their purchase and sale at any price the parties decide upon, or on their use as accounting units in which to keep books. This, and not a Utopian European Monetary Unit, seems to me now both the practicable and the desirable arrangement to aim at. To make the scheme effective it would be important, for reasons I state later, also to provide that banks in one country be free to establish branches in any of the others.

Government and legal tender

This suggestion may at first seem absurd to all brought up on the concept of 'legal tender'. Is it not essential that the law designate one kind of money as the legal money? This is, however, true only to the extent that, *if* the government does issue money, it must also say what must be accepted in discharge of debts incurred in that money. And it must also determine in what manner certain non-contractual legal obligations, such as taxes or liabilities for damage or torts, are to be discharged. But there is no reason whatever why people should not be free to make contracts, including ordinary purchases and sales, in any kind of money they choose, or why they should be obliged to sell against any particular kind of money.

There could be no more effective check against the abuse of money by the government than if people were free to refuse any money they distrusted and to prefer money in which they had confidence. Nor could there be a stronger inducement to governments to ensure the stability of their money than the knowledge that, so long as they kept the supply below the demand for it, that demand would tend to grow. Therefore, let us deprive governments (or their monetary authorities) of all power to protect their money against competition: if they can no longer conceal that their money is becoming bad, they will have to restrict the issue.

The first reaction of many readers may be to ask whether the effect of such a system would not, according to an old rule, be that the bad money would drive out the good. But this would be a misunderstanding of what is called Gresham's Law. This indeed is one of the oldest insights into the mechanism of money, so old that 2,400 years ago Aristophanes, in one of his comedies, could say that it was with politicians as it is with coins, because the bad ones drive out the good.[6] But the truth which apparently even today is not generally understood is that Gresham's Law operates *only* if the two kinds of money have to be accepted at a prescribed rate of exchange. Exactly the opposite will happen when people are free to exchange the different kinds of money at whatever rate they can agree upon. This was observed many times during the great inflations when even the most severe penalties threatened by governments could not prevent people from using other kinds of money – even commodities like cigarettes and bottles of brandy rather than the government money – which clearly meant that the good money was driving out the bad.[7]

Benefits of free currency system

Make it merely legal and people will be very quick indeed to refuse to use the national currency once it depreciates noticeably, and they will make their dealings in a currency they trust. Employers, in particular, would find it in their interest to offer, in collective agreements, not wages anticipating a foreseen rise of prices but wages in a currency they trusted and could make the basis of rational calculation. This would deprive government of the power to counteract excessive wage increases, and the unemployment they would cause, by depreciating their currency. It would also prevent employers from conceding such wages in the expectation that the national monetary authority would bail them out if they promised more than they could pay.

There is no reason to be concerned about the effects of such an arrangement on ordinary men who know neither how to handle nor how to obtain strange kinds of money. So long as the shopkeepers knew that they could turn it instantly at the current rate of exchange into whatever money they preferred, they would be only too ready to sell their wares at an appropriate price for any currency. But the malpractices of govern-ment would show themselves much more rapidly if prices rose only in terms of the money issued by it, and people would soon learn to hold the government responsible for the value of the money in which they were paid. Electronic calculators, which in seconds would give the equivalent of any price in any currency at the current rate, would soon be used everywhere. But, unless the national government all too badly mismanaged the currency it issued, it would probably be continued to be used in everyday retail transactions. What would be affected mostly would be not so much the use of money in daily payments as the willingness to *hold* different kinds of money. It would mainly be the tendency of all business and capital transactions rapidly to switch to a more reliable standard (and to base calculations and accounting on it) which would keep national monetary policy on the right path.

5 Long-run Monetary Stability

The upshot would probably be that the currencies of those countries trusted to pursue a responsible monetary policy would tend to displace gradually those of a less reliable character. The reputation of financial righteousness would become a jealously guarded asset of all issuers of money, since they would know that even the slightest deviation from the path of honesty would reduce the demand for their product.

I do not believe there is any reason to fear that in such a competition for the most general acceptance of a currency there would arise a tendency to deflation or an increasing value of money. People will be quite as reluctant to borrow or incur debts in a currency expected to appreciate as they will hesitate to lend in a currency expected to depreciate. The convenience of use is decidedly in favour of a currency which can be expected to retain an approximately stable value. If governments and other issuers of money have to compete in inducing people to *hold* their money, and make long-term contracts in it, they will have to create confidence in its long-run stability.

'The universal prize'

Where I am not sure is whether in such a competition for reliability any government-issued currency would prevail, or whether the predominant preference would not be in favour of some such units as ounces of gold. It seems not unlikely that gold would ultimately re-assert its place as 'the universal prize in all countries, in all cultures, in all ages', as Jacob Bronowski has recently called it in his brilliant book on *The Ascent of Man*,[8] if people were given complete freedom to decide what to use as their standard and general medium of exchange – more likely, at any rate, than as the result of any organised attempt to restore the gold standard.

The reason why, in order to be fully effective, the free international market in currencies should extend also to the services of banks is, of course, that bank deposits subject to cheque represent today much the largest part of the liquid assets of most people. Even during the last hundred years or so of the gold standard this circumstance increasingly prevented it from operating as a fully international currency, because any inflow or outflow in or out of a country required a proportionate expansion or contraction of the much larger superstructure of the national credit money, the effect of which falls indiscriminately on the whole economy instead of merely increasing or decreasing the demand for the particular goods which was required to bring about a new balance between imports and exports. With a truly international banking system, money could be transferred directly without producing the harmful process of secondary contractions or expansions of the credit structure.

It would probably also impose the most effective discipline on governments if they felt immediately the effects of their policies on the attractive-ness of investment in their country. I have just read in an English Whig tract more than 250 years old: 'Who would establish a Bank in an arbitrary country, or trust his money constantly there?'[9] The tract, incidentally, tells us that yet another 50 years earlier a great French banker, Jean Baptist Tavernier, invested all the riches he had amassed in his long rambles over the world in what the authors described as 'the barren rocks of Switzerland'; when asked why by Louis XIV, he had the courage to tell him that 'he was willing to have something which he could call his own!' Switzerland, apparently, laid the foundations of her prosperity earlier than most people realise.

Free dealings in money better than monetary unions

I prefer the freeing of all dealings in money to any sort of monetary union also because the latter would demand an international monetary authority which I believe is neither practicable nor even desirable – and hardly to be more trusted than a national authority. It seems to me that there is a very sound element in the widespread disinclination to confer sovereign powers, or at least powers to command, on any international authority. What we need are not international authorities possessing powers of direction, but merely international bodies (or, rather, inter-national treaties which are effectively enforced) which can prohibit certain actions of governments that will harm other people. Effectively to prohibit all restrictions on dealings in (and the possession of) different kinds of money (or claims for money) would at last make it possible that the absence of tariffs, or other obstacles to the movement of goods and men, will secure a genuine free trade area or common market – and do more than anything else to create confidence in the countries committing themselves to it. It is now urgently needed to counter that monetary nationalism which I first criticised almost 40 years ago[10] and which is becoming even more dangerous when, as a consequence of the close kinship between the two views, it is turning into monetary socialism. I hope it will not be too long before complete freedom to deal in any money one likes will be regarded as the essential mark of a free country.[11]

You may feel that my proposal amounts to no less than the abolition of monetary policy; and you would not be quite wrong. As in other connections, I have come to the conclusion that the best the state can do with respect to money is to provide a framework of legal rules within which the people can develop the monetary institutions that best suit them. It seems to me that if we could prevent governments from meddling with money, we would do more good than any government has ever done in this regard. And private enterprise would probably have done better than the best they have ever done.

I A Comment on Keynes, Beveridge, and Keynesian Economics

Lord Keynes has always appeared to me a kind of new John Law. Like Law, Keynes was a financial genius who made some real contributions to the theory of money. (Apart from an interesting and original discussion of the factors determining the value of money, Law gave the first satisfactory account of the cumulative growth of acceptability once a commodity was widely used as a medium of exchange.) But Keynes could never free himself from the popular false belief that, as Law expressed it, 'as the additional money will give work to people who were idle and enabled those already working to earn more, the output will increase and industry will prosper'.[12]

It was against this sort of view that Richard Cantillon and David Hume began the development of modern monetary theory. Hume in particular put the central point at issue by saying that, in the process of inflation, 'it is only in this interval or intermediate situation between the acquisition of money and the rise of prices, that the increasing quantity of gold and silver is favourable to industry'.[13] It is this work we shall have to do again after the Keynesian flood.

In one sense, however, it would be somewhat unfair to blame Lord Keynes too much for the developments after his death. I am certain he would have been – whatever he had said earlier – a leader in the fight against the present inflation. But developments, at least in Britain, were also mainly determined by the version of Keynesianism published under the name of Lord Beveridge for which (since he himself understood no economics whatever) his scientific advisers must bear the responsibility.

I have been blamed for charging Lord Keynes with a somewhat limited knowledge of economic theory, but the defectiveness of his views on the theory of international trade, for example, has often been pointed out. And the clearest proof seems to me to be the caricature of other theories which he presented, presumably in good faith, in order to refute them.

Notes

1 [The main section and sub-headings have been inserted to help readers, especially non-economists unfamiliar with Professor Hayek's writings, to follow the argument; they were not part of the original lecture. – ED.]

2 [This observation is amplified by Professor Hayek in a note, 'A Comment on Keynes, Beveridge, and Keynesian Economics', below, p. 257. – ED.]

3 John Hicks, *The Crisis in Keynesian Economics*, Oxford University Press, 1974, p. 1.

4 F. A. Hayek, *Profits, Interest and Investment*, Routledge & Kegan Paul, London, 1939, p. 63n.

5 F. A. Hayek, 'The Pretence of Knowledge', Nobel Memorial Prize Lecture 1974, reprinted in *Full Employment at Any Price?*, Occasional Paper 45, IEA, 1975, p. 37 (see below, ch. 6, p. 280 – quotation cited on p. 287).

6 Aristophanes, *Frogs*, 891–8, in Frere's translation:

> Oftentimes we have reflected on a similar abuse
> In the choice of men for office, and of coins for common use,
> For our old and standard pieces, valued and approved and tried,
> Here among the Grecian nations, and in all the world besides,
> Recognised in every realm for trusty stamp and pure assay,
> Are rejected and abandoned for the trash of yesterday,
> For a vile adulterated issue, drossy, counterfeit and base,
> Which the traffic of the city passes current in their place.

About the same time, the philosopher Diogenes called money 'the legislators' game of dice'!

7 During the German inflation after the First World War, when people began to use dollars and other solid currencies in the place of marks, a Dutch financier (if I rightly remember, Mr Vissering) asserted that Gresham's Law was false and the opposite true.

8 Jacob Bronowski, *The Ascent of Man*, BBC Publications, London, 1973.

9 Thomas Gordon and John Trenchard, *The Cato Letters*, letters dated 12 May 1722 and 3 February 1721 respectively, published in collected editions, London, 1724, and later.

10 *Monetary Nationalism and International Stability*, Longmans, London, 1937.

11 It may at first seem as if this suggestion were in conflict with my general support of fixed exchange rates under the present system. But this is not so. Fixed exchange rates seem to me to be necessary so long as national governments have a monopoly of issuing money in their territory in order to place them under a very necessary discipline. But this is of course no longer necessary when they have to submit to the discipline of competition with other issuers of money equally current within their territory.

12   John Law, *Money and Trade Considered with a Proposal for Supplying the Nations with Money*, W. Lewis, London, 1705. [*A Collection of Scarce and Valuable Tracts* (the Somers Collection of Tracts, Vol. XIII), John Murray, London, 1815, includes John Law's tract (1720 edition) at pp. 775–817; an extract from p. 812 reads: 'But as this addition to the money will employ the people that are now idle, and those now employed to more advantage, so the product will be increased, and manufacture advanced.' – ED.]

13   David Hume, *On Money* (Essay III).

5

Inflation: the Path to Unemployment

1 The Economic Consequences of Lord Keynes

The responsibility for current world-wide inflation, I am sorry to say, rests wholly and squarely with the economists, or at least with that great majority of my fellow economists who have embraced the teachings of Lord Keynes.

What we are experiencing are simply the economic consequences of Lord Keynes. It was on the advice and even urging of his pupils that governments everywhere have financed increasing parts of their expenditure by creating money on a scale which every reputable economist before Keynes would have predicted would cause precisely the sort of inflation we have got. They did this in the erroneous belief that this was both a necessary and a lastingly effective method of securing full employment.

'Seductive doctrine'

The seductive doctrine that a government deficit, as long as unemployment existed, was not only innocuous but even meritorious was of course most welcome to politicians. The advocates of this policy have long maintained that an increase of total expenditure which still led to an increase of employment could not be regarded as inflation at all. And now, when the steadily accelerating rise of prices has rather discredited

Published originally as a contribution to IEA Readings No. 14, *Inflation: Causes, Consequences, Cures* (1974). Reproduced by kind permission of the Editor and the author from the *Daily Telegraph*, 15 and 16 October 1974.

this view, the general excuse is still that a moderate inflation is a small price to pay for full employment: 'rather five per cent inflation than five per cent unemployment', as it has recently been put by the German Chancellor.

This persuades most people who do not see the grave harm which inflation does. It might seem – and even some economists have maintained – that all inflation does is to bring about some redistribution of incomes, so that what some lose others will gain, while unemployment necessarily means a reduction of aggregate real income.

This, however, disregards the chief harm which inflation causes, namely that it gives the whole structure of the economy a distorted, lopsided character which sooner or later makes a more extensive unemployment inevitable than that which that policy was intended to prevent. It does so by drawing more and more workers into kinds of jobs which depend on continuing or even accelerating inflation. The result is a situation of rising instability in which an ever-increasing part of current employment is dependent on continuing and perhaps accelerating inflation and in which every attempt to slow down inflation will at once lead to so much unemployment that the authorities will rapidly abandon it and resume inflation.

We are already familiar with the concept of 'stagflation' to describe that state in which the accepted rate of inflation no longer suffices to produce satisfactory employment. Politicians in that position have now little choice but to speed up inflation.

Disorganisation of economic activity

But this process cannot go on for ever, as an accelerating inflation soon leads to a complete disorganisation of all economic activity. Nor can this end be avoided by any effort to control prices and wages while the increase of the quantity of money continues: the particular jobs inflation has created depend on a continued rise of prices and will disappear as soon as that stops. A 'repressed' inflation, beside causing a still worse disorganisation of economic activity than an open one, has not even the advantage of maintaining that employment which the preceding open inflation has created.

We have in fact been led into a frightful position. All politicians promise that they will stop inflation *and* preserve full employment. But they *cannot* do this. And the longer they succeed in keeping up employment by continuing inflation, the greater will be the unemployment when the inflation finally comes to an end. There is no magic trick by which we can extricate ourselves from this position which we have created.

This does not mean that we need go through another period of unemployment as we did in the 1930s. That was due to the failure to prevent an actual shrinkage of the total demand for which there was no justification. But we must face the fact that in the present situation merely to stop the inflation or even to slow down its rate will produce substantial unemployment. Certainly nobody wishes this, but we can no longer avoid it and all attempts to postpone it will only increase its ultimate size.

The only alternative we have, and which, unfortunately, is a not unlikely outcome, is a command economy in which everyone is assigned his job; and though such an economy might avoid outright worklessness, the position of the great majority of workers in it would certainly be much worse than it would be even during a period of unemployment.

Market economy not at fault

It is not the market economy (or 'the capitalist system') which is responsible for this calamity but our own mistaken monetary and financial policy. What we have done is to represent on a colossal scale what in the past produced the recurring cycles of booms and depressions; to allow a long inflationary boom to bring about a misdirection of labour and other resources into employments in which they can be maintained only so long as inflation exceeds expectations. But while in the past the mechanism of the international monetary system brought such an inflation to a stop after a few years, we have managed to design a new system which allowed it to run on for two decades.

As long as we try to maintain this situation we are only making things worse in the long run. We can prevent a greater reaction than is necessary only by giving up the illusion that the boom can be prolonged indefinitely and by facing now the task of mitigating the suffering and preventing the reaction from degenerating into a deflationary spiral. It will chiefly be a task not of preserving existing jobs but of facilitating the opening of (temporary and permanent) new jobs for those who will inevitably lose their present ones.

We can no longer hope to avoid this necessity, and closing our eyes to the problem will not make it go away. It may well be true that because people have been taught that government can always prevent unemployment, its failure to do so will cause grave social disturbances.

But if this is so, we probably have it no longer in our power to prevent this.

2 Restructuring the Economy by Making Markets Work

In order to see clearly the causes of our troubles it is necessary to understand the chief fault of the theory which has been guiding monetary and financial policy during the past 25 years. It is the belief that all important unemployment is due to an insufficiency of aggregate demand and can be cured by an increase of that demand.

This is the more readily believed as it is true that some employment is due to that cause and that an increase in aggregate demand will in most circumstances lead to a temporary increase of employment. But not all unemployment is due to an insufficiency of total demand or would disappear if total demand were higher. And, worse, much of the employment which an increase of demand at first produces cannot be maintained by demand remaining at that higher level but only by a continued rise of demand.

This sort of unemployment which we temporarily 'cure' by inflation, but in the long run are making worse by it, is due to the misdirection of resources which inflation causes. It can be prevented only by a movement of workers from the jobs where there is an excess supply to those where there is a shortage. In other words, a continuous adjustment of the various kinds of labour to the changing demand requires a real labour market in which the wages of the different kinds of labour are determined by demand and supply.

Without a functioning labour market there can be no meaningful cost calculation and no efficient use of resources. Such a market can exist even with fairly strong trade unions so long as the unions bear the responsibility for any unemployment excessive wage demands will cause. But it disappears once government relieves the unions of this responsibility by committing itself to the maintenance of full employment at any price.

Rôle of the unions

This, incidentally, also answers the very confusing dispute about the rôle of the unions in causing inflation. There is, strictly speaking, no such thing as a cost-push inflation: all inflation is caused by excessive demand. To this extent the 'monetarists' led by Professor Milton Friedman are perfectly right. But unions can force a government committed to a Keynesian full employment policy to inflate in order to prevent the unemployment which their actions could otherwise cause; indeed, if it is believed that government will prevent a rise of wages from leading to unemployment, there is no limit to the magnitude of wage demands – and, indeed, even little reason for the employers to resist them.

There is a little more reason to question Professor Friedman's recommendation of indexing as a means to combat the current inflation. No doubt indexing could do a lot to mitigate the harm inflation does to such groups as pensioners or those who have retired on their savings. And it might even cure at the root such inflations as are due to the inability of a government to keep up revenue to cover current expenditure.

But it is not likely to remedy the present inflation which is due to all people together trying to buy more than there is on the market and insisting that they be given enough money to enable them to buy at current prices what they expect to get. In this they must always be disappointed by a new rise of prices caused by their demand, and the vicious circle can be broken only by people contenting themselves with a somewhat lower real buying power than that which they have been vainly chasing for so long. This effect, however, a general adoption of indexing would prevent. It might even make a continuous inflation inevitable.

But at present it is not chiefly wage demands that drive us into accelerating inflation – though they are part of the mechanism that does so. But people will learn before long that the increase of money wages is self-defeating. What is likely to drive us further on the perilous road will be the panicky reactions of politicians every time a slowing down of inflation leads to a substantial rise of unemployment. They are likely to react to it by resuming inflation and will find that every time it needs a larger dose of inflation to restore employment until in the end this medicine will altogether fail to work. It is this process which we must avoid at any price. It can be tolerated only by those who wish to destroy the market order and to replace it by a Communist or some other totalitarian system.

'Face the facts'

The first requirement, if we are to avoid this fate, is that we face the facts, and make people at large understand that, after the mistakes we have made, it simply is no longer in our power to maintain uninterrupted full employment. No economist who has lived through the experience of the 1930s will doubt that extensive and prolonged unemployment is one of the worst disasters which can befall a country. But all we can hope to do now is to prevent it from becoming too extensive and too prolonged and that it will be no more than an unavoidable period of transition to a state in which we can again hope to achieve the reasonable goal of a high and stable level of employment.

What the public must learn to understand if a rational policy is to be possible is that, whatever may be the fault of past governments, in the present position it is simply no longer in the power of government to maintain full employment and a tolerable productive organisation of the economy.

It will need great courage – and almost more understanding than one dares to hope for – on the part of the government to make people understand what the position is. We are probably approaching a critical test of democracy about the outcome of which one must feel apprehensive. One of the prime requirements of its successfully weathering this crisis is that the people are in time undeceived about the fateful illusion that there is a cheap and easy means of at the same time securing full employment and a continuous rapid rise of real wages. This can be achieved only by that steady restructuring of the use of all resources in adaptation to changing real conditions which the debauching of the monetary medium prevents and only a properly functioning market can bring about.

6

Full Employment at Any Price?

I Inflation, the Misdirection of Labour, and Unemployment

1 Inflation and Unemployment

After a unique 25-year period of great prosperity the economy of the Western world has arrived at a critical point. I expect that the experience of the period will enter history under the name of The Great Prosperity as the 1930s are known as The Great Depression. We have indeed succeeded, by eliminating all the automatic brakes which operated in the past, namely the gold standard and fixed rates of exchange, in maintaining the full and even over-employment which was created by an expansion of credit and in the end prolonged by open inflation, for a much longer time than I should have thought possible. But the inevitable end is now near, if it has not already arrived.

I find myself in an unpleasant situation. I had preached for 40 years that the time to prevent the coming of a depression is the boom. During

Published originally as IEA Occasional Paper No. 45 (1975). The first part of this chapter is a revised version of a lecture, delivered on 8 February 1975, to the 'Convegno Internazionale: Il Problema della Moneta Oggi', organised in commemoration of the 100th birthday of Luigi Einaudi by the Academia Nazionale dei Lincei at Rome, and to be published in the proceedings of that congress. Part II is the Alfred Nobel Memorial Lecture, delivered on 11 December 1974, at the Stockholm School of Economics: © copyright The Nobel Foundation, Stockholm.

the boom nobody listened to me. Now people again turn to me and ask how the consequences of a policy of which I had constantly warned can be avoided. I must witness the heads of the governments of all the Western industrial countries promising their people that they will stop the inflation *and* preserve full employment. But I know that they *cannot* do this. I even fear that such attempts, as President Ford has just announced, to postpone the inevitable crisis by a new inflationary push, may temporarily succeed and make the eventual breakdown even worse.

Three choices in policy

The disquieting but unalterable truth is that a false monetary and credit policy, pursued through almost the whole period since the last war, has placed the economic systems of all the Western industrial countries in a highly unstable position in which *anything* we can do will produce most unpleasant consequences. We have a choice between only three possibilities:

- To allow a rapidly accelerating open inflation to continue until it has brought about a complete disorganisation of all economic activity.
- To impose controls of wages and prices which will for a time conceal the effects of a continued inflation but would inevitably lead to a centrally-directed totalitarian economic system.
- Finally, to terminate resolutely the increase of the quantity of money which would soon, through the appearance of substantial unemployment, make manifest all the misdirections of labour which the inflation of the past years has caused and which the two other procedures would further increase.

Lessons of the Great Inflation

To understand why the whole Western world allowed itself to be led into this frightful dilemma, it is necessary to glance briefly back at two events soon after the First World War which have largely determined the views that have governed the policy of the post-war years. I want first to recall an experience which has unfortunately been largely forgotten. In Austria and Germany the Great Inflation had directed our attention to the connection between changes in the quantity of money and changes in the degree of employment. It especially showed us that the employment created by inflation diminished as soon as the inflation slowed down, and that the termination of the inflation always produced what came to be called a 'stabilisation crisis' with substantial unemployment. It was the insight into this connection which made me and some of my contemporaries from the outset reject and oppose the kind of full employment policy propagated by Lord Keynes and his followers.

I do not want to leave this recollection of the Great Inflation without adding that I have probably learnt at least as much if not more than I learnt from personally observing it by being taught to see – then largely by my teacher, the late Ludwig von Mises – the utter stupidity of the arguments then propounded, especially in Germany, to explain and justify the increases in the quantity of money. Most of these arguments I am now encountering again in countries, not least Britain and the USA, which then seemed economically better trained and whose economists rather looked down at the foolishness of the German economists. None of these apologists of the inflationary policy was able to propose or apply measures to terminate the inflation, which was finally ended by a man, Hjalmar Schacht, who firmly believed in a crude and primitive version of the quantity theory.

British origin of inflation as cure for unemployment

The policy of the recent decades, or the theory which underlies it, had its origin, however, in the specific experiences of Great Britain during the 1920s and 1930s. Great Britain had after what now seems the very modest inflation of the First World War, returned to the gold standard in 1925, in my opinion very sensibly and honestly, but unfortunately and unwisely at the former parity. This had in no way been required by classical doctrine: David Ricardo had in 1821 written to a friend[1] that 'I never should advise a government to restore a currency, which was depreciated 30 per cent, to par'. I ask myself often how different the economic history of the world might have been if, in the discussion of the years preceding 1925, even only one English economist had remembered and pointed out this long-published passage from Ricardo.

In the event, the unfortunate decision taken in 1925 made a prolonged process of deflation inevitable, which process might have been successful in maintaining the gold standard if it had been continued until a large part of the wages had been reduced. I believe this attempt was near success when in the world crisis of 1931 Britain abandoned it together with the gold standard, which was greatly discredited by this event.

2 Keynes's Political 'Cure' for Unemployment

Development of Keynesian ideas

It was during the period of extensive unemployment in Great Britain preceding the world-wide economic crisis of 1929–31 that John Maynard Keynes developed his basic ideas. It is important to note that this development of his economic thought happened in a very exceptional and almost unique position of his country. It was a period when, as a result of the big appreciation of the international value of the pound sterling, the real wages of practically all British workers had been substantially increased compared with the rest of the world, and British exporters had in consequence become substantially unable successfully to compete with other countries. In order to give employment to the unemployed it would therefore have been necessary either to reduce practically *all* wages or to raise the sterling prices of most commodities.

In the development of Keynes's thought it is possible to distinguish three distinct phases. First, he began with the recognition that it was necessary to reduce real wages. Second, he arrived at the conclusion that this was *politically* impossible. Third, he convinced himself that it would be vain and even harmful. The Keynes of 1919 had still understood that:

> There is no subtler, no surer means of overturning the existing basis of society than to debauch the currency. The process engages all the hidden forces of economic law on the side of destruction, and does it in a manner which not one man in a million is able to diagnose.[2]

His political judgement made him the inflationist, or at least avid anti-deflationist, of the 1930s. I have, however, good reason to believe that he would have disapproved of what his followers did in the post-war period. If he had not died so soon, he would have become one of the leaders in the fight against inflation.

'The fatal idea'

It was in that unfortunate episode of English monetary history in which he became the intellectual leader that he gained acceptance for the fatal idea: that unemployment is predominantly due to an insufficiency of aggregate demand compared with the total of wages which would have to be paid if all workers were employed at current rates.

This formula of employment as a direct function of total demand proved so extraordinarily effective because it seemed to be confirmed in some degree by the results of quantitative empirical data. In contrast, the alternative explanations of unemployment which I regard as correct could make no such claims. The dangerous effects which the 'scientistic' prejudice has had in this diagnosis is the subject of my Nobel lecture at Stockholm (part II of this chapter). Briefly, we find the curious situation that the (Keynesian) theory, which is comparatively best confirmed by statistics because it happens to be the only one which can be tested quantitatively, is nevertheless false. Yet it is widely accepted only because the explanation earlier regarded as true, and which I still regard as true, cannot *by its very nature* be tested by statistics.

3 The True Theory of Unemployment

The true, though untestable, explanation of extensive unemployment ascribes it to a discrepancy between the distribution of labour (and the other factors of production) between industries (and localities) and the distribution of demand among their products. This discrepancy is caused by a distortion of the system of *relative* prices and wages. And it can be corrected only by a change in these relations, that is, by the establishment in each sector of the economy of those prices and wages at which supply will equal demand.

The cause of unemployment, in other words, is a deviation from the equilibrium prices and wages which would establish themselves with a free market and stable money. But we can never know beforehand at what structure of relative prices and wages such an equilibrium would establish itself. We are therefore unable to measure the deviation of current prices from the equilibrium prices which make it impossible to sell part of the labour supply. We are therefore also unable to demonstrate a statistical correlation between the distortion of relative prices and the volume of unemployment. Yet, although not measurable, causes may be very effective. The current superstition that only the measurable can be important has done much to mislead economists and the world in general.

Keynes's temptations to the politicians

Probably even more important than the fashionable prejudices concerning scientific method which made the Keynesian theory attractive to professional economists were the temptations it held out for politicians. It offered them not only a cheap and quick method of removing a chief source of real human suffering. It also promised them release from the most confining restrictions that had impeded them in their striving for popularity. Spending money and budget deficits were suddenly represented as virtues. It was even argued persuasively that increased government expenditure was wholly meritorious, since it led to the utilisation of hitherto unused resources and thus cost the community nothing but brought it a net gain.

These beliefs led in particular to the gradual removal of all effective barriers to an increase in the quantity of money by the monetary authorities. The Bretton Woods agreement had tried to place the burden of international adjustment exclusively on the surplus countries, that is, to require them to expand but not to require the deficit countries to contract. It thus laid the foundation for a world inflation. But this was at least done in the laudable endeavour to secure fixed rates of exchange. Yet when the criticism of the inflation-minded majority of economists succeeded in removing this last obstacle to national inflation, no effective brake remained, as the experience of Britain since the late 1960s illustrates.

Floating exchanges, full employment, stable currency

It is, I believe, undeniable that the demand for flexible rates of exchange originated wholly from countries such as Britain some of whose economists wanted a wider margin for inflationary expansion (called 'full employment policy'). They have, unfortunately, later received support also from other economists who were not inspired by the desire for inflation but who seem to me to have overlooked the strongest argument in favour of fixed rates of exchange: that they constitute the practically irreplaceable curb we need to *compel* the politicians, and the monetary authorities responsible to them, to maintain a stable currency.

The maintenance of the value of money and the avoidance of inflation constantly demand from the politicians highly unpopular measures which they can justify to people adversely affected only by showing that government was compelled to take them. So long as the preservation of the external value of the national currency is regarded as an indisputable necessity, as it is with fixed exchange rates, politicians can resist the constant demands for cheaper credits, avoidance of a rise in interest rates, more expenditure on 'public works', and so on. With fixed exchanges a fall in the foreign value of the currency or an outflow of gold or foreign exchange reserves acted as a signal requiring prompt government action. With flexible exchange rates, the effect of an increase in the quantity of money on the internal price level is much too slow to be generally recognised or to be charged to those ultimately responsible for it. Moreover, the inflation of prices is usually preceded by a welcome increase in employment, and it may therefore even be welcomed because its harmful effects are not visible until later.

It is therefore easy to understand why, in the hope of restraining countries all too inclined towards inflation, others like Germany, even while noticeably suffering from imported inflation, hesitated in the post-war period to destroy altogether the system of fixed rates of exchange. For a time it seemed likely to restrain the temptation further to speed up inflation. But now that the system of fixed rates of exchange appears to have totally collapsed, and there is scarcely any hope that self-discipline might induce some countries to restrain themselves, little reason is left to adhere to a system that is no longer effective. In retrospect one may even ask whether, out of a mistaken hope, the German Bundesbank or the Swiss National Bank have not waited too long, and then raised the value of their currency too little. But in the long run I do not believe we shall regain a system of international stability without returning to a system of fixed exchange rates which imposes upon the national central banks the restraint essential if they are successfully to resist the pressure of the inflation-minded forces of their countries – usually including Ministers of Finance.

4 Inflation Ultimately Increases Unemployment

But why all this fear of inflation? Should we not try to learn to live with it, as some South American States seem to have done, particularly if, as some believe, this is necessary to secure full employment? If this were true and the harm done by inflation were only that which many people emphasise, we would have to consider this possibility seriously.

Why we cannot live with inflation

The answer, however, is twofold. *First*, such inflation, in order to achieve the goal aimed at, would have constantly to *accelerate*, and accelerating inflation would sooner or later reach a degree which makes all effective order of a market economy impossible. *Second*, and most important, in the long run such inflation makes much *more* unemployment inevitable than that which it was originally designed to prevent.

The argument often advanced that inflation produces merely a *redistribution* of the social product, while unemployment *reduces* it and therefore represents a worse evil, is thus false, because *inflation becomes the cause of increased unemployment.*

Harmful effects of inflation

I certainly do not wish to under-estimate the other harmful effects of inflation. They are much worse than anyone can conceive who has not himself lived through a great inflation. I count my first eight months in a job during which my salary rose to 200 times the initial amount as such an experience. I am indeed convinced that such a mismanagement of the currency is tolerated by the people only because, while the inflation proceeds, nobody has the time or energy to organise a popular rebellion.

What I want to say is that even the effects which every citizen experiences are not the worst consequence of inflation, which is usually not understood because *it becomes visible only when the inflation is past.* This must particularly be said to economists, politicians or others who like to point to the South American countries which have had inflations lasting through several generations and seem to have learnt to live with them. In these predominantly agrarian countries the effects of inflation are chiefly limited to those mentioned. The most serious effects that inflation produces in the labour markets of industrial countries are of minor importance in South America.

The attempts made in some of these countries, in particular Brazil, to deal with the problems of inflation by some method of indexing can, at best, remedy some of the consequences but certainly not the chief causes or the most harmful effects. They could not prevent the worst damage which inflation causes, that misdirection of labour which I must now consider more fully.

The misdirection of labour

Inflation makes certain jobs *temporarily* attractive. They will disappear when it stops or even when it ceases to accelerate at a sufficient rate. This result follows because inflation

(a) changes the distribution of the money stream between the various sectors and stages of the process of production, and
(b) creates expectation of a further rise of prices.

The defenders of a monetary full employment policy often represent the position as if a *single* increase of total demand were sufficient to secure full employment for an indefinite but fairly long period. This argument overlooks both the inevitable effects of such a policy on the distribution of labour between industries and those on the wage policy of the trade unions.

As soon as government assumes the responsibility to maintain full employment at whatever wages the trade unions succeed in obtaining, they no longer have any reason to take account of the unemployment their wage demands might have caused. In this situation every rise of wages which exceeds the increase in productivity will make necessary an increase in total demand if unemployment is not to ensue. The increase in the quantity of money made necessary by the upward movement of wages thus released becomes a *continuous* process requiring a constant influx of additional quantities of money. The additional money supply must lead to changes in the relative strength of demand for various kinds of goods and services. And these changes in relative demand must lead to further changes in relative prices and consequent changes in the direction of production and the allocation of the factors of production, including labour. I must leave aside here all the other reasons why the prices of different goods – and the quantities produced – will react differently to changes in the demand (such as elasticities – the speed with which supply can respond to demand).

The chief conclusion I want to demonstrate is that the longer the inflation lasts, the larger will be the number of the workers whose jobs depend on a *continuation* of the inflation, often even on a continuing *acceleration* of the rate of inflation – not because they would not have found employment without the inflation, but because they were drawn by the inflation into *temporarily* attractive jobs which after a slowing down or cessation of the inflation will again disappear.

The consequences are unavoidable

We ought to have no illusion that we can escape the consequences of the mistakes we have made.[3] Any attempt to preserve the jobs made profitable by inflation would lead to a complete destruction of the market order. *We have once again in the post-war period missed the opportunity to forestall a depression while there was still time to do so.* We have indeed used our emancipation from institutional restraints – the gold standard and fixed exchange rates – to act more stupidly than ever before.

But if we cannot escape the re-appearance of substantial unemployment, this is not the effect of a failure of 'capitalism' or the market economy, but exclusively due to our own errors which past experience and available knowledge ought to have enabled us to avoid. It is unfortunately only too true that the disappointment of expectations they have created may lead to serious social unrest. But this does not mean that we can avoid it. The most serious danger now is certainly that attempts, so attractive for the politicians, to postpone the evil day and thereby make things in the long run even worse, may still succeed. I must confess I have been wishing for some time that the inescapable crisis may come soon. And I hope now that any attempts made promptly to restart the process of monetary expansion will not succeed, and that we shall now be forced to face the choice of a new policy.

Temporary, not mass, unemployment

Let me, however, emphasise at once that, although I regard a period of some months, perhaps even more than a year, of considerable unemployment as unavoidable, this does not mean that we must expect another long period of mass unemployment comparable with the Great Depression of the 1930s, provided we do not commit very bad mistakes of policy. Such a development can be prevented by a sensible policy which does not repeat the errors responsible for the duration of the Great Depression.

But before I turn to what our future policy ought to be I want to reject emphatically a misrepresentation of my point of view. I certainly do not recommend unemployment as a *means* to combat inflation. But I have to advise in a situation in which *the choice open to us is solely between some unemployment in the near future and more unemployment at a later date.* What I fear above all is the *après nous la déluge* attitude of the politicians who in their concern about the next elections are likely to choose more unemployment later. Unfortunately, even some commentators, such as the writers of the *Economist*, argue in a similar manner and have called for 'reflation' when the increase in the quantity of money is still continuing.

5 What Can Be Done Now?

The first step

The first necessity now is to stop the increase of the quantity of money – or at least to reduce it to the rate of the real growth of production – and this cannot happen soon enough. Moreover, *I can see no advantage in a gradual deceleration*, although for purely technical reasons it may prove all we can achieve.

It does not follow that we should not endeavour to stop a real deflation when it threatens to set in. Although I do not regard deflation as the original cause of a decline in business activity, a disappointment of expectations has unquestionably tended to induce a process of deflation – what more than 40 years ago I called a 'secondary deflation'[4] – the effect of which may be worse, and in the 1930s certainly was worse, than what the original cause of the reaction made necessary, and which has no steering function to perform.

I have to confess that 40 years ago I argued differently. I have since altered my opinion – not about the theoretical explanation of the events but about the practical possibility of removing the obstacles to the functioning of the system by allowing deflation to proceed for a while.

I then believed that a short process of deflation might break the rigidity of money-wages (what economists have since come to call their 'rigidity downwards') or the resistance to the reduction of some particular money-wages, and that in this way we could restore relative wages determined by the market. This seems to me still an indispensable condition if the market mechanism is to function satisfactorily. But I no longer believe it is in practice possible to achieve it in this manner. I probably should have seen then that the last chance was lost after the British government in 1931 abandoned the attempt to bring costs down by deflation just when it seemed near success.

Prevent recession degenerating into depression

If I were today responsible for the monetary policy of a country I would certainly try to prevent a threatening deflation, that is, an absolute decrease of the stream of incomes, by all suitable means, and would announce that I intended to do so. This alone would probably be sufficient to prevent a degeneration of the recession into a long-lasting depression. The re-establishment of a properly functioning market would, however, still require a re-structuring of the whole system of relative prices and wages and a re-adjustment to the expectation of stable prices, which presupposes a much greater flexibility of wages than exists now. What chance we have to achieve such a determination of relative wage-rates by the market and how long it may take I dare not predict. But, although I recognise that a *general* reduction of money wages is politically unachievable, I am still convinced that the required adjustment of the structure of *relative* wages can be achieved without inflation only through the reduction of the money wages of some groups of workers, and therefore must be thus achieved.

From a longer point of view it is obvious that, once we have got over the immediate difficulties, we must not avail ourselves again of the seemingly cheap and easy method of achieving full employment by aiming at the maximum of employment which in the short run can be achieved by monetary pressure.

The Keynesian dream

The Keynesian dream is gone even if its ghost will continue to plague politics for decades. It is to be wished, though this is clearly too much to hope for, that the term 'full employment' itself, which has become so closely associated with the inflationist policy, should be abandoned – or that we should at least remember that it was the aim of classical economists long before Keynes. John Stuart Mill reports in his autobiography[5] how 'full employment with high wages' appeared to him in his youth as the chief *desideratum* of economic policy.

The primary aim: stable money, not unstable 'full' employment

What we must now be clear about is that our aim must be, not the maximum of employment which can be achieved in the short run, but a 'high and stable [i.e. *continuing*] level of employment', as one of the wartime British White Papers on employment policy phrased it.[6] This, however, we can achieve only through the re-establishment of a properly functioning market which, by the free play of prices and wages, establishes for each sector the correspondence of supply and demand.

Though it must remain one of the chief tasks of monetary policy to prevent wide fluctuations in the quantity of money or the volume of the income stream, the effect on employment must not be the dominating consideration guiding it. *The primary aim must again become the stability of the value of money.* The currency authorities must again be effectively protected against the political pressure which today forces them so often to take measures that are politically advantageous in the short run but harmful to the community in the long run.

Disciplining the monetary authorities

I wish I could share the confidence of my friend Milton Friedman who thinks that one could deprive the monetary authorities, in order to prevent the abuse of their powers for political purposes, of all discretionary powers by prescribing the amount of money they may and should add to circulation in any one year. It seems to me that he regards this as practicable because he has become used for statistical purposes to draw a sharp distinction between what is to be regarded as money and what is not. This distinction does not exist in the real world. I believe that, to ensure the convertibility of all kinds of near-money into real money, which is necessary if we are to avoid severe liquidity crises or panics, the monetary authorities must be given some discretion. But I agree with Friedman that we will have to try and get back to a more or less automatic system for regulating the quantity of money in ordinary times. His principle is one that monetary authorities ought to aim at, not one to which they ought to be tied by law. The necessity of 'suspending' Sir Robert Peel's Bank Act of 1844 three times within 25 years after it was passed ought to have taught us this once and for all.

And although I am not as optimistic as the Editor of the London *Times*, Mr William Rees-Mogg, who in a sensational article[7] (and now in a book)[8] has proposed the return to the gold standard, it does make me feel somewhat more optimistic when I see such a proposal coming from so influential a source. I would even agree that among the feasible monetary systems the international gold standard is the best, if I could believe that the most important countries could be trusted to obey the rules of the game necessary for its preservation. But this seems to me exceedingly unlikely, and no single country can have an effective gold standard: by its nature it is an international system and can function only as an international system.

It is, however, a big step in the direction of a return to reason when at the end of his book Mr Rees-Mogg argues that

> We should be tearing up the full employment commitment of the 1944 White Paper, a great political and economic revolution.
>
> This would until very recently have seemed a high price to pay; now it is no great price at all. There is little or no prospect of maintaining full employment with the present inflation, in Britain or in the world. The full employment standard became a commitment to inflation, but the inflation has now accelerated past the point at which it is compatible with full employment.[9]

Equally encouraging is a statement of the British Chancellor of the Exchequer, Mr Denis Healey, who is reported to have said:

> It is far better that more people should be in work, *even if that means accepting lower wages on average*, than that those lucky enough to keep their jobs should scoop the pool while millions are living on the dole.[10] (My italics.)

It would almost seem as if in Britain, the country in which the harmful doctrines originated, a reversal of opinion were now under way. Let us hope it will rapidly spread over the world.

II The Pretence of Knowledge

The particular occasion of this lecture, combined with the chief practical problem which economists have to face today, have made the choice of its topic almost inevitable. On the one hand, the still recent establishment of the Nobel Memorial Prize in Economic Sciences marks a significant step in the process by which, in the opinion of the general public, economics has been conceded some of the dignity and prestige of the physical sciences. On the other hand, economists are at this moment called upon to say how to extricate the free world from the serious threat of accelerating inflation which, it must be admitted, has been brought about by policies the majority of economists have recommended and even urged governments to pursue. We have indeed at the moment little cause for pride: as a profession we have made a mess of things.

The 'scientistic' attitude derived from the physical sciences[11]

It seems to me that this failure of economists to guide policy more successfully is closely connected with their propensity to imitate as closely as possible the procedures of the brilliantly successful physical sciences – an attempt which in our subject may lead to outright error. It is an approach that has come to be described as the 'scientistic' attitude – which, as I defined it some 30 years ago,

> ... is decidedly unscientific in the true sense of the word, since it involves a mechanical and uncritical application of habits of thought to fields different from those in which they have been formed.[12]

I want to begin by explaining how some of the gravest errors of recent economic policy are a direct consequence of this scientistic error.

The theory which has been guiding monetary and financial policy during the last 30 years, and which I contend is largely the product of such a mistaken conception of the proper scientific procedure, consists in the assertion that there exists a simple positive correlation between total employment and the size of the aggregate demand for goods and services; and it leads to the belief that we can permanently ensure full employment by maintaining total money expenditure at an appropriate level. Among the various theories advanced to account for extensive unemployment, this is probably the only one in support of which strong quantitative evidence can be adduced. I nevertheless regard it as fundamentally false, and to act upon it, as we now experience, as very harmful.

This brings me to the crucial issue. Unlike the position in the physical sciences, in economics and other disciplines that deal with what I call 'essentially complex' phenomena, the aspects of the events to be explained for which we can obtain quantitative data are necessarily limited and may not include the important ones. While in the physical sciences it is generally assumed, probably with good reason, that any important factor which determines the observed events will itself be directly observable and measurable, in the study of such 'essentially complex' phenomena as the market, which depend on the actions of many individuals, all the circumstances that will determine the outcome of a process, for reasons I shall explain later, *will hardly ever be fully known or measurable*. And while in the physical sciences the investigator will be able to measure, on the basis of a *prima facie* theory, what he thinks important, in the social sciences what is treated as important is often that which happens to be accessible to measurement. This is sometimes carried to the point where it is demanded that our theories must be formulated in such terms that they refer only to measurable magnitudes.

It can hardly be denied that such a demand quite arbitrarily limits the facts that are to be admitted as possible causes of the events in the real world. This view, which is often quite naïvely accepted as required by scientific procedure, has some rather paradoxical consequences. We know, of course, about the market and similar social structures, very many facts that we cannot measure and on which indeed we have only some very imprecise and general information. And because the effects of these facts in any particular instance cannot be confirmed by quantitative evidence, they are simply disregarded by those sworn to admit only what they regard as scientific evidence. And they thereupon happily proceed on the fiction that the factors they can measure are the only relevant ones.

The correlation between aggregate demand and total employment, for instance, may be only approximate; but as it is the *only* one on which we have quantitative data, it is accepted as the only causal connection that counts. On this standard there may thus well exist better 'scientific' evidence for a false theory, which will be accepted because it appears as more 'scientific', than for a valid explanation, which is rejected because there is no sufficient quantitative evidence for it.

The chief cause of unemployment

Let me illustrate this by a brief sketch of what I regard as the chief true cause of extensive unemployment – an account which will also explain why such unemployment cannot be lastingly cured by the inflationary policies recommended by the now fashionable theory. The correct explanation appears to me to be the existence of discrepancies between the distribution of demand among the different goods and services and the allocation of labour and other resources among the production of those outputs. We possess a fairly good 'qualitative' knowledge of the forces by which a correspondence between demand and supply in the different sectors of the economic system is brought about, of the conditions under which it will be achieved, and of the factors likely to prevent such an adjustment. The separate steps in the account of this process rely on facts of everyday experience, and few who take the trouble to follow the argument will question the validity of the factual assumptions, or the logical correctness of the conclusions drawn from them. We have indeed good reason to believe that unemployment indicates that the structure of *relative* prices and wages has been distorted (usually by monopolistic or governmental price-fixing), and that to restore equality between the demand for and the supply of labour in all sectors changes of relative prices and wages and some transfers of labour will be necessary.

But when we are asked for quantitative evidence for the particular structure of prices and wages that would be required to assure a smooth continuous sale of the products and services offered, we must admit that we have no such information. We know, in other words, the *general* conditions in which what we call, somewhat misleadingly, an 'equilibrium' will establish itself; but we never know the *particular* prices or wages that would exist if the market were to bring about such an equilibrium. We can merely say in which conditions we can expect the market to establish prices and wages at which demand will equal supply. But we can never produce statistical information that would show how much the prevailing prices and wages *deviate* from those that would secure a continuous sale of the current supply of labour. This account of the causes of unemployment is an empirical theory, in the sense that it might be proved false: for example, if with a constant money supply, a general increase of wages did not lead to unemployment. But it is certainly not the kind of theory we could use to obtain specific numerical predictions concerning the rates of wages, or the distribution of labour, to be expected.

Why should we in economics, however, have to plead ignorance of the sort of facts on which, in the case of a physical theory, a scientist would certainly be expected to give precise information? It is probably not surprising that people impressed by the example of the physical sciences should find this position very unsatisfactory and should insist on the standards of proof they find there. The reason for this state of affairs, as I have briefly indicated, is that the social sciences, like much of biology but unlike most of the physical sciences, have to deal with structures of *essential* complexity, that is, whose characteristic properties can be exhibited only by models made up of relatively large numbers of variables. Competition, for example, is a process which will produce certain results only if it proceeds among a fairly *large* number of acting persons.

In some inquiries, particularly where problems of a similar kind arise in the physical sciences, the difficulties can be overcome by using, not specific information about the individual elements, but data about the relative frequency, or the probability, of the occurrence of the various distinctive properties of the elements. But this is true only where we have to deal with what has been called by Dr Warren Weaver (formerly of the Rockefeller Foundation), with a distinction that ought to be much more widely understood, 'phenomena of unorganised complexity', in contrast to those 'phenomena of organised complexity' with which we have to deal in the social sciences.[13] Organised complexity here means that the character of the structures showing it depends not only on the properties of the individual elements of which they are composed, and the relative frequency with which they occur, but also on the manner in which the individual elements are connected with one another. In explaining the working of such structures we cannot for this reason replace the information about the individual elements by statistical information, but require full information about each element if from our theory we are to derive specific predictions about individual events. Without such specific information about the individual elements we shall be confined to what on another occasion I have called mere 'pattern predictions' – predictions of some of the general attributes of the structures that will form themselves, but not containing specific statements about the individual elements of which the structures will be made up.[14]

This is particularly true of our theories accounting for the determination of the systems of relative prices and wages that will form themselves on a well-functioning market. Into the determination of these prices and wages will enter the effects of particular information possessed by every one of the participants in the market process – a sum of facts which in their totality cannot be known to the scientific observer or to any other single brain. It is indeed the source of the superiority of the market order, and the reason why, so long as it is not suppressed by the powers of government, it regularly displaces other types of order, that in the resulting allocation of resources it uses more of the knowledge of particular facts which exists only dispersed among uncounted persons, than any one person can possess. But because we, the observing scientists, can thus never *know* all the determinants of such an order, and in consequence also cannot know at which particular structure of prices and wages demand would everywhere equal supply, we also cannot measure the deviations from that order. Nor can we statistically test our theory that it is the deviations from that 'equilibrium' system of prices and wages which makes it impossible to sell certain products and services at the prices at which they are offered.

Mathematical method in economics: uses and limitations

Before I continue with my immediate concern, the effects of all this on the employment policies currently pursued, allow me to define more specifically the inherent limitations of our numerical knowledge that are so often overlooked. I want to do this to avoid giving the impression that I generally reject the mathematical method in economics. I regard it indeed as the great advantage of the mathematical technique that it allows us to describe, by algebraic equations, the general character of a pattern even where we are ignorant of the numerical values determining its particular manifestation. Without this algebraic technique we could scarcely have achieved that comprehensive picture of the *mutual inter-dependencies* of the different events in a market. It has, however, led to the illusion that we can use this technique to determine and predict the *numerical values* of those magnitudes; and this has led to a vain search for quantitative or numerical constants.

This happened despite that the modern founders of mathematical economics had no such illusions. It is true their systems of equations describing the pattern of a market equilibrium are so framed that, *if* we were able to fill in all the blanks of the abstract formulae, that is, *if* we knew all the parameters of these equations, we could calculate the prices and quantities of all commodities and services sold. But, as Vilfredo Pareto, one of the founders of this theory, clearly stated, its purpose cannot be 'to arrive at a numerical calculation of prices' because, as he said, it would be 'absurd' to assume that we could ascertain all the data.[15] Indeed, the chief point was seen by those remarkable anticipators of modern economics, the Spanish schoolmen of the 16th century, who emphasised that what they called *pretium mathematicum*, the mathematical price, depended on so many particular circumstances that it could never be known to man but was known only to God.[16] I sometimes wish that our mathematical economists would take this to heart. I must confess that I still doubt whether their search for measurable magnitudes has made significant contributions to our *theoretical understanding* of economic phenomena – as distinct from their value as a *description* of particular situations. Nor am I prepared to accept the excuse that this branch of research is still very young: Sir William Petty, the founder of econometrics, was after all a somewhat senior colleague of Sir Isaac Newton in the Royal Society![17]

There may be few instances in which the superstition that only measurable magnitudes can be important has done positive harm in the economic field; but the present problem of inflation and employment is a very serious one. Its effect has been that what is generally the true cause of extensive unemployment has been disregarded by the scientistically-minded majority of economists, because its operation could not be confirmed by directly observable relations between measurable magnitudes. Instead, an almost exclusive concentration on quantitatively measurable *surface* phenomena has produced a policy that has made matters worse.

It has, of course, to be readily admitted that the kind of theory I regard as the true explanation of unemployment is of somewhat limited content because it allows us to make only very general predictions of the *kind* of events we must expect in a given situation. But the effects on policy of the more ambitious constructions have not been very fortunate. I confess that I prefer true but imperfect knowledge, even if it leaves much undetermined and unpredictable, to a pretence of exact knowledge that is likely to be false. The credit gained for seemingly simple but false theories by their apparent conformity with recognised scientific standards may, as the present instance shows, have grave consequences.

Macro-economic solution for unemployment may cause resource-misallocation and intensify unemployment

Indeed, in the case discussed, the very measures which the dominant 'macro-economic' theory has recommended as a remedy for unemployment, namely the increase of aggregate demand, have become a cause of a very extensive misallocation of resources which is likely to make later large-scale unemployment inevitable. The continuous injection of additional amounts of money at points of the economic system where it creates a temporary demand which must cease when the increase of the quantity of money stops or slows down, together with the expectation of a continuing rise of prices, draws labour and other resources into employments which can last only so long as the increase of the quantity of money continues at the same rate – or perhaps even only so long as it continues to accelerate at a given rate. What this policy has produced is not so much a level of employment that could not have been brought about in other ways as a distribution of employment which cannot be maintained indefinitely and which after some time can be maintained only by a rate of inflation that would rapidly lead to a disorganisation of all economic activity. The truth is that by a mistaken theoretical view we have been led into a precarious position in which we cannot prevent substantial unemployment from re-appearing: not because, as my view is sometimes misrepresented, this unemployment is deliberately brought about as a means to combat inflation, but because it is now bound to occur as a deeply regrettable but *inescapable* consequence of the mistaken policies of the past as soon as inflation ceases to accelerate.

I must, however, now leave these problems of immediate practical importance introduced chiefly to illustrate the momentous consequences that may follow from errors concerning abstract problems of the philosophy of science. There is as much reason to be apprehensive about the long-run dangers created in a much wider field, by the uncritical acceptance of assertions which have the *appearance* of being scientific, as there is in the problems I have just discussed.

When science is unscientific

What I mainly wanted to show by the topical illustration is that, certainly in my subject, but I believe also generally in the sciences of man, what looks superficially like the most scientific procedure is often the most unscientific, and, beyond this, that in these other activities there are definite limits to what we can expect science to achieve. This means that to entrust to science – or to deliberate control according to scientific principles – more than scientific method can achieve may have deplorable effects. The progress of the natural sciences in modern times has of course so much exceeded all expectations that any suggestion that there may be some limits to it is bound to arouse suspicion. This insight will be especially resisted by all who have hoped that our increasing power of prediction and control, generally regarded as the characteristic result of scientific advance, applied to the processes of society, would soon enable us to mould it entirely to our liking. It is indeed true that, in contrast to the exhilaration which the discoveries of the physical sciences tend to produce, the insights we gain from the study of society more often have a dampening effect on our aspirations; and it is perhaps not surprising that the more impetuous younger members of our profession are not always prepared to accept this truth. Yet the confidence in the unlimited power of science is only too often based on a false belief that the scientific method consists in the application of a ready-made technique, or in imitating the form rather than the substance of scientific procedure, as if one needed only to follow some cooking recipes to solve all social problems. It sometimes almost seems as if the *techniques* of science were more easily learnt than the *thinking* that shows us what the problems are and how to approach them.

The conflict between what, in its present mood, the public expects science to achieve in satisfaction of popular hopes and what is really in its power is a serious matter. Even if all true scientists recognised the limitations of what they can do in human affairs, so long as the public expects more there will always be some who will pretend, and perhaps honestly believe, that they can do more to meet popular demands than is really in their power. It is often difficult enough for the expert, and certainly in many instances impossible for the layman, to distinguish between justified and unjustified claims advanced in the name of science. The enormous publicity recently given by the media to a report pronouncing in the name of science on *The Limits to Growth*, and the silence of the same media about the devastating criticism this report has received from the competent experts,[18] must make one feel somewhat apprehensive about the use to which the prestige of science can be put. But it is by no means only in economics that far-reaching claims are made for a more scientific direction of all human activities and the desirability of replacing spontaneous processes by 'conscious human control'. If I am not mistaken, psychology, psychiatry, and some branches of sociology, and still more the so-called philosophy of history, are even more affected by what I have called the scientistic prejudice, and by specious claims of what science can achieve.[19]

If we are to safeguard the reputation of science, and to prevent the arrogation of knowledge based on a superficial similarity of procedure with that of the physical sciences, much effort will have to be directed toward debunking such arrogations, some of which have by now become the vested interests of established university departments. We cannot be grateful enough to such modern philosophers of science as Sir Karl Popper for giving us a test by which we can distinguish between what we may and may not accept as scientific – a test which I am sure some doctrines now widely accepted as scientific would not pass. There are some special problems, however, in connection with those essentially complex phenomena of which social structures are so important an instance, which make me wish to conclude by restating in more general terms the reasons why in these fields not only are there absolute obstacles to the prediction of specific events, but why to act as if we possessed scientific knowledge enabling us to transcend them may itself become a serious obstacle to the advance of the human intellect.

The obstacles to prediction

The chief point we must remember is that the vast and rapid advance of the physical sciences took place in fields where it proved that explanation and prediction could be based on laws which accounted for the observed phenomena as functions of comparatively *few* variables – either particular facts or relative frequencies of events. This may even be the ultimate reason why we single out these realms as 'physical' in contrast to those more highly organised structures I have here called 'essentially complex' phenomena. There is no reason why the position must be the same in the latter as in the former fields. The difficulties we encounter in essentially complex phenomena are not, as one might at first suspect, difficulties about formulating theories to explain the observed events – although they also cause special difficulties about testing proposed explanations and therefore about eliminating bad theories. They are due to the chief problem which arises when we apply our theories to any particular situation in the real world. A theory of essentially complex phenomena must refer to a *large* number of particular facts, all of which must be ascertained before we can derive a prediction from it, or test it.

Once we have succeeded in this task there should be no particular difficulty about deriving testable predictions. With the help of modern computers, it should be easy enough to insert these data into the appropriate blanks of the theoretical formulae and to derive a prediction. The real difficulty, to the solution of which science has *little* to contribute and which is sometimes indeed *insoluble*, consists in the ascertainment of the particular facts.

A simple example will show the nature of this difficulty. Consider a ball game played by a few people of approximately equal skill. If we knew a few particular facts in addition to our general knowledge of the ability of the individual players, such as their state of attention, their perceptions and the state of their hearts, lungs, muscles, etc. at each moment of the game, we could probably predict the outcome. Indeed, if we were familiar both with the game and the teams, we should probably have a fairly shrewd idea on what the outcome will depend. But we shall not of course be able to ascertain those facts, and in consequence the result of the game will be outside the range of the scientifically predictable however well we may know what effects particular events would have on the result of the game. This does not mean that we can make no predictions at all about the course of the game. If we know the rules of the different games we shall, in watching one, very soon know which game is being played, and what kinds of actions we can and cannot expect. But our capacity to predict will be confined to such *general* characteristics of the events to be expected, and will not include the capacity of predicting *particular* individual events.

This explanation corresponds to what I have called earlier the mere pattern predictions to which we are increasingly confined as we penetrate from the realm where relatively simple laws prevail into the range of phenomena where organised complexity rules. As we advance, we find more and more frequently that we can in practice ascertain some, but not all, of the particular circumstances which determine the outcome of a given process. In consequence, we are able to predict some, but not all, of the properties of the result we have to expect. Often all we shall be able to predict will be some abstract characteristic of the pattern that will appear – relations between kinds of elements about which individually we know very little. Yet, as I am anxious to repeat, we will still achieve predictions which can be falsified and which therefore satisfy Popper's test of empirical significance.

Of course, compared with the precise predictions we have learnt to expect in the physical sciences, this sort of mere pattern prediction is a second best with which we do not like to have to be content. Yet the danger against which I want to warn is precisely the belief that it is necessary to achieve more in order to have a claim to be accepted as scientific. This way lies charlatanism and worse. To act on the belief that we possess the knowledge and the power that enable us to shape the processes of society entirely to our liking, knowledge which in the real world we do *not* possess, is likely to make us do much harm.

Power to coerce may impede spontaneous forces

In the physical sciences there may be little objection to trying to do the impossible; we might even feel that we ought not to discourage the over-confident because their experiments may after all produce new insights. But in the social sciences the erroneous belief that the exercise of some power would have beneficial consequences is likely to lead to a new power to *coerce* other men being conferred on some authority. Even if such power is not in itself bad, its exercise is likely to impede the functioning of those spontaneous ordering forces by which, without understanding them, man is in the real world so largely assisted in the pursuit of his aims. We are only beginning to understand on how subtle a communications system the functioning of an advanced industrial society is based. This communications system, which we call the market, turns out to be a more efficient mechanism for digesting dispersed information than any that man has deliberately designed.

If man is not to do more harm than good in his efforts to improve the social order, he will have to learn that, in this, as in all other fields where essential complexity of an organised kind prevails, *he cannot acquire the full knowledge which would make mastery of the events possible.* He will therefore have to use what knowledge he can achieve, not to shape the results as the craftsman shapes his handiwork, but rather to cultivate a growth by providing the appropriate environment, as the gardener does for his plants.

There is danger in the exuberant feeling of ever-growing power which the advance of the physical sciences has engendered and which tempts man to try – 'dizzy with success', to use a characteristic phrase of early communism – to subject not only our natural but also our human environment to the control of a human will. The recognition of the insuperable limits to his knowledge ought indeed to teach the student of society a lesson of humility which should guard him against becoming an accomplice in man's fatal striving to control society – a striving which makes him not only a tyrant over his fellows, but may well make him destroy a civilisation which no brain has designed but which has grown from the free efforts of millions of individuals.

III No Escape: Unemployment Must Follow Inflation[20]

The primary duty today of any economist who deserves the name seems to me to repeat on every occasion that the present unemployment is the direct and inevitable consequence of the so-called full employment policies pursued for the last 25 years. Most people still believe mistakenly that an increase in aggregate demand will remove unemployment for some time. Nothing therefore short of the realisation that this remedy, though usually effective in the short run, produces much more unem-ployment later will prevent the public from exerting irresistible pressure to resume inflation as soon as unemployment substantially increases.

To understand this basic truth is to recognise that the majority of economists whose advice governments have been following everywhere in Britain and the rest of the Western world during this period have thoroughly discredited themselves and ought to do penance in sackcloth and ashes. What was almost unquestioned orthodoxy for close to 30 years has been thoroughly discredited. And the present economic crisis also marks a severe setback in the authority of economics – or at least the long overdue collapse of the Keynesian bubble of the fashionable doctrine that has dominated opinion for a generation. I am fully convinced that before we can hope to return to reasonable stability, not to mention lasting prosperity, we must exorcise the Keynesian incubus. By this I mean less what John Maynard Keynes himself taught – because you can find in Keynes, as in Marx, almost anything – than the teaching of those Keynesians who, as Professor Joan Robinson recently wrote, 'sometimes had some trouble in getting Maynard to see what the point of his revolution really was'.[21]

Keynes confirmed business belief in high demand

The conquest of opinion by Keynesian economics is mainly due to the fact that its argument conformed with the age-old belief of the businessman that his prosperity depended on consumers' demand. The plausible but erroneous conclusion derived from his individual experience in business that general prosperity could be maintained by keeping general demand high, against which economic theory had been arguing for generations, was suddenly again made respectable by Keynes. And since the 1930s it has been embraced as obvious good sense by a whole generation of economists brought up on the teaching of his school. It has had the effect that for a quarter of a century we have systematically employed all available methods of increasing money expenditure, which in the short run creates additional employment but at the same time leads to misdirections of labour that must ultimately result in extensive unemployment.

'Secondary depression' and monetary counter-measures

This fundamental connection between inflation and unemployment is obscured because, although (except during an actual deflation, i.e. a decrease of the quantity of money) insufficient demand is normally *not* the primary cause of unemployment, unemployment may itself become the cause of an absolute shrinkage of aggregate demand which in turn may bring about a further increase of unemployment and thus lead to a cumulative process of contraction in which unemployment feeds on unemployment. Such a 'secondary depression' caused by an induced deflation should of course be prevented by appropriate monetary counter-measures. (The difficult question, which I can only briefly mention here, is how this can be done without producing further misdirections of labour.) At this moment, however, our chief task is still to prevent attempts to combat the unemployment made inevitable through mis-directions of labour by a renewed spurt of inflation, which would only increase these misdirections and thus in the long run make matters worse.

Difficult to discover the misdirected labour in 'the long prosperity'

A short exposition cannot do justice to the complexity of the facts in a further important problem. In past booms followed by depressions the misdirections of labour were comparatively easy to trace because the expansion of credit during the boom served almost exclusively industrial investment. But during the recent long prosperity since the end of the War, which was maintained by the removal of all automatic checks on continued inflation (such as the gold standard, fixed exchange rates, relieving deficit countries from the necessity to contract, and providing extra international liquidity), the additional demand financed by inflation has been much more widely dispersed and is therefore much more difficult to trace. Its effect on the allocation of resources in general and especially of labour would have to be investigated separately for each country and part of the period; and I am by no means clear where the most important over-developments would be found. The places where the misplaced and in consequence now *dis*placed workers can find lasting employment can be discovered only by letting the market operate freely.

Revival must come from sustainable (profitable) investment

In general it is probably true to say that an equilibrium position will most effectively be approached if consumers' demand is prevented from falling substantially by providing employment through public works, from which workers will wish to move as soon as they can to other and better-paid occupations, not by directly stimulating investment and similar expenditure which will draw labour into jobs they will expect to be permanent but must cease as soon as the source of this expenditure dries up.

We must certainly expect the recovery to come from a revival of investment. But we want investment of the kind which will prove profitable and can be continued when a new position of fair stability and a high level of employment has been achieved. Neither a subsidisation of investment nor artificially low interest rates are likely to achieve this position. And least of all is the desirable (i.e. stable) form of investment to be brought about by stimulating consumers' demand.

The belief that, in order to make new investment profitable consumers' demand must increase is part of the same widespread fallacy to which the businessman is especially prone. It is true only of investment designed to increase output by using the *same* techniques as hitherto employed, but not of the only sort of investment which can increase productivity per head of worker by equipping a given labour force with *more* capital equipment. Such intensification of capital use is indeed encouraged by relatively *low* product (consumer good) prices (which make it necessary to save on labour costs) and discouraged by high ones. This is one of the elementary connections between wages and investment wholly overlooked in Keynesian economics.[22]

Monetarism and the mechanical (macro) quantity theory

The contention that a general rise of prices such as we in the Western world have experienced in recent years is wholly due to, and made possible solely by, an excessive increase in the quantity of money, and that, therefore, governmental monetary policy is wholly responsible for it, is today usually described as the 'monetarist' position. It seems to me in this general form incontrovertible, even though it is also true that what has led governments to such a policy was chiefly the activity of trade unions and similar activities by other monopolistic bodies (such as the oil cartel). But in a narrower sense 'monetarist' is today frequently used to describe the expositors of a somewhat mechanical form of the quantity theory of the value of money which in my opinion tends to over-simplify the theoretical argument.

My chief objection against this theory is that, as what is called a 'macro-theory', it pays attention only to the effect of changes in the quantity of money on the general price level and not to the effects on the structure of relative prices. In consequence, it tends to disregard what seem to me the most harmful effects of inflation, the misdirection of resources it causes and the unemployment which ultimately results from it.

Nevertheless, for most practical purposes I regard this simple form of the quantity theory as a decidedly helpful guide and agree that we should not forget that the great inflations of the past, particularly those in Germany of the early 1920s and the late 1940s, were effectively stopped by men[23] who acted on this somewhat crude form of the quantity theory. But, though this over-simplified explanation of events seems to me inadequate to account for some of the deleterious effects of changes in the quantity of money, I emphasised as long as nearly 45 years ago, when I attempted to remedy these defects, that

> ... it would be one of the worst things which could befall us if the general public should ever again cease to believe in the elementary propositions of the quantity theory[24]

(then represented chiefly by the economists Irving Fisher and Gustav Cassel). But exactly this has happened as the result of the persuasive powers of Lord Keynes to whose proposals for combatting the depression of the 1930s the traditional views had been an obstacle.

Cantillon and Keynes

The defects of what became the traditional approach had indeed been pointed out 200 years earlier when Richard Cantillon had argued against John Locke's similar mechanical quantity theory that

> ... he realised well that the abundance of money makes everything dear, but he did not analyse how that takes place. The great difficulty of that analysis consists in the discovery by what path and in what proportion the increase of money raises the price of things.[25]

This analysis Cantillon was the first to attempt, and in time the examination of the course through which an inflow of additional money alters the *relative* demand for different commodities and services led to an explanation of how inflation results in a misdirection of resources, and particularly labour which becomes 'redundant' as soon as inflation slows down or even ceases to accelerate. But this promising stream of thought was smothered by the Keynesian flood which threw economists back to a state of knowledge that had been surpassed long before, and re-opened the gates to errors of government policy of which our grandparents would have been ashamed.

Present inflation engineered by government badly advised

The present inflation has been deliberately brought about by government on the advice of economists. The British Labour Party, as early as 1957, in its proposals for a National Pension Fund, dealt with the problem of future price movements by the assumption that prices would double between 1960 and 1980[26] – then an alarming prospect but now of course already far surpassed. As long ago as 1948, a highly influential textbook of economics[27] could plead that a 5 per cent per annum increase of prices was innocuous (which means that prices would double in less than 13 years). What these and other economists overlooked was that the purpose which they approved required an accelerating inflation, and that any accelerating inflation sooner or later becomes unbearable. Inflation at a constant rate soon comes to be anticipated in ordinary business trans-actions, and then merely harms the recipients of fixed contractual incomes but does no good.

'Inflation': true and false

Much confusion is of course caused in current discussion by a constant misuse of the term 'inflation'. Its original and proper meaning is an excessive increase of the quantity of money which will normally lead to an increase of prices. But even a general rise of prices, for instance one brought about by a shortage of food caused by bad harvests, is not inflation. Nor would a general rise of prices caused by a shortage of oil and other sources of energy that led to an absolute reduction of consumption be properly called inflation – if this shortage had not been made the excuse of a further increase in the quantity of money. There may also be considerable inflation that considerably harms the working of the market without any rise of prices – if this effect is prevented by controls. Indeed such a 'repressed' inflation tends to disorganise all economic activity even more than open inflation. Moreover, it has no beneficial effects whatever even in the short run (except for the receivers of the additional money), and leads straight to a centrally directed economy.

Inflation and unemployment: over-eating and indigestion

Let me repeat in conclusion that inflation has of course many other bad effects, much more grave and painful than most people understand who have not lived through one; but that the most serious and at the same time the least understood is that in the long run it inevitably produces extensive unemployment. It is simply not true, as some economists have suggested, that so long as unemployment exists, an increase in aggregate demand does only good and no harm. That may be true in the short run but not in the long run. We do not have the choice between inflation and unemployment, as little as we can choose between over-eating and indigestion: though over-eating may be very pleasant while it proceeds, the indigestion will follow.

Notes

1   David Ricardo to John Wheatley, 18 September 1821, reprinted in Piero Sraffa (ed.), *The Works of David Ricardo*, Cambridge University Press, Vol. IX, 1952, p. 73.
2   *The Economic Consequences of the Peace* (1919), reprinted in *The Collected Writings of John Maynard Keynes*, Macmillan for the Royal Economic Society, Vol. II, 1971, p. 149.
3   I should make it clear that, although I was addressing an audience in Italy, what I am saying certainly also applies to Britain and most other Western countries. There is little sign so far of this truth being understood in Britain.
4   Defined and discussed below on pp. 292–3. I recall that the phrase was frequently used in the LSE Seminar from the 1930s.
5   J. Stillinger (ed.), *Autobiography and other Writings*, Houghton Mifflin, Boston, 1969.
6   *Employment Policy*, Cmd 6527, HMSO, May 1944, Foreword.
7   'Crisis of Paper Currencies: Has the Time Come for Britain to Return to the Gold Standard?', *The Times*, 1 May 1974.
8   *The Reigning Error: the Crisis of World Inflation*, Hamish Hamilton, London, 1974.
9   *Ibid.*, p. 112.
10   Speech at East Leeds Labour Club reported in *The Times*, 11 January 1975.
11   [The sub-headings have been inserted to help readers, especially non-economists unfamiliar with Professor Hayek's writings, to follow the argument; they were not part of the original Nobel Lecture. – ED.]

12   'Scientism and the Study of Society', *Economica*, August 1942, reprinted in *The Counter-Revolution of Science*, Glencoe, Ill., 1952, p. 15 of this reprint.

13   Warren Weaver, 'A Quarter Century in the Natural Sciences', *The Rockefeller Foundation Annual Report 1958*, Ch. I, 'Science and Complexity'.

14   Cf. my essay, 'The Theory of Complex Phenomena', in M. Bunge (ed.), *The Critical Approach to Science and Philosophy. Essays in Honor of K. R. Popper*, New York, 1964, and reprinted (with additions) in my *Studies in Philosophy, Politics and Economics*, Routledge & Kegan Paul, London, and University of Chicago Press, Chicago, 1967.

15   V. Pareto, *Manuel d'economie politique*, 2nd edn, Paris, 1927, pp. 223–24.

16   Cf., e.g., Luis Molina, *De iustitia et iure*, Cologne, 1596–1600, tom. II, disp. 347, no. 3, and particularly Johannes de Lugo, *Disputationum de iustitia et iure tomus secundus*, Lyon, 1642, disp. 26, sect. 4, no. 40.

17   [Petty, 1623–87; Newton, 1642–1727. – ED.]

18   *The Limits to Growth: A Report of the Club of Rome's Project on the Predicament of Mankind*, New York, 1972; for a systematic examination of this document by a distinguished economist cf. Wilfred Beckerman, *In Defence of Economic Growth*, London, 1974, and, for a list of earlier criticisms by experts, Gottfried Haberler, *Economic Growth and Stability*, Los Angeles, 1974, who rightly calls their effect 'devastating'.

19   I have given some illustrations of these tendencies in other subjects in my inaugural lecture as Visiting Professor at the University of Salzburg, *Die Irrtümer des Konstruktivismus und die Grundlagen legitimer Kritik gesellschaftlicher Gebilde*, Munich, 1970, now re-issued for the Walter Eucken Institute, at Freiburg im Breisgau, by J. C. B. Mohr, Tübingen, 1975.

20   The following contains essentially additional points which I found necessary to insert in various lectures I gave during the month of April 1975 at various places in the United States on the general subject treated in the first part of this chapter.

21   Joan Robinson, 'What has become of the Keynesian Revolution?', in Milo Keynes (ed.), *Essays on John Maynard Keynes*, Cambridge University Press, 1975, p. 125.

22   [It is a central element in the Austrian theory of capital. – ED.]

23   Schacht and Erhard respectively.

24   *Prices and Production*, Routledge, London, 1931, p. 3. E. von Böhm-Bawerk used to speak of 'the indestructible core of truth in the quantity theory'.

25   Richard Cantillon, *An Essay on the Nature of Commerce in General*, Henry Higgs (ed.), Macmillan, London, 1931, Part I, Chapter 6.

26   *National Superannuation: Labour's Policy for Security in Old Age*, published by the Labour Party, London, 1957, pp. 104 and 109.

27   'If price increases could be held down to, say, less than 5 per cent per year, such a mild steady inflation need not cause too great concern.' (Paul A. Samuelson, *Economics: an Introductory Analysis*, McGraw-Hill, first edn, 1948, p. 282.)

7

The Repercussions of Rent Restriction

1 Introduction

The problem of rent control is still frequently judged only in terms of its impact on landlord and tenant, so that other far-reaching repercussions on the whole economic system are largely ignored or underrated. Even when some notice is taken of them, a distorted and sometimes totally false view spills over from popular misconceptions even into learned debates. It is here that some drastic re-thinking is needed.

What I shall try to do, therefore, is to deal in turn with the major consequences of statutory rent restrictions and the reduction of rents below market prices through the government financing of building construction. I shall start with their impact on the general supply of accommodation to rent and on the main types of dwellings, then go on to consider their effects on how the supply is distributed among people in search of a home, on income distribution, and on the pattern of production in general, with particular reference to the supply of capital and the effect on wage levels. My terms of reference require me to concentrate entirely on the control of domestic rents, without going into the closely related and most important question of the impact of rent regulation on business premises, which I have previously discussed in a similar context.[1]

If my account of the impact of rent restrictions seems exaggerated in any particular, I would emphasise that my thoughts are attuned to the Viennese scene. The ways in which these conditions differ from those in

This essay was adapted from a lecture delivered in 1930 and published in *Schriften des Vereins für Sozialpolitik*, 182, Munich, 1930. The English translation was published as a contribution to IEA Readings No. 7, *Verdict on Rent Control* (1972).

Germany are well known. The best way to dramatise this contrast is by pointing out that it will be another two years before the average Viennese rent reaches a temporary peak equivalent to 30 per cent of pre-war rents, despite there being at present no government powers to allocate or assign accommodation, in brief, no thorough-going state control.

Even so, I believe my principal reflections to be equally valid in a German context. Basically, deductions which can more easily be drawn from Vienna than elsewhere must also hold good where less severe forms of rent restriction are practised. The theory can be worked out by pure reason; all that Vienna provides is a convenient source of illustration. Far from exaggerating the consequences, they would be still more striking were it not for the decline in Vienna's population.

2 The Unique Characteristic of Housing

A unique feature of price control in housing compared with that in other goods and services is that war-time housing regulations have been retained and enforced ever since. The reason is not that housing is more 'necessary' than, say, food, nor that it has become harder or more costly to supply than other necessaries, but simply that, unlike almost all other consumer goods, it is a *durable* commodity which, once produced, remains available for many decades, and is therefore in some ways more vulnerable to state control than, say, bacon or potatoes.

It is precisely because of this unique feature of housing that the most unwelcome of all the effects of price-pegging, its effect on supply, is neither generally felt nor even generally recognised. We are faced with the problem of evaluating the significance of rent controls not merely as temporary but as permanent expedients. On a shorter view we could allow ourselves to assess their effects on the distribution and enlargement of the existing housing *stock*. Instead we must tackle the underlying problem, that of meeting *indefinitely* an emergent demand for homes at repressed rents.

Elasticities of demand and supply

We pay too little attention to the phenomenal rise in demand for homes which must occur every time rents fall below the level at which they would settle in an unfettered market. It is not merely a matter of the undoubted elasticity of demand in the housing market, reacting as it does every time lower building costs enable rents to be reduced with a corresponding rise in demand. The housing shortage which inevitably follows every statutory limitation of rent levels is directly related to the difficulty of finding new accommodation. It turns the occupation of a dwelling into a capital asset and encourages a tenant to hang on to his home even when he would surrender it at the reduced price provided he could be sure of finding another home when he wanted one.

In these circumstances a large unsatisfied demand for housing was obviously bound to emerge even without an increase in population, and the only way to bridge this gap was by the government financing of house-building. When, as in Vienna and Austria generally, there is in addition a big difference between statutory rents and rents which would prevail in the open market, the prospect of fully satisfying the demand for homes at depressed rents seems totally illusory. Despite a decline in population of one-seventh and an increase in housing stock of something like one-tenth (there are no reliable figures), no-one can pretend that the demand for housing is less than it was. That depressed rents are largely responsible for the increased demand for homes in Germany as well, and that the current housing shortage is to that extent a product of rent restriction, can also be seen from the decline in population density in almost every city in the country since the War. I shall return to the changing contemporary significance of such estimates of average population density.

Government supply in long run

Over and above this supply gap, which can be met only by government (or municipal) building schemes, we have to take into account the demands generated by population expansion, and further – and here are the basic problems of housing controls as a permanent institution – the whole range of demand created by the misallocation of the available stock of rentable accommodation. State control as an *emergency* measure could jog along contentedly enough with new building intended to supplement the housing stock built by private enterprise. In the *long term*, however, if public finance is being used to build homes the demand for which has increased due to a lowering of rents, it will ultimately have to be applied to *all* new building of houses to let. Hence – and the literature on the subject shows that this is worth emphasising – it is not enough to build publicly-financed homes in the hope that they will constitute an *additional* supply; if the aim is to keep rents *permanently* depressed, then for as long as rents are held below market rates it will be necessary to use public money to provide the *total* supply.

This development not only raises complex financial questions. Very few government authorities will want to assume responsibility in this way for all types of housing. In general, it will prove necessary to limit government building to the more modest types of dwelling, with the natural corollary that they will be the only types to enjoy rent protection. Limiting the applicability of rent regulations in this way to particular classes of dwellings, however, gives rise to other difficulties too often overlooked. For if public building operations and the supply of below-cost homes are to be confined, as they must be, to the classes of dwelling for which society is prepared to shoulder full responsibility indefinitely, they must also inevitably cater for the social class whose lot society wishes to ease, and not for the better-off. Hence it is futile to think that resources currently deemed appropriate to public expenditure on building can be used both to make up the short-fall of homes for the poorest sections of the community and *at the same time* to erect homes of better than average quality for the majority of the population. Better standards can be achieved with public funds (where there is sufficient surplus finance) to put up a number of model homes. But every attempt to depress rents even in this latter category below the levels required to pay off capital and interest will founder, unless there is available enough public money to meet the demand for all housing in this class indefinitely.

It is worth noting an unfortunate side-effect of some significance which will occur even when government finance is confined to building homes for the poorest sections, that is, those whose needs alone it can hope to satisfy. I refer to the relatively large gap that will emerge between rents for the best housing that government money can build and for the privately constructed alternative. A large number of people will therefore inevitably settle for a home of poorer quality than they would have occupied if rents had shown a smooth progression instead of such a disproportionate variation.

3 Effects on Distribution

So much for the ways in which rent restrictions affect the quantity and composition of available housing. How do they affect its distribution? Most experts have gone no further than to repeat and briefly illustrate the *cliché* that housing conditions are 'fossilised' by rent controls. An associated phenomenon seems to account for most of the 'far-reaching effects' I have mentioned.

The assumption of this further argument is that rent regulations will continue as at present for homes of all classes, and that the housing shortage created by rent restriction will inevitably persist. While this situation continues, the attitude to changing circumstances of anyone with a low-rental home will be governed by the conditions before rent regulation came into force. Clearly, such a distribution of available homes to rent, understandable though it may be on historical grounds, must conform less and less to diverse changing needs the longer the controls have been in force. Clearly, also, the implications of such a limitation for the mobility of manpower must be harmful.

Extent of 'fossilisation'

Before I examine these implications, however, I should first like to consider the true extent of this 'fossilisation', and where we should look for a thaw, if any. Some adjustment is made, for example, when the occupier of a controlled tenancy sub-lets or 'sells' his tenancy (in fact if not in law); in other words, when he transmits his controlled tenancy in exchange for money, and in cases – and these are in the majority – where an exchange takes place between two homes of different standards. For reasons explained, by no means all the tenants who would take smaller homes, given the chance under free market rents, will sub-let the corresponding portion of their existing dwellings or welcome an exchange. The only possible result is that a proportionately smaller share of the housing stock becomes available to those who must depend on satisfying their requirements by sub-renting, buying, or exchanging property than if they were competing freely for their share with all the other home-seekers on the open market.

Thus the interplay between supply and demand must be weighted against the tenant in those partial markets where prices are free and here too rents demanded will be higher than in an open market. The growing section of the community which neither enjoys controlled tenancies nor is catered for by government-financed building is thus worse off than if there were no protective legislation at all. In practice, this means that many younger people pay a form of tribute to their elders still living in their pre-war homes; and this subsidy may amount to more than the rent they would be paying a landlord if there were no controlled tenancies.

In practice, very few can avail themselves of this means of restoring mobility, and it therefore plays only a minor rôle. For the majority, it is a harsh and rigid fact of life that tenants cling to their dwellings, thereby preventing the adaptation of housing on offer to changing requirements in terms of size, position, and standards. As a result, while there are isolated instances of population densities so divergent as to make a mockery of statistical averages, there are disproportionately more acute housing shortages where average densities are truly comparable, that is, where the number of homes on offer is comparable, than there would be in the open market.

Immobilising labour

The restrictions on the mobility of manpower caused by rent controls mean not only that available accommodation is badly used to satisfy diverse housing requirements. They also have implications for the deployment and recruitment of labour to which too little attention is paid.

In normal times regional switches in industrial manpower requirements entail considerable labour migration and, despite the unusually large changes in industry in the past decade, migrations have been blocked by rent controls. Left to itself, and given an unfettered wage structure, this immobility would prevent wages in different regions from evening themselves out, and cause marked variations between the regions.

As things stand, however, collectively negotiated wage settlements largely rule out such variations, and two other results therefore follow. First, the wage-earner will choose to commute rather than move whenever his new place of work is within reach of his home, either on a daily or a weekly basis, even though he may find this mode of living by no means satisfactory. The wage-earner who is prevented from moving will have to spend extra time and money, which represent a cut in pay, further aggravated because regional differences have been eliminated. From the economic standpoint, this and all other expenditures incurred by people because they are 'wedded' to their homes are downright wasteful. B. Kautsky[2] points out that the cause of Vienna's increased tram traffic, which doubled between 1913 and 1928 at a time of diminishing population, can only have been this inhibited mobility. P. Vas,[3] admittedly with some exaggeration, estimates that 'the additional fares squeezed out of the Viennese public by rent control alone' amounted to at least two-thirds of the annual outlay on new building in the city.

Commuting or unemployment?

Commuting, however, is not always a feasible alternative to moving house, and if it is not, the result is unemployment. Joseph Schumpeter, writing in *Deutsche Volkswirt*, once gave forceful expression to the importance of the correlation between lack of mobility of labour and unemployment, an importance which cannot be rated too highly. I shall merely mention one example of it which came to my notice recently.

A manufacturer of my acquaintance with a factory in a small town some five hours from Vienna and an office in Vienna itself went to the labour exchange in Vienna to ask for an electrical fitter for his provincial factory. Twenty or so fitters, some of whom had been out of work for a long time, applied for the vacancy, but every one of them withdrew rather than give up a protected tenancy in Vienna for unprotected works accommodation. Weeks later the industrialist had still not found his fitter. Every manufacturer in Austria with a factory outside the main industrial centres can tell you countless similar stories.

I would almost go as far as to say that when the reduced rents policy succeeds in providing low-cost homes for *all-comers* the repercussions will be even more disastrous. We should not forget that city-dwellers, who form the bulk of those living in rented accommodation, are not the only ones who move. Every successful attempt to provide low-cost rented accommodation in an urban area must also accentuate the drift from the countryside to the towns. No-one would wish, whether for economic or for social reasons, artificially to encourage the growth of mammoth cities. Yet such is the inevitable consequence of inhibiting rent increases which act as a useful brake on this drift to the towns. The greatest harm must come from aiding it in boom periods, as unemployment must inevitably shoot up in any subsequent recession. In practice, even when rents have been buoyed up by a flourishing economy, this has also had its good side.

Incidentally, it is questionable, to put it no stronger, whether one should set out to make it easier for the poorer sections of the community to have children at the expense of the more prosperous, or to improve the lot of the urban population at the expense of the rural. Yet this is the inevitable outcome of a policy of federal or provincial subsidies which aid city growth and prevent the size of households from adjusting naturally to incomes.

(There is one last aspect closely connected with the wasteful distribution of available accommodation: the way it obscures genuine trends in demand both for location and quality. I deal with it below.)

Effect on income distribution

There is only one more point I should like to consider fully about the effects of rent restrictions on income distribution: their effect on wage levels. On no subject is there more muddled thinking. Intractable this problem in analysis may be, especially allowing for the indirect effects, but it is nonetheless vital to show how groundless is the popular belief that rent protection results in lower wages. It is astonishing to see even Pribram,[4] in his contribution to the earlier literature on the subject, propounding this belief as self-evident, with no attempt at substantiation.

What I have in mind are wage levels relative to other values, not increases in purchasing power for the individual wage-earner relative to the cost of housing. One can understand the lay person construing the proposition 'If I have to pay more in rent then I must be paid more in wages' as meaning that higher wages must follow in the wake of higher rents. But an economist who comes to this conclusion must suddenly have abandoned his scientific thought processes. Pribram's remarks indeed show this clearly, for he writes:

> since ... after controlled rents had been *adjusted* by law to wages ... statutory rights and not economic justice were what *determined* rents, all those commodities in whose cost wages were a component went down in price ...

This passage suffices to show that Pribram has decided not to analyse wage formation, on the ground that there is no need for it, and to substitute a notional 'just' wage. Indeed this is the only way his argument can be made to hang together; yet on it is based the popularly held belief in the efficacy of rent control as a stimulus to production.

In my own mind I am clear beyond all doubt that a cost theory such as Pribram probably has in mind, even as a relatively short-term expedient tailored to fit the present circumstances, does not stand up to the evidence. If we appraise the present state of the labour market, ruled as it is by collective bargaining, our starting-point is that to every wage bracket there corresponds a given number of wage-earners. It follows that the scale of wage increases the unions can push through depends on the strength of 'workers' solidarity', that is, on whether unemployment benefit is generous enough to deter those who would be priced out of their jobs from accepting work for less than the new rates. There is no need to point out that even if rents were higher industry could not employ more than a given number of work-people within a given wage bracket.

Nor should it be assumed that an all-round increase in rents and other prices would substantially alter the position of the unions.

Conversely, what is certain is that to an unemployed worker a controlled tenancy is the equivalent of a substantially higher unemployment benefit. In other words, rent controls have the same effect as a rise in unemployment benefit in reducing pressure on the labour market from the unemployed. Accordingly, it can be argued more forcefully that wages are *raised* rather than restrained by rent control – and that this is more important than its effect on the supply of workers.

Admittedly this applies only if there is an all-round increase in rents and all other prices, and it is probable that, if rents were suddenly to soar, as they would do if controls were abruptly lifted, such a psychological change would come over the working population that the unions might venture to press wage claims leading to a rate of unemployment higher than would previously have been tolerated. However, this has nothing in common with the generally accepted view that rent controls help to keep production costs down.

Indirect effects on demand

Moreover, the direct effects of rent controls on the supply of manpower through their influence on wages are grossly exaggerated, in whichever direction one believes them to operate.

A far larger rôle is played by specific indirect effects on demand, which influence industry's ability to pay higher wages. This form of wage-pegging, which is ultimately due to rent control, is totally different from its depressant effect on wages, which has been given such prominence, and can only be regarded as harmful. The effects I have in mind are principally those which come into play in a rather roundabout way, via the investment of capital. They are reinforced by a host of other uneconomic practices, some already touched on and some that remain to be mentioned, such as the distortions and inefficient deployment of available productive resources which rent control brings in its wake: such practices inevitably bring down the demand price of human labour.

4 Effect on Supply of Capital for Investment

Current housing policies affect the supply of investment capital to the economy in two ways. First, the supply of new capital is reduced because income from housing is insufficient to repay existing loans. This is of much importance to industry, since in present circumstances a good deal of this amortisation would not have been ploughed back into housing but would have become available to the rest of the economy, at least for a transitional period. Second, and more important, as a result of public building schemes immense sums were used at one time for purposes other than those best designed to increase human productivity, that is, those which would have been served in the normal course of events but for the housing policies followed.

Public building investment distorts resource allocation

The importance of the absorption of resources by public building is best shown by comparing the amount spent in Vienna alone on domestic building (at least 700 million schillings) with the market value of Austria's entire share capital as quoted on the Vienna Stock Exchange which, the Austrian Institute for Market Research has calculated, amounted to 961 million schillings in 1929. Given the subsequent 25 per cent drop in share prices, the total value cannot now be much over 700 million schillings.

Even so, we are very far from having bridged the housing 'gap'. Can one doubt that, allowing for federal and provincial expenditure on domestic housing and for all the administrative expenses of operating the present policy, an outlay which exceeds the total value of Austria's industrial investment capital must have major repercussions? Even assuming that, after taxation, only part of this capital would have gone to industry, this state of affairs cannot fail to affect human productivity, and hence wage levels.

When we try to assess this deployment of capital, or indeed to assess housing policies as a whole, our attitude to one question is crucial. Anyone who believes that the economic difficulties, especially the heavy unemployment, of the post-war period can successfully be combatted by stimulating consumption, that there is no shortage of the means of consumption but that the obstacle to the fullest use of available resources is that consumers' incomes are too low, and who consequently looks to public works of every kind to tone up the economy in the long term, takes a more benign view than I do of the present outlay on housing and the tendency inherent in present-day housing policies to push up consumption at the expense of capital formation.

There is unfortunately no space for a criticism of this most dangerous of the prevalent errors of economic theory which, originating in America, is steadily gaining more ground.

Homes not provided for the right people

Quite apart from the repercussions of draining off capital from other sectors of the economy, a further question is whether the present outlay on housing succeeds in satisfying housing requirements as well under the present restrictive system as would an identical outlay under a free market system.

This brings me to the question postponed earlier, and by the same token to one of the gravest problems of present housing policies. For what we saw earlier of the uneconomic distribution of existing accommodation applies with equal force to building operations with no free market prices to guide them. My argument is in no way affected should rent restrictions not be applied to new building. It is rather that the needs of those who happen not to have any accommodation at present and who accordingly head the queue for new construction do not coincide with the needs which would come to light if existing accommodation were distributed rationally. It would make sounder sense to apportion some of the available accommodation among the homeless, and to build new homes on a completely different pattern and in different areas, that is, homes for which real demand exceeds supply.

At present we really have no idea how much housing is required, of what size, or where. So instead of building with a view to supplementing the existing range of homes, we carry on as if new home-seekers had no interest whatever in existing accommodation, and as if the housing needs of tenants in controlled dwellings were immutably fixed for all time. For example, suppose that quite fortuitously a rural or urban district has a number of young couples looking for homes; in present circumstances homes will be built even though far more people are already living there than want to do so and even though the homes required would soon become available if mobility were restored. Alternatively, homes may be built for families with children simply because there are many such families without suitable accommodation; but at the same time there may be many older couples occupying homes which no longer correspond to their needs and which would be suitable for families.

The tremendous waste entailed in such arbitrary building must call seriously in doubt the proposition, partly supported by C. Kruschwitz,[5] that rent restrictions should only be abolished when supply and demand have balanced themselves out; indeed it leads us to question the very idea that this balance can ever be achieved in such conditions. Before the War, that is, independently of restrictive legislation, Adolf Weber noted that

> ... the basic cause of housing difficulties is ... the variance between the extreme flexibility of present-day economic relationships and the rigidity of the housing market.[6]

Do we really stand a chance of eliminating our present housing shortage while we persist in denying even to new building the possibility of responding to changing needs?

Value of theoretical analysis

The specific object of my paper was to give a systematic picture of the repercussions of restrictive rent legislation. If this account seems to boil down to a catalogue of iniquities to be laid at the door of rent control, that is no mere coincidence, but inevitable because it stems from both a theoretical and a liberal treatment of the problem, which are one and the same. For I doubt very much whether theoretical research into the same problems carried out by someone of a different politico-economic persuasion than myself could lead to different conclusions. Therefore, if theory brings to light nothing but unfavourable conclusions, it must indicate that though the immediate benefits of rent control, for which it was introduced in the first place, are obvious to everyone, theory is needed to uncover the unintentional consequences which intervention brings in its wake.

That these unlooked-for consequences are incidentally unwelcome should surprise no one. Everyone is naturally at liberty to weigh for himself the benign against the damaging consequences of rent control. Nor is recognition of the damaging consequences in itself tantamount to opposition to rent control. What *is* necessary is to know them for what they are before venturing an opinion for or against.

However, if in my concluding remarks I am to draw any lessons for future policy from our investigations, then I am bound to say that, having weighed the advantages against the drawbacks, I have come to the conclusion that the indispensable condition for an escape from our present troubles is a speedy return to an open market in housing.

5 Transition to an Open Market

Even so, given agreement on that ultimate goal, we are still left with the question of how best to use our knowledge of present conditions to regulate the transitional period. A conviction that an open market is *per se* the most desirable condition is of course far from an assertion that the immediate abolition of rent control as things are is the most effective method of achieving it.

Dangers of sudden lifting of controls

Indeed, precisely because rent control means so much more than that tenants pay less rent than they would do otherwise, because it means that available accommodation is distributed quite differently from the way it would be in an open market, it follows that the freeing of the market would not only bring an extra charge on the tenant but also cause changes in the pattern of distribution.

Were controls to be lifted suddenly, these changes would inevitably take place on such a scale that the market would be utterly disorganised, with all the resulting dangers. It would suddenly become apparent not only that there was a serious imbalance between supply and demand, but also that prices for a particular kind of home in particular localities had risen out of all proportion to their value. The worst of the pressure would doubtless fall on small dwellings, as the demand for them by people obliged to leave their larger homes owing to rent increases would be considerably higher than the demand from those with the means to move into the relatively cheaper larger homes thus vacated. This pressure would be aggravated by the absence of a ceiling on rents. Attempts would undoubtedly be made to push rents up to grotesque levels, and in the initial confusion they would probably succeed.

In my view, the remedy is not to raise rents gradually, as is generally suggested, up to the critical point, by which I mean the point which would establish prices on the open market, and thus harmonise supply and demand, which would provide freedom of movement, and which would be reached virtually instantaneously. For the transition to go through smoothly, some prior correction of existing distribution patterns is called for.

The only solution I can envisage is to try to create as large an open market as possible alongside a temporary retention of controls in specific cases. In other words, the proposal is progressively to enlarge as far as possible the existing free-market sector catering for non-controlled tenancies, sub-letting and home-buying. A basis for this already exists since, as explained earlier, an ever-increasing proportion of the population no longer enjoys the benefits of rent control. What is now needed is to block the transfer of protection, so that new home-seekers start off on the right footing, thus avoiding misdirection of future demand and also putting the maximum number of existing dwellings on the free market, but without creating a new demand by the eviction of tenants.

I hope this basic outline of the subject will be found adequate. It leaves me free to indicate in 'verbal shorthand' those measures which I think offer the best hope of achieving this end.

Practical measures

Plainly the first step must be to detach tenancy protection from *property* and attach it to *persons*, by which I mean to an occupier or his *bona fide* dependants. The inheritance or transmission of a protected *tenancy* would then cease. The next stage would be to remove controls from the largest dwellings, followed by dwellings large in relation to family size, and lastly from homes previously sub-let or sub-divided, when a landlord chooses to divide up a building rather than to let it as a self-contained unit. The conversion into flats of existing large dwellings ought to be especially encouraged, although probably little encouragement would be needed to persuade landlords to let freely part of a building formerly wholly subject to rent control. The supply of homes could be speeded up by the imposition of a tax or similar levy on the rental income not only of occupied but also of unoccupied property. Another move designed to ease the tenant's position transitionally *vis-à-vis* the market in the face of legislation weighted in favour of the landlord would be to require landlords to give long notice periods, while allowing tenants to give shorter ones.

What is of supreme importance, however, is that all subsequent building operations should align their prices with the rents which emerge from these partial markets. With this in view some public aid might need to be given to building merely to stop rents in particular areas and for certain types of housing from rising above the levels to which private enterprise building could ultimately be expected to bring them.

Even so, money from whatever source should be applied only where at least a market return on investment is to be expected, and when public money is used the rents asked should be no lower than foreseeable average rents after the abolition of rent control. And if, in order to keep rents down, public money is to be used at all, the lesson we must draw is that it should be used exclusively to build the very smallest and cheapest of homes.

Notes

1   F. A. Hayek, 'Das Mieterschutzproblem: Nationalökonomische Betrachtungen', *Bibliothek für Volkswirtschaft und Politik*, No. 2, Vienna, 1929. To a large extent what follows is based on the earlier, more detailed study.
2   B. Kautsky, *Schriften des Vereins für Sozialpolitik*, 17 III, 1930, p. 70 *et seq.*
3   P. Vas, *Die Wiener Wohnungszwangswirtschaft von 1917–1927*, Jena, 1928, p. 35.
4   Pribram, *Schriften des Vereins für Sozialpolitik*, 177, I, 1930, p. 48.
5   Carl Kruschwitz, *Schriften des Vereins für Sozialpolitik*, 177, I, 1930, p. 48.
6   Adolf Weber, *Die Wohnungsproduktion*, Tübingen, 1914, p. 354.

8

1980s Unemployment and the Unions

1 Employment and Inflation

British sentiments on unemployment and opinions on the effective remedies for it have been shaped by a unique historical experience that has
given rise to a persuasive but false theory which for a generation has
dominated discussion. The unique situation was created by Britain's
decision after World War I to return to gold at the pre-war parity. This
was a very honest decision for the banker of the world which may have
seemed necessary to preserve that position. But it proved a very unwise
decision, at least when it was decided to achieve this result slowly and
gradually. It had certainly not been understood what it would mean to
drag out over a decade the process of adapting internal prices and wages
to world levels.

The United States had set a different example. There, in the short
period of less than a year, from the middle of 1920 to the middle of 1921,
monetary policy succeeded in bringing wholesale prices down by 44 per
cent, thereby restoring the value of the dollar to its pre-war level. The
suffering during this period was great, but the foundations for a speedy
resumption of prosperity were laid: in the following two years industrial
production rose by 63 per cent and the national product by 23 per cent.

Painful consequences for Britain of restoring the gold standard in 1925

Britain chose otherwise. Though the clear determination of the Government to restore the gold standard made it possible to do so as early as

Published originally as Hobart Paper No. 87, 2nd Edition, IEA (1984).

1925, internal prices and wages were then still far from being adapted to the international level. To maintain this parity, a slow and highly painful process of deflation was initiated, bringing lasting and extensive unemployment, to be abandoned only when it became intolerable when intensified by the world crisis of 1931 – but, I am still inclined to believe, just at a time when the aim of that painful struggle had been nearly achieved.

During this period, which fashioned the outlook of the next generation, Britain found herself in the exceptional position, as an effect of the policy pursued, that all wages in the export industries on which the people depended for their livelihood were too high. In these conditions it was indeed approximately true that a rise of total demand would have been an effective way of lastingly removing most of the unemployment. The idea that general employment was determined by the relation of aggregate demand for final products prevailing in a given country (or monetary community) to the costs of the supply of goods, true enough under the special conditions of the time, unfortunately then came to dominate the monetary theory of the following generations and was applied in wholly different circumstances in which it became very misleading.

While the possibility of selling different quantities of *one* commodity depends of course on the magnitude of the demand for it, the possibility of selling a collection of a wide variety of different commodities is not in any simple manner related to the sum of the demands for all of them together. If the composition (or distribution) of the demand for the various products is very different from that of their supply, no magnitude of total demand will assure that the market is cleared. The wider the difference between the composition of the demand and that of the supply, the more the achievement of a correspondence between the whole of demand and the whole of supply can be brought about *only* by a change in the relative quantities, *and* this, in turn, only by a change in the relative prices of the different products and services, including wages. This is a major problem even if we think only of the possible discrepancies of demand and supply of all the final products – or what the economists are in the habit of calling the 'horizontal' dimension of the structure of production. But the complexity becomes immense when we include in our considerations the fact that all that is done at any one time does not serve the wants of one single point of time but the wants of many future dates, and that at each of these 'stages' varying expectations of the future will cause independent and different fluctuations of demand and supply. Once one comprehends this truth, the belief that a management of aggregate final demand can secure lasting full employment must look very naïve; and it seems inevitable that a policy based on such a crude conception would be bound in the end to make things worse rather than better.

Closeness of match of distribution of demand and supply determines aggregate employment

The rate of general employment thus depends on the degree of correspondence between the distribution of demand and the distribution of supply. And it is the distribution of supply which must adapt itself to the distribution of demand – even more than elsewhere in a country largely dependent on exports, over the demands for which it has no control. Aggregate demand may well exceed the aggregate price of all goods and services offered, yet this will not create full employment if in the sectors in which demand exceeds supply the already employed obstruct the entry of additional workers by claiming all the surplus as gain for themselves. Nor will people move out of the sector with a relative deficiency of demand unless it is clear that they cannot all hope to continue to earn there the wages they used to receive.

The disappearance of *some* employment opportunities is a necessary feature not only of any progressive but even of a stationary economy operating in a changing environment. If every firm were forced to continue employing its whole staff at the terms originally agreed upon, it would indeed have to continue until it went down with all hands, dragging down even those for whom it might have continued to provide a living. This appears to happen in Japan, where security of job while the firm lasts seems to produce a frequency of bankruptcies unequalled elsewhere.

One of the most vivid memories of my many defeats is of a discussion at the London Economic Club some 30 or 40 years ago when I let myself be silenced by a retort of Mr R. G. Hawtrey, as he then was, to the effect that what I apparently wanted were 'bigger and better bankruptcies'. I am not sure that Britain would not have attained a stronger position if she had allowed this. People seem to forget that the bankruptcy of a company need not mean the disappearance of its productive *equipment* but merely the replacement of an unsuccessful *management* by a new one.

Jobs are from the beginning a product of the market. In the long run only the market can provide ever new jobs which in a changing world must be constantly found to maintain all those whom the market in the first instance enabled to live by selling their labour. The numbers which can be maintained by transferring to them income taken by taxation from others is limited. And this is what has to be done to keep people employed who are given a larger share of the product than they contribute. Nobody can claim a moral right to employment at a particular wage, unless there is opportunity profitably to employ him at such wages. The problem today is that access to such employment is denied to him by the monopolistic organisations of his fellows. All opportunities for employment are a creation of the market and the classical ideal of 'full employment at high wages' (J. S. Mill) can be achieved only by a functioning market on which the wages offered for different kinds of work tell the worker where, in the circumstances of the moment, he can make the largest contribution to the social product.

Trade unions obstruct adaptation of relative prices (especially wages) to the distribution of demand

It is the continuous change of *relative* market prices and particularly wages which alone can bring about that steady adjustment of the proportions of the different efforts to the distribution of demand, and thus a steady flow of the stream of products. It is this incessant adaptation of relative wages to the ever-changing magnitudes, at which in each sector demand will equal supply, which the trade unions have set out to inhibit. Wages are no longer to be determined by demand and supply but by alleged considerations of justice, which means in effect not only simply custom and tradition but increasingly sheer power. The market is thereby deprived of the function of guiding labour to where it can be sold.

Unemployment inevitable

It is inevitable that this obstruction of the market should produce extensive unemployment. And if it had not been for a scapegoat to which responsibility could be diverted, even the members of the trade unions would long ago have been forced to admit that the policies of the unions were, under normal conditions, the sole cause of extensive lasting unemployment as well as the chief obstacle to a faster rise of the income of the workers. This scapegoat, raised by the persuasive voice of Lord

Keynes to the position of a generally accepted dogma, was 'aggregate demand' depending on the supply of money.

The scapegoat possessed a certain plausibility because of the unique experience of Britain half a century ago, when it was indeed true that policy had created a situation where the *general* wage level of Britain was too high and the unemployment could have been cured by increasing aggregate demand by lowering the external value of sterling.

It was a great historical misfortune that this special experience had directed attention to a more painless remedy which, however, could be employed effectively only in the special circumstances of that time. This view, however, pleased the traditional sympathy of the British public with the efforts of the trade unions by relieving them of the responsibility for the bad effects of their efforts. Most people were happy to learn that government had the power, and therefore the exclusive responsibility, to secure full employment. But this release of the trade unions from the responsibility for the effects of their actions also removed the chief restraint on the abuse of their power.

In post-World War II Britain it was no longer the general level of money wages which was too high. It should indeed have been higher with a free market for labour in which monopolistic groups could not deprive others of their chances. It is the wages maintained by the closed shops whose barriers prevented the rest from earning as much as they might have done which keeps the productivity of the majority of British workers low. Once the opportunity to earn more in a particular trade becomes the exclusive property of those already employed there, successes of individual enterprises are likely to be taken out by its present staff in the form of higher wages rather than leading to additional employment.

Inflation, employment, and trade unions: Britain, 1980s

The problem of inflation, the problem of employment, and the problem of the excessive power of the trade unions have become inseparable in present-day Britain. Although seen as a problem of economic cause and effect, there is no such thing as 'cost-push inflation'. The only effect of an excessive rise of wages (or of the price of anything else) would be that what is offered cannot be sold. *Politically* the problem of trade union power is the primary problem because, so long as government has the control of the supply of money, it will be forced to resort to the palliative of inflation which temporarily disguises the effects of a rise of wages on employment but leads to cumulative arrears of omitted adaptations which merely store up later trouble.

Indeed, the reliance on monetary expansion as a cure for unemployment would not be so harmful if it were merely a temporary palliative, ineffective to cure the underlying causes. What makes it so dangerous is that it actually and continuously makes matters worse. It not only preserves the existing but leads to a continuous accumulation of further misdirections of efforts which ought to have been currently corrected. *Monetary demand not based on real earnings can last only so long as the additions to the supply of money grow.*

The palliative (monetary expansion) is the pernicious poison (inflation)

But the palliative, so tempting to the politician, proves to be a poison, and, because it is habit-forming, pernicious even in the smallest doses. Although one hesitates to use this worn metaphor, the whole situation as well as the moral issues involved are much the same as those presented by some habit-forming drug which can produce a passing state of euphoria necessarily followed by withdrawal symptoms of severe depression. People who advocate its use as a stimulant, except in an acute political emergency, are simply quacks. There is only one important difference between the individual and the political problem: while a human patient may under medical direction last through a protracted treatment, no political community will long bear the suffering connected with such a slow cure.

Surprising as it may seem, these after-effects of inflation have been much neglected by economists. They were mainly concerned with its *current* effects on the relation between debtors and creditors, with the suffering of all those whose income was determined by long-term contracts, including wage-earners, and with the general injustice of the arbitrary redistribution of incomes which inflation causes while it proceeds. This is the effect which everybody soon learns to see, the source of general complaint, and it seems of all that most economists are aware of who think exclusively in terms of the effects of *average* prices. For them inflation is an evil which can be slowly and gradually reduced, and in the fight against which every slowing-down of the rate of inflation is a gain. But the chief penalty for past inflation must be paid so long as it is being reduced and for some time after it has been stopped.

To reduce present unemployment by inflation always becomes the cause of greater unemployment later, because the effect of making possible a postponement of necessary adaptations is cumulative and in the course of time creates an amount of maladjustment which nobody is prepared to face. The artificial demand brought about by increasing the amount of money is simply misleading: it attracts workers into employments which cannot be maintained except by *accelerating* inflation. The crucial point that must be recognised is that it is not the *size* of total demand but the *distribution* of demand which decides whether a level of employment can be maintained. There is no substitute for a flexible wage structure. The vain search for a palliative while preserving the unions' strength is the chief source of Britain's economic decline.

If in the short run inflation reduces unemployment, in the long run its accumulated effects will make much more unemployment inevitable than it temporarily reduced. To see this result it is necessary to understand fully the process through which for a time a general rise of prices can make activities profitable which are bound to fail as soon as inflation *ceases to accelerate*. This is particularly important in order to refute the uncomprehending or malicious allegations in Britain that unemployment is now deliberately created as a means to stop inflation. Unemployment has been made inevitable by past inflation; it has merely been *postponed* by accelerating inflation. *But those responsible for the present unemployment are those who caused the inflation, not those who are trying to stop it.* To postpone this any further could merely make the eventual outcome worse. It is simply not within human power to postpone the evil day indefinitely. An inflationary boom must collapse sooner or later with the consequence of large-scale unemployment.

Inflation cannot be accelerated indefinitely. Though even a fairly rapidly depreciating money will still serve as a means of calculation, it ceases to do so once the rate of depreciation exceeds a certain speed. When prices begin to double every year, and then every month or every week, and finally every day (and I have seen this happen), the money in terms of which this occurs is discarded by the public. But once acceleration of inflation is accepted as indispensable to maintain employment, this point must eventually be reached. What then puts an end to it is that people refuse to sell for this sort of money and other means of exchange take the place of those which government provided.

Repressed inflation via price controls or incomes policy more damaging than open inflation

The expedient which is likely to postpone this inevitable ultimate outcome for a long time at the price of even more damage done is widely thought to be price controls. I have been preaching on this topic for years that if anything is worse than an open inflation it is a repressed inflation, an increase in the quantity of money which proceeds but by legal price-fixing is prevented from showing any effects on prices. If an *open* inflation severely distorts the steering function of the market, a *repressed* inflation completely suspends it. Price-fixing or an incomes policy means no less than a transition from a market economy to a planned economy with all its inevitable consequences.

Britain in the 1980s

The acute problem for Britain at present is still whether to stop inflation dead instantly or to protract the process of reducing it over months or years, and the answer to this must depend on our insight about how inflation operates which we had begun discussing. The crucial point was that it can preserve its stimulating effect only so long as it accelerates, and that as soon as it ceases to accelerate all the misdirections of production which it has caused will show themselves. In practice, terminating the acceleration of inflation, and even more gradually reducing the rate of inflation, must have an effect very similar to deflation. It will cause the same widespread disappointment of expectations and force the suspension of activities which had been kept going by prices turning out to be higher than they ought to have been.

The difference between the two phenomena is that, while we can always prevent deflation, once we have embarked on an accelerating inflation we will sooner or later be forced to stop it, if not earlier at least when people refuse to hold or even accept the money with its fast-dwindling buying power. And since any inflation, however modest at first, can help employment only so long as it accelerates, adopted as a means of reducing unemployment, it will do so for any length of time only while it accelerates.

'Mild' steady inflation cannot help – it can lead only to outright inflation

That inflation at a constant rate soon ceases to have any stimulating effect, and in the end merely leaves us with a backlog of delayed adaptations, is the conclusive argument against the 'mild' inflation represented as beneficial even in standard economics textbooks. Those who advocate, or even are merely prepared to tolerate, mild inflation are inevitably driven to support more and more inflation. Nor is anything gained by merely reducing inflation to a 'reasonable' rate. *Inflation must be stopped dead*, because the trouble about it is precisely that its stimulating effect can be preserved only by accelerating it. Once a given rate of inflation is generally *expected*, it no longer stimulates but only continues to preserve some of the misdirections of efforts it has caused. But so long as it is believed that general employment is determined by a monetary policy which in the long run will only make matters worse, to begin with a mild expansion will invariably lead to outright inflation.

Slowly falling inflation with high unemployment likely to fail in an industrial democracy

Considered as a purely technical problem of monetary policy, we have of course the choice whether we wish to reduce inflation slowly and gradually or instantly. In neither case can we escape causing thereby for a time extensive unemployment. This has been made inescapable by what has happened earlier. For a short time the amount of unemployment may be even higher when the termination of inflation is effected quickly than it will ever be during the long process of a gradual return. Politically, however, we may not be able to choose. A drastic cut, however painful, will be tolerable and would be patiently submitted to if there were hope of recovery in the near future. I do not believe that any democratic government can stay the course of a slow reduction of inflation over years – at least not in a highly industrialised country. Even 20 per cent unemployment would probably be borne for six months if there existed confidence that it would be over at the end of such a period. But I doubt whether any government could persist for two or three years in a policy that meant 10 per cent unemployment for most of that period. Such efforts will prove vain and the suffering wasted if public opinion makes it necessary to break it off before the desired result has been achieved.

I am of course fully aware of the immense problem of public finance involved in being suddenly deprived of the means for covering a budget deficit which the creation of money has provided. But, however difficult, it can be solved and must be solved if the last chance of avoiding a final collapse of the British economy is to be taken. Though a real balancing of the budget requires a period of some length, the necessary borrowing does not have to be based on increasing the circulation of sterling.

At a time when the ordinary citizen is in desperate difficulty to find an opportunity for stable investments of his savings, a large government loan in terms of a new stable unit could be raised very cheaply and bring into the government's pockets funds which the citizen would probably otherwise spend. As I have suggested on another occasion (*The Times*, 13 June 1980):

> Large amounts could probably be raised at perhaps 3 or even $2\frac{1}{2}$ per cent if a public which no longer knows what to do with its savings were offered such an opportunity. It seems to me that the British government, perhaps undeservedly, still enjoys a reputation for honesty which may make an experiment of this sort a great success. The 'solids', in terms of which the loan would be issued, would have to be defined as, and be redeemable in, so much of a bundle of other currencies as would at the time be required to buy on the world market a 'basket' of a wide range of internationally traded raw materials in precisely stated quantitative combinations. Ultimately the unit might become, if necessary, the basis of a new British currency.

2 The Telecommunications System of the Market

Many people seem to believe that freedom consists of being able to do whatever they like and still enjoy all the benefits of an advanced society in which they must co-operate with others. But modern society, which rests on a far-ranging division of labour, could not prosper – or even survive for long – if it allowed the mass of its members that kind of freedom. Its relative opulence requires all of us to observe an impersonal discipline. More than once in our lifetimes, some of us have to do things we may dislike – changing our jobs, our homes, or our neighbourhoods, or accepting a smaller income than we had come to expect, and so on. And all this is hard to bear because it seems the consequence of causes and events a long way off about which we know nothing: a change of habit in another industry or a technical invention in another country. Nobody is morally entitled to claim a share in the wealth which such a society produces unless he is prepared to obey the discipline of other people's wants or other countries' production methods that are ultimately the sources of our wealth.

Producing the desired commodity in the most economic way at the required time is what counts, not 'working hard'

With an extensive 'division of labour', in which we all specialise in producing goods and services, we must be ready to change the nature or direction of our efforts, or accept less than our accustomed income, in response to unforeseen circumstances and unforeseen changes in them. All *economic* problems are caused by *unforeseen* events. Otherwise we could simply continue doing what we decided long ago without ever having to change our work, our industry, or our homes.

In an economic system whose productivity, in this sense of producing what others want, rests on a world-wide division of labour and special-isation, the size of the national product will depend not on individuals 'working hard' but on making the 'right' (desired) things in the 'right' (most economic) manner and at the 'right' time (required by the consumer in the market which may be hundreds or thousands of miles away in other continents). The way in which at any one time the individual can make the largest contribution to the product of society and thereby maximise his share of that product in the form of wages, salaries, etc., will depend on the new opportunities opening up from day to day for thousands of workers in other occupations with whom he co-operates in producing something – often without knowing it – or from consumers whose demands he serves – usually without knowing them at all.

Market prices convey information to change course

Each individual can rarely know the conditions which make it desirable, for him as well as for others, to do one thing rather than another, or to do it in one way rather than another. *It is only through the prices he finds in the market that he can learn what to do and how*. Only they, constantly and unmistakably, can inform him what goods or services he ought to produce in his own interest as well as the general interest of his community or country as a whole. The 'signal' which warns him that he must alter the direction or nature of his effort is frequently the discovery that he can no longer sell the fruits of his effort at prices which leave a surplus over costs. This signalling apparatus works as much for the employed worker as for the professional or business man.

In a free society nobody can compel another person to continue in his job. And, in most instances, he will have alternatives open to him. Yet signals which nobody has deliberately set will often inform him that what he has been producing, and what he would readily continue producing as industriously as before, will no longer earn him as much as it has done, or as much as he could earn elsewhere in another job or industry. The signals may thus tell him that he may even earn nothing at all if he continues in what he has been producing. All the conscientious devotion in the world will earn nothing for the workers making Triumph motor-cycles if the motor-cyclists in Britain and overseas want other cycles.

For anyone earning his living in the market, which means most of us, the most valuable contribution he can make at any time will depend on thousands of continually changing conditions of which he can have no direct knowledge. It is nevertheless possible for him to make whatever decisions are most advantageous both to himself and the community at large because the open market conveys to him, through its prices, the information he requires to make the right decisions and choices. The prices are thus the indispensable signals that communicate to him the effects of events with which he cannot himself be directly acquainted.

Division of labour and technology constantly changing

The division of labour among individuals, firms, or countries is not once-for-all but a complex, balanced structure which must continuously change to perform its function. It is a fatal mistake, frequently made by engineers or other natural scientists, to imagine there are long-lasting, technically determined production methods which are superior to all others, and that these make it possible to continue the use of the factors in rigid quantitative proportions. It is not 'good technology' which determines productivity but the right choice among the many tech-nologies available. This is an economic, not a technological, problem.

The vast increase in output and living standards made possible by the wide-ranging division of labour in the modern Western world is chiefly the result of goods and services being produced by those best able to do so and of their using the means of production which sacrifice as little as necessary of other goods or services that could have been produced with the resources, so that their 'opportunity costs' are minimised.

It is solely through the effects which unknown, remote events have on prices that the individual employer, producer or dealer can take account of changes in the conditions in which raw materials are produced, in the demand for some final products for which his contribution is needed, or in technology. Such events will sometimes affect only indirectly, and at many removes, the activity with which he is directly concerned. And that indirect route takes the form of substituting objects which have become relatively cheaper for other objects which have become relatively dearer.

Efficient use of resources guided unconsciously by remote control of millions unknown to one another

All effort to make the best use of available resources is thus guided by a sort of remote control. The signals which inform individuals what they should produce are not deliberately set by anyone. They are the joint result of all the individuals using, for their own purposes, the detailed information they know. And the prices which guide them are formed by incorporating all the effects of their demands and supplies.

What prices tell everybody is the rate at which (or the proportion in which) other people can (for their own purposes) substitute a quantity of one commodity for quantities of another. If any commodity is worth more to an individual relatively to another commodity than the current market rate, he can exchange it to the extent he desires. In doing so he will affect the price and contribute his mite of information to the signals. It is thus the consequent tendency towards similarity of all internal rates of substitution of different persons (counting all the costs of passing goods from one person's control to another's) which secures the most efficient use of resources. This result is achieved through using the knowledge possessed by the participants in the market, whether they know one another or not. Each individual can thus produce his output at the least cost in terms of the products that others, in consequence, will lack and want.

Far-ranging division of labour made possible only by self-steering market process

It is as if all participants in the market had before them the current results of a giant computer into which each of them, in the light of the available data, could feed his own offers and demands by pressing a few buttons. But such a computer would be helpful only if everybody had full access to it all the time and was committed to buy and sell what was on offer or in demand, so that nobody could manipulate the market by false information. In practice, the real market attains only an approximation to this ideal, but it is as close an approximation as we can achieve with the imperfect information available.

Although Adam Smith told us 200 years ago in *The Wealth of Nations* that

> ... this division of labour, from which so many advantages are derived, is not originally the effect of any human wisdom, which foresees and intends the general opulence to which it gives occasion,

most people, especially 'social engineers', still conceive of it as something designed, or at least designable, such as the division of labour within a single factory. Smith himself contributed to this misconception by deriving his most famous illustration from the organisation of pin-making by several workers each doing a specialised job. Adam Smith clearly understood but did not fully explain that the division of labour among many people who know nothing of each other is made possible only by the market. It would develop through such a self-steering process *only because it uses more information than any directing agency could ever possess.*

Modern societies can produce as much as they do because everybody is informed by market prices of the highest costs at which it is worthwhile producing any particular commodity or service. And each producer can find out how and whether he can produce at such costs only because he can calculate his own costs in comparison with the prices that reflect all the other uses to which the resources he employs might be put.

Production for satisfaction of known wants impossible with extensive division of labour

Because the division of labour is among millions of people who do not even know of the existence of most of the others for whom and in co-operation with whom they unwittingly work, their aim becomes impersonal and, in a sense, abstract. The aim of the efforts of all can no longer be the satisfaction of *known* demands, for they have no knowledge of the subsequent use of their products. The aim must therefore become solely the yield from the sale of their products on the market. To obtain such a return, each individual must seek to meet the demands of other people at least as cheaply as anyone else does. Everybody's effort must thus be directed at producing goods and services at costs as much as possible *below* current prices. The *difference* between costs and returns, which we disdainfully call 'gain' or 'profit', thus becomes the true measure of the social usefulness to others of our efforts. And production at a loss, when costs exceed the yield, becomes an offence against the best use of resources. And this is especially true when it means, as it so often does, that someone else's resources are being misused.

The difference between obeying and not obeying the signals of prices and costs is, therefore, the difference between productive and unproductive effort – between effort which increases and effort which diminishes the national product. We might also call it the difference between socially beneficial and anti-social activities.

Market prices are not perfect but the best available

This analysis is not substantially modified by the undeniable truth that even the most perfect market prices do not take into account *all* the circumstances we would wish – often described as 'external' conditions. But where we have to adapt production to many more events than we can be aware of, a signal which takes account of most of them is better than none. Travellers do not throw away the map of a strange country they have to cross because they find it is not wholly accurate.

Only free prices send reliable signals; administered prices mislead

Only prices at which everyone is free to buy and sell as much as he wants and his means allow can operate as reliable guides. Only if all owners or users of goods can take part in the dealings will all requirements and all opportunities be taken into account. Prices fixed by political authority, or prices influenced by controls on demand and supply – such as rationing, subsidies, special taxes – do not guide in the right direction but generally mislead because they distort the information about supply and consumer demand and, moreover, add a political element that has little to do with reflecting technical possibilities or satisfying consumers.

Monopoly prices can be made least harmful by maintaining competition

Prices may, for a time, be fixed by a monopolist who owes his position not to privilege conferred upon him by government, but to his superior efficiency which nobody else can equal. Consumers have scarcely any right to force such a producer to do as well as he can if he is already doing better than anybody else in his industry. We can only make it necessary for all producers to do at least as well as those producers whom we pay the same price for the same product. But the use of power to restrict competition, or to deny new producers access to a market in order to keep prices at a desired figure, will prevent some relevant information about conditions of supply from being taken into account.

Contrary to a widespread belief, unless it is sheltered from competition by government protection, a big business has no more power than anyone else to fix prices arbitrarily. It is subject to the same disciplines of supply and demand. And if such a firm mistakes the signals, it will, fortunately, fail – at least so long as government does not bail it out, as has recently happened in Britain.

Pursuit of gain creates indirect incentives to serve others

The pursuit of gain is thus the only way in which men can serve the requirements of others whom they do not know, and adjust their efforts to circumstances they cannot directly observe. The pursuit of gain is held in bad repute, because it does not have as its aim the *visible* benefit of others and may be successfully guided by purely selfish motives. Yet the source of the strength of the market order is that it uses the immediate concerns of individuals to make them serve needs that are more important than they can know. It is not because a man's aims are 'selfish' but because they are his own that he can contribute, through his free decisions guided by the signals of prices, more to the welfare of others than if that were his direct goal. His efforts may not be the most beneficial to his *immediate* neighbours – and for that reason may not make him popular among them – but he will thus serve society at large much better than he could in any other way.

Discovering relevant information only through competition: the
telecommunications of the market

In this manner, the market not only matches millions of separate efforts to one another so that, on the whole, the demand for a commodity or a service (including, of course, labour) will approximately correspond to its supply at market prices. The market also obliges and enables all participants – buyers and sellers – to obtain a given output from a *minimum* of resources available to them. Put another way, it induces everyone to obtain from a given input of resources as *large* a proportion of the social product as possible.

They can do this only because they can calculate, in terms of the costs of labour, capital, etc., the cheapest way of producing what they can expect to sell at a known price. Without prices determined by competition, in which the variegated knowledge and requirements of millions are reflected, effective calculation would be impossible. Prices administered by central authority, as in Russia and Poland (or Britain and the USA), on the other hand, which must be based on much less information than that reflected by competitive prices, are often likely to show a surplus on activities which are socially loss-making, or vice versa. They therefore cause massive misdirection of human and natural resources in producing commodities or services that the people do not want.

With given competitive prices, each participant in the productive process can attempt to produce, from any given quantity of resources, as large an output as can be achieved. The use of the existing but dispersed information about detailed circumstances, where nobody can always know who possesses that information, requires competition as the process of *selection* which finds ('discovers') the possessor of the relevant information. Only the telecommunications system of the market can enable the participants to discover which method of production is cheapest, in terms of the other commodities or services we should like, and for which the resources could have been used.

British 'anti-economics' in the use of productive resources

All economising in production means that we use less of one resource and more of another: materials, energy, equipment, or human labour. This process always requires constant adaptation to new circumstances since, as I have argued, all economic problems are problems of adaptation to *unknown* and *unforeseen* change.

Producing cheaply means using as few resources as possible, measured in terms of the rates (prices) at which different products could be substituted for each other in their various uses. And reducing costs means setting free resources which could produce more elsewhere. In any particular instance, the primary aim must therefore always be to use as few resources as possible for a given output. Only as a result of producing as cheaply as possible will people have income to spare to pay for the work of others. The secret of productivity which makes it possible to employ many at high wages is for each producer to do his job with the use of as few resources as possible.

In Britain the unfortunate experience of long periods of unemployment, due to exceptional historical, and not necessarily recurring, circumstances, has made the people forget this fundamental truth. It has led them to behave as if the direct aim of economic activity were to use as *many* resources as possible. It has come to be thought in Britain that a prime task of economic policy was the protection of *existing* jobs. This fundamental reversal of the truth has developed into a sort of anti-economics which has misrepresented the chief social goal to be the use of as *large* a quantity of resources as possible.

Job creation and credit expansion are the creators of unemployment

This view of economic policy finds support in the statistical nonsense, common in Western countries since the War, of measuring the social product in terms of costs. In a country like Britain, heavily dependent on selling its products to the rest of the world, this whole approach must have the opposite effect on employment from the one intended. Government efforts – which are politically unavoidable under the prevailing form of unlimited democracy – to enable workers to retain employment which has become unprofitable at existing wages only increase the backlog of necessary job adjustments. Sooner or later, the backlog must lead to unemployment. And the longer it is deferred, the more the unemployment.

Attempts in recent years to achieve full employment through credit expansion – to draw workers into jobs which can last only so long as inflation progressively accelerates – have, moreover, markedly exacerbated that effect. To consider the manipulation of aggregate demand as a means of securing an efficient use of resources, i.e. of directing them where they ought to be used, is anti-economics. Britain has been brought to her present plight, not because of the lack of skill or industry of the individual worker, but because government and labour organisations, in order to appease groups of workers, have tried to relieve them of the necessity for adjustments by removing the inducements (and rewards) of changing their jobs.

Competition essential for controlling costs

In the absence of a competitive market in which freely determined prices inform all producers of the socially cheapest way of producing commodities or services, and at what prices other producers can supply them, costs easily get out of control. Without the help of such information-creating prices, managers, who tend to be concerned chiefly about the physical process of production and are perhaps fascinated by the beauty of the technique employed, can quickly let the outlay on production rise to double what it would otherwise be. This lack of market information means that twice as much could have been produced from the amount of resources consumed.

Neither does this reduction of output below potential measure the whole loss a country may suffer as a result of a distorted price structure. For a firm or country producing for sale in competition with others, costs higher than the necessary level by perhaps only one or two per cent may mean the complete loss of the business, and therefore of the whole income derived from it.

It is by this constant pressure that competition leaves buyers and sellers in the market no choice but to make use of *all* the available possibilities in combining resources to avoid unnecessary costs. The absence of this pressure on producers and suppliers is certain to raise costs unnecessarily. A country which lives on imports, like Britain, may thus become unable to pay for them.

3 Three Options for Policy

There are three attitudes which organised power can take towards the extensive division of labour required in an advanced society.

Refine the legal framework – especially to catch 'externalities'

First, legislation and government may cultivate the market – as they did for a long time, without really understanding its requirements. Through trial and error they could gradually develop the framework of private and criminal law required by the system of private property. Assisted by a better understanding of the working of the market, we might continue these efforts to improve the legal framework where we find it defective. In particular, the current delimitation of property rights may not catch the 'external' effects that at present are not adequately taken into account by prices.

Emulate or 'correct' the market by central planning – but impossible to agree on objectives

Secondly, the public authority might try to emulate the market's allocation of resources by a system of central direction. Such a system of collectivist economic planning has, for a long time, exercised intense fascination for many people. It was thought the way to achieve not only a more efficient economic process but also a more just distribution of incomes. But the initial hope soon had to be abandoned when it was realised that no planning authority could ever use all the information about detailed circumstances that is dispersed among hundreds of thousands of individuals, to anything like the extent to which the market uses it day by day.

Even attempts to 'correct' the prices set by the market, through the intervention of authority, must founder. It is impossible sensibly to correct a signal (price) that conveys information on the combined effects of changes in supply and demand of which the authority itself does not know. The hope of achieving a more just distribution of incomes in this way is doomed to disappointment. Not only could few people agree on what a just distribution of incomes would be. Even more serious, any attempt to reward people according to some principle of merit or 'need', instead of according to the value of their services to their fellows (which may be very different), would make voluntary collaboration in the efficient use of resources impossible.

Syndicalist or corporativist organisation of interest groups is anti-social

Thirdly, there is the syndicalist–corporativist response. This amounts to a systematic obstruction and sabotage of price determination through the competitive market by organised sectional interests that are permitted to use power and coercion to maintain their monopoly. In almost all instances their aim is to secure for their members a larger share of the social income. Yet, at the same time, the restrictive methods they employ reduce that total. They are therefore anti-social in the only proper sense of the word. By bringing about a larger loss to the community, they secure for themselves a smaller gain. Yet these practices are today common in Britain among groups whose membership probably adds up to a large proportion of the population.

Central direction and monopoly domination combined in futile 'incomes policies'

It is scarcely an exaggeration to say that, while we still owe our current living standards chiefly to the operation of an increasingly mutilated market system, economic policy is guided almost entirely by a combination of the two views whose object is to destroy the market: the planning ambitions of doctrinaire socialist intellectuals and the restrictionism of trade unions and trade associations. This paradox continues although, until the most recent times, the market order has again and again produced the outstanding successes around the world, while no attempt to determine the division of labour by either central planning or monopolies has ever succeeded. What today is called an 'incomes policy' is merely an attempt to reconcile these two policies, equally hostile to the market, in a futile endeavour to combat inflation. Every effort in this direction constitutes a new blow at the competitiveness of British industry.

The market as liberator: minimises coercion and fraud

From a human viewpoint the perhaps most profound advantage of the market over alternative methods of directing the use of resources is that it virtually eliminates the use of force and the coercion of men by other men. This result is in marked contrast to the inexorable subjection to superiors which is an essential and indispensable ingredient of socialism and monopoly.

It may be true that, in the last century in communities with only a single factory or mine, the local manager could exercise an almost dictatorial power over the workers. The distance-annihilating increase in mobility occasioned by modern communications, and particularly by the motor-car, has removed this subjection to monopoly. But, in general, probably never in the whole of recorded history was the exercise of arbitrary power and the personal subjection of human beings to the power of others reduced so much as during the second half of the last century – that period which we like to call, contemptuously and misleadingly, the age of *laissez-faire*. Compared with the feudalism of the preceding centuries, it gave a degree of individual freedom to the working population previously unknown in the history of civilisation. During that period, any citizen of the Western industrial countries could proudly claim he was not irrevocably subject to any man's orders.

Collectivism and syndicalism destroy freedom and wealth

The two alternative systems, on the other hand, require a return to coercion without rule. They demand personal submission to a superior to whom a man is assigned, or to dependence on an organised group of special interests whose pleasure determines whether a man is allowed to earn his living in a particular way. The two systems are bound to destroy not only personal freedom but also the wealth on which the group members base their demands. This is so because that wealth is founded on the use of widely dispersed information, which is created only if everybody is allowed to employ his own knowledge for his own purposes and if prices are formed in a free market so as to convey to him the information he requires to fit his efforts into the general pattern of economic activity.

The market rewards what should be done to satisfy consumer preferences, not what is done by producers

It is this highly sensitive, though somewhat delicate, instrument that makes possible an efficient use of resources. But the would-be reformers want to destroy it because they will not understand that something which has never been deliberately designed but has grown through a process of selective evolution can achieve more than rational direction ever could. Their main complaint is that the market order distributes benefits with little regard to justice. In a sense, this is true and even necessary, because the prices paid for different individuals' services are not designed as a reward for what they have done but function as an indicator of what they ought to do. The prices paid for services are not a 'just' reward for effort but a neutral indicator of where they require to be applied.

Planned efficiency could be no more 'just' than market efficiency

The director of a planned society who wanted to secure an efficient use of resources, and to use wages as an inducement to workers to go where they were required, could be no more just than the market. A steering mechanism to achieve adaptation to unforeseen changes cannot be 'just'. Adaptation to an unknown number of unforeseen events, which in their totality cannot be known to anybody but to which all submit under the same abstract rules, cannot be designed. It is therefore incapable of being 'just'.

Social usefulness is not and cannot be apportioned according to any principles of justice. If we want to induce people to offer what will produce the largest contribution to the requirements of others, we must allow them to earn incomes that correspond to their performance, rather than to their merits or needs.

Marx stood reality on its head: the labour value error of classical economics

The guide rôle of prices, which Adam Smith clearly understood, was later obscured by the labour theory of value of Ricardo, the two Mills and Karl Marx. They inverted the true causal relationship. Instead of showing that prices informed producers how much labour it was worth putting into an object, they taught that the value of a product was determined by the labour invested in it. It is this inversion of the true functional relationship of value (informing people how much cost it is worthwhile incurring to produce things) into the belief that values are a result of people having invested costs in producing them that incapacitates Marxists from ever understanding the function of the market.

This error of classical theory, from which British (or, at least, Cambridge) economics never quite recovered, bears some responsibility for the recent economic decline of Britain. To reverse it requires recognition of the market as a communication system which achieves something that no other known system could possibly achieve.

The harmful legacy of our moral instincts

Our inherited moral feelings constitute the stubborn obstacle to the moral approval of the market system to which we owe our wealth. They demand that we consciously aim at benefiting other known persons; in contrast, the beneficial effects of our efforts on other people in the market society are mostly unknown to us and cannot guide us. In order to do most good the individual must let himself be guided by abstract and impersonal signs. He cannot consciously aim at the most gain for others, but only at the most gain for himself and his associates.

This rule of conduct conflicts with the moral instincts we have inherited from the face-to-face society in which the human race for centuries lived hundreds of times longer than in the exchange society of the last 200 years. These moral instincts derive from the small hunting group of 50 or so men, and from the later tribal society in which the concern of each for the known needs of his fellows was essential for the survival of the group.

To these inherited and deeply ingrained emotions, the incentives which make us work for the market give little gratification. The restraints the legal order places on them – such as the respect for another's property, the keeping of promises, and the responsibility for torts – often appear meaningless. So long as independent artisans, craftsmen, tradesmen, or merchants numerically predominated in society and shaped opinion, their daily acquaintance with the market taught them its rules, and the commercial standards it had developed were widely accepted. But among employees of large organisations, who have little acquaintance with the market and to whom the rôle of prices as essential signals is largely incomprehensible, the ancestral emotions of morality and justice have re-emerged. The clamour today is for *visible* 'justice' – an allocation of rewards for recognisable merits and 'needs'.,

Contrived 'social justice' is meaningless; justice develops spontaneously if it generates behaviour that benefits all

This desire is not only irreconcilable with the signalling and guide functions of prices and, in consequence, destructive of the market. It also raises moral problems to which traditional moral principles provide no answers. The formula which is widely believed to provide an answer, namely, 'social justice', proves when tested to be wholly devoid of content. Beneficial conceptions of justice will develop naturally and persist in a society when they secure conduct which benefits the members of the group which practises them, not when attempts to make them prevail are imposed by force.

Pursuit of private gain guided by abstract rules of honest conduct does more good for others

The rules of just individual conduct which the law enforces, and which essentially require honesty, have gained wide acceptance in the Western world because they impartially improved the chances of all individuals to obtain a larger command over the worldly goods for which they strive. But most people find it difficult to understand that the pursuit of gain guided solely by abstract rules of honest conduct may do more good for others we do not know than a conscious, deliberate attempt to do good to them. Yet we in the Western world would certainly never have achieved our present standard of living if individuals had allowed moral feelings about good intentions to prevail, and had consequently forced people to aim at satisfying the needs of individuals they knew directly.

Return to a less impersonal society would be a return to poverty

We ought, perhaps, to understand that many well-intentioned, 'compassionate' people dislike this impersonal, abstract society into which they are born and which provides insufficient gratification for their altruistic emotions. But a return to the primitive forms of society for which they yearn, in which doing good can be expressed directly in everyday life, would also mean a return to the extreme poverty which has been abolished in the Western world. The poverty, moreover, would be much more severe if the present millions of population had to be fed by a process of deliberate direction of the use of resources to satisfy the wants of people known personally to all producers by hand or brain.

Competition: a 'game' of discovery that creates wealth by skill and chance

The competitive search for adaptation to an uncertain future induces us to try to use as fully as possible the dispersed knowledge of continually changing detailed information. This process necessarily becomes a sort of game in which individual success usually depends on a combination of skill and luck which can never be clearly distinguished. The right thing for the individual to do at a given moment – what is both in his own and in the general interest – must depend on the accidental position into which history has placed him. We have learned to play this game of *discovery*, which we call 'competition', because the communities that experimented with it and gradually improved its rules have flourished above others. Consequently they have been imitated. But the outcome of the game, the rules of which require people to take the fullest advantage of the opportunities that come their way to serve both themselves and others, can be no more 'just' than that of any game of chance.

All we can ask is that the players behave honestly and do not cheat, and that the rules are the same for all. But we cannot make even the starting positions the same if the game is to serve its purpose of inducing people to make the best of their peculiar knowledge of circumstances and their peculiar skills. If the abstract signals of prices are to give correct guidance, the value which the services required have for consumers must be offered to *all* potential suppliers alike, irrespective of their 'needs' or merits. Those whose position and knowledge enable them to make the most gain must be tempted into the game, in order that their competition brings down prices for everyone else. If the individual is to be free to decide what to produce, he must be paid, whether the result of his efforts is due to skill or luck. To try to make this remuneration correspond to what is imagined to be 'socially just' would thus, in practice, be anti-social and destructive of the national wealth.

High-minded men intent on doing visible good would destroy wealth

An economist necessarily becomes a student of conflicts of values. He must constantly draw attention to the existence of such conflicts which people, in their dreams of good works, tend to ignore. He must warn them not to under-estimate the importance of those values of protection against destitution and starvation which are now largely assured and taken for granted, and not to sacrifice them to the lure of new ones – selfless compassion or 'caring' – which are not yet realised.

What the economist is thus sometimes obliged to tell people is that to follow the advice of what are commonly regarded as 'good men', because their views appeal to deeply ingrained moral emotions, may destroy the whole framework within which those new ambitions of doing good seem to be achievable. Unfortunately, the real goodness of a moral view does not depend on the high-mindedness of its exponents. The good done in everyday life would be undermined by acting on high-minded advice because it would destroy the peaceful co-operation of free men using their own knowledge for their own purposes.

Moral rules prove themselves in time by demonstrating that they conduce to the general welfare of all members of society as a whole, not by benefiting particular high-minded groups that wish to impose their notion of what is moral upon society. In other words, what is good for society does not necessarily correspond with the advice proffered by those individuals who are regarded as good, even if they are revered as near-saintly. It is determined by the welfare of the community which practises the moral rules. A set of moral beliefs supported by the moral leaders of a society, theological or secular, may become a grave obstacle to the achievement of such necessary requirements of a coherent society as peace and good prospects for individuals to attain the goals for which they strive and which conduce to the benefit of all.

The interaction of morals and institutions

In a society of free men, such non-viable morals are likely to disappear with the decline of the community which practises them. It is different once they become embedded in its institutions. A vague idea like that of 'social justice' will lead to the creation of an apparatus charged with putting right by force what is thought to be wrong. Such institutions, expected to apply a moral code that does not exist, come under irresistible pressure from many sectional interests to remedy their respective social grievances. This pressure forces the institutions to invent new rules which satisfy the sectional demands, but which increasingly obstruct the functioning of the self-ordering market mechanism. In this process, unclear moral ideas lead to the creation of national (and now, increasingly, even international) institutions which are then under a political necessity to design new rules that may have very little to do with the initial moral aims which led to their creation. I sometimes wonder whether this interaction, in which moral beliefs create institutions which, in turn, produce moral conceptions very different from those which gave rise to the institutions, is not the true story of the rise and fall of civilisations.

Examples of such national and international institutions are minimum wages depriving juveniles and immigrants of chances of jobs, or support by the International Labour Office depriving under-developed countries of the possibility of competition.

Recovery of Britain requires rejection of 'high-minded' politicians; political determination of income has wasted resources and destroyed wealth

This conclusion raises a further question: Can a people which finds it has developed destructive morals save itself? If those precepts have remained 'moral' in the *true* sense of the word – that they are not enforced by organised power – then no doubt self-salvation is still possible. But it will require the decline of the influence of the groups which led opinion, and their place will have to be taken by others who are prepared to disregard such *harmful* principles. The struggle for the recovery of Britain may thus mean a struggle against those long regarded as the 'good' people, whose 'social conscience' led them to try to impose some ideal design on the distribution of incomes. These are the politicians in all parties, in the trade unions, supported by well-meaning but muddled people in high places.

There is, of course, no reason why, in a community with the degree of wealth generally achieved by Western nations, we should not be able to provide *outside* the market a uniform minimum income for all adults who, for one reason or another, cannot earn more in the market. But, in view of the extent to which in Britain today relative wages and prices are determined politically, it must be wondered how the country can still produce anything at all at prices which have to be internationally competitive. And it is impossible not to be pessimistic about the future of Britain until the basic source of the inability to earn more from international trade is removed. The threat that the weakness may be made even worse by further resort to central direction and planning, advocated by some politicians, raises not only economic but also political spectres.

Keynes wrong again: aiming for heaven makes life hell

Some people still place trust in the belief that the sound basic instincts of the British people will protect the nation from such a course. But this confidence is justified only so long as individuals are free to select or reject moral ideas according to whether they enhance or damage the health of the community.

It is different when ideals are forced upon them by the coercive powers of government. National character certainly shapes institutions, but, in the long run, institutions also shape national character. It is, therefore, a dangerous delusion to believe, as Lord Keynes wrote to me at the end of his comments on my 1944 book, *The Road to Serfdom*, that

> ... dangerous acts can be done safely in a community which thinks and feels rightly which would be the way to hell if they were executed by those who think and feel wrongly.

I fear that the German poet Friedrich Hölderlin saw more clearly when, almost 150 years earlier, he wrote:

> What has always made the state a hell on earth has been precisely that man has tried to make it his heaven.

4 The Trade Unions and Britain's Economic Decline

So far I have discussed the general principles of a market economy. I now turn to what is widely recognised as the crucial debility in Britain's economic future but which is usually regarded as politically insoluble.

Trade unions, in their present form, have become part of the British way of life, and their power has become politically sacrosanct. But economic decline has also become part of the British way of life, and few people are willing to accept that as sacrosanct. Many British people are beginning to see the connection between the two. Yet this insight is in such conflict with what most of them believe the trade unions have achieved for the mass of wage-earners that they cannot see a remedy. This dilemma overlooks the unique privileges the unions enjoy in Britain, which have placed them in a position where they are forced to be anti-social, as even one of their friends, Baroness Wootton, has had to admit.

False claims to benefit the population as a whole

Unions have gained the public support they still enjoy by their pretence of benefiting the working population at large. They probably did achieve this aim in their early years when more or less immobile workers sometimes faced a single factory-owner. I do not, of course, deny the trade unions their historical merits or question their right to exist as voluntary organisations. Indeed, I believe that everybody, unless he has voluntarily renounced it, ought to have the right to join a trade union. But neither ought anyone to have the right to force others to do so. I am even prepared to agree that *everybody* ought to have the *right* to strike, so far as he does not thereby break a contract or the law has not conferred a monopoly on the enterprise in which he is engaged. But I am convinced that nobody ought to have the right to *force* others to strike.

Trade unions' legal privileges obstruct working-class prosperity

Such would be the position if the general principles of law applicable to all other citizens applied also to the trade unions and their members. But in 1906, in a typical act of buying the swing-vote of a minority, the then Liberal Government passed the Trade Disputes Act which, as A. V. Dicey justly put it (in *Law and Public Opinion in England* 1914), conferred

> ... upon a trade union a freedom from civil liability for the commission of even the most heinous wrong by the union or its servant, and in short confer[red] upon every trade union a privilege and protection not possessed by any other person or body of persons, whether corporate or incorporate. ... [it] makes the trade union a privileged body exempted from the ordinary law of the land. No such privileged body has ever before been created by an English Parliament [and] it stimulates among workmen the fatal illusion that [they] should aim at the attainment not of equality, but of privilege.

These legalised powers of the unions have become the biggest obstacle to raising the living standards of the working class as a whole. They are the chief cause of the unnecessarily big differences between the best- and worst-paid workers. They are the prime source of unemployment. They are the main reason for the decline of the British economy in general.

Trade union members gain by exploiting other workers

The crucial truth, which is not generally understood, is that all the powers employed by individual trade unions to raise the remuneration of their members rest on depriving other workers of opportunities. This truth was apparently understood, in the past, by the more reasonable trade union leaders. Twenty-three years ago, the then chairman of the Trades Union Congress could still say that he did

> ... not believe that the trade union movement of Great Britain can live for much longer on the basis of compulsion. Must people belong to us or starve, whether they like our policies or not? No. I believe the trade union card is an honour to be conferred, not a badge which signifies that you have got to do something whether you like it or not. We want the right to exclude people from our union if necessary, and we cannot do this on the basis of 'Belong or Starve'.

Thus Mr Charles (now Lord) Geddes.

There has evidently been a complete change. The present ability of any trade union to obtain better terms for its members rests chiefly on its legalised power to *prevent other workers from earning as good an income as they otherwise might.* It is thus maintained, literally, by the exploitation of those not permitted to do work that they would like to do. The élite of the British working class may still profit as a result, although even this has now become doubtful. But they certainly derive their relative advantage by keeping workers who are *worse* off from improving their position. These groups acquire their advantage at the expense of those they prevent from bettering themselves by doing work in which they could earn more – though somewhat less than those who claim a monopoly.

Free society threatened by union curtailment of access to jobs

If a free society is to continue, no monopoly can be allowed to use physical force to maintain its privileged position and to threaten to deprive the public of essential services that other workers are able and willing to render. Yet all the most harmful practices of British trade unions derive from their being allowed forcefully to prevent outsiders from offering their services to the public on their own terms. The chief instances of such legal powers are intimidatory picketing, preventing non-members from doing particular kinds of jobs such as 'demarcation' rules, and the closed shop. Yet all these restrictive practices are prohibited in most of the more prosperous Western countries.

Union restrictive practices have hurt the working man

It is more than doubtful, however, whether in the long run these selfish practices have improved the real wages of even those workers whose unions have been most successful in driving up their relative wages – compared with what they would have been in the absence of trade unions. It is certain, and could not be otherwise, that the average level of attainable real wages of British workers as a whole has thereby been substantially lowered. Such practices have substantially reduced the productivity potential of British labour generally. They have turned Britain, which at one time had the highest wages in Europe, into a relatively low-wage economy.

British price structure paralysed by political wage determination

A large economy can be prosperous only if it relies on competitive prices to co-ordinate individual effort by condensing all the information fed into the market by many thousands of individuals. The effect of the present system of wage determination in Britain is that the country no longer has an internal price structure to guide the economic use of resources. This is almost entirely due to the rigidity of politically determined wages. If it is no longer possible to know the most efficient use of the natural talents of the British people, it is because relative wages no longer reflect the relative scarcity of skills. Even their relative scarcity is no longer determined by objective facts about the real conditions of supply and demand, but by an artificial product of the arbitrary decisions of legally tolerated monopolies.

Impersonal nature of market decisions makes them acceptable

Prices or wages cannot be a matter of 'justice' if the economic system is to function. Whether it is necessary for maintaining or increasing the national income to draw people into tool-making or services, or to discourage entry into entertainment or sociological research, has nothing to do with the 'justice' or the merits or the 'needs' of those affected. In the real world, nobody can know where people are required but the market, which absorbs and digests the myriad bits of information possessed by all who buy or sell in it. And it is precisely because the decision is not the opinion of an identifiable person (like a Minister or Commissar) or a group of men (like a Cabinet or Politbureau) but results from impersonal signals in a process that no individual or group can control, that makes it tolerable. It would be unbearable if it were the decision of some authority which assigned everyone to his job and determined his reward.

British governments have supported union coercion

I would be prepared to predict that the average worker's income would rise fastest in a country where relative wages are flexible, and where the exploitation of workers by monopolistic trade union organisations of specialised groups of workers is effectively outlawed. Such exploitation is, however, the chief source of power of individual labour unions in Britain. The result of thus freeing the labour market would inevitably be a structure of relative wages very different from the traditional one now preserved by union power. This result will have to come about if the British economy is to stop decaying.

While a functioning market and trade unions with coercive powers cannot co-exist, yet it is only in the free system of the market that the unions can survive. Yet the unions are destroying the free market through their legalised use of coercion. The widespread use of force to gain at the expense of others has not only been tolerated but also supported by British governments, on the false pretence that it enhances justice and benefits the most needy. Not only is the opposite true; the effect of this tolerance and support of union coercion is to reduce everybody's potential income – except that of trade union officials.

Trade unions' legal privileges the chief cause of unemployment

Impeding increases in productivity and hence real wage growth is not the worst effect of current trade union practices. Even more serious is the extent to which they have become the chief cause of unemployment, for which the market economy is then blamed.

The volume of employment is not a function of the *general* wage level but of the structure of *relative* wages. The contrary belief, still widely held in Britain by economists and politicians, is due to a unique experience of this country. It arose after Britain returned to the gold standard in 1925 at the pre-war parity between sterling and gold, when wages, which had risen considerably during the wartime inflation, proved generally too high for the country to maintain its exports. It was in that very special atmosphere that discussion about the relationship between wages and unemployment started, and the belief came to be held that the crucial factor was the general level of wages. The writings of Keynes unfortunately seemed to support this error.

The situation after 1925 was entirely exceptional. The normal cause of recurrent waves of widespread unemployment is rather a discrepancy between the way in which demand is distributed between products and services, and the proportions in which resources are devoted to producing them. Unemployment is the result of divergent changes in the direction of demand and the techniques of production. If labour is not deployed according to demand for products, there is unemployment. But the most common cause is that, because of excessive credit expansion, over-investment has been encouraged and too many resources have been drawn into the production of capital goods, where they can be employed only so long as the expansion continues or even accelerates. And credit is expanded to appease trade unions that fear their members will lose their jobs, even though it is they themselves who forced wages too high to enable the workers to find jobs at these excessive rates of pay.

Full employment requires continual changes in relative wages

Once such a misdirection of resources has taken place, tolerably full employment can be restored only by redirecting some of them to other uses. This is, of necessity, a slow process, even when wages are flexible. And so long as substantial unemployment prevails in such a large sector of the economy, it is likely to set up a cumulative process of deflation. Even maintaining total final demand cannot provide a cure, because it will not create employment in the over-expanded capital industries. The unemployment there will continue to operate as a persistent drain on the income stream. It cannot be stopped, or lastingly compensated for, by the expenditure of new paper money printed for the purpose or created in other ways. The attempt to cure it by adding to the supply of money must lead to accelerating inflation. Yet this has been the futile policy of recent British governments.

Such unemployment can be effectively cured only by redirecting workers to jobs where they can be lastingly employed. In a free society, this redirection requires a change in relative wages to make prospects less attractive in occupations or industries where labour is in surplus and more attractive where the demand for labour is expanding. This is *the essential mechanism which alone can correct a misdirection of labour* once it has occurred in a society where workers are free to choose their jobs.

Short of very special circumstances such as those after 1925, there is no reason why it should ever be necessary for the general level of wages to fall. But it is not possible to keep a market economy working *at full speed*, which is what the workers would like, without *some* wages occasionally falling while others rise. Full employment cannot be maintained by preserving a conventional, outdated wage structure, but only by adjusting wages in each sector to changing demands – raising some wages by lowering others.

Keynes's responsibility for 'the final disaster'

The final disaster we owe mainly to Lord Keynes. His erroneous conception that employment could be directly controlled by regulating aggregate demand through monetary policy shifted responsibility for employment from the trade unions to government. This error relieved trade unions of the responsibility to adjust their wage demands so as to sell as much work as possible, and misrepresented full employment entirely as a function of government monetary policy. For 40 years it has thus made the price mechanism ineffective in the labour market by preventing wages from acting as a signal to workers and employers. As a result there is divided responsibility: the trade unions are allowed to enforce their wage demands without regard to the effect on employment, and government is expected to create the demand at which the available supply of work can be sold at the prevailing (or even higher) wages. Inevitably the consequence is continuous and accelerating inflation.

Futility of negotiating reform with union leaders until deprived of legal privileges

It is an illusion to imagine that the problems Britain now faces can be solved by negotiation with the present trade union leaders. They owe their power precisely to the scope for abusing the privileges which the law has granted them. It is the rank and file of the workers, including many trade union members, who ultimately suffer from this abuse. I believe they could be helped to understand this cause of their suffering. Their support must be obtained if the system that is destroying Britain's wealth and well-being is to be changed.

One of the more recent general secretaries of the Trades Union Congress, the late George Woodcock, wrote about 'the fear and dislike in which many of our own people seem to hold our own trade unions'. A political party in which trade unions have a major constitutional rôle cannot strike at the source of their power. If I were responsible for the policy of the Conservative Party, I would rather be defeated at the polls than be charged with policy but without a clear mandate to remove the legal sources of excessive trade union power. This a trade union party, of course, can never do. The only hope is that an appeal to a large number of workers over the heads of their present leaders will lead to the demand for a reduction in their powers.

No salvation for Britain until union privileges are revoked

There can be no salvation for Britain until the special privileges granted to the trade unions three-quarters of a century ago are revoked. Average real wages of British workers would undoubtedly be higher, and their chances of finding employment better, if the wages paid in different occupations were again determined by the market and if all limitations on the work an individual is allowed to do were removed.

Britain can improve her position in the world market, and hence the price in work effort at which her population can be fed, only by allowing the market to bring about a restructuring of her whole internal price system. What is ossified in Britain is not the skill of her entrepreneurs or workers, but the price structure and the indispensable discipline it imposes. The present British economic system no longer signals what has to be done and no longer rewards those who do it or penalises those who fail to do it.

5 Reform of Trade Union Privilege the Price of Salvation in the 1980s[1]

Sometimes one is forced to doubt whether it is still doctrinaire blindness rather than sinister intention that leads politicians in Britain and elsewhere to invert the truth. One of the most glaring examples has been the attempt to represent the present British trade unions as free institutions. They were when they fought for freedom of association and thereby gained the support of all believers in liberty. They unfortunately retained the support of some naïve pseudo-liberals after they had become the only privileged institution licensed to use coercion without law.

The coercion on which their present power rests is the coercion of other workers who are deterred by the threat of violence from offering their labour on their own terms. The coercion of enterprise is always secondary, and operates through depriving other workers of their opportunities.

'Open enemies'

The unions have of course now become the open enemies of the ideal of freedom of association by which they once gained the sympathy of the true liberals. Freedom of association means the freedom to decide whether one wants to join an association or not. Such freedom no longer exists for most workers. The present unions offer to a skilled worker only the choice between joining and starving, and it is solely by keeping non-members out of jobs that they can raise the wages of particular groups of workers above the level they would reach in a free market.

There are certainly many useful tasks unions can perform with respect to the internal organisations of enterprises – questions on which the arrangements of large organisations depend. But they cease to operate beneficially when they are conceded the power of keeping non-members out of a job, or refuse to work with others who prefer different contracts from those which they obtain for their members. The higher wages the unions can thus obtain for those who can be employed at their terms are gained at the expense of those who cannot be thus employed.

Like all other monopolistic control of prices its main effect is to suspend the process which brings about the balancing of demand and supply in the different sectors of economic activity. It is in this way that the licensed use of force by the trade unions to determine a structure of relative wages which the individual unions or smaller groups of workers regard as attainable has become the chief obstacle to a high and stable level of employment.

It is a complete inversion of the truth to represent the unions as improving the prospect of employment at high wages. They have become in Britain the chief cause of unemployment and the falling standard of living of the working class.

I prefer to believe it is doctrinaire blindness rather than a devious attempt to destroy the existing order which can make a politician deny this obvious truth. For a country depending for its livelihood on international trade the endeavour to shelter relative wages against the forces of the international market can have no other effect than growing unemployment at falling real wages. Britain has been led into a position in which it has become impossible to know how its labour force can be deployed most productively.

The Foot confusion

It was the most extraordinary part of Michael Foot's outburst a year or two ago that he represented unions as simultaneously a part of free institutions and the restriction of their coercive powers as a cause of unemployment. The reason why I believe that the licence to use coercion conceded to unions some 70 years ago should be withdrawn is precisely that their actions have become the chief cause of unemployment. They bring this about in two ways. The first is the obvious one of an increased demand for some product being absorbed by an increase of the wages of the workers already employed in it rather than by an influx of additional workers, leaving out in the cold those in the industries from which demand has turned.

The second way is less understood but even more serious because it is more permanent. At wages higher than those which would prevail in a free market, employers must, in order to be able to pay them, use the limited amount of capital that is available in a manner which will require fewer workers for a given output. It is true that higher wages can enforce 'rationalisation': they bring this about by making it necessary to use the available capital for equipping a smaller number of workers with more capital per head, leaving correspondingly less for the rest.

J. M. Keynes's palliative

All this had been well understood long ago. It was initially only J. M. Keynes's despair about the political impossibility of making wages again flexible which led him to resort to the palliative of temporarily reducing real wages by inflation. But one may thus for a time evade the difficulties caused by a rigid wage *level*, but not those caused by an artificially fixed structure of *relative* wages. This is what apparently even some of the more experienced trade union leaders are beginning to understand, but what the illusionists and demagogues of the Labour Party refuse to recognise.

In an ever-changing world there is as little chance of the market for labour ever being cleared with rigid relative wages based on some traditional standards as there would be for the different commodities at rigid relative prices. And the power to stop the whole supply of an essential element of production is, of course, the power to kill enterprise. There will usually exist some reserves which can sustain life for a time even after an enterprise has been mortally wounded. However, I fear in many instances the process of capital shrinkage is merely temporarily concealed by inflation but will manifest itself as soon as inflation stops, as it must sooner or later.

It will then be vain to ask government to preserve the existing jobs. The government can do nothing to force the world to buy British goods. Indeed, the pressure on it to secure particular jobs is the most certain means progressively to reduce the productivity of British workers and their earning power in international exchange.

Fools' paradise

Britain can scarcely hope to be self-sufficient even with general prosperity; but she can certainly not be a wealthy country without constant redirection of efforts which in recent times have been so lamentably impeded by the political necessity of enabling people to carry on as before by providing the means out of the pockets of others. The longer we allow the number to grow in their present employment while producing what the world market will not buy at prices adequate to maintain them at their present level, the greater will be the ultimate catastrophe when the fools' paradise collapses.

There is no hope of Great Britain maintaining her position in international trade – and for her people that means no hope of maintaining their already reduced standard of living – unless the unions are deprived of their coercive powers. So long as they possess them, even the wisest union leaders can, as we see every day, be forced by little groups to exercise them. This is killing enterprise after enterprise and causing a continuous dissipation of capital, the full effect of which we have not yet experienced. As a result of a mistake of legislation in the past they have Britain by the throat and cannot understand they are killing the goose which lays the golden eggs.

I am not qualified to judge what is today politically possible. That depends on prevailing opinion. All I can say with conviction is that, *so long as general opinion makes it politically impossible to deprive the trade unions of their coercive powers, an economic recovery of Great Britain is also impossible.*

It is sufficiently alarming when one watches developments in Britain from the inside. But one is reduced to complete despair when one observes what is happening in the rest of the world while Britain remains paralysed by the consequences of the privileges irresponsibly conceded to the trade unions by law. When one watches how even Japan is now being beaten in ever more fields by South Korea and other newcomers who have discovered the benefits of free markets, one cannot but shudder when one asks how in a few years' time Britain is to get the food to feed her people.

Will Britain pay the price of the union 'sacred cow'?

This is not merely a question of whether Britain can do without Japanese or Korean cars or other products. It is a question of how other people can be made to buy British ships, or shoes, or steel, or textiles, or chemicals, when not only Japanese and Korean factories and shipyards produce them more efficiently and cheaply, but more and more other people surpass Britain in an astounding versatility – and when not only British scientists and engineers but increasingly also skilled British workers find that they can do better in countries whose business structure has not been ossified by trade union restrictions.

A drastic change may still provide an outlet, but after another decade during which nobody dares to touch the sacred cow, it will certainly be too late.

Note

1 An edited version of an article, 'The Powerful Reasons for Curbing Union Powers', published in *The Times*, 10 October 1978.

9

The Confusion of Language in Political Thought

1 Introduction

Modern civilisation has given man undreamt of powers largely because, without understanding it, he has developed methods of utilising more knowledge and resources than any one mind is aware of. The fundamental condition from which any intelligent discussion of the order of all social activities should start is the constitutional and irremediable ignorance both of the acting persons and of the scientist studying this order, of the multiplicity of particular, concrete facts which enter this order of human activities because they are known to *some* of its members. As the motto on the title page expresses it, 'man has become all he is without understanding what happened'.[1] This insight should not be a cause of shame but a source of pride in having discovered a method that enables us to overcome the limitations of individual knowledge. And it is an incentive deliberately to cultivate institutions which have opened up those possibilities.

The great achievement of the 18th-century social philosophers was to replace the naïve constructivist rationalism of earlier periods,[2] which interpreted all institutions as the products of deliberate design for a foreseeable purpose, by a critical and evolutionary rationalism that examined the conditions and limitations of the effective use of conscious reason.

We are still very far, however, from making full use of the possibilities which those insights open to us, largely because our thinking is governed by language which reflects an earlier mode of thought. The important problems are in large measure obscured by the use of words which imply

Published originally as IEA Occasional Paper No. 20 (1968).

anthropomorphic or personalised explanations of social institutions. These explanations interpret the general rules which guide action directed at particular purposes. In practice such institutions are successful adaptations to the irremediable limitations of our knowledge, adaptations which have prevailed over alternative forms of order because they proved more effective methods for dealing with that incomplete, dispersed knowledge which is man's unalterable lot.

The extent to which serious discussion has been vitiated by the ambiguity of some of the key terms, which for lack of more precise ones we have constantly to use, has been vividly brought home to me in the course of a still incomplete investigation of the relations between law, legislation, and liberty on which I have been engaged for some time. In an endeavour to achieve clarity I have been driven to introduce sharp distinctions for which current usage has no accepted or readily intelligible terms. The purpose of the following sketch is to demonstrate the importance of these distinctions which I found essential and to suggest terms which should help us to avoid the prevailing confusion.

2 Cosmos and Taxis

The achievement of human purposes is possible only because we recognise the world we live in as orderly. This order manifests itself in our ability to learn, from the (spatial or temporal) parts of the world we know, rules which enable us to form expectations about other parts. And we anticipate that these rules stand a good chance of being borne out by events. Without the knowledge of such an order of the world in which we live, purposive action would be impossible.

This applies as much to the social as to the physical environment. But while the order of the physical environment is given to us independently of human will, the order of our social environment is partly, but only partly, the result of human design. The temptation to regard it *all* as the intended product of human action is one of the main sources of error. The insight that *not all order that results from the interplay of human actions is the result of design* is indeed the beginning of social theory. Yet the anthropomorphic connotations of the term 'order' are apt to conceal the fundamental truth that all deliberate efforts to bring about a social order by arrangement or organisation (i.e. by assigning to particular elements specified functions or tasks) take place within a more comprehensive spontaneous order which is not the result of such design.

While we have the terms 'arrangement' or 'organisation' to describe a *made* order, we have no single distinctive word to describe an order which has formed *spontaneously*. The ancient Greeks were more fortunate in this respect. An arrangement produced by man deliberately putting the elements in their place or assigning them distinctive tasks they called *taxis*, while an order which existed or formed itself independent of any human will directed to that end they called *cosmos*. Though they generally confined the latter term to the order of nature, it seems equally appropriate for any spontaneous social order and has often, though never systematically, been used for that purpose.[3] The advantage of possessing an unambiguous term to distinguish this kind of order from a made order should outweigh the hesitation we may feel about endowing a social order which we often do not like with a name which conveys the sense of admiration and awe with which man regards the cosmos of nature.

The same is in some measure true of the term 'order' itself. Though one of the oldest terms of political theory, it has been somewhat out of fashion for some time. But it is an indispensable term which, on the definition we have given it – a condition of affairs in which we can successfully form expectations and hypotheses about the future – refers to objective facts and not to values. Indeed, the first important difference between a spontaneous order or *cosmos* and an organisation (arrangement) or *taxis* is that, not having been deliberately made by men, a *cosmos* has no purpose.[4] This does not mean that its existence may not be exceedingly serviceable in the pursuit of many purposes: the existence of such an order, not only in nature but also in society, is indeed indispensable for the pursuit of any aim. But the order of nature and aspects of the social order not being deliberately created by men, cannot properly be said to have a purpose, though both can be used by men for many different, divergent and even conflicting purposes.

While a *cosmos* or spontaneous order has thus no purpose, every *taxis* (arrangement, organisation) presupposes a particular end, and men forming such an organisation must serve the same purposes. A *cosmos* will result from regularities of the behaviour of the elements which it comprises. It is in this sense endogenous, intrinsic or, as the cyberneticians say, a 'self-regulating' or 'self-organising' system.[5] A *taxis*, on the other hand, is determined by an agency which stands outside the order and is in the same sense exogenous or imposed. Such an external factor may induce the formation of a spontaneous order also by imposing upon the elements such regularities in their responses to the facts of their environment that a spontaneous order will form itself. Such an indirect method of securing the formation of an order possesses important advantages over the direct method: it can be applied in circumstances where what is to affect the order is not known as a whole to anyone. Nor is it necessary that the rules of behaviour within the *cosmos* be deliberately created: they, too, *may* emerge as the product of spontaneous growth or of evolution.

It is therefore important to distinguish clearly between the spontaneity of the order and the spontaneous origin of regularities in the behaviour of elements determining it. A spontaneous order may rest in part on regularities which are not spontaneous but imposed. For policy purposes there results thus the alternative whether it is preferable to secure the formation of an order by a strategy of indirect approach, or by directly assigning a place for each element and describing its function in detail.

Where we are concerned solely with the alternative social orders, the first important corollary of this distinction is that in a *cosmos* knowledge of the facts and purposes which will guide individual action will be those of the acting individuals, while in a *taxis* the knowledge and purposes of the organiser will determine the resulting order. The knowledge that can be utilised in such an organisation will therefore always be more limited than in a spontaneous order where all the knowledge possessed by the elements can be taken into account in forming the order without this knowledge first being transmitted to a central organiser. And while the complexity of activities which can be ordered as a *taxis* is necessarily limited to what can be known to the organiser, there is no similar limit in a spontaneous order.

While the deliberate use of spontaneous ordering forces (that is, of the rules of individual conduct which lead to the formation of a spontaneous general order) thus considerably extends the range and complexity of actions which can be integrated into a single order, it also reduces the power anyone can exercise over it without destroying the order. The regularities in the conduct of the elements in a *cosmos* determine merely its most general and abstract features. The detailed characteristics will be determined by the facts and aims which guide the actions of individual elements, though they are confined by the general rules within a certain permissible range. In consequence, the concrete content of such an order will always be unpredictable, though it may be the only method of achieving an order of wide scope. We must renounce the power of shaping its particular manifestations according to our desires. For example, the position which each individual will occupy in such an order will be largely determined by what to us must appear as accident. Though such a *cosmos* will serve all human purposes to some degree, it will not give anyone the power to determine whom it will favour more and whom less.

In an arrangement or *taxis*, on the other hand, the organiser can, within the restricted range achievable by this method, try to make the results conform to his preferences to any degree he likes. A *taxis* is necessarily designed for the achievement of particular ends or of a particular hierarchy of ends; and to the extent that the organiser can master the information about the available means, and effectively control their use, he may be able to make the arrangement correspond to his wishes in considerable detail. Since it will be *his* purposes that will govern the arrangement, he can attach any valuation to each element of the order and place it so as to make its position correspond to what he regards as its merits.

Where it is a question of using limited resources known to the organiser in the service of a unitary hierarchy of ends, an arrangement or organisation (*taxis*) will be the more effective method. But where the task involves using knowledge dispersed among and accessible only to thousands or millions of separate individuals, the use of spontaneous ordering forces (*cosmos*) will be superior. More importantly, people who have few or no ends in common, especially people who do not know one another or one another's circumstances, will be able to form a mutually beneficial and peaceful spontaneous order by submitting to the same abstract rules, but they can form an organisation only by submitting to somebody's concrete will. To form a common *cosmos* they need agree only on abstract rules, while to form an organisation they must either agree or be made to submit to a common hierarchy of ends. Only a *cosmos* can thus constitute an open society, while a political order conceived as an organisation must remain closed or tribal.

3 Nomos and Thesis

Two distinct kinds of rules or norms correspond respectively to *cosmos* or *taxis* which the elements must obey in order that the corresponding kind of order be formed. Since here, too, modern European languages lack terms which express the required distinction clearly and unambiguously, and since we have come to use the word 'law' or its equivalents ambiguously for both, we shall again propose Greek terms which, at least in the classic usage of 5th and 4th century Athens BC, conveyed approximately the required distinction.[6]

By *nomos* we shall describe a universal rule of just conduct applying to an unknown number of future instances and equally to all persons in the objective circumstances described by the rule, irrespective of the effects which observance of the rule will produce in a particular situation. Such rules demarcate protected individual domains by enabling each person or organised group to know which means they may employ in the pursuit of their purposes, and thus to prevent conflict between the actions of the different persons. Such rules are generally described as 'abstract' and are independent of individual ends.[7] They lead to the formation of an equally abstract and end-independent spontaneous order or *cosmos*.

In contrast, we shall use *thesis* to mean any rule which is applicable only to particular people or in the service of the ends of rulers. Though such rules may still be general to various degrees and refer to a multiplicity of particular instances, they will shade imperceptibly from rules in the usual sense to particular commands. They are the necessary instrument of running an organisation or *taxis*.

The reason why an organisation must to some extent rely on rules and not be directed by particular commands only also explains why a spontaneous order can achieve results which organisations cannot. By restricting actions of individuals only by general rules they can use information which the authority does not possess. The agencies to which the head of an organisation delegates functions can adapt to changing circumstances known only to them, and therefore the commands of authority will generally take the form of general instructions rather than of specific orders.

In two important respects, however, the rules governing the members of an organisation will necessarily differ from rules on which a spontaneous order rests: rules for an organisation presuppose the assignment of particular tasks, targets or functions to individual people by commands; and most of the rules of an organisation will apply only to the persons charged with particular responsibilities. The rules of organisation will therefore never be universal in intent or end-independent, but always subsidiary to the commands by which rôles are assigned and tasks or aims prescribed. They do not serve the spontaneous formation of an abstract order in which each individual must find his place and is able to build up a protected domain. The purpose and general outline of the organisation or arrangement must be determined by the organiser.

This distinction between the *nomoi* as universal rules of conduct and the *theseis* as rules of organisation correspond roughly to the familiar distinction between private (including criminal) and public (constitutional and administrative) law. There exists much confusion between these two kinds of rules of law. This confusion is fostered by the terms employed and by the misleading theories of legal positivism (in turn the consequence of the predominant rôle of public lawyers in the development of jurisprudence). Both represent the public law as in some sense primary and as alone serving the public interest; while private law is regarded, not only as secondary and derived from the former, but also as serving not general but individual interests. The opposite, however, would be nearer the truth. Public law is the law of organisation, of the superstructure of government originally erected only to ensure the enforcement of private law. It has been truly said that public law passes, but private law persists.[8] Whatever the changing structure of government, the basic structure of society resting on the rules of conduct persists. Government therefore owes its authority and has a claim to the allegiance of the citizens only if it maintains the foundations of that spontaneous order on which the working of society's everyday life rests.

The belief in the pre-eminence of public law is a result of the fact that it has indeed been deliberately created for particular purposes by acts of will, while private law is the result of an evolutionary process and has never been invented or designed as a whole by anybody. It was in the sphere of public law where law-making emerged while, for millennia, in the sphere of private law development proceeded through a process of law-finding in which judges and jurists endeavoured to articulate the rules which had already for long periods governed action and the 'sense of justice'.

Even though we must turn to public law to discover which rules of conduct an organisation will in practice enforce, it is not necessarily the public law to which the private law owes its authority. Insofar as there is a spontaneously ordered society, public law merely organises the apparatus required for the better functioning of that more comprehensive spontaneous order. It determines a sort of superstructure erected primarily to protect a pre-existing spontaneous order and to enforce the rules on which it rests.

It is instructive to remember that the conception of law in the sense of *nomos* (i.e. of an abstract rule not due to anybody's concrete will, applicable in particular cases irrespective of the consequences, a law which could be 'found' and was not made for particular foreseeable purposes) has existed and been preserved together with the ideal of individual liberty only in countries such as ancient Rome and modern Britain, in which the development of private law was based on case law and not on statute law, that is, was in the hands of judges or jurists and not of legislators. Both the conception of law as *nomos* and the ideal of individual liberty have rapidly disappeared whenever the law came to be conceived as the instrument of a government's own ends.

What is not generally understood in this connection is that, as a necessary consequence of case-law procedure, law based on precedent must consist exclusively of end-independent abstract rules of conduct of universal intent which the judges and jurists attempt to distil from earlier decisions. There is no such built-in limitation to the norms established by a legislator; and he is therefore less likely to submit to such limitations as the chief task which occupies him. For a long time before alterations in the *nomos* were seriously contemplated, legislators were almost exclusively concerned with laying down the rules of organisation which regulate the apparatus of government. The traditional conception of the law as *nomos* underlies ideals like those of the Rule of Law, a Government under the Law, and the Separation of Powers. In consequence, when representative bodies, initially concerned solely with matters of government proper, such as taxation, began to be regarded also as the sources of the *nomos* (the private law, or the universal rules of conduct), this traditional concept was soon replaced by the idea that law was whatever the will of the authorised legislator laid down on particular matters.[9]

Few insights more clearly reveal the governing tendencies of our time than understanding that the progressive permeation and displacement of private by public law is part of the process of transformation of a free, spontaneous order of society into an organisation or *taxis*. This transformation is the result of two factors which have been governing development for more than a century: on the one hand, of the increasing replacement of rules of just individual conduct (guided by 'commutative justice') by conceptions of 'social' or 'distributive' justice, and on the other hand, of the placing of the power to lay down *nomoi* (i.e. rules of just conduct) in the hands of the body charged with the direction of government. It has been largely this fusion of these two essentially different tasks in the same 'legislative' assemblies which has almost wholly destroyed the distinction between law as a universal rule of conduct and law as an instruction to government on what to do in particular instances.

The socialist aim of a just distribution of incomes must lead to such a transformation of the spontaneous order into an organisation; for only in an organisation, directed towards a common hierarchy of ends, and in which the individuals have to perform assigned duties, can the conception of a 'just' reward be given meaning. In a spontaneous order nobody 'allocates', or can even foresee, the results which changes in circumstances will produce for particular individuals or groups, and it can know justice only as rules of just individual conduct but not in results. Such a society certainly presupposes the belief that justice, in the sense of rules of just conduct, is not an empty word – but 'social justice' must remain an empty concept so long as the spontaneous order is not wholly transformed into a totalitarian organisation in which rewards are given by authority for merit earned in performing duties assigned by that authority. 'Social' or 'distributive' justice is the justice of organisation but meaningless in a spontaneous order.

4 A Digression on Articulated and Non-articulated Rules

Though the distinction to be considered next is not quite on the same plane with the others examined here, it will be expedient to insert some remarks on the sense in which we are employing the term 'rule'. As we have used it, it covers two distinct meanings the difference between which is often confused with or concealed by the more familiar and closely related distinction between written and unwritten, or between customary and statute, law. The point to be emphasised is that a rule may effectively govern action in the sense that from knowing it we can predict how people will act, without it being known as a verbal formula to the actors. Men may 'know how' to act, and the manner of their action may be correctly described by an articulated rule, without their explicitly 'knowing that' the rule is such and such; that is, they need not be able to state the rule in words in order to be able to conform to it in their actions, or to recognise whether others have or have not done so.

There can be no doubt that, both in early society and since, many of the rules which manifest themselves in consistent judicial decisions are not known to anyone as verbal formulae, and that even the rules which are known in articulated form will often be merely imperfect efforts to express in words principles which guide action and are expressed in approval or disapproval of the actions of others. What we call the 'sense of justice' is nothing but that capacity to act in accordance with non-articulated rules, and what is described as finding or discovering justice consists in trying to express in words the yet unarticulated rules by which a particular decision is judged.

This capacity to act, and to recognise whether others act, in accordance with non-articulated rules probably always exists before attempts are made to articulate such rules; and most articulated rules are merely more or less successful attempts to put into words what has been acted upon before, and will continue to form the basis for judging the results of the application of the articulated rules.

Of course, once particular articulations of rules of conduct have become accepted, they will be one of the chief means of transmitting such rules; and the development of articulated and unarticulated rules will constantly interact. Yet it seems probable that no system of articulated rules can exist or be fully understood without a background of unarticulated rules which will be drawn upon when gaps are discovered in the system of articulated rules.

This governing influence of a background of unarticulated rules explains why the application of general rules to particular instances will rarely take the form of a syllogism, since only articulated rules can serve as explicit premises of such a syllogism. Conclusions derived from the articulated rules only will not be tolerated if they conflict with the conclusions to which yet unarticulated rules lead. Equity develops by the side of the already fully articulated rules of strict law through this familiar process.

There is in this respect much less difference between the unwritten or customary law which is handed down in the form of articulated verbal rules and the written law, than there is between articulated and unarticulated rules. Much of the unwritten or customary law may already be articulated in orally transmitted verbal formulae. Yet, even when all law that can be said to be explicitly known has been articulated, this need not mean that the process of articulating the rules that in practice guide decisions has already been completed.

5 Opinion and Will, Values and Ends

We come now to a pair of important distinctions for which the available terms are particularly inadequate and for which even classical Greek does not provide us with readily intelligible expressions. Yet the substitution by Rousseau, Hegel, and their followers down to T. H. Green, of the term 'will' for what older authors had described as 'opinion',[10] and still earlier ones contrasted as *ratio* to *voluntas*, was probably the most fateful terminological innovation in the history of political thinking.

This substitution of the term 'will' for 'opinion' was the product of a constructivist rationalism[11] which imagined that all laws were invented for a known purpose rather than the articulation or improved formulation of practices that had prevailed because they produced a more viable order than those current in competing groups. The term 'opinion' at the same time became increasingly suspect because it was contrasted with incontrovertible knowledge of cause and effect and a growing tendency to discard all statements incapable of proof. 'Mere opinion' became one of the chief targets of rationalist critique; 'will' seemed to refer to rational purposive action, while 'opinion' came to be regarded as something typically uncertain and incapable of rational discussion.

Yet the order of an open society and all modern civilisation rests largely on opinions which have been effective in producing such an order long before people knew why they held them; and in a great measure it still rests on such beliefs. Even when people began to ask how the rules of conduct which they observed might be improved, the effects which they produced, and in the light of which they might be revised, were only dimly understood. The difficulty lay in the fact that any attempt to assess an action by its foreseeable results in the particular case is the very opposite of the function which opinions about the permissibility or non-permissibility of a kind of action play in the formation of an overall order.

Our insight into these circumstances is much obscured by the rationalistic prejudice that intelligent behaviour is governed exclusively by a knowledge of the relations between cause and effect, and by the associated belief that 'reason' manifests itself only in deductions derived from such knowledge. The only kind of rational action constructivist rationalism recognises is action guided by such considerations as 'If I want X then I must do Y'. Human action, however, is in fact as much guided by rules which limit it to permissible kinds of actions – rules which generally preclude certain *kinds* of actions irrespective of their foreseeable particular results. Our capacity to act successfully in our natural and social environment rests as much on such knowledge of what *not* to do (usually without awareness of the consequences which would follow if we did it) as on our knowledge of the particular effects of what we do. In fact, our positive knowledge serves us effectively only thanks to rules which confine our actions to the limited range within which we are able to foresee relevant consequences. It prevents us from overstepping these limits. Fear of the unknown, and avoidance of actions with unforeseeable consequences, has as important a function to perform in making our actions 'rational' in the sense of successful as positive knowledge.[12] If the term 'reason' is confined to knowledge of positive facts and excludes knowledge of the 'ought not', a large part of the rules which guide human action so as to enable the individuals or groups to persist in the environment in which they live is excluded from 'reason'. Much of the accumulated experience of the human race would fall outside what is described as 'reason' if this concept is arbitrarily confined to positive knowledge of the rules of cause and effect which govern particular events in our environment.

Before the rationalist revolution of the 16th and 17th centuries, however, the term 'reason' included and even gave first place to the knowledge of appropriate rules of conduct. When *ratio* was contrasted with *voluntas*, the former referred pre-eminently to opinion about the permissibility or non-permissibility of the kinds of conduct which *voluntas* indicated as the most obvious means of achieving a particular result.[13] What was described as reason was thus not so much knowledge that in particular circumstances particular actions would produce particular results, but a capacity to avoid actions of a kind whose foreseeable results seemed desirable, but which were likely to lead to the destruction of the order on which the achievements of the human race rested.

We are familiar with the crucial point that the general order of society into which individual actions are integrated results not from the concrete purposes which individuals pursue but from their observing rules which limit the range of their actions. It does not really matter for the formation of this order what are the concrete purposes pursued by the individuals; they may in many instances be wholly absurd, yet so long as the individuals pursue their purposes within the limits of those rules, they may in doing so contribute to the needs of others. It is not the purposive but the rule-governed aspect of individual actions which integrates them into the order on which civilisation rests.[14]

To describe the content of a rule, or of a law defining just conduct, as the expression of a *will*[15] (popular or other) is thus wholly misleading. Legislators approving the text of a statute articulating a rule of conduct, or legal draftsmen deciding the wording of such a bill, will be guided by a will aiming at a particular result; but the particular form of words is not the content of such a law. *Will* always refers to particular actions serving particular ends, and the will ceases when the action is taken and the end (terminus) reached. But nobody can have a *will* in this sense concerning what shall happen in an unknown number of future instances.

Opinions, on the other hand, have no purpose known to those who hold them – indeed, we should rightly suspect an opinion on matters of right and wrong if we found that it was held for a purpose. Most of the beneficial opinions held by individuals are held by them without their having any known reasons for them except that they are the traditions of the society in which they have grown up. *Opinion* about what is right and wrong has therefore nothing to do with *will* in the precise sense in which it is necessary to use the term if confusion is to be avoided. We all know only too well that our will may often be in conflict with what we think is right, and this applies no less to a group of people aiming at a common concrete purpose than to any individual.

While an act of will is always determined by a particular concrete *end* (terminus) and the state of willing ceases when the end is achieved, the manner in which the end is pursued does also depend on *dispositions* which are more or less permanent properties of the acting person.[16] These dispositions are complexes of built-in rules which say either which kinds of actions will lead to a certain kind of result or which are generally to be avoided. This is not the place to enter into a discussion of the highly complex hierarchical structure of those systems of dispositions which govern our thinking and which include dispositions to change dispositions, etc., as well as those which govern all actions of a particular organism and others which are only evoked in particular circumstances.[17]

What is of importance is that among the dispositions which will govern the manner of action of a particular organism there will always be, in addition to dispositions to the kind of actions likely to produce particular results, many negative dispositions which rule out some kinds of action. These inhibitions against types of actions likely to be harmful to the individual or the group are probably among the most important adaptations which all organisms, and especially all individuals living in groups, must possess to make life possible. 'Taboos' are as much a necessary basis of successful existence of a social animal as positive knowledge of what kind of action will produce a given result.

If we are systematically to distinguish the *will* directed to a particular *end* (terminus) and disappearing when that particular end has been reached, from the *opinion* in the sense of a lasting or permanent disposition towards (or against) *kinds* of conduct, it will be expedient to adopt also a distinct name for the generalised aims towards which *opinions* are directed. It is suggested that among the available terms the one which corresponds to *opinion* in the same way in which *end* corresponds to *will* is the term *value*.[18] It is of course not used currently only in this narrow sense; and we are all apt to describe the importance of a particular concrete end as its value. Nevertheless, at least in its plural form *values*, the term seems as closely to approach the needed meaning as any other term available.

It is therefore expedient to describe as values what may guide a person's actions throughout most of his life as distinct from the concrete ends which determine his actions at particular moments. Values in this sense, moreover, are largely culturally transmitted and will guide the action even of persons who are not consciously aware of them, while the end which will most of the time be the focus of conscious attention will normally be the result of the particular circumstances in which he finds himself at any moment. In the sense in which the term 'value' is most generally used it certainly does not refer to particular objects, persons, or events, but to attributes which many different objects, persons, or events may possess at different times and different places and which, if we endeavour to describe them, we will usually describe by stating a rule to which these objects, persons or actions conform. The importance of a value is related to the urgency of a need or of a particular end in the same manner in which the universal or abstract is related to the particular or concrete.

It should be noted that these more or less permanent dispositions which we describe as *opinions about values* are something very different from the emotions with which they are sometimes connected. Emotions, like needs, are evoked by and directed towards particular concrete objects and rapidly disappear with their disappearance. They are, unlike opinions and values, *temporary* dispositions which will guide actions with regard to particular things but not a framework which controls all actions. Like a particular end, an emotion may overpower the restraints of opinion which refer not to the particular but to the abstract and general features of the situation. In this respect opinion, being abstract, is much more akin to knowledge of cause and effect and therefore deserves to be included with the latter as part of reason.

All moral problems, in the widest sense of the term, arise from a conflict between a knowledge that particular desirable results can be achieved in a given way and the rules which tell us that some *kinds* of actions are to be avoided. It is the extent of our ignorance which makes it necessary that in the use of knowledge we should be limited and refrain from many actions whose unpredictable consequences might place us outside the order within which alone the world is tolerably safe for us. It is only thanks to such restraints that our limited knowledge of positive facts serves us as a reliable guide in the sea of ignorance in which we move. The actions of a person who insisted on being guided only by calculable results and refused to respect opinions about what is prudent or permissible would soon prove unsuccessful and in this sense irrational to the highest degree.

The understanding of this distinction has been badly blurred by the words at our disposal. But it is of fundamental importance because the possibility of the required agreement, and therefore of a peaceful existence of the order of an Open Society, rests on it. Our thinking and our vocabulary are still determined largely by the problems and needs of the small group concerned with specific ends known to all its members. The confusion and harm caused by the application of these conceptions to the problems of the Open Society are immense. They have been preserved particularly through the dominance in moral philosophy of a Platonic tribalism which in modern times has received strong support from the preference of people engaged in empirical research for the problems of the observable and tangible small groups and from their distaste for the intangible, more comprehensive order of the social cosmos – an order which can be only mentally reconstructed but never intuitively perceived or observed as a whole.

The possibility of an Open Society rests on its members possessing common opinions, rules and values, and its existence becomes impossible if we insist that it must possess a common will issuing commands directing its members to particular ends. The larger the groups within which we hope to live in peace, the more the common values which are enforced must be confined to abstract and general rules of conduct. The members of an Open Society have and can have in common only *opinions* on values but *not a will* on concrete ends. In consequence, the possibility of an order of peace based on agreement, especially in a democracy, rests on coercion being confined to the enforcement of abstract rules of just conduct.

6 Nomocracy and Teleocracy

The first two of the distinctions we have drawn (in sections 2 and 3) have been conveniently combined by Professor Michael Oakeshott into the two concepts of *nomocracy* and *teleocracy*,[19] which need now hardly any further explanation. A *nomocracy* corresponds to our *cosmos* resting entirely on general rules or *nomoi*, while a *teleocracy* corresponds to a *taxis* (arrangement or organisation) directed towards particular ends or *teloi*. For the former the 'public good' or 'general welfare' consists solely in the preservation of that abstract and end-independent order which is secured by obedience to abstract rules of just conduct: that

> ... public interest which is no other than common right and justice excluding all partiality or private interest [which may be] called the empire of laws and not of men.[20]

For a teleocracy, on the other hand, the common good consists of the sum of the particular interests, that is, the sum of the concrete foreseeable results affecting particular people or groups. It was this latter conception which seemed more acceptable to the naïve constructivist rationalism whose criterion of rationality is a recognisable concrete order serving known particular purposes. Such a teleocratic order, however, is incompatible with the development of an Open Society comprising numerous people having no known concrete purposes in common; and the attempt to impose it on the grown order of a nomocracy leads back from the Open Society to the Tribal Society of the small group. And since all conceptions of the 'merit' according to which individuals should be 'rewarded' must derive from concrete and particular ends towards which the common efforts of a group are directed, all efforts towards a 'distributive' or 'social' justice must lead to the replacement of the nomocracy by a teleocracy, and thus to a return from the Open to the Tribal Society.

7 Catallaxy and Economy

The instance in which the use of the same term for two different kinds of order has caused most confusion, and is still constantly misleading serious thinkers, is probably that of the use of the word 'economy' for both the deliberate arrangement or organisation of resources in the service of a unitary hierarchy of ends, such as a household, an enterprise, or any other organisation including government, and the structure of many inter-related economies of this kind which we call a social, or national, or world 'economy' and often also simply an 'economy'. The ordered structure which the market produces is, however, not an organisation but a spontaneous order or cosmos, and is for this reason in many respects fundamentally different from that arrangement or organisation originally and properly called an economy.[21]

The belief, largely due to this use of the same term for both, that the market order ought to be made to behave as if it were an economy proper, and that its performance can and ought to be judged by the same criteria, has become the source of so many errors and fallacies that it seems necessary to adopt a new technical term to describe the order of the market which spontaneously forms itself. By analogy with the term *catallactics* which has often been proposed as a replacement for the term 'economics' as the name for the theory of the market order, we could describe that order itself as a *catallaxy*. Both expressions are derived from the Greek verb *katallatein* (or *katallassein*) which, significantly, means not only 'to exchange' but also 'to receive into the community' and 'to turn from enemy into friend'.[22]

The chief aim of this neologism is to emphasise that a *catallaxy* neither ought nor can be made to serve a particular hierarchy of concrete ends, and that therefore its performance cannot be judged in terms of a sum of particular results. Yet all the aims of socialism, all attempts to enforce 'social' or 'distributive' justice, and the whole of so-called 'welfare economics', are directed towards turning the *cosmos* of the spontaneous order of the market into an arrangement or *taxis*, or the *catallaxy* into an economy proper. Apparently the belief that the catallaxy ought to be made to behave as if it were an economy seems so obvious and unquestionable to many economists that they never examine its validity. They treat it as the indisputable presupposition for rational examination of the desirability of any order, an assumption without which no judgement of the expediency or worth of alternative institutions is possible.

The belief that the efficiency of the market order can be judged only in terms of the degree of the achievement of a known hierarchy of particular ends is, however, wholly erroneous. Indeed, since these ends are in their totality not known to anybody, any discussion in such terms is necessarily empty. The discovery procedure which we call competition aims at the closest approach we can achieve by any means known to us to a somewhat more modest aim which is nevertheless highly important: namely a state of affairs in which all that is in fact produced is produced at the lowest possible costs. This means that of that particular combination of commodities and services which will be produced more will be made available than could be done by any other known means; and that in consequence, though the share in that product which the different individuals will get is left to be determined by circumstances nobody can foresee and in this sense to 'accident', each will get for the share he wins in the game (which is partly a game of skill and partly a game of chance) as large a real equivalent as can be secured. We allow the individual share to be determined partly by luck in order to make the total to be shared as large as possible.

The utilisation of the spontaneous ordering forces of the market to achieve this kind of optimum, and leaving the determination of the relative shares of the different individuals to what must appear as accident, are inseparable. Only because the market induces every individual to use his unique knowledge of particular opportunities and possibilities for his purposes can an overall order be achieved that uses in its totality the dispersed knowledge which is not accessible as a whole to anyone. The 'maximisation' of the total product in the above sense, and its distribution by the market, cannot be separated because it is through the determination of the prices of the factors of production that the overall order of the market is brought about. If incomes are not determined by factor pricing within the output, then output cannot be maximised relative to individual preferences.

This does not preclude, of course, that *outside* the market government may use distinct means placed at its disposal for the purpose of assisting people who, for one reason or another, cannot through the market earn a minimum income. A society relying on the market order for the efficient use of its resources is likely fairly soon to reach an overall level of wealth which makes it possible for this minimum to be at an adequate level. But it should not be achieved by manipulating the spontaneous order in such a manner as to make the income earned on the market conform to some ideal of 'distributive justice'. Such efforts will reduce the total in which all can share.

8 Demarchy and Democracy

This, unfortunately, does not exhaust the neologisms which seem necessary to escape the confusion which dominates current political thought. Another instance of the prevailing confusion of language is the almost universal use of the term 'democracy' for a special kind of democracy which is by no means a necessary consequence of the basic ideal originally described by that name. Indeed, Aristotle questioned whether this form should even be called 'democracy'.[23] The appeal of the original ideal has been transferred to the particular form of democracy which now prevails everywhere, although this is very far from corresponding to what the original conception aimed at.

Initially the term 'democracy' meant no more than that whatever ultimate power there is should be in the hands of the majority of the people or their representatives. *But it said nothing about the extent of that power.* It is often mistakenly suggested that any ultimate power must be unlimited. From the demand that the *opinion* of the majority should prevail it by no means follows that their *will* on particular matters should be unlimited. Indeed, the classical theory of the separation of powers presupposes that the 'legislation' which was to be in the hands of a representative assembly should be concerned only with the passing of 'laws' (which were presumed to be distinguishable from particular commands by some intrinsic property), and that particular decisions did not become laws (in the sense of *nomoi*) merely because they emanated from the 'legislature'. Without this distinction the idea that a separation of powers involved the attribution of particular functions to distinct bodies would have been meaningless and indeed circular.[24]

If the legislature only can make new law and can do nothing else but make law, whether a particular resolution of that body is valid law must be determinable by a recognisable property of that resolution. Its source alone does not constitute a sufficient criterion of validity.

There can be no doubt that what the great theorists of representative government and of liberal constitutionalism meant by law when they demanded a separation of powers was what we have called *nomos*. That they spoiled their aim by entrusting to the same representative assemblies also the task of making laws in another sense, namely that of the rules of organisation determining the structure and conduct of government, is another story which we cannot further pursue here. Nor can we further consider the inevitable consequence of an institutional arrangement under which a legislature which is not confined to laying down universal rules of just conduct must be driven by organised interests to use its power of 'legislation' to serve particular private ends. All we are here concerned with is that it is not necessary that the supreme authority possesses this sort of power. To limit power does *not* require that there be another power to limit it. If all power rests on *opinion*, and opinion recognises no other ultimate power than one that proves its belief in the justice of its actions *by committing itself to universal rules* (the application of which to particular cases it cannot control), the supreme power loses its authority as soon as it oversteps these limits.

The supreme power thus need not be an unlimited power – it may be a power which loses the indispensable support of opinion as soon as it pronounces anything which does not possess the substantive character of *nomos* in the sense of a universal rule of just conduct. Just as the Pope is deemed to be infallible only *dum ex cathedra loquitur*, that is, so long as he lays down dogma and not in his decision of particular matters, so a legislature may be supreme only when it exercises the capacity of legislating in the strict sense of stating the valid *nomos*. And it can be so limited because there exist objective tests (however difficult they may be to apply in particular instances) by which independent and impartial courts, not concerned with any particular aims of government, can decide whether what the legislature resolves has the character of a *nomos* or not, and therefore also whether it is binding law. All that is needed is a court of justice which can say whether the acts of the legislature do or do not possess certain formal properties which every valid law must possess. But this court need possess no positive power to issue any commands.

The majority of a representative assembly may thus well be the *supreme* power and yet not possess *unlimited* power. If its power is limited to acting as (to revive another Greek term which appealed both to the 17th-century English theorists of democracy and to John Stuart Mill)[25] *nomothetae*, or as the setters of the *nomos*, without power to issue particular commands, no privilege or discrimination in favour of particular groups which it attempted to make law would have the force of law. This sort of power would simply not exist because whoever exercised supreme power would have to prove the legitimacy of its acts by committing itself to universal rules.

If we want democratic determination not only of the coercive rules which bind the private citizen as well as the government, but also of the administration of the government apparatus, we need some representative body to do the latter. But this body need not and should not be the *same* as that which lays down the *nomos*. It should itself be *under* the *nomos* laid down by another representative body, which would determine the limits of the power which this body could not alter. Such a governmental or directive (but in the strict sense *not* legislative) representative body would then indeed be concerned with matters of the *will* of the majority (i.e. with the achievement of a particular concrete purpose) for the pursuit of which it would employ governmental powers. It would not be concerned with questions of *opinion* about what was right and wrong. It would be devoted to the satisfaction of concrete foreseeable needs by the use of separate resources set aside for the purpose.

The fathers of liberal constitutionalism were surely right when they thought that in the supreme assemblies concerned with what they regarded as legislation proper, that is, with laying down the *nomos*, those coalitions of organised interests which they called factions and which we call parties should have no place. Parties are indeed concerned with matters of concrete *will*, the satisfaction of the particular interest of the people who combine to form them, but legislation proper should express *opinion* and therefore not be placed in the hands of representatives of particular interests but in the hands of a representative sample of the prevailing opinion, persons who should be secured against all pressure of particular interests.

I have elsewhere suggested[26] a method of electing such a representative body that would make it independent of the organised parties though they would still remain necessary for the effective democratic conduct of government proper. It requires the election of members for long periods after which they would not be re-eligible. To make them nevertheless representative of current opinion a representation by age groups might be used: each generation electing once in their lives, say, in their 40th year, representatives to serve for 15 years and thereafter assured of continued occupation as lay judges. The law-making assembly would then be composed of men and women between 40 and 55 (and thus probably of an average age somewhat lower than the existing representative assemblies!), elected by their contemporaries after they had opportunity to prove themselves in ordinary life, and required on election to abandon their private occupations for an honorific position for the rest of their active life.

Such a system of election by the contemporaries (who usually are the best judges of a person's ability) would come nearer to producing that ideal of the political theorists, a senate of wise and honourable men, than any system yet tried. The restriction of the power of such a body to legislation proper would for the first time make possible that real separation of powers which has never yet existed, and with it a true government under the law and an effective rule of law. The governmental or directive assembly, on the other hand, subject to the law laid down by the former, and concerned with the provision of particular services, might well continue to be elected on established party lines.

Such a basic change in existing constitutional arrangements presupposes that we finally shed the illusion that the safeguards men once painfully devised to prevent abuse of government power are all unnecessary once that power is placed in the hands of the majority of the people. There is no reason whatever to expect that an omnipotent democratic government will always serve the general rather than particular interests. Democratic government free to benefit particular groups is bound to be dominated by coalitions of organised interests, rather than serve the general interest in the classical sense of 'common right and justice, excluding all partial or private interests'.

It is greatly to be regretted that the word democracy should have become indissolubly connected with the conception of the unlimited power of the majority on particular matters.[27] But if this is so we need a new word to denote the ideal which democracy originally expressed, the ideal of a rule of the popular *opinion* on what is just, but not of a popular *will* concerning whatever concrete measures seem desirable to the coalition of organised interests governing at the moment. If democracy and limited government have become irreconcilable conceptions, we must find a new word for what once might have been called limited democracy. We want the *opinion* of the *demos* to be the ultimate authority, but not allow the naked power of the majority, its *kratos*, to do rule-less violence to individuals. The majority should then *rule* (*archein*) by 'established *standing laws*, promulgated and known to the people, and not by extemporary decrees'.[28] We might perhaps describe such a political order by linking *demos* with *archein* and call *demarchy* such a limited government in which the opinion but not the particular will of the people is the highest authority. The particular scheme considered above was meant to suggest one possible way to secure such a *demarchy*.

If it is insisted upon that democracy must be unlimited government, I do indeed *not* believe in democracy, but I am and shall remain a profoundly convinced demarchist in the sense indicated. If we can by such a change of the name free ourselves from the errors that have unfortunately come to be so closely associated with the conception of democracy, we might thereby succeed in avoiding the dangers which have plagued democracy from its very beginning and have again and again led to its destruction. It is the problem which arose in the memorable episode of which Xenophon tells us, when the Athenian Assembly wanted to vote the punishment of particular individuals and

> ... the great numbers cried out that it was monstrous if the people were to be prevented from doing whatever they wished ... Then the Prytanes, striken with fear, agreed to put the question – all of them except Socrates, the son of Sophroniskus; and he said that in no case would he act except in accordance with the law.[29]

Notes

1   The passage from Gianbattista Vico used as a motto is taken from G. Ferrari (ed.), *Opere*, 2nd edn, Milan, 1854, Vol. V, p. 183.
2   Cf. my *Studies in Philosophy, Politics, and Economics*, London and Chicago, 1967, especially Chapters 4, 5 and 6, as well as my lecture 'Dr Bernard Mandeville', *The Proceedings of the British Academy, 1966* LII, London, 1967.
3   For example, J. A. Schumpeter, *History of Economic Analysis*, New York, 1954, p. 67, where he speaks of A. A. Cournot and H. von Thünen as the first two authors 'to visualise the general inter-dependence of all economic

quantities and the necessity of representing this cosmos by a system of equations'.

4   The only passage known to me in which the error, usually only implicit, that 'order supposes an end' is explicitly stated in these words occurs, significantly, in the writings of Jeremy Bentham: 'An Essay on Political Tactics', first published in Bowring (ed.), *Works*, Vol. II, p. 399.

5   The idea of the formation of spontaneous or self-determining orders, like the connected idea of evolution, has been developed by the social sciences before it was adopted by the natural sciences and here developed as cybernetics. This is beginning to be seen by the biologists. For example, G. Hardin, *Nature and Man's Fate*, 1959, Mentor edn, New York, 1961, p. 54: 'But long before [Claude Bernard, Clerk Maxwell, Walter B. Cannon or Norbert Wiener] Adam Smith had just as clearly used the idea [of cybernetics]. The "invisible hand" that regulates prices to a nicety is clearly this idea. In a free market, says Smith in effect, prices are regulated by negative feedback.'

6   *Thesis* must not be confused with *thesmos*, a Greek term for 'law' older than *nomos* but, at least in classical times, meaning rather the law laid down by a ruler than the impersonal rules of conduct. *Thesis*, by contrast, means the particular act of setting up an arrangement. It is significant that the ancient Greeks could never make up their minds whether the proper opposite to what was determined by nature (*physei*) was what was determined *nomo* or what was determined *thesei*. On this problem see Chapter 6 of the volume of essays and the lecture mentioned in note 2, above.

7   The end-independent character of rules of just conduct has been demonstrated clearly by David Hume and most systematically developed by Immanuel Kant. Cf. D. Hume, 'An Enquiry Concerning the Principles of Morals', in T. H. Green and T. H. Grose (eds.), *Essays, Moral, Political, and Literary*, London, 1875, Vol. II, p. 273: 'the benefit resulting from [the social virtues of justice and fidelity] is not the consequence of every individual single act; but arises from the whole scheme of system concurred in by the whole, or the greater part of society. General peace and order are the attendants of justice or a general abstinence from the possessions of others: But a particular regard to the particular right of one individual citizen may frequently, considered in itself, be productive of pernicious consequences. The result of the individual act is here, in many instances, directly opposite to that of the whole system of actions; and the former may be extremely hurtful, while the latter is, to the highest degree advantageous.' See also his *Treatise on Human Nature* (same edn), Vol. II, p. 318: 'It is evident, that if men were to regulate their conduct by the view of a particular *interest*, they would involve themselves in endless confusion.' For I. Kant see the excellent exposition in Mary Gregor, *Laws of Freedom*, Oxford, 1963, especially pp. 38–42 and 81.

8   H. Huber, *Recht, Staat, und Gesellschaft*, Bern, 1954, p. 5: 'Staatsrecht vergeht, Privatrecht besteht'.

9   A revealing description of the difference between the law with which the judge is concerned and the law of modern legislation is to be found in an essay by the distinguished American public lawyer P. A. Freund in R. B. Brandt (ed.), *Social Justice*, Spectrum Books, New York, 1962, p. 94: 'The judge addresses himself to standards of consistency, equivalence, predictability, the legislator to fair shares, social utility, and equitable distribution'.

10   The term 'opinion' has been most consistently used in this sense by David Hume, particularly in *Essays, loc. cit.*, Vol. I, p. 125: 'It may be further said that, though men be much governed by interest, yet even interest itself, and all human affairs, are entirely governed by *opinion*'; and *ibid.*, p. 110: 'As force is always on the side of the governed, the governors have nothing to support themselves but opinion. It is therefore on opinion only that government is founded; and this maxim extends to the most despotic military government as well as the most free and popular.' It seems that this use of the term 'opinion' derives from the great political debates of the 17th century; this is at least suggested by the text of a broadside of 1641 with an engraving by Wenceslas Hollar (reproduced as frontispiece to Vol. I of William Haller (ed.), *Tracts on Liberty in the Puritan Revolution 1638–1747*, New York, 1934) which is headed 'The World is Ruled and Governed by Opinion'.

11   The Cartesian foundations of Rousseau's thinking in these respects are clearly brought out in Robert Derathé, *Le rationalisme de J.-J. Rousseau*, Paris, 1948.

12   The extension of knowledge is largely due to persons who transcended these limits, but of those who did many more probably perished or endangered their fellows than added to the common stock of positive knowledge.

13   John Locke, *Essays on the Law of Nature* (1676), W. von Leyden (ed.), Oxford, 1954, p. 111: 'By reason ... I do not think is meant here that faculty of the understanding which forms trains of thought and deduces proofs, but certain definite principles of action from which spring all virtues and whatever is necessary for the proper moulding of morals ... reason does not so much establish and pronounce this law of nature as search for it and discover it. ... Neither is reason so much the maker of that law as its interpreter'.

14   The distinction between what we call here the 'purposive' and the 'rule-governed' aspects of action is probably the same as Max Weber's distinction between what he calls *zweckrational* and *wertrational*. If this is so it should, however, be clear that hardly any action could be guided by only either the one or the other kind of consideration, but that considerations of the effectiveness of the means according to the rules of cause and effect will normally be combined with considerations of their appropriateness according to the normative rules about the permissibility of the means.

15   This is a confusion against which the ancient Greeks were protected by

their language, since the only word they had to express what we describe as willing, *bouleuomai*, clearly referred only to particular concrete actions. (M. Pohlenz, *Der Hellenische Mensch*, Göttingen, 1946, p. 210.)

16 Cf. Chapter 3 of my *Studies in Philosophy, Politics, and Economics, op. cit.*

17 It is the basic mistake of particularistic utilitarianism to assume that rules of just conduct aim at particular concrete ends and must be judged by them. I know of no clearer expression of this fundamental error of constructivist rationalism than the statement by Hastings Rashdall (*The Theory of Good and Evil*, London, 1948, Vol. I, p. 148) that 'all moral judgements are ultimately judgements as to the value of ends'. This is precisely what they are *not*. They do not refer to concrete ends but to kinds of action or, in other words, they are judgements about means based on a presumed probability that a kind of action will produce undesirable effects but are applicable in spite of our factual ignorance in most particular instances of whether they will do so or not.

18 Cf. W. Shakespeare, *Troilus and Cressida*, II, 2, 52:

> 'But value dwells not in particular will;
> It holds its estimate and dignity
> As well wherein 'tis precious of itself
> As in the prizer.'

19 So far as I know these terms have been used by Professor Oakeshott only in his oral teaching but not in any published work. For reasons which will become clear in Section 8, I should have preferred to employ the term *nomarchy* rather than *nomocracy*, if the former were not too easily confused with 'monarchy'.

20 James Harrington, *The Prerogative of Popular Government* (1658), in J. Toland (ed.), *The Oceana and His Other Works*, London, 1771, p. 224.

21 I now find somewhat misleading the definition of the science of economics as 'the study of the disposal of scarce means towards the realisation of given ends', which has been so effectively expounded by Lord Robbins and which I should long have defended. It seems to me appropriate only to that preliminary part of catallactics which consists in the study of what has sometimes been called 'simple economies' and to which also Aristotle's *Oeconomica* is exclusively devoted: the study of the dispositions of a single household or firm, sometimes described as the economic calculus or the pure logic of choice. (What is now called economics but had better be described as catallactics Aristotle described as *chrematistike* or the science of wealth.) The reason why Robbins's widely accepted definition now seems to me to be misleading is that the ends which a *catallaxy* serve are not *given* in their totality to anyone, that is, are not known either to any individual participant in the process or to the scientist studying it.

22 See H. G. Liddell and R. Scott, *A Greek–English Lexicon*, new edn, Oxford, 1940, s.v. *Katallásso*.

23   Aristotle, *Politics*, Iv IV 4, 1,292a, Loeb, Rackham (ed.), Cambridge, Mass., and London, 1950, p. 303: 'And it would seem a reasonable criticism to say that such a democracy is not a constitution at all; for where the laws do not govern there is no constitution, as the law ought to govern all things while the magistrates control particulars, and we ought to judge this to be constitutional government; if then democracy really is one of the forms of constitution, it is manifest that an organisation of this kind, in which all things are administered by resolutions of the assembly, is not even a democracy in the proper sense, for it is impossible for a voted resolution to be a universal rule.'

24   Cp. above what is said under 'Nomos and Thesis' on the difference between private and public law; and on what follows now also the important work by M. J. C. Vile, *Constitutionalism and the Separation of Powers*, Clarendon Press, Oxford, 1967.

25   Cf. Philip Hunton, *A Treatise on Monarchy*, London, 1643, p. 5, and John Stuart Mill, *On Liberty and Considerations of Representative Government*, R. B. McCallum (ed.), Oxford, 1946, p. 171.

26   Most recently in 'The Constitution of a Liberal State', *Il Politico*, 1967.

27   Cf. R. Wollheim, 'A Paradox in the Theory of Democracy', in P. Laslett and W. G. Runciman (eds), *Philosophy, Politics, and Society*, 2nd series, London, 1962, p. 72: 'the modern conception of democracy is of a form of government in which no restriction is placed on the governing body'.

28   John Locke, *Second Treatise on Government*, sect. 131, P. Laslett (ed.), Cambridge, 1960, p. 371.

29   Xenophon, *Hellenica*, I, Vii, 15, Loeb ed. by C. L. Brownson, Cambridge, Mass., and London, 1918, p. 73.

10

Economic Freedom and Representative Government

1 The Seeds of Destruction

Thirty years ago I wrote a book[1] which, in a manner which many regarded as unduly alarmist, described the dangers that the then visible collectivist tendencies created for personal freedom. I am glad that these fears so far have not materialised, but I do not think this has proved me wrong. In the first instance I did not, as many misunderstood me, contend that if government interfered at all with economic affairs it was bound to go the whole way to a totalitarian system. I was trying to argue rather what in more homely terms is expressed by saying 'if you don't mend your principles you will go to the devil'.

Post-war revival: the 'Great Prosperity'

In the event developments since the war, in Britain as well as in the rest of the Western world, have gone much less in the direction which the prevalent collectivist doctrines seemed to suggest was likely. Indeed, the first 20 years after the War saw a revival of a free market economy much stronger than even its most enthusiastic supporters could have hoped. Although I like to think that those who worked for this consummation in the intellectual sphere, such as Harold Wincott, to whose memory this lecture is dedicated, have contributed to it, I do not overrate what intellectual debate can achieve. At least as important were probably the experiences of Germany, relying on a market economy, rapidly becoming the strongest economic power of Europe – and to some extent the

The Fourth Wincott Memorial Lecture, published originally as IEA Occasional Paper No. 39 (1973).

practical efforts for a removal of the obstacles to international trade, such as GATT and perhaps in some measure the intentions if not the practice of the EEC.

The result was the Great Prosperity of the last 20 to 25 years which, I fear, will in the future appear as an event as unique as the Great Depression of the 1930s now appears to us. To me at least it seems clear that, until six or eight years ago, this prosperity was due entirely to the freeing of the spontaneous forces of the economic system and not, as in the later years, to inflation. Since this is today often forgotten I may perhaps remind you that, in the most remarkable burst of prosperity of this period, that of the German Federal Republic, the average annual rise of prices remained below 2 per cent until 1966.

I believe that even this modest rate of inflation would not have been necessary to secure the prosperity, and indeed that we should all today have better prospects of continuing prosperity if we had been content with what was achieved without inflation and had not attempted to stimulate it further by an expansionist credit policy. Instead such a policy has created a situation in which it is thought necessary to impose controls which will destroy the main foundations of the prosperity, namely the functioning market. Indeed, the measures supposedly necessary to combat inflation – as if inflation were something which attacks us and not something which we create – threaten to destroy the free economy in the near future.

Inflation: the threat to freedom

We find ourselves in the paradoxical situation that, after a period during which the market economy has been more successful than ever before in rapidly raising living standards in the Western world, the prospects of its continuance even for the next few years must appear slight. I have indeed never felt so pessimistic about the chances of preserving a functioning market economy as I do at this moment – and this means also of the prospects of preserving a free political order. Although the threat to free institutions now comes from a source different from that with which I was concerned 30 years ago, it has become even more acute than it was then.

That a systematically pursued incomes policy means the suspension of the price mechanism and before long the replacement of the market by a centrally directed economy seems to me beyond doubt. I cannot here discuss the ways in which we may still avoid this course, or the chances that we may still do so. Although I regard it as at this time the chief duty of every economist to fight inflation – and to explain why a repressed inflation is even worse than an open inflation – I devote this lecture to another task. As I see it, inflation has merely speeded up the process of the destruction of the market economy which has been going on for other reasons, and brought much nearer the moment when, seeing the economic, political and moral consequences of a centrally directed economy, we shall have to think how we can re-establish a market economy on a firmer and more durable basis.

2 The Danger of Unlimited Government

For some time I have been convinced that it is not only the deliberate attempts of the various kinds of collectivists to replace the market economy by a planned system, nor the consequences of the new monetary policies, which threaten to destroy the market economy: the political institutions prevailing in the Western world necessarily produce a drift in this direction which can be halted or prevented only by changing these institutions. I have belatedly come to agree with Joseph Schumpeter who 30 years ago argued[2] that there was an irreconcilable conflict between democracy and capitalism – except that it is not democracy as such but the particular forms of democratic organisation, now regarded as the only possible forms of democracy, which will produce a progressive expansion of governmental control of economic life even if the majority of the people wish to preserve a market economy.

Majority rule and special interests

The reason is that it is now generally taken for granted that in a democracy the powers of the majority must be unlimited, and that a government with unlimited powers will be forced, to secure the continued support of a majority, to use its unlimited powers in the service of special interests – such groups as particular traders, the inhabitants of particular regions, etc. We shall see this most clearly if we consider the situation in a community in which the mass of the people are in favour of a market order and against government direction, but, as will normally happen, most of the groups wish an exception to be made in their favour. In such conditions a political party hoping to achieve and maintain power will have little choice but to use its powers to buy the support of particular groups. They will do so not because the majority is interventionist, but because the ruling party would not retain a majority if it did not buy the support of particular groups by the promise of special advantages. This means in practice that even a statesman wholly devoted to the common interest of all the citizens will be under the constant necessity of satisfying special interests, because only thus will he be able to retain the support of a majority which he needs to achieve what is really important to him.

The root of the evil is thus the unlimited power of the legislature in modern democracies, a power which the majority will be constantly forced to use in a manner that most of its members may not desire. What we call the will of the majority is thus really an artefact of the existing institutions, and particularly of the omnipotence of the sovereign legislature, which by the mechanics of the political process will be driven to do things that most of its members do not really want, simply because there are no formal limits to its powers.

It is widely believed that this omnipotence of the representative legislature is a necessary attribute of democracy because the will of the representative assembly could be limited only by placing another will above it. Legal positivism, the most influential current theory of jurisprudence, particularly represents this sovereignty of the legislature as logically necessary. This, however, was by no means the view of the classical theorists of representative government. John Locke made it very clear that in a free state even the power of the legislative body should be limited in a definite manner, namely to the passing of laws in the specific sense of general rules of just conduct equally applicable to all citizens. That all coercion would be legitimate only if it meant the application of general rules of law in this sense became the basic principle of liberalism. For Locke, and for the later theorists of Whiggism and the separation of powers, it was not so much the source from which the laws originated as their character of general rules of just conduct equally applicable to all which justified their coercive application.

What is law?

This older liberal conception of the necessary limitation of all power by requiring the legislature to commit itself to general rules has, in the course of the last century, been replaced gradually and almost imperceptibly by the altogether different though not incompatible conception that it was the approval of the majority which was the only and sufficient restraint on legislation. And the older conception was not only forgotten but no longer even understood. It was thought that any substantive limitation of the legislative power was unnecessary once this power was placed in the hands of the majority, because approval by it was regarded as an adequate test of justice. In practice this majority opinion usually represents no more than the result of bargaining rather than a genuine agreement on principles. Even the concept of the arbitrariness which democratic government was supposed to prevent changed its content: its opposite was no longer the general rules equally applicable to all but the approval of a command by the majority – as if a majority might not treat a minority arbitrarily.

3 The Fundamental Principle

Today it is rarely understood that the limitation of all coercion to the enforcement of general rules of just conduct was the fundamental principle of classical liberalism, or, I would almost say, its definition of liberty. This is largely a consequence of the fact that the substantive (or 'material') conception of law (as distinguished from a purely formal one) which underlies it, and which alone gives a clear meaning to such ideas as that of the separation of powers, of the rule of law or of a government under the law, had been rarely stated explicitly but merely tacitly presupposed by most of the classical writers. There are few passages in their 17th- and 18th-century writings in which they explicitly say what they mean by 'law'. Many uses of the term, however, make sense only if it is interpreted to mean exclusively general rules of just conduct and not every expression of the will of the duly authorised representative body.

Tyranny of majorities

Though the older conception of law survives in limited connections, it is certainly no longer generally understood, and in consequence has ceased to be an effective limit on legislation. While in the theoretical concept of the separation of powers the legislature derived its authority from the circumstance that it committed itself to general rules and was supposed to impose only general rules, there are now no limits on what a legislature may command and so claim to be 'law'. While its power was thus once supposed to be limited not by a superior will but by a generally recognised principle, there are now no limits whatever. There is therefore also no reason why the coalitions of organised interests on which the governing majorities rest should not discriminate against any widely disliked group. Differences in wealth, education, tradition, religion, language, or race may today become the cause of differential treatment on the pretext of a pretended principle of social justice or of public necessity. Once such discrimination is recognised as legitimate, all the safeguards of individual freedom of the liberal tradition are gone. If it is assumed that whatever the majority decides is just, even if what it lays down is not a general rule, but aims at affecting particular people, it would be expecting too much to believe that a sense of justice will restrain the caprice of the majority: in any group it is soon believed that what is desired by the group is just. And since the theoreticians of democracy have for over a hundred years taught the majorities that whatever they desire is just, we must not be surprised if the majorities no longer even ask whether what they decide is just. Legal positivism has powerfully contributed to this development by its contention that law is not dependent on justice but determines what is just.

Mirage of 'social justice'

Unfortunately, we have not only failed to impose upon legislatures the limitations inherent in the necessity of committing themselves to general rules. We have also charged them with tasks which they can perform only if they are not thus limited but are free to use coercion in the discriminatory manner that is required to assure benefits to particular people or groups. This they are constantly asked to do in the name of what is called social or distributive justice, a conception which has largely taken the place of the justice of individual action. It requires that not the individuals but 'society' be just in determining the share of individuals in the social product; and in order to realise any particular distribution of the social product regarded as just it is necessary that government directs individuals in what they must do.

Indeed, in a market economy in which no single person or group determines who gets what, and the shares of individuals always depend on many circumstances which nobody could have foreseen, the whole conception of social or distributive justice is empty and meaningless; and there will therefore never exist agreement on what is just in this sense. I am not sure that the concept has a definite meaning even in a centrally directed economy, or that in such a system people would ever agree on what distribution is just. I am certain, however, that nothing has done so much to destroy the juridical safeguards of individual freedom as the striving after this mirage of social justice. An adequate treatment of the topic of this lecture would indeed presuppose a careful dissection of this ideal which almost everybody seems to believe to have a definite meaning but which proves more completely devoid of such meaning the more one thinks about it. But the main subject of this lecture is what we have to do, if we ever again get a chance, to stop those tendencies inherent in the existing political systems which drive us towards a totalitarian order.

Compatibility of collective wants

Before I turn to this main problem, I should correct a widespread misunderstanding. The basic principle of the liberal tradition, that all the coercive action of government must be limited to the enforcement of general rules of just conduct, does not preclude government from rendering many other services for which, except for raising the necessary finance, it need not rely on coercion. It is true that in the 19th century a deep and not wholly unjustified distrust of government often made liberals wish to restrain government much more narrowly. But even then, of course, certain collective wants were recognised which only an agency possessing the power of taxation could satisfy. I am the last person to deny that increased wealth and the increased density of population have enlarged the number of collective needs which government can and should satisfy. Such government services are entirely compatible with liberal principles so long as,

firstly, government does not claim a monopoly and new methods of rendering services through the market (e.g. in some now covered by social insurance) are not prevented;
secondly, the means are raised by taxation on uniform principles and taxation is not used as an instrument for the redistribution of income; and,
thirdly, the wants satisfied are collective wants of the community as a whole and not merely collective wants of particular groups.

Not every collective want deserves to be satisfied: the desire of the small bootmakers to be protected against the competition of the factories is also a collective need of the bootmakers, but clearly not one which in a liberal economic system could be satisfied.

Nineteenth-century liberalism in general attempted to keep the growth of these service activities of government in check by entrusting them to local rather than central government in the hope that competition between the local authorities would control their extent. I cannot consider here how far this principle had to be abandoned and mention it only as another part of the traditional liberal doctrine whose rationale is no longer understood.

I had to consider these points to make it clear that those checks on government activity with which for the rest of this lecture I shall be exclusively concerned refer only to its powers of coercion but not to the necessary services we today expect government to render to the citizens.

I hope that what I have said so far has made it clear that the task we shall have to perform if we are to re-establish and preserve a free society is in the first instance an intellectual task: it presupposes that we not only recover conceptions which we have largely lost and which must once again become generally understood, but also that we design new institutional safeguards which will prevent a repetition of the process of gradual erosion of the safeguards which the theory of liberal constitutionalism had meant to provide.

4 The Separation of Powers

The device to which the theorists of liberal constitutionalism had looked to guarantee individual liberty and the prevention of all arbitrariness was the separation of powers. If the legislature laid down only general rules equally applicable to all and the executive could use coercion only to enforce obedience to these general rules, personal liberty would indeed be secure. This presupposes, however, that the legislature is confined to laying down such general rules. But, instead of confining parliament to making laws in this sense, we have given it unlimited power simply by calling 'law' everything which it proclaims: a legislature is now not a body that makes laws; a law is whatever is resolved by a legislature.

This state of affairs was brought about by the loss of the old meaning of 'law' and by the desire to make government democratic by placing the direction and control of government in the hands of the legislatures, which are in consequence constantly called upon to order all sorts of specific actions – to issue commands which are called laws, although in character they are wholly different from those laws to the production of which the theory of the separation of powers had intended to confine the legislatures.

The concept of 'lawyer's law'

Although the task of designing and establishing new institutions must appear difficult and almost hopeless, the task of reviving and making once more generally understood a lost concept for which we no longer have even an unambiguous name is perhaps even more difficult. It is a task which in this case has to be achieved in the face of the contrary teaching of the dominant school of jurisprudence. I will try briefly to state the essential characteristics of laws in this specific narrow sense of the term before I turn to the institutional arrangements which would secure that the task of making such laws be really separated from the tasks of governing.

A good way is to consider the peculiar properties which judge-made law possesses of necessity, while they belong to the products of legislatures in general only in so far as these have endeavoured to emulate judge-made law. It is no accident that this concept of law has been preserved much longer in the common law countries whereas it was rarely understood in countries which relied wholly on statute law.

This law consists essentially of what used to be known as 'lawyer's law' – which is and can be applied by courts of justice and to which the agencies of government are as much subject as are private persons. Since this judge-made law arises out of the settlement of disputes, it relates solely to the relations of acting persons towards one another and does not control an individual's actions which do not affect others. It defines the protected domains of each person with which others are prohibited from interfering. The aim is to prevent conflicts between people who do not act under central direction but on their own initiative, pursuing their own ends on the basis of their own knowledge.

These rules must thus apply in circumstances which nobody can foresee and must therefore be designed to cover a maximum number of future instances. This determines what is commonly but not very helpfully described as their 'abstract' character, by which is meant that they are intended to apply in the same manner to all situations in which certain generic factors are present and not only to particular designated persons, groups, places, times, etc. They do not prescribe to the individuals specific tasks or ends of their actions, but aim at making it possible for them so mutually to adjust their plans that each will have a good chance of achieving his aims. The delimitation of the personal domains which achieve this purpose is of course determined chiefly by the law of property, contract, and torts, and the penal laws which protect 'life, liberty, and property'.

Limits to coercion

An individual who is bound to obey only such rules of just conduct as I have called these rules of law in this narrow sense is free in the sense that he is not legally subject to anybody's commands, that within known limits he can choose the means and ends of his activities. But where everybody is free in this sense each is thrown into a process which nobody controls and the outcome of which for each is in large measure unpredictable. Freedom and risk are thus inseparable. Nor can it be claimed that the magnitude of each individual's share of the national income, dependent on so many circumstances which nobody knows, will be just. But nor can these shares meaningfully be described as unjust. We must be content if we can prevent them from being affected by unjust actions. We can of course in a free society provide a floor below which nobody need fall, by providing outside the market for all some insurance against misfortune. There is indeed much we can do to improve the framework within which the market will operate beneficially. But we cannot in such a society make the distribution of incomes correspond to some standard of social or distributive justice, and attempts to do so are likely to destroy the market order.

But if, to preserve individual freedom, we must confine coercion to the enforcement of general rules of just conduct, how can we prevent legislatures from authorising coercion to secure particular benefits for particular groups – especially a legislature organised on party lines where the governing majority frequently will be a majority only because it promises such special benefits to some groups? The truth is of course that the so-called legislatures have *never* been confined to making laws in this narrow sense, although the theory of the separation of powers tacitly assumed that they were. And since it has come to be accepted that not only legislation but also the direction of current government activities should be in the hands of the representatives of the majority, the direction of government has become the chief task of the legislatures. This has had the effect not only of entirely obliterating the distinction between laws in the sense of general rules of just conduct and laws in the sense of specific commands, but also of organising the legislatures not in the manner most suitable for making laws in the classical sense but in the manner required for efficient government, that is above all on party lines.

Representative government driven to serve sectional interests

Now, I believe we are right in wanting both legislation in the old sense and current government to be conducted democratically. But it seems to me it was a fatal error, though historically probably inevitable, to entrust these two distinct tasks to the same representative assembly. This makes the distinction between legislation and government, and thereby also the observance of the principles of the rule of law and of a government under the law, practically impossible. Though it may secure that every act of government has the approval of the representative assembly, it does not protect the citizens against discretionary coercion. Indeed, a representative assembly organised in the manner necessary for efficient government, and not restrained by some general laws it cannot alter, is bound to be driven to use its powers to satisfy the demands of sectional interests.

It is no accident that most of the classical theorists of representative government and of the separation of powers disliked the party system and hoped that a division of the legislature on party lines could be avoided. They did so because they conceived of the legislatures as concerned with the making of laws in the narrow sense, and believed that there could exist on the rules of just conduct a prevalent common opinion independent of particular interests. But it cannot be denied that democratic *government* requires the support of an organised body of representatives, which we call parties, committed to a programme of action, and a similarly organised opposition which offers an alternative government.

Separate legislative assembly

It would seem the obvious solution of this difficulty to have two distinct representative assemblies with different tasks, one a true legislative body and the other concerned with government proper, i.e. everything except the making of laws in the narrow sense. And it is at least not inconceivable that such a system might have developed in Britain if at the time when the House of Commons with the exclusive power over money bills achieved in effect sole control of government, the House of Lords, as the supreme court of justice, had obtained the sole right to develop the law in the narrow sense. But such a development was of course not possible so long as the House of Lords represented not the people at large but a class.

On reflection, however, one realises that little would be gained by merely having two representative assemblies instead of one if they were elected and organised on the same principles and therefore also had the same composition. They would be driven by the same circumstances which govern the decisions of modern parliaments and acting in collusion would probably produce the same sort of authorisation for whatever the government of the day wished to do. Even if we assume that the legislative chamber (as distinguished from the governmental one) were restricted by the constitution to passing laws in the narrow sense of general rules of just conduct, and this restriction were made effective through the control by a constitutional court, little would probably be achieved so long as the legislative assembly were under the same necessity of satisfying the demands of particular groups which force the hands of the governing majorities in today's parliaments.

Specific interests and permanent principles

While for the governmental assemblies we should want something more or less of the same kind as the existing parliaments, whose organisation and manner of proceeding have indeed been shaped by the needs of governing rather than the making of laws, something very different would be needed for the legislative assembly. We should want an assembly not concerned with the particular needs of particular groups but rather with the general permanent principles on which the activities of the community were to be ordered. Its members and its resolutions should represent not specific groups and their particular desires but the prevailing opinion on what kind of conduct was just and what kind was not. In laying down rules to be valid for long periods ahead this assembly should be 'representative of', or reproduce a sort of cross-section of, the prevailing opinions on right and wrong; its members should not be the spokesmen of particular interests, or express the 'will' of any particular section of the population on any specific measure of government. They should be men and women trusted and respected for the traits of character they had shown in the ordinary business of life, and not dependent on the approval by particular groups of electors. And they should be wholly exempt from the party discipline necessary to keep a governing team together, but evidently undesirable in the body which lays down the rules that limit the powers of government.

Membership of legislative assembly

Such a legislative assembly could be achieved if, *first*, its members were elected for long periods, *secondly*, they were not eligible for re-election after the end of the period, and, *thirdly*, to secure a continuous renewal of the body in accord with gradually changing opinions among the electorate, its members were not all elected at the same time but a constant fraction of their number replaced every year as their mandate expired; or, in other words, if they were elected, for instance, for 15 years and one 15th of their number replaced every year. It would further seem to me expedient to provide that at each election the representatives should be chosen by and from only one age-group so that every citizen would vote only once in his life, say in his 40th year, for a representative chosen from his age-group.

The result would be an assembly composed of persons between their 40th and their 55th year, elected after they had opportunity to prove their ability in ordinary life (and, incidentally, of an average age somewhat below that of contemporary parliaments). It would probably be desirable to disqualify those who had occupied positions in the governmental assembly or other political or party organisations and it would also be necessary to assure to those elected for the period after their retirement some dignified, paid and pensionable position, such as lay-judge or the like.

The advantage of an election by age-groups, and at an age at which the individuals could have proved themselves in ordinary life, would be that in general a person's contemporaries are the best judges of his character and ability; and that among the relatively small numbers participating in each election the candidates would be more likely to be personally known to the voters and chosen according to the personal esteem in which they were held by the voters – especially if, as would seem likely and deserve encouragement, the anticipation of this common task led to the formation of clubs of the age-groups for the discussion of public affairs.

5 Advantages of Legislative Separation

The purpose of all this would of course be to create a legislature which was not subservient to government and did not produce whatever laws government wanted for the achievement of its momentary purposes, but rather which with the law laid down the permanent limits to the coercive powers of government – limits within which government had to move and which even the democratically elected governmental assembly could not overstep. While the latter assembly would be entirely free in determining the organisation of government, the use to be made of the means placed at the disposal of government and the character of the services to be rendered by government, it would itself possess no coercive powers over the individual citizens. Such powers, including the power to raise by taxation the means for financing the services rendered by government, would extend only to the enforcement of the rules of just conduct laid down by the legislative assembly. Against any overstepping of these limits by government (or the governmental assembly) there would be open an appeal to a constitutional court which would be competent in the case of conflict between the legislature proper and the governmental bodies.

A further desirable effect of such an arrangement would be that the legislature would for once have enough time for its proper task. This is important because in modern times legislatures frequently have left the regulation of matters which might have been effected by general rules of law to administrative orders and even administrative discretion simply because they were so busy with their governmental tasks that they had neither time for nor interest in making law proper. It is also a task which requires expert knowledge which a long-serving representative might acquire but is not likely to be possessed by a busy politician anxious for results which he can show his constituents before the next election. It is a curious consequence of giving the representative assembly unlimited power that it has largely ceased to be the chief determining agent in shaping the law proper, but has left this task more and more to the bureaucracy.

I must not, however, make you impatient by pursuing further the details of this Utopia – though I must confess that I have found fascinating and instructive the exploration of the new opportunities offered by contemplating the possibility of separating the truly legislative assembly from the governmental body. You will rightly ask what the purpose of such a Utopian construction can be if by calling it thus I admit that I do

not believe it can be realised in the foreseeable future. I can answer
in the words of David Hume in his essay on 'The Idea of a Perfect
Commonwealth', that

> in all cases, it must be advantageous to know what is the most perfect in
> the kind, that we may be able to bring any real constitution or form of
> government as near it as possible, by such gentle alterations and inno-
> vations as may not give too great a disturbance to society.

Notes

1 *The Road to Serfdom*, Routledge, 1944.
2 *Capitalism, Socialism and Democracy*, Allen & Unwin, 1943 (Unwin University Books No. 28, 3rd edn, 1950).

11

Will the Democratic Ideal Prevail?

I interpret the question we are trying to answer in this collection of essays as: How long can government continue to increase its powers over the economy without harmful long-term consequences that would be difficult to check or to reverse by the procedures of democracy? My answer is to analyse the working of the democratic process as it becomes exposed to the importunities of pressure groups. This analysis is a short statement of the diagnosis on which I have been working for some years.

It is no longer possible to ignore that more and more thoughtful and well-meaning people are slowly losing their faith in what was to them once the inspiring ideal of democracy.

This is happening at the same time as, and in part perhaps in consequence of, a constant extension of the field to which the principle of democracy is being applied. But the growing doubts are clearly not confined to these obvious abuses of a political ideal: they concern its true core. Most of those who are disturbed by their loss of trust in a hope which has long guided them, wisely keep their mouths shut. But my alarm about this state makes me speak out.

It seems to me that the disillusionment which so many experience is not due to a failure of the principle of democracy as such but to our having tried it the wrong way. It is because I am anxious to rescue the true ideal from the miscredit into which it is falling that I am trying to find out the mistake we made and how we can prevent the bad consequences we have observed of democratic procedure.

Published originally as a contribution to *The Coming Confrontation: Will the Open Society Survive to 1989?*, Hobart Paperback No. 12, IEA (1978).

1   A 'Bargaining' Democracy

To avoid disappointment, of course, any ideal has to be approached in a sober spirit. In the case of democracy in particular we must not forget that the word refers solely to a particular method of government. It meant originally no more than a certain procedure for arriving at political decisions, and tells us nothing about what the aims of government ought to be. Yet, as the only method of peaceful change of government which men have yet discovered, it is nevertheless precious and worth fighting for.

Yet it is not difficult to see why the outcome of the democratic process in its present form must bitterly disappoint those who believed in the principle that government should be guided by the opinion of the majority.

Though some still claim this is now the case, it is too obviously not true to deceive observant persons. Never, indeed, in the whole of history were governments so much under the necessity of satisfying the particular wishes of numerous special interests as is true of governments today. Critics of present democracy like to speak of 'mass-democracy'. But if democratic government were really bound to what the masses agreed upon there would be little to object to. The cause of the complaints is not that the governments serve an agreed opinion of the majority, but that they are bound to serve the several interests of a conglomerate of numerous groups. It is at least conceivable, though unlikely, that an autocratic government will exercise self-restraint; but an omnipotent democratic government simply cannot do so. If its powers are not limited, it simply cannot confine itself to serving the agreed views of the majority of the electorate. It will be forced to bring together and keep together a majority by satisfying the demands of a multitude of special interests, each of which will consent to the special benefits granted to other groups only at the price of their own special interests being equally considered. Such a bargaining democracy has nothing to do with the conceptions used to justify the principle of democracy.

2   The Playball of Group Interests

When I speak here of the necessity of democratic government being limited, or more briefly of limited democracy, I do not, of course, mean that the part of government conducted democratically should be limited, but that *all* government, especially if democratic, should be limited. The reason is that democratic government, if nominally omnipotent, becomes as a result exceedingly weak, the playball of all the separate interests it has to satisfy to secure majority support.

How has the situation come about?

For two centuries, from the end of absolute monarchy to the rise of unlimited democracy, the great aim of constitutional government had been to limit all governmental powers. The chief principles gradually established to prevent all arbitrary exercise of power were the separation of powers, the rule or sovereignty of law, government under the law, the distinction between private and public law, and the rules of judicial procedure. They all served to define and limit the conditions under which any coercion of individuals was admissible. Coercion was thought to be justified only in the general interest. And only coercion according to uniform rules equally applicable to all was thought to be in the general interest.

All these great liberal principles were given second rank and were half forgotten when it came to be believed that democratic control of government made unnecessary any other safeguards against the arbitrary use of power. The old principles were not so much forgotten as their traditional verbal expression deprived of meaning by a gradual change of the key words used in them. The most important of the crucial terms on which the meaning of the classical formulae of liberal constitutionalism turned was the term 'Law'; and all the old principles lost their significance as the content of this term was changed.

3 Laws versus Directions

To the founders of constitutionalism the term 'Law' had had a very precise narrow meaning. Only from limiting government by law in this sense was the protection of individual liberty expected. The philosophers of law in the 19th century finally defined it as rules regulating the conduct of persons towards others, applicable to an unknown number of future instances and containing prohibitions delimiting (but of course not specifying) the boundaries of the protected domain of all persons and organised groups.

After long discussions, in which the German jurisprudents in particular 'had at last elaborated this definition of what they called 'law in the material sense', it was in the end suddenly abandoned for what now must seem an almost comic objection. Under this definition the rules of a constitution would not be law in the material sense.

They are, of course, not rules of conduct but rules for the organisation of government, and like all public law are apt to change frequently while private (and criminal) law can last.

Law was meant to prevent unjust conduct. Justice referred to principles equally applicable to all and was contrasted to all specific commands or privileges referring to particular individuals and groups. But who still believes today, as James Madison could 200 years ago, that the House of Representatives would be unable to make any 'law which will not have its full operation on themselves and their friends, as well as the great mass of society'?

What happened with the apparent victory of the democratic ideal was that the power of laying down laws and the governmental power of issuing directions were placed into the hands of the same assemblies. The effect of this was necessarily that the supreme governmental authority became free to give itself currently whatever laws helped it best to achieve the particular purposes of the moment. But it necessarily meant the end of the principle of government *under* the law. While it was reasonable enough to demand that not only legislation proper but also governmental measures should be determined by democratic procedure, placing both powers into the hands of the same assembly (or assemblies) meant in effect return to unlimited government.

It also invalidated the original belief that a democracy, because it had to obey the majority, could do only what was in the general interest. That would have been true of a body which could give only *general* laws or decide on issues of truly *general* interest. But it is not only *not* true but outright *impossible* for a body which has unlimited powers and must use them to buy the votes of particular interests, including those of some small groups or even powerful individuals. Such a body, which does not owe its authority to demonstrating its belief in the justice of its decisions by committing itself to general rules, is constantly under the necessity of rewarding the support by the different groups by special advantages conceded to them.

4 Laws and Arbitrary Government

The result of this development was not merely that government was no longer under the law. It also brought it about that the concept of law itself lost its meaning. The so-called legislature was no longer (as John Locke had thought it should be) confined to giving laws in the sense of general rules. *Everything* the 'legislature' resolved came to be called 'law', and it was no longer called 'legislature' because it gave laws, but 'laws' became the name for everything which emanated from the 'legislature'. The hallowed term 'law' thus lost all its old meaning, and it became the name for the commands of what the fathers of constitutionalism would have called arbitrary government. Government became the main business of 'legislature' and legislation subsidiary to it.

The term 'arbitrary' no less lost its classical meaning. The word had meant 'rule-less' or determined by particular will rather than according to recognised rules. In this true sense even the decision of an autocratic ruler may be lawful, and the decision of a democratic majority entirely arbitrary. Even Rousseau, who is chiefly responsible for bringing into political usage the unfortunate conception of 'will', understood at least occasionally that, to be just, this will must be *general in intent*. But the decisions of the majorities in contemporary legislative assemblies need not, of course, have that attribute. Anything goes, so long as it increases the number of votes supporting governmental measures.

An omnipotent sovereign parliament, not confined to laying down general rules, means that we have an arbitrary government. What is worse, a government which cannot, even if it wished, obey any principles, but must maintain itself by handing out special favours to particular groups. It must *buy* its authority by discrimination. Unfortunately, the British Parliament which had been the model for most representative institutions also introduced the idea of the sovereignty (i.e. omnipotence) of Parliament. But the sovereignty of the law and the sovereignty of an unlimited Parliament are irreconcilable. Yet today, when Mr Enoch Powell claims that 'a Bill of Rights is incompatible with the free constitution of this country', Mr Callaghan hastens to assure him that he understands that and agrees with Mr Powell.[1]

It turns out that the Americans 200 years ago were right and an almighty Parliament means the death of the freedom of the individual. Apparently a free constitution no longer means the freedom of the individual but *a licence to the majority in Parliament to act as arbitrarily as it pleases*. We can either have a free Parliament or a free people.

Personal freedom requires that all authority is restrained by long-run principles which the opinion of the people approves.

5 From Unequal Treatment to Arbitrariness

It took some time for those consequences of unlimited democracy to show themselves.

For a while the traditions developed during the period of liberal constitutionalism continued to operate as a restraint on the extent of governmental power. Wherever these forms of democracy were imitated in parts of the world where no such traditions existed, they invariably, of course, soon broke down. But in the countries with longer experience with representative government the traditional barriers to arbitrary use of power were at first penetrated from entirely benevolent motives. Discrimination to assist the least fortunate did not seem to be discrimination. (More recently we even invented the nonsense word 'underprivileged' to conceal this.) But in order to put into a more equal material position people who are inevitably very different in many of the conditions on which their worldly success depends, it is necessary to treat them unequally.

Yet to break the principle of *equal treatment under the law* even for charity's sake inevitably opened the floodgates to arbitrariness. To disguise it the pretence of the formula of 'social justice' was resorted to; nobody knows precisely what it means, but for that very reason it served as the magic wand which broke down all barriers to partial measures. Dispensing gratuities at the expense of somebody else *who cannot be readily identified* became the most attractive way of buying majority support. But a parliament or government which becomes a charitable institution thereby becomes exposed to irresistible blackmail. And it soon ceases to be the 'deserts' but becomes exclusively the 'political necessity' that determines which groups are to be favoured at general expense.

This legalised corruption is not the fault of the politicians; they cannot avoid it if they are to gain positions in which they can do any good. It becomes a built-in feature of any system in which majority support authorises special measures assuaging particular discontents. Both a legislature confined to laying down general rules and a governmental agency which can use coercion only to enforce general rules that it cannot change can resist such pressure; an omnipotent assembly cannot.

Deprived of all power of discretionary coercion, government might, of course, still discriminate in rendering services — but this would be less harmful and could be more easily prevented. But once central government possesses no power of discriminatory coercion, most services could be and probably should be delegated to regional or local corporations competing for inhabitants by providing better services at lower costs.

6 Separation of Powers to Prevent Unlimited Government

It seems clear that a nominally unlimited ('sovereign') representative assembly must be progressively driven into a steady and unlimited extension of the powers of government. It appears equally clear that this can be prevented only by dividing the supreme power between two distinct democratically elected assemblies, i.e. by applying the principle of the separation of powers on the highest level.

Two such distinct assemblies would, of course, have to be differently composed if the *legislative* one is to represent the *opinion* of the people about which sorts of government actions are just and which are not, and the other, *governmental* assembly were to be guided by the *will* of the people on the particular measures to be taken within the frame of rules laid down by the first. For this second task — which has been the main occupation of existing parliaments — their practices and organisation have become well adapted, especially with their organisation on party lines which is indeed indispensable for conducting government.

But it was not without reason that the great political thinkers of the 18th century were without exception deeply distrustful of party divisions in a true legislature. It can hardly be denied that the existing parliaments are largely unfit for legislation proper. They have neither the time nor the right to approach it.

I have on various occasions sketched a possible organisation for such a democratic legislature and hope soon to publish a full account of it.[2] This plan, which I have worked out over many years, is, however, unquestionably only one way in which the aim can be achieved. Here I am concerned solely with the general principle on which I have no remaining doubts: the absolute necessity of dividing in some manner the supreme power between two different and mutually wholly independent democratic assemblies with entirely distinct and sharply separated functions.

A reform of the House of Lords might offer an opportunity for a move in that direction.

If this solution of dividing supreme power into two independent democratic assemblies, or some better device, is not applied in the next 10 years or so, the public loss of faith in the ideal of democracy itself will continue to evaporate, especially if government acquires even more power over economic life and even more power to dispense arbitrary, discriminate benefits to group interests, that will, in turn, therefore, be increasingly disposed to organise pressure on it. The end-result must be either the collapse of political democracy or a renewed recognition by the majority, which suffers from such sectional favours, to re-assert the supremacy of institutions that serve the general will.

Notes

1 House of Commons, 17 May 1977. There would in fact be no need for a catalogue of protected rights, but merely of the single restriction of all governmental power that no coercion was permissible except to enforce obedience to laws as defined before. That would include all the recognised fundamental rights and more.

2 See Chapters 7, 8 and 10 of my *New Studies in Philosophy, Politics, Economics and the History of Ideas* (Routledge & Kegan Paul, London, 1978), and the third volume of my *Law, Legislation and Liberty: The Political Order of a Free People* (Routledge & Kegan Paul, 1979).

Index